Kitchens and Kitchenware

Jane H. Celehar

Photography by Ed Johnson Productions
Columbus, Ohio

Cover Design by Heather Miller
Make Up by Mary Jane Strouf

ISBN 0-87069-425-1
Library of Congress Catalog
Card Number 84-051254

10 9 8 7 6 5 4 3 2 1

Published by

Wallace-Homestead Book Company
580 Water's Edge Road
Lombard, Illinois 60148

One of the ABC PUBLISHING Companies

Acknowledgments

I am particularly indebted to my friend Janet Hutton for all the help, time, and encouragement she has given throughout this project! I'd also like to thank Janet for illustrating the trademarks.

A special thank-you to my friends Mildred and George Tuttle, who were so generous with their support information and the use of their collection and resources of books and catalogs.

To my friends Judy and Tom Jones, who provided valuable resource material and the use of their collection, I am most appreciative.

Next I want to thank Mr. Kenneth E. Johnson, the son of Edward H. Johnson, the founder of the A. & J. Manufacturing Company, Binghamton, New York. Mr. Johnson provided me with invaluable identification, dating, and background information.

My gratitude is also extended to Donna Davis, Ruth Dillon, and Roger McDaniels for allowing me to use their items in this book, and to Sue Outterson for proofreading.

To Ed Johnson, photographer for both of my books, thank you for doing such wonderful work.

Thank you, Liz Fletcher, for being a most understanding editor and friend and for all your encouragement and suggestions.

Finally, my thanks and appreciation to all those people, libraries, and companies who provided valuable assistance, information, and cooperation.

Contents

Introduction

Even before my first book, *Kitchens and Gadgets*, was released, I found I had acquired much information that was not included in it. This, along with the encouragement of my editor Liz Fletcher, inspired me to start my next book. *Kitchens and Kitchenware* is a broad, in-depth look at that special room, the kitchen, and its furnishings. Everything is different from *Kitchens and Gadgets* but can be readily used as an adjunct to it.

After extensive research, it was time to decide how to put all this new information together. I finally decided the best and most understandable way was to present it by decades instead of by separate chapters on the kitchen, gadgets, appliances, etc.

Kitchens and Kitchenware starts at the turn of the century and covers fifty years, showing the evolution of the kitchen in the first half of the twentieth century.

Electric and gas power, mechanization, and social changes all had tremendous effects on the kitchen. Historical and pictorial changes in the kitchen and its equipment are illustrated.

The book goes from the large, inefficient kitchen where work was done by domestic servants, to the efficient "servantless" kitchen with modern gadgets and appliances, both large and small. The book includes the history of the mechanization of appliances—for example, the changes from a handheld toaster to an automatic one.

Tools, gadgets, manufacturers, trademarks, etc., are not repeated from the book *Kitchens and Gadgets 1920 to 1950*. The history of the manufacturers and the trademarks are in separate listings.

Pictures illustrate how the decorative scheme of the kitchen changed through the years. Reproduced advertisements and pages from old catalogs clearly let us see what was available in the past.

Microwave ovens, food processors, molded plastic, and computers seem commonplace today. It is hoped that we will appreciate living in the 1980s by looking into the past through the kitchen door.

Pricing Kitchen Collectibles

This book covers a broad range of kitchen collectibles. The author has not attempted to price the varied items that fall into special categories all their own. Some items such as graniteware, have soaring prices, making it difficult to keep up with the trends. Fiesta Ware, Hall Pottery, Depression glass, etc., are also specialty collectibles. Aluminum cookware is becoming collectible, but not enough information is available at this writing. Dollhouses and complete sets of kitchen toys are better covered by toy specialists.

The prices listed serve only as a guide of "asking" prices. Values will vary depending on the source, local demand, geographic location, availability, quality, and condition. The final judge is YOU, the buyer.

The fun of collecting is searching for your particular interest and then finding it. The people you will meet along the way and the information you will gather are the special rewards of being a collector. Happy hunting!

The Old-Fashioned Kitchen, 1900 to 1920

At the dawn of the twentieth century, a new, exciting world lay ahead. Tremendous changes would touch the home, especially the kitchen. Let's look back to 1900 to see what transpired.

At the turn of the century, housekeeping was a time-consuming, back-breaking job. In the average-size town, the home probably did not have electricity. The old-fashioned kitchen was dominated by the range. Unless gas was available, cooking would have been done on a cast iron, iron-wood combination, or coal range; all were inconvenient and inefficient. Flatirons were heated on the stove, toast was made on an open fire or in the oven. All beating was done by hand.

The kitchen lacked adequate storage and often had no provision for keeping fresh food unless there was an icebox or "cooler." The cooler was a passage in the wall, fitted with strong wire shelves. In summer, cool air was carried from below ground up to the roof, where food could be stored for a time.

Almost everything was stored in a pantry, requiring a

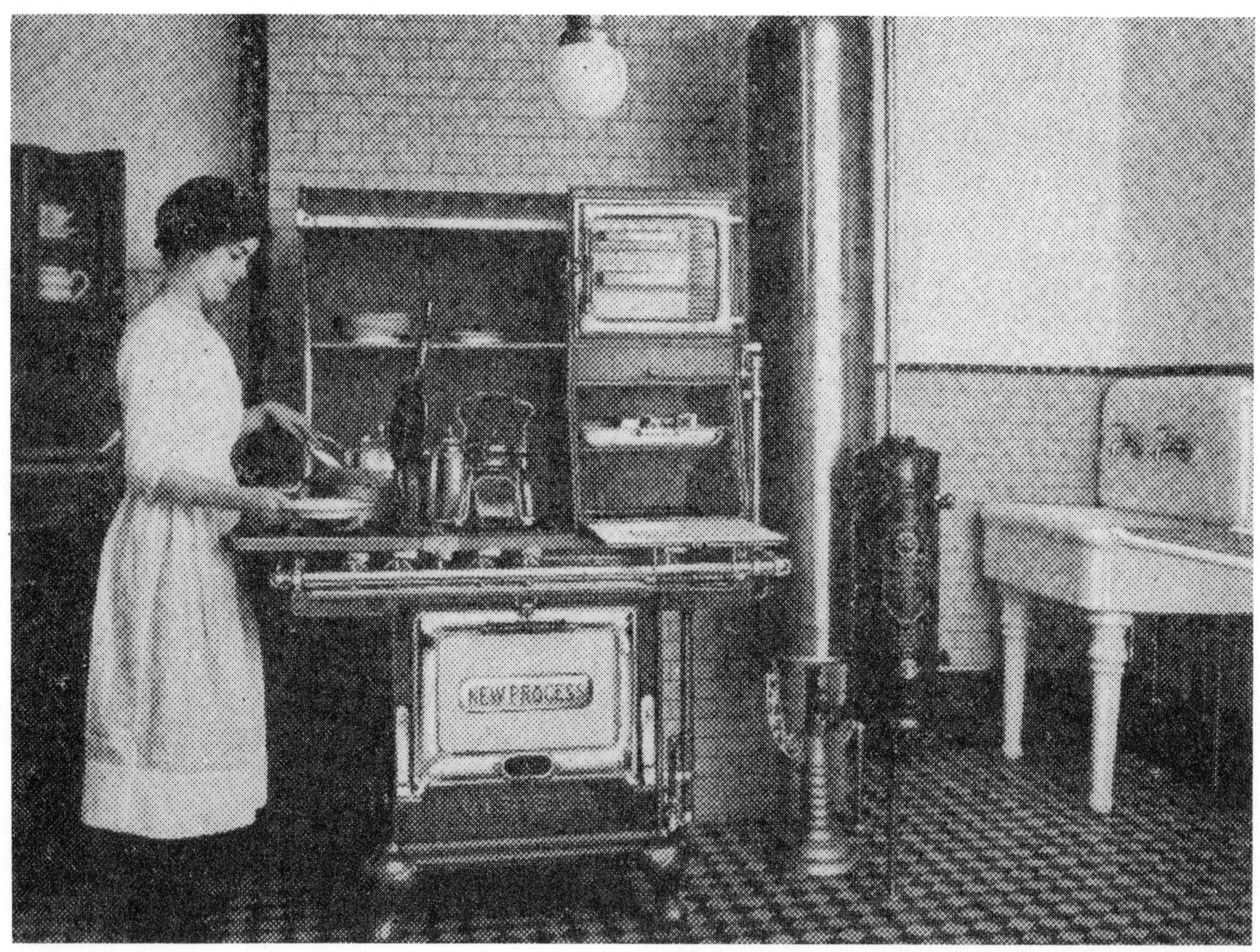

The "modern" early 1900s gas kitchen with a gas range and water heater. Notice the single ceiling light, tiled walls, and the porcelain-enamel sink on four legs. This was pictured in the *Kitchen Talk* booklet of the New Process Stove Company.

lot of trips and endless miles of walking. It took a great deal of walking, stooping, and bending to prepare a family meal in the large, old-fashioned kitchen.

At the turn of the century, the homemaker had little time on her hands after washing, ironing, sewing, cleaning, cooking, and caring for the children, unless she was fortunate enough to have servants to ease her work. A respectable woman's place was in the home. She was not permitted to vote, and politics were not open to her; besides, she was worn out from the full-time schedule at home.

In 1902, in *Good Housekeeping*, Ethelwyn Wetherald defined drudgery: "To drudge is to do in a spiritless manner work that is monotonous, irksome, compulsory, heavy and brainless."

By 1900, there were cries against the long hours and hard work for the housekeeper. The gas stove caused many changes, as it helped reduce work time and made cooking easier. The physical problems of the past century were beginning to be replaced by social concerns. With the time saved in household labor, women were able to get out of the house. Mrs. Rebecca D. Lowe of the General Federation of Women's Clubs said in 1900 that the sphere for the woman was not just the home, but the whole world.

Domestic scientist Catherine Beecher noted the "servant problem" in the mid 1800s, and by the 1900s, the public became aware that servants were considered inferior. In many cases, wages were not the problem; in fact, they were high compared to those of unskilled labor. Board and lodging were added to wages, leaving clothing a servant's only expense. In some cases the employer even supplied uniforms. However, young girls would rather have worked in a factory with fewer benefits in order to have regular hours, evenings free, and more independence.

There were many magazine articles advocating the abolition of the permanent working class, an accepted situation today. One magazine in 1901 suggested it was time for the maid to be hired on a business basis, with defined duties and hours, and that she be treated as a member of the family.

The prize-winning model kitchen in the 1901 *Good Housekeeping* contest. Mrs. C. H. Truesdell was the winner. She said features of this kitchen were attractive for either the modest or expensive home.

The Truesdell room was 14′ × 17½′. This included the pantry, which was a pass closet between the dining room and kitchen. The pantry had shelves for china, plus drawers and cupboards. A closet held extension leaves for the dining room and kitchen tables and a work table with tip bins and breadboards sat beneath a high window.

The range was in the center of the kitchen, in front of the chimney projection. It almost concealed the hot water boiler (a real luxury at that time) on the left. On the other side was a cupboard to hold pots and pans, tins, cereal, coffee, tea, etc. On the lower shelves, there was room for iron and graniteware.

Mrs. Truesdell felt that her white enameled sink was attractive under a high window, which provided necessary light. Two windows at the other end of the room also let in light and provided ventilation. The sink and the range each had an electric light on a swing bracket. The windows had olive green shades (adding a touch of color) and silkaline sash curtains. Next to the sink was a wood box that could be filled from the shed. The refrigerator was to the right of the wood box and sink. Mrs. Truesdell preferred her linoleum floor, in wood tones, over a hardwood floor because it was easier to clean and more comfortable to walk on. A plant or two provided more color.

After making the practical test of using the kitchen without a maid, Mrs. Truesdell found that it was a convenient, step-saving room.

Mrs. Truesdell, like others, probably feared the use of tin food containers, believing acidic foods would dissolve the tin and cause illness. Sanitary safeguards were not yet in place, and adulterated products by unscrupulous canners caused the responsible canners to fight for better laws. The 1906 Federal Food and Drugs Act sought to protect the public from the sale of harmful, spoiled, impure, infected, or otherwise adulterated food, drugs, and cosmetics. Washing and sterilizing were standardized. The establishment of the National Canners Association brought about a research laboratory for studying canning technology. The machinery was developed in this first decade of the twentieth century to make the cans we are familiar with today.

The Federal Food and Drugs Act of 1906 had a positive effect on the canning industry. By 1910, housewives had begun to lay aside their prejudice that canned goods were unsafe and were buying fifteen times as many canned goods as they had in 1900.

In the early years of the century, life was becoming easier with gas ranges and aluminum cookware. Packaged products, such as cereal, Nabisco wafers, and "quick and easy" Minute tapioca and Jell-o were becoming familiar in the home. Advertising in periodicals informed the housewife of these new convenient foods.

The following are samples of grocery prices between 1900 and 1910 from *This Fabulous Century:*

Fresh: Apples 30¢ a peck, eggs 12¢ a dozen, butter 18¢ a pound.

Canned: Golden cream corn 10¢, tomatoes 20¢, sliced peaches 25¢.

Staples: Tea 40¢, coffee 15¢ a pound, sugar $5.80 for 100 pounds, salt 20¢ for 100 pounds, gelatine 15¢.

Before World War I, the housewife was still doing a majority of food preparation herself. The domestic scientist became the home economist in 1908. The Cooperative Agricultural Extension was formed, providing instructions and practical demonstrations to train rural women to make the most of their resources.

Home economists told of the need for the "efficient" kitchen, an idea that captured the public's interest around 1910. By then the giddy young woman — the Gibson girl—was all freshness and good grooming, wearing a shirtwaist and a skirt that might reveal an ankle. If she wasn't yet free from domestic labor, she could at least imagine a time when she might be. A new image of the American woman evolved!

More innovations were introduced to the American woman in three years (1909 to 1912) than in the previous three decades. They included electricity, the new source of power; home appliances; the automobile; and a greater variety of foods. The housewife was informed quickly through advertising!

Christine Frederick told homemakers in 1914 to "Have A Step Saving Kitchen," a smaller version of the large kitchen. It would be a workroom to save time and labor, creating efficient and happy workers. Industry-proven efficiency methods were applied to the kitchen. As the size of appliances decreased, the kitchen became smaller, too.

Mrs. C. S. Parker, in a 1917 *Woman's Home Companion*, said 92 percent of the women in the United States did their own housework. She decided that if this was true, she was going to have a step-saving, convenient kitchen that would be a joy to work in.

Her kitchen was white; the only color came from the cream-colored drainboards and the dark red floor, which had been made of a mixture of sawdust and concrete. To prevent dust from collecting, Mrs. Parker did not use curtains or mats, and her cupboards went all the way to the ceiling.

The stove was in the middle of the room, backed up to the projection of the living-room chimney. The pantry was opposite the stove. A mixing cabinet was between the stove and the sink. The U-shaped sink with drainboard counter was a step-saving arrangement for removing dishes from the breakfast table, then washing, air drying, and putting them away, all in three steps. The breakfast alcove was her joy. It was used not just for breakfast, but for lunch and dinner too.

"The Handy Alcove Kitchen" illustrated in *Woman's Home Companion* in 1917. "A joy to the woman who does her own work."

The cozy breakfast alcove set the tone for the whole room.

This shows the beginning of the "pantry," which stands directly opposite the stove.

The U-shaped arrangement of the sink and drainboards is illustrated.

The 1918 booklet *Helpful Hints For Linoleum Salesmen* said, "Economy of time, energy and materials is highly desirable in any workshop. The kitchen (the workshop of the house) should combine these requirements with the appearance of perfect cleanliness, a workable order or arrangement and a degree of attractiveness. All fundamental qualities of a linoleum floor are effective to a high degree in solving this problem...."

Social changes had a great effect on the kitchen. Many were direct results of the onset of mass production and World War I. Factories during the "war to end all wars" drew domestic workers from the home, leaving the housewife to do her own work. The electric motor made it possible for industries to open up new areas of the country, because they were no longer dependent on steam for power. This meant the migration of workers, lured by the promise of a new future. Many of these people had been domestic workers before World War I.

The knowledge that women could do the same work as men became clear during World War I. This fact, plus a political awareness through the cause of the suffragettes, led to the "emancipation" of the American woman. The housewife demanded a solution to the household drudgery that she was now personally enduring.

This 1918 kitchen featured Armstrong's linoleum flooring. The floor and curtains offered the only color in this small, sanitary white kitchen. (Courtesy Armstrong World Industries, Inc.)

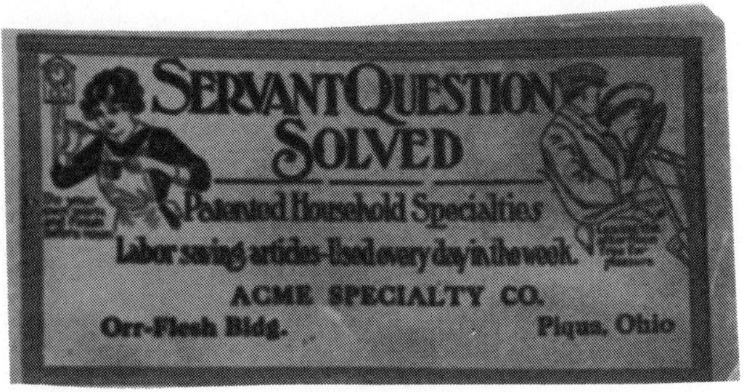

The cover of an early 1900s "Household Specialties" catalog.

Gadgets

Beaters. There were three types of beaters: fixed, rotary, and mechanical.

The inventor of this beater was George L. Raymond of Binghamton, New York. The patent application was filed January 18, 1907, and the patent, number 868,124, was granted October 15, 1907. The *Patent Gazette* said: "The combination of three wires to form wings, pivot and spiral of an egg beater, and the enclosing of the spiral portion of said wires when so formed in the handle, the upper part of which handle contains a spiral spring, and the lower part of which is capped by a trifurcated ferrule." Sometime later a single four-wing beater was manufactured.

This type of beater, with a blackwood handle, was sold from about 1915 to 1922. It was invented by E. H. Johnson, who filed a patent application September 5, 1915. On December 18, 1917, it received patent number 1,250,889.

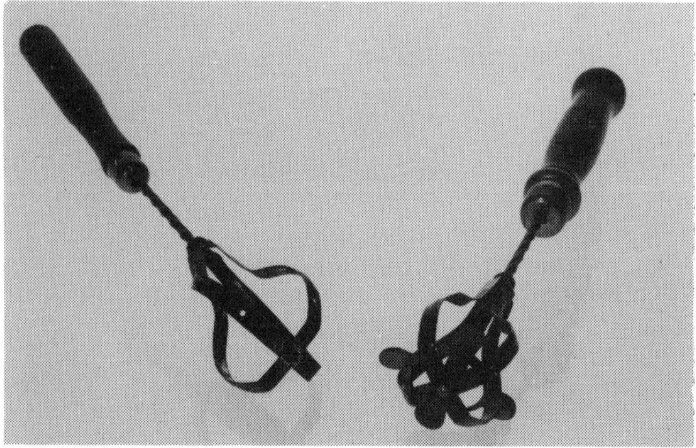
Left: Natural handle mechanical beater marked on ferrule: "The A. & J. PATD Oct.16'07 Other Pats Pending made in USA." This beater operated with an up-and-down motion like a top. The double wire wings are attached to a metal spring extending into the handle.

Right: The ferrule was marked: "A. & J. Patented Made in U.S.A. It has four solid wings with a four-leaf, perforated, nonmoveable tin insert that allows the liquid to flow through." **$9-15**

The Sterling Beater was a mechanical beater that operated on the spinning principle with an up-and-down motion.

Can openers. As the grocer's shelves offered more types of canned goods, homemakers needed more can openers.

Cutting tools. The noodle cutter was used to create dainty dishes for the table. An advertisement said it would appeal to every housekeeper. The retail price was 25¢.

Knives. A saw-back knife, a combination of serrated knife and saw, was something new in the knife line in the early 1900s. It could be used as a bread or cake knife and also for cutting up meat for home use. With its serrated edge, it never needed to be sharpened, and it cut bread better and more easily. It could be purchased for 35¢.

Note: Do not sharpen a serrated knife with an electric sharpener.

Mashers. The fruit and vegetable press, also known as a ricer, mashes and removes the skins of boiled potatoes all in one operation. Many people think it is the only way to ensure that there will be no lumps in mashed potatoes.

Meat tenderers. A meat ax was useful for cutting joints in meat and poultry, and for cracking soupbones.

In the Acme Specialty Company catalog, this was called a family cleaver and meat tenderer. "Every housewife will admit that a good meat cleaver is a necessity in her kitchen. A meat tenderer is just as necessary. Here we have both combined in one, well made, neat and attractive article." It was said to be designed for home use and indispensable in every kitchen. The cleaver was made of crucible steel that was oiled and tempered. The cutting edge was ground for sharpness, and the waterproof handle was made of black rubberoid. This indispensable tool sold for 45¢.

The Sterling eggbeater was offered by the Acme Specialty Company. They said: "Is practically automatic and is operated with one hand, leaving the other hand free to add ingredients ...only beater that can be used in an ordinary cup." **$8-14**

Sterling Can Opener

A good Can Opener is a necessity
in every home

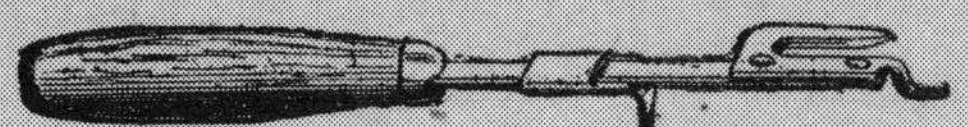

The Sterling is one of the best all-around can opener on the market.

DIRECTIONS

For opening a round can insert the point in the center of the can top, then lower handle until sliding knife touches can. Then adjust sliding knife to edge of can and by bearing down on handle you can force blade through the tin. Then draw handle around until the top is cut out. Do not touch the sliding knife after forcing it through the tin. For opening a square can, force knife or end of can opener through the can top and near the edge, working it forward with an up and down pressure

RETAIL PRICE 20 CENTS, POSTAGE 3 CENTS

The Sterling Can Opener was sold by the Acme Specialty Company for round and square cans. "A good can opener is a necessity in every home." **$3-8**

PERFECT NOODLE CUTTER

EASY TO MAKE NOODLES NOW ! One of the most dainty dishes provided for the table is Noodles. There has been a long felt want for a device to cut them, as the old method is very tedious and cumbersome work.

It is a simple little article, but it does the work to perfection. Easy to handle and always cuts them in regular even strips as shown in the picture.

Push the Perfect Noodle Cutter over the dough and the Noodles are ready for the Kettle. It is an article that will appeal to every housekeeper.

Agents will readily see what a field there is for this device. Every household wants noodles to eat but they don't get them often enough because of the trouble to cut, etc.

Agents, here is your opportunity to handle a live article.

RETAIL PRICE 25 CENTS POSTAGE 3 CENTS

16

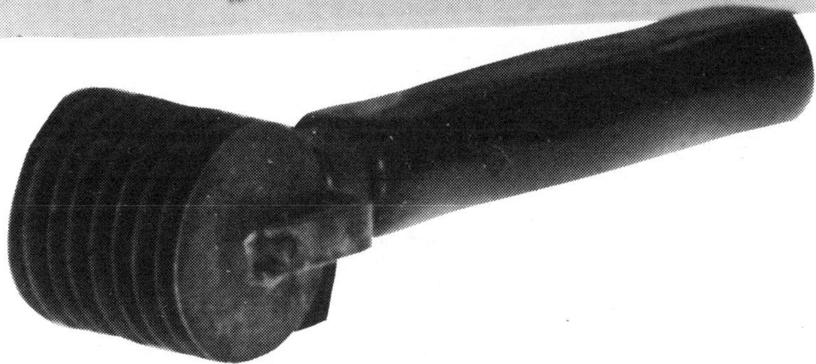

The unmarked noodle cutter has a black wooden enamel handle. The advertisement is from the Acme Specialty Company catalog. The retail price was 25¢. It told the agents that this was their opportunity to handle a "live" article. **$3-6.50**

The "Queen of the Kitchen Combination" could be used to core apples, cut biscuits, cut the center out of doughnuts, cut cookies, or separate eggs. **$12-20**

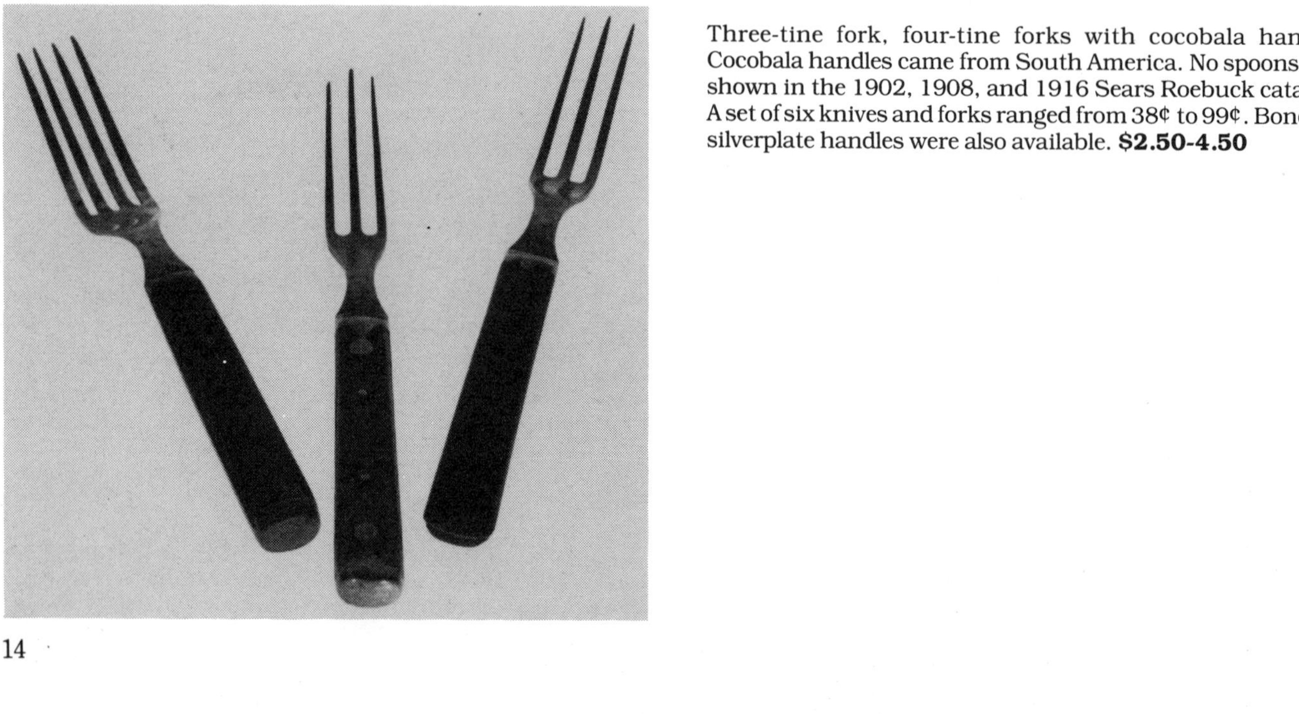

Three-tine fork, four-tine forks with cocobala handles. Cocobala handles came from South America. No spoons were shown in the 1902, 1908, and 1916 Sears Roebuck catalogs. A set of six knives and forks ranged from 38¢ to 99¢. Bone and silverplate handles were also available. **$2.50-4.50**

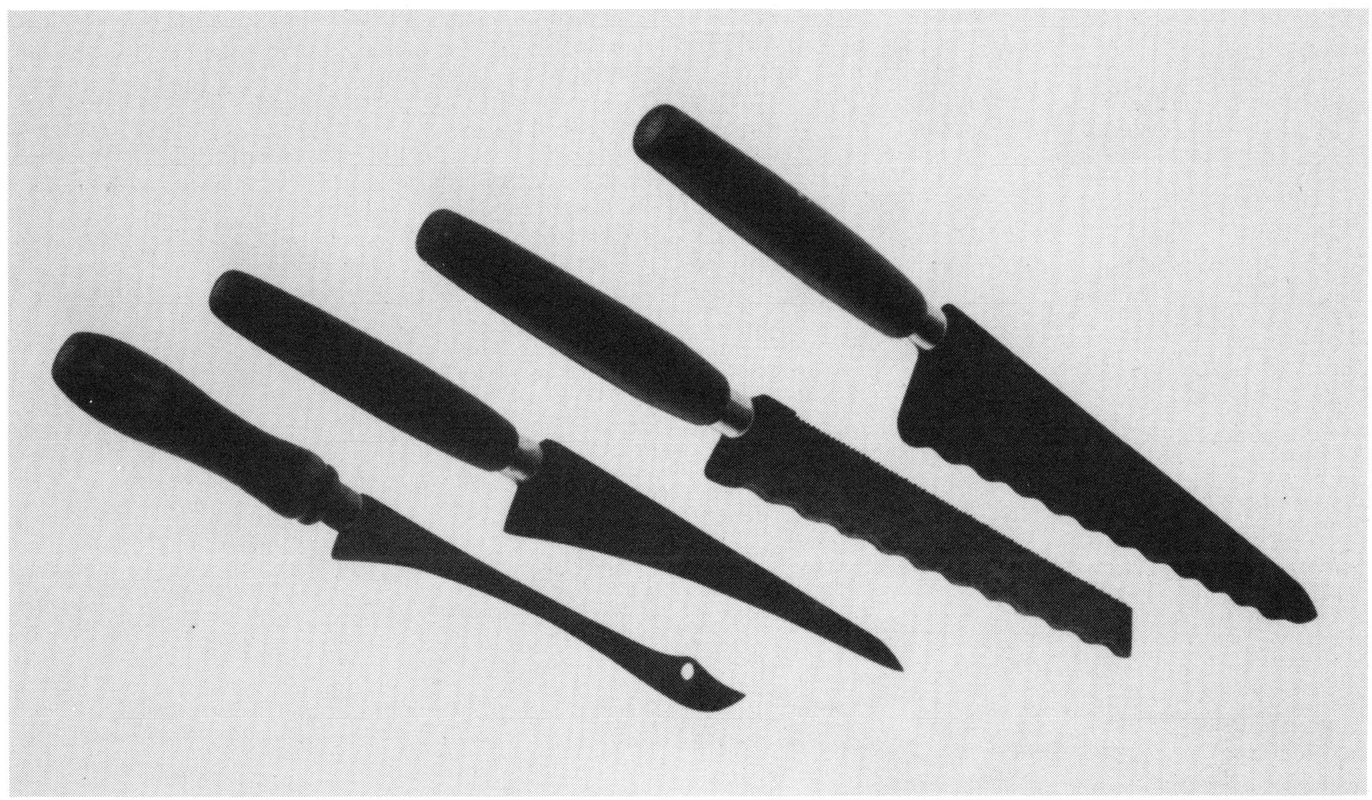

Bread knives with black wooden handles that needed no sharpening. Left to right:

New System Bakery, Woodsfield, Ohio (scalloped edge).

Unmarked. Serrated edge — scalloped edge. In 1918, Sears Roebuck bread knives were sold for 11¢ or 34¢. They would cleanly slice a hot or cold loaf of bread. Utility knives with black wooden handles were for all purposes.

Marked CHCO. It is a carving and utility knife.

An unmarked carving-utility knife. **$6-9**

A. & J. mechanical double potato masher with black enamel handle. This masher operates on the same principle as a spinning top, with an up-and-down motion. **$8.50-15**

On one handle: "King Seamless-Cup Press." On other side: "Cin'ti Galv. Co." This is a ricer, masher, fruit and vegetable press. **$9.50-12**

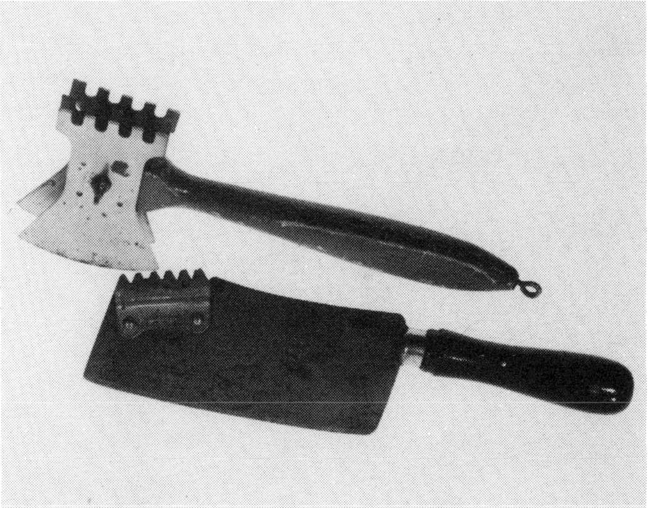

Meats could be tenderized by pounding them, breaking down tough muscle fibers.

"Pat. Apr. 4, 1911; M. H. Tyler Mfg. Co. Muncie, Indiana," marked on natural wooden handle.

Marked: "Meat Tenderer; Pat. 4-8-07; Superior Warranted." A combination meat tenderer and cleaver. It is made of crucible steel and has a rubberoid handle. **$6-10**

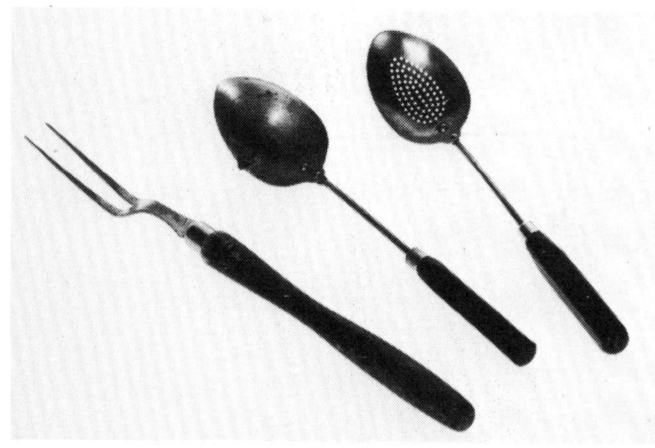

A fork is useful to test the tenderness of meats and vegetables. Metal spoons can be used for mixing, stirring, straining, and tasting. Left to right:

A. & J. fork.

"A. & J.; Patented Made in U.S.A." Measuring spoon marked from one teaspoon to one tablespoon.

"Pat'd. A. & J." Strainer spoon. **$3-5**

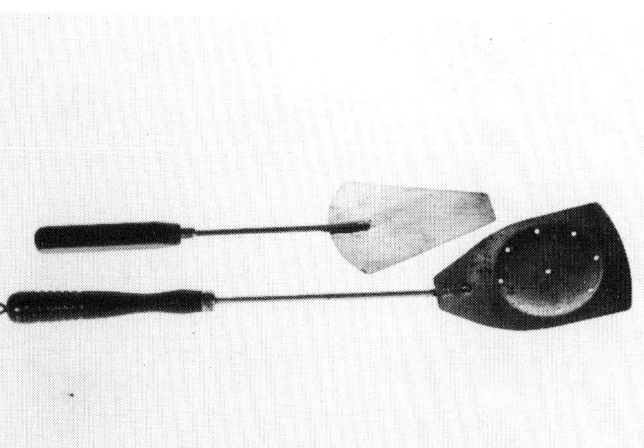

Turners were useful for turning hamburgers and pancakes. Slotted turners were handy for lifting foods that needed to drain.

A. & J. turner, unmarked turner. **$3-6.50**

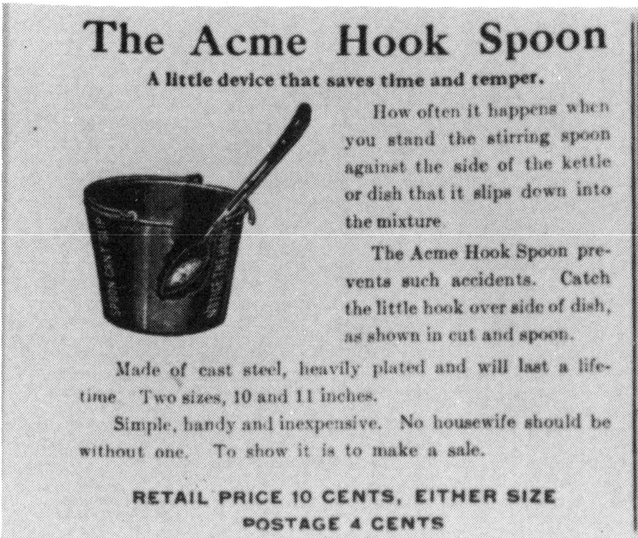

The Acme Hook Spoon was sold by the Acme Specialty Company in the early 1900s for 10¢. This device saved time and temper by hooking on the side of pan, preventing it from slipping into the mixture. **$4-7**

The colorful duster is made of many colored pieces of material. The burner is marked: "Sterno Canned Heat; To extinguish push burner aside and place this plate over can opening."

The burner holds a can of canned heat in a metal frame that has a movable flame adapter. **Burner, $4-7.50**

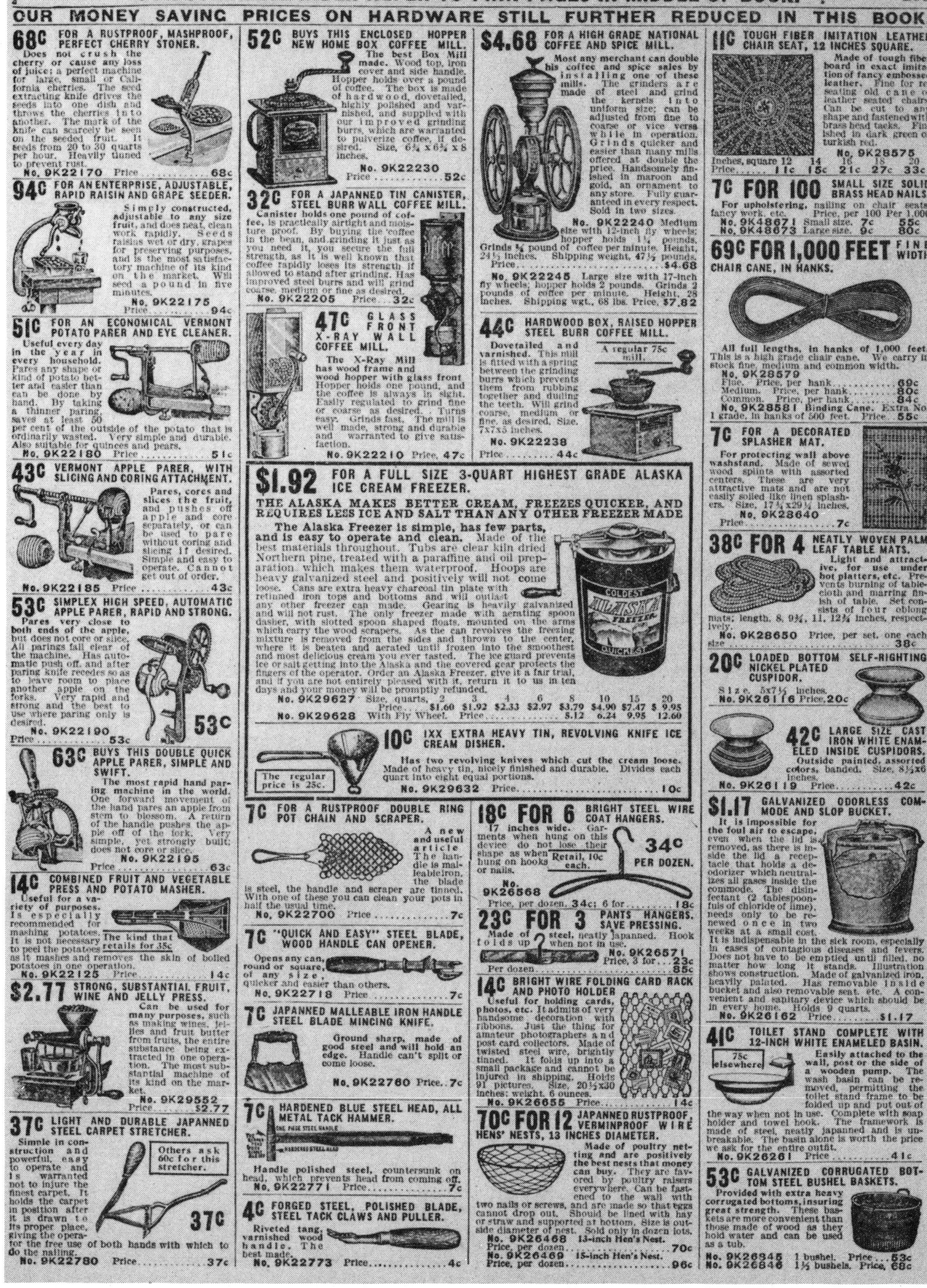

2 FOR COMPLETE INDEX REFER TO PINK PAGES IN MIDDLE OF BOOK. 469

OUR MONEY SAVING PRICES ON HARDWARE STILL FURTHER REDUCED IN THIS BOOK.

68c FOR A RUSTPROOF, MASHPROOF, PERFECT CHERRY STONER.

Does not crush the cherry or cause any loss of juice; a perfect machine for large, small or California cherries. The seed extracting knife drives the seeds into one dish and throws the cherries into another. The mark of the knife can scarcely be seen on the seeded fruit. It seeds from 20 to 30 quarts per hour. Heavily tinned to prevent rust.

No. 9K22170 Price 68c

94c FOR AN ENTERPRISE, ADJUSTABLE, RAPID RAISIN AND GRAPE SEEDER.

Simply constructed, adjustable to any size fruit, and does neat, clean work rapidly. Seeds raisins wet or dry, grapes for preserving purposes, and is the most satisfactory machine of its kind on the market. Will seed a pound in five minutes.

No. 9K22175 Price 94c

51c FOR AN ECONOMICAL VERMONT POTATO PARER AND EYE CLEANER.

Useful every day in the year in every household. Pares any shape or kind of potato better and easier than can be done by hand. By taking a thinner paring, saves at least 50 per cent of the outside of the potato that is ordinarily wasted. Very simple and durable. Also suitable for quinces and pears.

No. 9K22180 Price 51c

43c VERMONT APPLE PARER, WITH SLICING AND CORING ATTACHMENT.

Pares, cores and slices the fruit, and pushes off apple and core separately, or can be used to pare without coring and slicing if desired. Simple and easy to operate. Cannot get out of order.

No. 9K22185 Price 43c

53c SIMPLEX HIGH SPEED, AUTOMATIC APPLE PARER, RAPID AND STRONG.

Pares very close to both ends of the apple, but does not core or slice. All parings fall clear of the machine. Has automatic push off, and after paring knife recedes so as to leave room to place another apple on the forks. Very rapid and strong and the best to use where paring only is desired.

No. 9K22190 Price 53c

53c

63c BUYS THIS DOUBLE QUICK APPLE PARER, SIMPLE AND SWIFT.

The most rapid hand paring machine in the world. One forward movement of the hand pares an apple from stem to blossom. A return of the handle pushes the apple off of the fork. Very simple, yet strongly built; does not core or slice.

No. 9K22195 Price 63c

14c COMBINED FRUIT AND VEGETABLE PRESS AND POTATO MASHER.

Useful for a variety of purposes. Is especially recommended for mashing potatoes. It is not necessary to peel the potatoes as it mashes and removes the skin of boiled potatoes in one operation.

The kind that retails for 35c

No. 9K22125 Price 14c

$2.77 STRONG, SUBSTANTIAL FRUIT, WINE AND JELLY PRESS.

Can be used for many purposes, such as making wines, jellies and fruit butter from fruits, the entire substance being extracted in one operation. The most substantial machine of its kind on the market.

No. 9K29552 Price $2.77

37c LIGHT AND DURABLE JAPANNED STEEL CARPET STRETCHER.

Simple in construction and powerful, easy to operate and is warranted not to injure the finest carpet. It holds the carpet in position after it is drawn to its proper place, giving the operator the free use of both hands with which to do the nailing.

Others ask 60c for this stretcher.

37c

No. 9K22780 Price 37c

52c BUYS THIS ENCLOSED HOPPER NEW HOME BOX COFFEE MILL.

The best Box Mill made. Wood top, iron cover and side handle. Hopper holds over a pound of coffee. The box is made of hardwood, dovetailed, highly polished and varnished, and supplied with our improved grinding burrs, which are warranted to pulverize coffee, if desired. Size, 6¾ x 6¾ x 8 inches.

No. 9K22230 Price 52c

32c FOR A JAPANNED TIN CANISTER, STEEL BURR WALL COFFEE MILL.

Canister holds one pound of coffee, is practically airtight and moisture proof. By buying the coffee in the bean, and grinding it just as you need it, you secure the full strength, as it is well known that coffee rapidly loses its strength if allowed to stand after grinding. Has improved steel burrs and will grind coarse, medium or fine as desired.

No. 9K22205 Price 32c

47c GLASS FRONT X-RAY WALL COFFEE MILL.

The X-Ray Mill has wood frame and wood hopper with glass front. Hopper holds one pound, and the coffee is always in sight. Easily regulated to grind fine or coarse as desired. Turns easy. Grinds fast. The mill is well made, strong and durable and warranted to give satisfaction.

No. 9K22210 Price, 47c

$4.68 FOR A HIGH GRADE NATIONAL COFFEE AND SPICE MILL.

Most any merchant can double his coffee and spice sales by installing one of these mills. The grinders are made of steel and grind the kernels into uniform size; can be adjusted from fine to coarse or vice versa while in operation. Grinds quicker and easier than many mills offered at double the price. Handsomely finished in maroon and gold, an ornament to any store. Fully guaranteed in every respect. Sold in two sizes.

No. 9K22240 Medium size with 12-inch fly wheels; hopper holds 1¼ pounds. Grinds ¾ pound of coffee per minute. Height, 24½ inches. Shipping weight, 47½ pounds. Price $4.68

No. 9K22245 Large size with 17-inch fly wheels; hopper holds 2 pounds. Grinds 2 pounds of coffee per minute. Height, 28 inches. Shipping wgt., 68 lbs. Price, $7.82

44c HARDWOOD BOX, RAISED HOPPER STEEL BURR COFFEE MILL.

A regular 75c mill.

Dovetailed and varnished. This mill is fitted with a spring between the grinding burrs which prevents them from rubbing together and dulling the teeth. Will grind coarse, medium or fine, as desired. Size, 7x7x5 inches.

No. 9K22238 Price 44c

$1.92 FOR A FULL SIZE 3-QUART HIGHEST GRADE ALASKA ICE CREAM FREEZER.

THE ALASKA MAKES BETTER CREAM, FREEZES QUICKER, AND REQUIRES LESS ICE AND SALT THAN ANY OTHER FREEZER MADE

The Alaska Freezer is simple, has few parts, and is easy to operate and clean. Made of the best materials throughout. Tubs are clear kiln dried Northern pine, treated with a paraffine and oil preparation which makes them waterproof. Hoops are heavy galvanized steel and positively will not come loose. Cans are extra heavy charcoal tin plate with retinned iron tops and bottoms and will outlast any other freezer can made. Gearing is heavily galvanized and will not rust. The only freezer made with aerating spoon dasher, with slotted spoon shaped floats, mounted on the arms which carry the wood scrapers. As the can revolves the freezing mixture is removed from the sides and thrown to the center, where it is beaten and aerated until frozen into the smoothest and most delicious cream you ever tasted. The ice guard prevents ice or salt getting into the Alaska and the covered gear protects the fingers of the operator. Order an Alaska Freezer, give it a fair trial, and if you are not entirely pleased with it, return it to us in ten days and your money will be promptly refunded.

	Size, quarts	2	3	4	6	8	10	15	20
No. 9K29627	Price	$1.60	$1.92	$2.33	$2.97	$3.79	$4.90	$7.47	$ 9.95
No. 9K29628	With Fly Wheel. Price					5.12	6.24	9.95	12.60

10c IXX EXTRA HEAVY TIN, REVOLVING KNIFE ICE CREAM DISHER.

The regular price is 25c.

Has two revolving knives which cut the cream loose. Made of heavy tin, nicely finished and durable. Divides each quart into eight equal portions.

No. 9K29632 Price 10c

7c FOR A RUSTPROOF DOUBLE RING POT CHAIN AND SCRAPER.

A new and useful article. The handle is malleable iron, the blade is steel, the handle and scraper are tinned. With one of these you can clean your pots in half the usual time.

No. 9K22700 Price 7c

7c "QUICK AND EASY" STEEL BLADE, WOOD HANDLE CAN OPENER.

Opens any can, round or square, of any size, quicker and easier than others.

No. 9K22718 Price 7c

7c JAPANNED MALLEABLE IRON HANDLE STEEL BLADE MINCING KNIFE.

Ground sharp, made of good steel and will hold an edge. Handle can't split or come loose.

No. 9K22760 Price .. 7c

7c HARDENED BLUE STEEL HEAD, ALL METAL TACK HAMMER.

Handle polished steel, countersunk on head, which prevents head from coming off.

No. 9K22771 Price 7c

4c FORGED STEEL, POLISHED BLADE, STEEL TACK CLAWS AND PULLER.

Riveted tang, varnished wood handle. The best made.

No. 9K22773 Price 4c

18c FOR 6 BRIGHT STEEL WIRE COAT HANGERS.

17 inches wide. Garments when hung on this device do not lose their shape as when hung on hooks or nails.

Retail, 10c each.

34c PER DOZEN.

No. 9K26568 Price, per dozen, 34c; 6 for 18c

23c FOR 3 PANTS HANGERS. SAVE PRESSING.

Made of steel, neatly japanned. Hook folds up when not in use.

No. 9K26571 Price, 3 for ... 23c

Per dozen 85c

14c BRIGHT WIRE FOLDING CARD RACK AND PHOTO HOLDER

Useful for holding cards, photos, etc. It admits of very handsome decoration with ribbons. Just the thing for amateur photographers and post card collectors. Made of twisted steel wire, brightly tinned. It folds up into a small package and cannot be injured in shipping. Holds 91 pictures. Size, 20½x30 inches; weight, 6 ounces.

No. 9K26655 Price 14c

70c FOR 12 JAPANNED RUSTPROOF, VERMINPROOF WIRE HENS' NESTS, 13 INCHES DIAMETER.

Made of poultry netting and are positively the best nests that money can buy. They are favored by poultry raisers everywhere. Can be fastened to the wall with two nails or screws, and are made so that eggs cannot drop out. Should be lined with hay or straw and supported at bottom. Size is outside diameter of nest. Sold only in dozen lots.

No. 9K26468 13-inch Hen's Nest. Price, per dozen 70c

No. 9K26469 15-inch Hen's Nest. Price, per dozen 96c

11c TOUGH FIBER IMITATION LEATHER CHAIR SEAT, 12 INCHES SQUARE.

Made of tough fiber board in exact imitation of fancy embossed leather. Fine for reseating old cane or leather seated chairs. Can be cut to any shape and fastened with brass head tacks. Finished in dark green or turkish red.

No. 9K28575

Inches, square	12	14	16	18	20
Price	11c	15c	21c	27c	33c

7c FOR 100 SMALL SIZE SOLID BRASS HEAD NAILS.

For upholstering, nailing on chair seats, fancy work, etc.

		Price, per 100	Per 1,000
No. 9K48671	Small size.	7c	55c
No. 9K48673	Large size.	9c	80c

69c FOR 1,000 FEET FINE WIDTH CHAIR CANE, IN HANKS.

All full lengths, in hanks of 1,000 feet. This is a high grade chair cane. We carry in stock fine, medium and common width.

No. 9K28579

Fine. Price, per hank 69c

Medium. Price, per hank 80c

Common. Price, per hank 84c

No. 9K28581 Binding Cane. Extra No. 1 grade, in hanks of 500 feet. Price 55c

7c FOR A DECORATED SPLASHER MAT.

For protecting wall above washstand. Made of sewed wood splints with assorted centers. These are very attractive mats and are not easily soiled like linen splashers. Size, 17¼x29½ inches.

No. 9K28640 Price 7c

38c FOR 4 NEATLY WOVEN PALM LEAF TABLE MATS.

Light and attractive, for use under hot platters, etc. Prevents burning of tablecloth and marring finish of table. Set consists of four oblong mats; length, 8, 9¾, 11, 12¾ inches, respectively.

No. 9K28650 Price, per set, one each size 38c

20c LOADED BOTTOM SELF-RIGHTING NICKEL PLATED CUSPIDOR.

Size, 5x7½ inches.

No. 9K26116 Price, 20c

42c LARGE SIZE CAST IRON WHITE ENAMELED INSIDE CUSPIDORS.

Outside painted, assorted colors, banded. Size, 8½x6 inches.

No. 9K26119 Price 42c

$1.17 GALVANIZED ODORLESS COMMODE AND SLOP BUCKET.

It is impossible for the foul air to escape, even when the lid is removed, as there is inside the lid a receptacle that holds a deodorizer which neutralizes all gases inside the commode. The disinfectant (2 tablespoonfuls of chloride of lime), needs only to be renewed once in two weeks at a small cost. It is indispensable in the sick room, especially in cases of contagious diseases and fevers. Does not have to be emptied until filled, no matter how long it stands. Illustration shows construction. Made of galvanized iron, heavily painted. Has removable inside bucket and also removable seat, etc. A convenient and sanitary device which should be in every home. Holds 9 quarts.

No. 9K26162 Price $1.17

41c TOILET STAND COMPLETE WITH 12-INCH WHITE ENAMELED BASIN.

75c elsewhere

Easily attached to the wall, post or the side of a wooden pump. The wash basin can be removed, permitting the toilet stand frame to be folded up and put out of the way when not in use. Complete with soap holder and towel hook. The framework is made of steel, neatly japanned and is unbreakable. The basin alone is worth the price we ask for the entire outfit.

No. 9K26261 Price 41c

53c GALVANIZED CORRUGATED BOTTOM STEEL BUSHEL BASKETS.

Provided with extra heavy corrugated bottoms, insuring great strength. These baskets are more convenient than those made of wood as they hold water and can be used as a tub.

No. 9K26845 1 bushel. Price ... 53c

No. 9K26846 1½ bushels. Price, 68c

An assortment of kitchen hardware from the 1908 Sears Roebuck catalog. (Courtesy Sears, Roebuck and Company.)

Small Appliances

Electric casseroles and chafing dishes. Sometime during the first decade of the 1900s, electric casserole and chafing dishes appeared on the market. Landers, Frary and Clark was one manufacturer.

Electric coffeemakers. Landers, Frary and Clark introduced its first electric appliance, the "Universal" percolator, in 1908. It had an innovation called the "cold water pump," which allowed "perking" to start in two or three minutes. This was much faster than other percolators, which didn't start perking until the whole pot of water came to a boil.

An electric percolator sold for $4.50 in the 1916 Sears Roebuck catalog.

The first glass Silex coffeemaker was introduced in 1914. Silex meant: "Sanitary and Interesting method of making Luscious coffee. It is Easy to operate on account of its being X-ray transparent."

Electric corn poppers. Corn popping has been a favorite American pastime since the first Thanksgiving with the Indians. The first electric corn popper appeared in 1907; the manufacturer is unknown. It was said to work when connected to a light socket, and was to have been completely safe.

Electric egg cookers. Sears Roebuck's 1916 catalog illustrated an electric egg cooker for $2.45.

Irons. By the turn of the century, cast iron irons were usually hollow and filled with hot coal, charcoal, or a heated slug. Or, they might be "sad-irons." Three other types were acetylene gas, alcohol, and gasoline.

There were many different sizes of flat irons. They were heavy to lift and too hot to hold comfortably. Using them was pure drudgery. In 1871, one of the first major improvements was patented by a woman, Mrs. Potts. Her iron had a clip-on walnut handle that was not hot to hold and could be transferred from one iron to another. While one iron was in use, others were heated on the fire.

In 1890, they were sold by the Enterprise Manufacturing Company in sets of three for $4.50. By 1902, they were sold by Sears Roebuck at a reduced price of $2.83 for a complete set.

In 1862, Henry W. Seely invented the first electric iron, but it was not practical. Inventors began to work on designing electric irons once electric power companies were established in 1890. In 1903, Earl Richardson developed an electric iron with a "hot point," which was the origin of the Hotpoint trademark that became a part of General Electric in 1918.

Electric irons quickly became popular because they eased the drudgery of ironing. Before they came on the market, ironing meant heating and using various weights of heavy flat irons for different stages of the job, all the while enduring the discomfort of the heat.

General Electric sold an EvenHeat electric iron in 1913 for $4.25. The first iron with a detachable cord was offered by General Electric.

"Landers, Frary and Clark, New Britain, Connecticut," is marked on this four-egg electric egg cooker, which appears to have been used only for boiling eggs. **$12-15**

An example of one of Mrs. Pott's irons. (Courtesy Mildred Tuttle.) **$8-22 Set $15-28**

As electricity became more available, more electric appliances entered the marketplace. World War I encouraged the expansion of electric utilities for war production. Great strides were made in the next two decades in the development of electrical appliances.

Electric mixers. The invention of the small electric motor proved to be a key factor in the history of kitchen

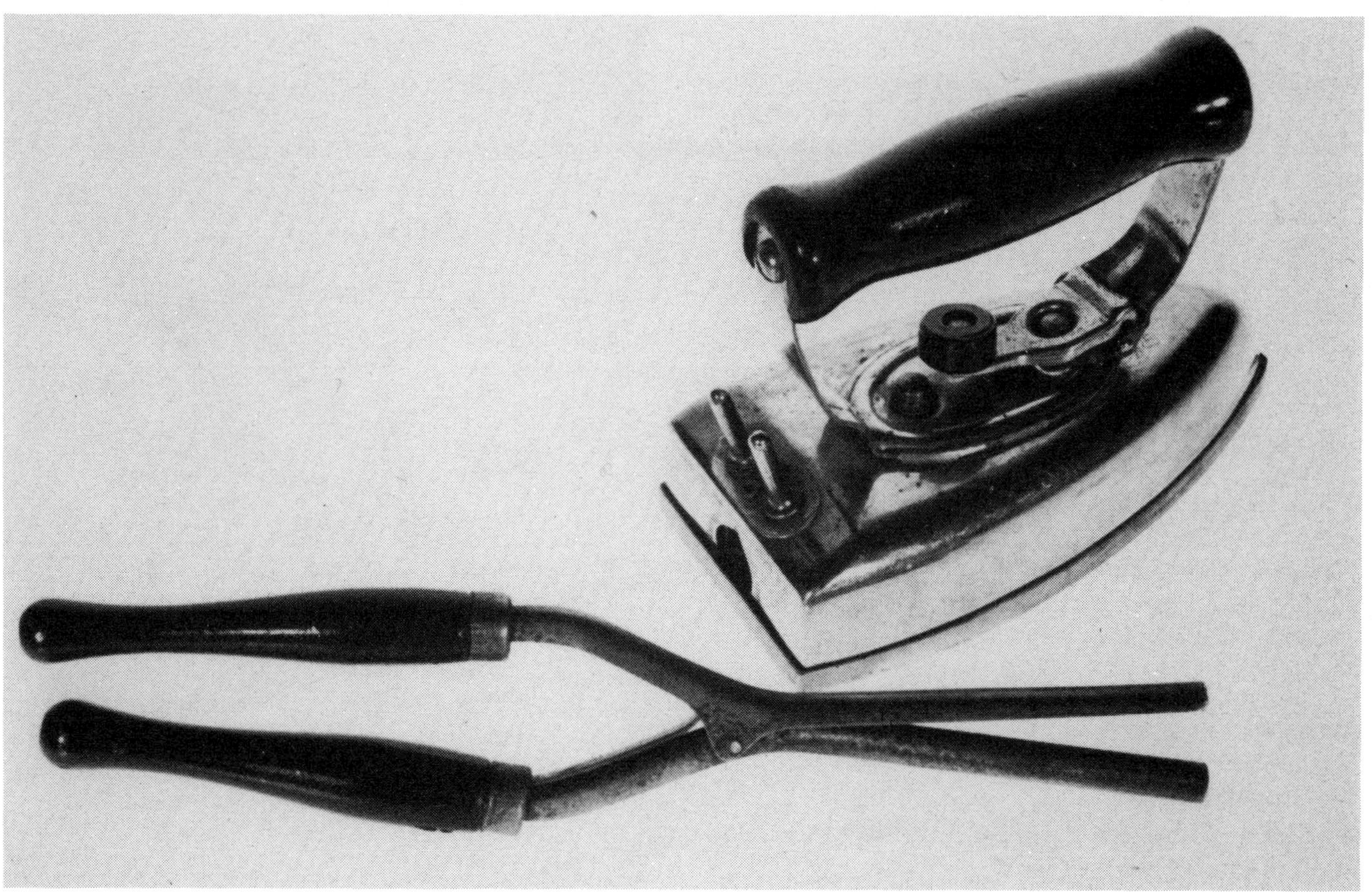

An electric traveling iron with curling iron, marked around inset of heater: "Universal, Landers, Frary & Clark; Volts 106/114 No. E 9021 Amps. 3.2." The iron was patented September 23, 1913. A curling iron heated this way was easier and cleaner to use than one heated over an oil lamp or gas stove ...no soot! **$6.50-10**

gadgets. The mixer-beater was one of the first appliances to be power driven.

One of the earliest domestic mixer-beaters, "Universal" was offered by Landers, Frary and Clark in 1918. It was simply a hand-driven beater with a small motor strapped on it. It had fixed beaters.

Toasters. Wire toasters with shorter wooden handles were used over the heat of coal or wood stoves starting in the 1890s.

The Knoblock Pyramid Toaster was patented in 1909. This top-of-the-range toaster was popular because it was easy to use, economical, and could be used on a gas, oil, or gasoline stove. It was said to be capable of toasting four slices of bread on the slanted sides in two minutes, and at the same time a pot of tea or coffee could be boiled on the flat top. It sold at Sears Roebuck for 23¢.

The popularity of the pyramid tin toaster has continued through the years. It is still being made today by Bromwell, a division of Leigh Products. The Bromwell Wire Goods Company, in business since 1819, is the oldest houseware company in the United States. Sears Roebuck sold the Perfect wire toaster for 21¢ in 1916.

General Electric and Westinghouse introduced the first electric toasters in 1909. These early toasters were completely open, toasting the bread on one side only. The electric toaster was quite an innovation — it made it possible to have toast anytime and it didn't have to be used in the kitchen. However, it needed to be watched or you could end up with burnt toast. A frugal housewife would take it to the sink and scrape off the burnt side. Once the first side was toasted, it had to be turned over manually.

"Do you like brown toast but find it unusually dried out? Does it so quickly it doesn't dry out. The perforated top can be used as a warming rack for toast or coffee pot." The electric toaster described in this copy sold for $1.45 and $1.95 according to an ad appearing in the 1916 Sears-Roebuck catalog.

Electric waffle irons and sandwich grills. The electric waffle iron appeared in 1918 when Landers, Frary and Clark introduced their model for $15. A waffle iron with a heat indicator was developed in 1920 by another company.

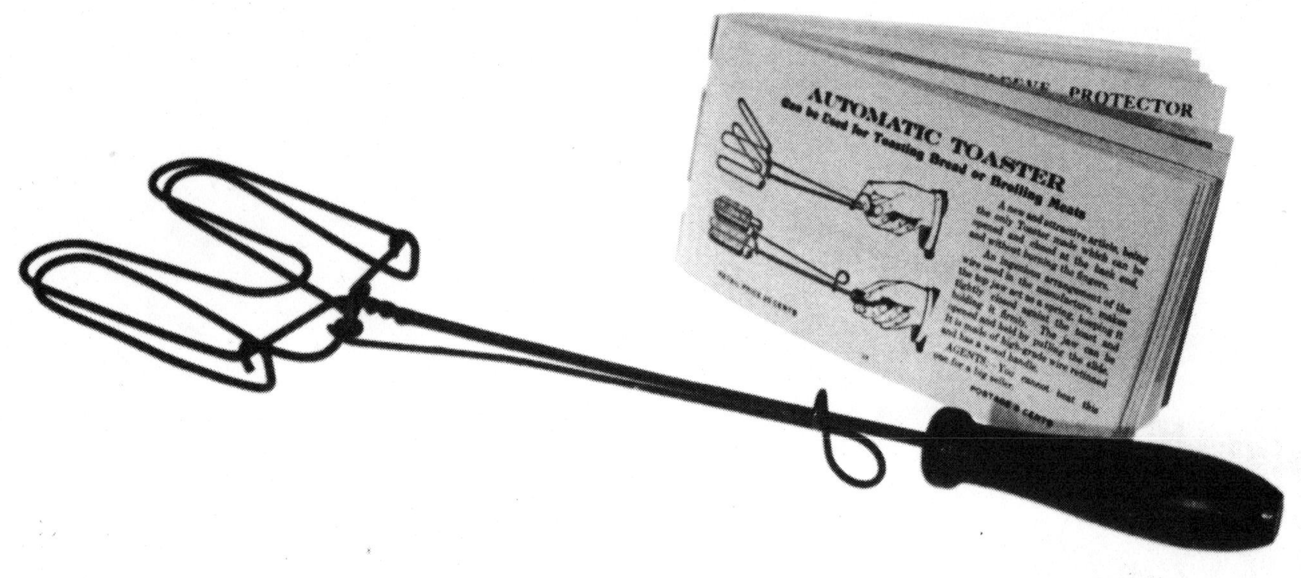

This black-handled, unmarked hand toaster was called an Automatic Toaster because it was said to be the only toaster that could be opened and closed at the back without burning the fingers. It was available in the early 1900s. **$6-8**

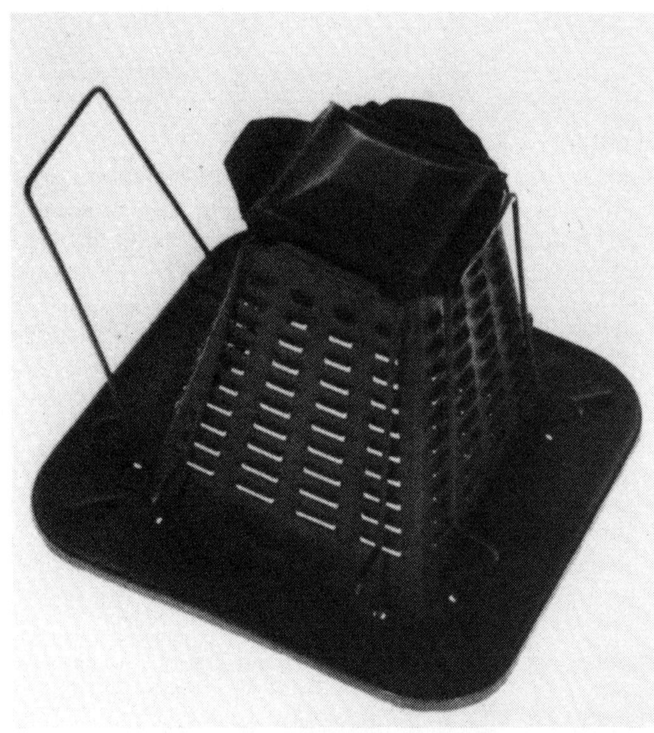

An early tin pyramid toaster. (Courtesy Mildred Tuttle.) **$7-15**

Turnover Toaster, marked: "Style no. 284032-A; Patented 8-25-14; Westinghouse Elec. & Mfg. Co. East Pittsburgh, Pa. U.S.A. 100-120 V. 550 Watts." Attached cord. **$12-18**

Toaster marked: "Thermax; volts 108 No. E 3946 amps. 45; Landers, Frary and Clark New Britain, Conn. U.S.A. Pat. Applied For." Has removable cord. **$10-15**

UNIVERSAL

Christmas Gifts

A Landers, Frary and Clark 1918 advertisement for their Universal appliances.

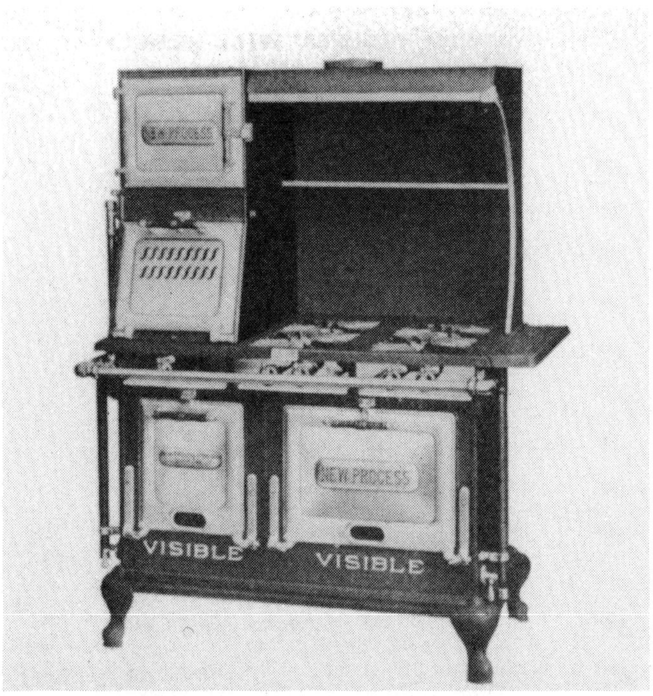

An early 1900 gas stove manufactured by the New Process Stove Company, Division of American Stove Company, Cleveland, Ohio. This model had two baking ovens (upper and lower), a broiling and boiling compartment, a warming oven, and cooking top.

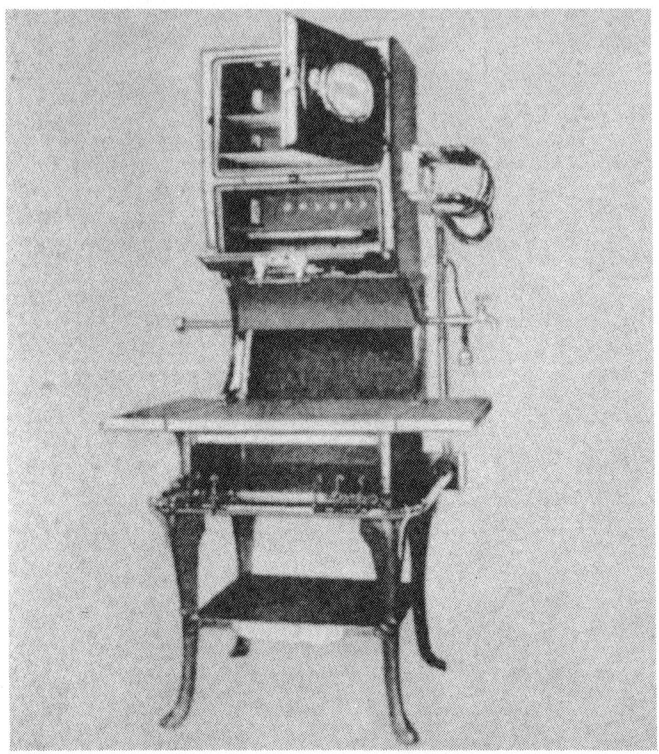

One of the first commercial electric ranges, c. 1910. It had an oven unit on top of the range, with a warming shelf below. The range had only two burners.

Large Appliances

Dishwashers. In 1899, an American housewife, Mrs. Cochran of Indiana, invented a domestic dishwashing machine. It was a wooden tub that was wheeled over to the sink, filled with dirty dishes, and then with hot water from a bucket. The handle was cranked to provide power to a set of air plungers, which drove water over the dishes. In 1914, it was fitted with an electric motor to become the first automatic dishwasher. "Automatic" meant the motor drove the washers. The machine had to be filled by hand and drained afterward.

In 1910 at the New York State Fair, a hand-cranked mechanical dishwasher was exhibited by the Walker Company of Syracuse, New York. This company persevered with the problem of automatically filling and draining the water until the electric dishwasher as we know it today was developed.

Ranges. Wood- and coal-burning stoves were popular at the turn of the century. Gas ranges, which had been available since the mid 1800s, were also beginning to be popular and had many advantages over wood and coal stoves. Combination coal and gas ranges were still offered after World War I.

The advantages of a gas stove were many compared to a wood or coal stove. Gas was clean burning and required no carrying or hauling since it was piped directly into the range. Fire started in an instant with no wasted fuel. And best of all, it saved time and labor.

Early gas and electric ranges copied the design of coal stoves. The manufacture of electric ranges on a commercial scale began in 1910 with the Hughes Electric Range, developed by George A. Hughes, founder of the Hughes Electric Heating Company. In 1918, he sold his company to General Electric and became president of a new company called General Electric Appliance Company (known as Hotpoint today because of a merger with the Hotpoint Company of California). In 1910, the Garland Gas Range had four burners with a side oven and broiler and sat on four legs.

Early electric ranges were neither satisfactory nor successful for several reasons: few homes had electric power, the range was not a constant source of energy; it was slow cooking, and it needed many repairs.

A significant device for the housewife was the oven regulator. It was invented in 1913 and was offered on some of American Stove Company's models in 1915, equipped with the Lorain Red Wheel Regulator. The first were not as easy for the housewife to use because the wheel was numbered from one to eleven, and the cook had to follow the direction book carefully. Later models solved this problem by reflecting true temperatures, allowing the housewife to set the indicator at 350 and know that the oven would remain at 350 degrees.

Refrigerators. Iceboxes had been used since the 1840s to refrigerate food, operating on the principle that the cake of ice in the top part of the icebox absorbed heat when it melted, and the heavier cool air flowed downward to the food compartments.

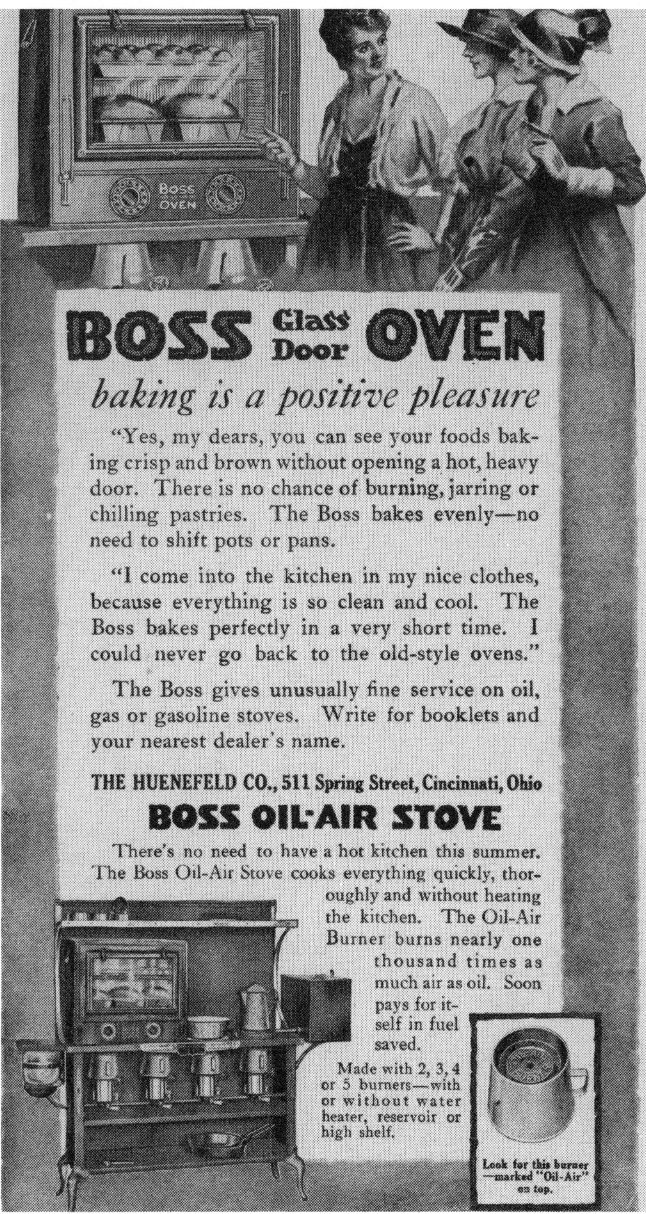

The 1917 Boss Oil-Air Stove with its glass door oven. Oil and kerosene ranges had been available since the late 1800s and were most often used in rural areas.

This New Range Is A Wonder For Cooking

Although it is less than four feet long it can do every kind of cooking for any ordinary family by gas in warm weather, or by coal or wood when the kitchen needs heating.

There is absolutely no danger in this combination, as the gas section is as entirely separate from the coal section as if placed in another part of the kitchen.

Note the two gas ovens above—one for baking, glass paneled and one for broiling, with white enamel door.

Gold Medal Glenwood

The large oven below has the Indicator and is heated by coal or wood.

See the cooking surface when you want to rush things—five burners for gas and four covers for coal.

When in a hurry both coal and gas ovens can be operated at the same time, using one for meats and the other for pastry—It

"Makes Cooking Easy"

Write for handsome free booklet 123 that tells all about it.

Weir Stove Co., Taunton, Mass.

Makers of the Celebrated Glenwood Coal, Wood and Gas Ranges, Heating Stoves and Furnaces.

In 1917, the Weir Stove Company advertised Glenwood, a combination coal/wood and gas range that posed no danger, because the gas section was entirely separate from the coal section. It had two gas ovens on top for baking and broiling and a large coal/wood oven below. When in a hurry, homemakers could use both the coal and gas ovens at the same time. Plus, there were five gas burners or four wood burners on top.

Ferdinand Carre introduced the forerunner of the household refrigerator in 1860 with his artificial ice machine. Mechanized refrigeration was possible when it was reduced to a compact size and had a built-in motor with thermostatic control.

The Domelre was the first successful air-cooled refrigerator. It was styled like the icebox, with the addition of a compressor unit on top, and was sold in 1913 and 1914.

Around 1916 to 1917, the large corporations started production of electric refrigerators, beginning with Kelvinator in 1916, followed by Frigidaire (called Guardian) in 1917. The first refrigerator cost $900.

A 1917 Rapid Fireless Cooker manufactured by the William Campbell Company of Detroit, Michigan. Every meal could be cooked in it.

Ask Your Dealer Why the "GLACIER" is a Sanitary Refrigerator

ASK him why the ice consumption is unusually low. Ask him why it properly preserves foods. Ask him why you should have one in your home.

And he will tell you that the "Glacier's" interior linings are one-piece porcelain. Being one piece, with no cracks or crevices, hard as flint, they are easily kept clean and, consequently, sanitary. He will tell you that, after years of experimenting, testing and trying, the manufacturers found cocoa fibre to be the best obtainable material for insulation and as perfect insulation is absolutely essential to the low consumption of ice, cocoa fibre, with dead air space, is used in all "Glacier" Refrigerators.

Proper sanitation, circulation and insulation are absolutely necessary to the perfect preservation of foods, and as good, wholesome food means good health, we have embodied the necessary essentials in the "Glacier"— sanitary interior with perfect insulation. Your dealer, then, will tell you that for appearance' sake, for health's sake, you will want a "Glacier" in your home.

The "Glacier" Refrigerator

Is a sound, well made Refrigerator, built for a lifetime of useful service. The "Glacier" is built with this in mind: To produce a refrigerator that will satisfy you, the user, in every particular — in appearance, in the wholesome preservation of food, in its ability to be easily cleaned, and to preserve economically — and we know that in the "Glacier" when you have given it every test, you will find all this.

Write today for catalog and the name of your nearest dealer.

NORTHERN REFRIGERATOR COMPANY
782 CROFTON AVENUE, S. W. GRAND RAPIDS, MICHIGAN

In 1917, the ad for the Glacier refrigerator tells why it was sanitary and its ice consumption was low... it was porcelain lined. Other refrigerators (iceboxes) in 1917 were the Belding Hall, which was stone-lined; the McCray, which was glass-lined and sold for $30 and up; and the Seeger, the original siphon refrigerator.

An ice refrigerator with an unusual shape was the 1917 White Frost Refrigerator manufactured by the White Frost Refrigerator Company, Jackson, Michigan. The company claimed it made the only round, white enameled refrigerator on earth. It was insulated with cork, had revolving shelves, move-easy casters, and a crystal clear water cooler with removable top.

Ice refrigerators range from $175 to $650 depending on the condition, the number of doors, and the size.

▶
The 1908 Sears Roebuck catalog shows ice refrigerators, from the smallest at $4.45 to the largest economy northern elm double door at $17.95. (Courtesy Sears, Roebuck and Company.)

$4.45 ECONOMY REFRIGERATORS AND ICE CHESTS

At $4.45 to $17.95 we offer wonderful values in this line of Economy Refrigerators and Ice Chests. Solid cast brass trimmings, galvanized steel inside linings and shelves, removable drain pipe, patented drip cup and swinging front baseboard. Convenient in arrangement, they are excellent preservers of food with an economical consumption of ice. Constructed on the best scientific principles, with a perfect insulation and circulation, they combine utility, cleanliness, solidity and durability.

THIS ICE CHEST we furnish in five different sizes, all built with a thick outer case of thoroughly seasoned northern elm, high gloss golden finish. The inner walls are built in the same perfect manner as the refrigerators and are economical in the use of ice. They are lined with a good quality galvanized steel and have galvanized steel shelves and ice rack. They are equipped with drain pipe, drip cup and finished first class throughout. While an ice chest does not have the cold dry air circulation like our refrigerators, yet they are excellent preservers of food and will give satisfaction. We recommend the purchase of one of our high grade refrigerators because of the greater convenience in handling the food and ice, the cold dry air circulation which keeps the provision chambers perfectly dry, always cold and will preserve the food better with less consumption of ice. Securely crated and shipped direct from factory in Southern Michigan.

Catalogue No.	Width	Depth	Height	Shipping Weight	Price
1K551	24⅞ inches	16¾ inches	24½ inches	70 pounds	$ 4.45
1K553	31¾ inches	21⅛ inches	25¾ inches	93 pounds	6.75
1K555	36¾ inches	24¾ inches	30⅞ inches	130 pounds	9.45
1K556	40¾ inches	26¾ inches	33⅛ inches	185 pounds	11.25

THIS IS A CONVENIENT, attractive and desirable refrigerator, substantially built and has our perfect insulated walls by which the ice is protected and the food preserved. The ice chamber is lined with galvanized steel and the bottom protected by a corrugated ice rack.

THE FOOD CHAMBER is lined with a good quality of galvanized steel and has double paneled door with heavy cast brass hinges and patent lock, with adjustable strike which allows the door to close with a slam, making an airtight joint; fitted with patent drain pipe and drip cup.

THE OUTER CASE is made of thoroughly seasoned northern elm, high gloss golden finish and having a swinging front baseboard. We use better material, the galvanized steel linings are heavier, the hardwood case better constructed, and the insulation and circulation of the cold dry air more perfect than the ordinary refrigerators sold by other dealers. The preservation of the food and the saving of ice will almost equal the value of the refrigerator in a single season.

SELECT ANY REFRIGERATOR from this line and send us your order, subject to ten days' trial, and we will guarantee the refrigerator which we will send you to give splendid satisfaction.

Catalogue No.	Width	Depth	Height	Ice Capacity	Shipping Weight	Price
1K560	24¾ inches	16⅛ inches	39¼ inches	35 pounds	100 pounds	$6.85
1K561	26⅞ inches	17⅞ inches	41¼ inches	45 pounds	110 pounds	8.75
1K562	27⅞ inches	18½ inches	43⅛ inches	60 pounds	125 pounds	9.65

We furnish No. 1K562 refrigerator with a porcelain lined water cooler, faucet and glass holder as shown in the illustration at $2.50 extra. The water cooler reduces the capacity of the ice chamber.

ACCESSIBLE, CLEANABLE, DURABLE.

THIS REGRIGERATOR requires but a small floor space, yet has roomy ice and provision chambers. An ice saver, a food saver and a space saver. The outer case is made of thoroughly seasoned northern elm, high gloss golden finish. Note the massive double paneled doors fitted with heavy cast brass hinges and our patent locks and strike. The doors can be closed with a slam and the joints are airtight. The ice chamber door opens from the front, a convenience in filling and chopping the ice. The floor of the food chamber is on a level with the bottom of the door, making it easy to clean. The ice and food chambers are lined with galvanized steel and fitted with drain pipe and drip cup. Has swing front baseboard.

THE INSULATED inner walls, the perfect system of dry air circulation, keep the provision chamber cold, dry and wholesome. An excellent preserver of the food with an economical consumption of ice; built to give superiority in general construction, convenience and refrigeration; securely crated and shipped from factory in Southern Michigan.

Catalogue No.	Width	Depth	Height	Ice Capacity	Shipping Weight	Price
1K571	24⅛ inches	18 inches	49¾ inches	50 pounds	120 pounds	$10.25
1K572	28 inches	19 inches	55½ inches	75 pounds	160 pounds	12.75

ECONOMY REFRIGERATOR $14.35

ECONOMY LARGE DOUBLE DOOR FAMILY REFRIGERATOR

COLD, DRY AND ROOMY. PERFECT INSULATION, PERFECT CIRCULATION AND PERFECT PRESERVATION OF THE FOOD.

THE REFRIGERATOR has an ice capacity of 100 pounds and is a splendid size for large families. It has beautifully carved northern elm case, in high gloss golden finish. Solid brass hinges and locks, and the best quality galvanized steel linings, galvanized ice rack and provision shelves. It has a removable waste pipe and our improved trap to prevent the entrance of warm air. A swinging front baseboard.

IT HAS OUR PERFECT SCIENTIFIC INSULATION, which makes it wonderfully economical for natural or artificial ice. The ice chamber is of ample capacity. The double doors to the provision chamber assist in maintaining a low temperature, as well as saving in ice, as when but one door is open at a time less warm air enters the refrigerators. Built with a view to convenience, economy and satisfactory service and every inch of space carefully utilized.

THIS REFRIGERATOR IS SURE TO PLEASE YOU.

No. 1K581

It is solid and substantial in appearance and elegant in finish and the decorations add greatly to its appearance.

Catalogue No.	Width	Depth	Height	Ice Capacity	Shipping Weight	Price
1K581	35¾ inches	21⅛ inches	45¾ inches	100 pounds	165 pounds	$14.35

ECONOMY REFRIGERATOR $17.95

LARGE DOUBLE DOORS. CONVENIENCE, CLEANLINESS, COLDNESS.

No. 1K575

DO NOT BUY A REFRIGERATOR TOO SMALL. It should be large enough to hold several days' supply of provisions and an ample supply of ice. This refrigerator has an ice capacity of 125 pounds and will readily hold a 100-pound piece of average dimensions with room to spare. The food chamber is large, roomy and convenient. The ice chamber doors in front make it easy of access. The perfectly insulated walls and galvanized steel linings, the perfect duplex circulation of the cold dry air from the ice chamber downward through the food chamber, passing and repassing in a constant flow, will keep provisions and milk fresh, sweet and pure. The outer case is made of thoroughly seasoned northern elm, high gloss golden finish. Doors have thick raised moulded panels and fitted with heavy cast brass hinges and patent adjustable locks and strikes. Has swing front baseboard, removable drain pipe and hinged drip cup. Shipped direct from factory in Southern Michigan.

Catalogue No.	Width	Depth	Height	Ice Capacity	Shipping Weight	Price
1K575	36¾ inches	19¾ inches	50¾ inches	125 pounds	195 pounds	$17.95

EXCEPTIONAL VALUES IN HIGH GRADE KITCHEN CABINETS

COMPARISON OF OUR KITCHEN CABINETS WILL SHOW EVERY ONE LOWER IN PRICE THAN THE SAME QUALITY CAN BE PURCHASED ELSEWHERE. WE CHALLENGE ANY FIRM ON EARTH TO FURNISH KITCHEN CABINETS THE EQUAL OF OURS IN QUALITY AT THE PRICE WE ASK

THE KITCHEN CABINETS we display this season, for beauty of design, high quality of material, construction and finish and convenience of arrangement and extraordinary value are positively unequaled. The excellent features embodied in the design and construction of our kitchen cabinets are the result of practical experience and careful study. They supply the need for every article used in the kitchen. Each cabinet is provided with ample bin drawer and shelf space. You will find every kitchen cabinet from the cheapest to the highest priced is perfectly constructed from specially selected materials and extra well finished. You will find every kitchen cabinet we sell to be made of better material, better constructed and better finished, more lasting and in every way more satisfactory than kitchen cabinets turned out of the average factory and sold by the average retail dealer. The illustrations will give you some idea of the convenience of arrangement and general appearance, but they must be seen, examined and compared with kitchen cabinets that sell at much higher prices to understand and appreciate the wonderful values.

OUR DESIGNS are strictly up to date. They are the result of the most careful and painstaking efforts. We offer you the same advantage of selection as you can find in any of the largest furniture stores in the cities with the added convenience of making your selection in your own home. The excellent practical features embodied in these splendid kitchen cabinets will be readily recognized by every housekeeper. While it is impossible for any illustration to bring out the beauty of design, the color, or the handsome smooth carvings, yet by a careful reading of the descriptions and close examination of the illustrations, which are exact reproductions of the photograph of the article, you can form a correct idea of the design.

THE WONDERFUL UTILITY of all of these splendid high grade Kitchen Cabinets will be readily recognized. A place is provided for everything used in the kitchen. Everything needed for the preparation of the meal is within easy reach of the busy housewife.

THE FINISH. The finish is a light natural color. The surface is perfectly sawed and smooth and the varnish coating brings out the beautiful natural grain of the wood.

READ WHAT WE SAY ABOUT OUR KITCHEN CABINETS ON PRECEDING PAGE.

Our Big Bargain Cabinet

No. 1K512 This Cabinet is an illustration of the wonderful saving to our customers, not only in this article, but in every other that we offer. Base is made of white maple, natural finish, with a white basswood table top. Size, 25x45 inches. Height of entire cabinet, 50 inches. It has two dustproof flour bins with wooden bottoms, two drawers partitioned for cutlery, and a removable carving and kneading board. Lower part of legs are detachable and placed inside drawers for convenience in shipping. Top has a double paneled back, a roomy top shelf, below which are seven drawers for holding various commodities used in the kitchen. We furnish the base of this cabinet without the top section if desired. Order one of our cabinets, place it beside any other cabinet offered at anywhere near our price, and if you do not find our cabinet double the value of the other, return it to us and we will cheerfully refund your purchase price and transportation charges. Shipped direct from factory in Southern Michigan.

Price, complete cabinet. Shipping weight, 135 pounds........ **$5.45**
Price, without top section, shipping weight, 95 pounds...... **3.65**

No. 1K511 We can furnish this Kitchen Cabinet without the top section, size, 25x44 inches. It is made of birch, natural finish. While we are confident that it will prove far superior in quality to any cabinet offered by any other dealer at the price, we do not recommend it. At the slight difference in price, order one of the better grade maple cabinets which you will find a far better investment and which difference in price is actually represented in the cost of material and labor. Shipping weight, 95 pounds. Price........ **$2.95**

Kitchen Cabinet, Reduced from $7.95 to $6.98.

No. 1K514 This handsome high grade Kitchen Cabinet is made of specially selected, thoroughly air seasoned and kiln dried hard white maple, natural finish. The table top on the base, size, 25x48 inches, is made of basswood, with moulded edges. Height entire cabinet, 55 inches. Base has large dustproof flour bin with wooden bottom, holding 60 pounds of flour, to the left are two roomy drawers for utensils and commodities. The two top drawers are for cutlery, linen, etc., fitted with two sliding chopping and kneading boards which can be taken out and placed on top for convenience in using. Top section has roomy top shelf, one large and two small drawers and two deep drawers for spice cans, packages, utensils, and various commodities used in every kitchen. All drawers and bins are perfect fitting and can be taken out for airing and cleaning. This cabinet cannot be bought in stores for less than $1'.00 to $12.00. Shipped direct from factory near Grand Rapids, Michigan.

Price, complete cabinet. Shipping weight, 185 pounds.... **$6.98**
Price. without top section Shipping weight, 125 pounds.... **5.25**

$7.85 for This High Grade Kitchen Cabinet.

No. 1K538 This Kitchen Cabinet at $7.85 is the equal of any cabinet offered by others at $12.00 to $13.00. Made of selected thoroughly seasoned hard white maple, natural finish, with a white basswood table top, with moulded edges on the base section. Size, 28x44 inches. Entire cabinet is 66 inches high. It has a large dustproof sliding bin which holds 70 pounds of flour, a spacious cupboard for pots, pans, etc., a cutlery drawer, linen drawer and a removable carving and kneading board finished on both sides. Top section has a roomy cupboard, four small shelves, a large shelf, and a combination shelf and plate rack on top. The construction is strictly first class throughout. Convenient and commodious arrangement will be fully appreciated by every housekeeper, as a place is provided for almost every article needed in the kitchen. The legs are detachable, the turned part being doweled into the frame posts which adds to the convenience in handling and using. Securely crated and shipped direct from factory near Grand Rapids, Mich. Our price for this kitchen cabinet represents a big saving to our customers.

Price, complete cabinet. Shipping weight, 155 pounds.... **$7.85**
Price, without top section. Shipping weight, 95 pounds.... **4.65**

The articles displayed are not included with the cabinet.

This Splendid Kitchen Cabinet, $10.85.

No. 1K521 This High Grade Kitchen Cabinet is made of white maple, natural finish. Base has a 26x48-inch table top, with moulded edges, made of basswood for ease in cleaning. Entire cabinet is 60 inches high. Extra large bin has wooden bottom and will hold 60 pounds of flour. Note the five roomy drawers for linen, knives, forks and various utensils and commodities. Has a removable kneading and chopping board, smooth finished on both sides, which can be taken out and placed on top of the base for convenience in using. Top section has a broad shelf, below which are six drawers for sugar, spices, packages, etc., and a large cupboard for coffee cans, bottles, etc. Drawers and bins can be removed for cleaning and airing. The high quality of cabinet construction, together with the practical arrangement, makes this strictly high grade kitchen cabinet wonderful value at our price. Compare this kitchen cabinet with those generally sold by others at $16.00 to $18.00. Shipped direct from factory in Grand Rapids, Mich. Shipping weight, about 195 pounds.

Price, complete cabinet.. **$10.85**

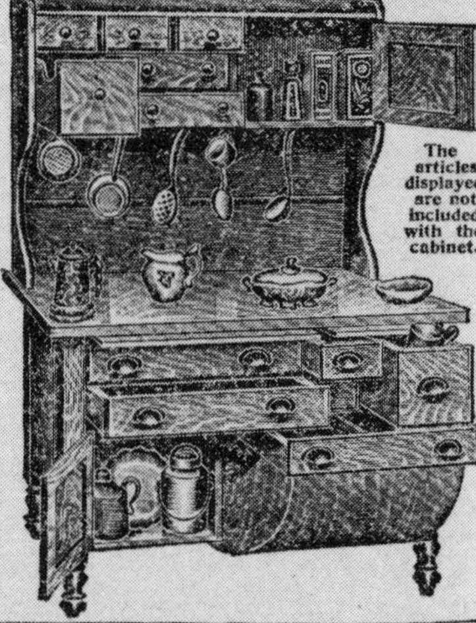

The articles displayed are not included with the cabinet.

No. 1K523 This high grade Kitchen Cabinet is a splendid example of convenience of arrangement in kitchen cabinet construction. It is made of specially selected hard white maple, thoroughly air seasoned and kiln dried, finished natural color. Entire height of cabinet, 72 inches. The base has a white wood top with moulded edges, size 25x50 inches. It has two dustproof flour bins with wood bottoms each holding 50 pounds of flour, between which are two deep drawers for linen and packages. Two long drawers above are convenient receptacles for cooking spoons, knives, forks and various other utensils used in every kitchen. Fitted with one kneading and one chopping board finished on both sides and can be removed and placed on top for convenience in using. The legs are detachable, the turned part being doweled into the square posts, which adds to the convenience and safety in handling and shipping. The top section combines excellence and beauty of design with a convenient and practical arrangement, which cannot be excelled. Cupboards with shelves and glass doors affording ample space for dishes, spice cans, coffee and tea canisters and a variety of packages and commodities within easy reach of the busy housewife. Note the tilting sugar bin in the center and spacious shelf below. Shipped direct from factory in Southern Michigan.

Price, as illustrated Shipping weight, 240 pounds........... **$11.75**
Price, base only. Shipping weight, 130 pounds........... **5.85**

The articles displayed are not included with the cabinet.

The articles displayed are not included with the cabinet.

This Magnificent High Grade Kitchen Cabinet Reduced from $13.45 to $12.95.

No. 1K525 Exceptionally attractive in design, strictly high grade in material, construction and finish, the equal of kitchen cabinets generally sold at $20.00 to $22.00. Made of specially selected, thoroughly air seasoned and kiln dried hard white maple, with a white wood platform on base with moulded edges. Entire height of cabinet, 70 inches; width of base, 25x50 inches. We call your special attention to the spacious and convenient arrangement of the compartments in the base. A roomy cupboard with double doors, to the left of which is a large flour bin which will hold 75 pounds of flour. In center two drawers for knives, forks, spoons, etc., either side of which is a spacious drawer for utensils, linen, etc. It has two removable chopping and kneading boards. In the top section is a cupboard with glass door and shelf, two tilting bins for sugar and salt, two drawers and a small cupboard. In the convenient and commodious arrangement, high quality of material and construction. This cabinet cannot be excelled. Remember the freight charges on a kitchen cabinet will amount to almost nothing as compared to what you will save in price when you buy from us. Comparison of our kitchen cabinets will show every one 30 to 40 per cent lower in price than the same quality can be bought elsewhere. Shipped direct from factory near Grand Rapids, Mich.

Price, complete cabinet. Shipping weight, 255 pounds........ **$12.95** | Price, without top section. Shipping weight, 160 pounds.......... **$7.95**

READ WHAT WE SAY ABOUT OUR KITCHEN CABINETS ON PRECEDING PAGE.

Kitchen cabinets range from $350 to $700 for hardwood to $200 to $350 for a painted finish in very good condition.

The 1908 Sears Roebuck catalog offered kitchen cabinets from a sale price of $2.95 up to the best, the Wilson Kitchen Cabinets, which were more elegant walnut pieces and sold for $13.95 to $19.95. (Courtesy Sears, Roebuck and Company.)

THE WILSON KITCHEN CABINETS

THE BEST KITCHEN CABINETS MADE REGARDLESS OF NAME, MAKE OR PRICE

THE KITCHEN AND THE KITCHEN CABINET. The kitchen is the workshop of the home. The work of the kitchen rightly understood and properly done is the most important of the entire household. System in the office, the store and the factory is a very valuable asset. Why is it not valuable in the kitchen? The housewife without the help of a kitchen cabinet with the cooking utensils and materials within easy reach, takes ten steps where one should suffice. The hours of drudgery will be turned into minutes of pleasure with the convenience of one of our Wilson Kitchen Cabinets. Our Wilson Kitchen Cabinet does for the woman and her kitchen what modern machinery and labor saving devices do for the bread winners of the family. Our Wilson Kitchen Cabinet holds, in a convenient and practical way, all the materials and utensils used in cooking. Any one of these cabinets is, in fact, a whole kitchen, occupying the floor space of a kitchen table, making the cooking easy, sanitary and economical, **insuring the best results. Every workman does better work with good tools than with poor ones.**

IN THESE FOUR WILSON CABINETS is attained the absolute perfection of kitchen cabinet construction. The newest and best ideas of arrangement have been carefully and conscientiously worked out. Embodied in their splendid detail of arrangement are practical suggestions from thousands of America's best housekeepers. Compact, roomy and convenient, a place for everything used in the kitchen and everything always in place. We challenge any other firm on earth to furnish kitchen cabinets their equal in solidity of construction, elegance of design, completeness of detail, honesty of material, beauty of finish and painstaking workmanship. Made in Grand Rapids, Michigan, by one of the best, most favorably known and reliable makers of strictly high grade, dependable furniture. They are the perfect product of the best skilled workmanship from the highest grade materials obtainable at any price.

THE SATIN WALNUT used in the construction of these splendid kitchen cabinets is a thoroughly air seasoned and kiln dried Northern hardwood, specially adapted to kitchen cabinet construction, possessing perfect strength, solidity and a beautiful grain. The so called "satin walnut finish," offered by many other dealers, is but a poor imitation of the genuine satin walnut used in our Wilson Kitchen Cabinets. It is a coarser, softer wood and does not possess the perfect wearing qualities and handsome close grain of genuine satin walnut. The genuine satin walnut used in our Wilson Kitchen Cabinets is specially selected from the choicest lumber, thoroughly tested; will not warp, check or split and will hold its color for a lifetime.

THE FINISH on these magnificent kitchen cabinets is a beautiful color with a rich high gloss golden brown. It has a velvety sheen which harmonizes with all surroundings and to produce which requires special care by the best skilled and experienced workmen. The surfaces are carefully rubbed and sanded until perfectly even and smooth, after which the best wood filler and special finishing coatings are applied. The resulting surface is as smooth as glass and when thoroughly dry and hardened will not be affected by the varying temperature and steam in the kitchen.

THE WORKMANSHIP. Each cabinet is so constructed that the top section can be detached from the base section for convenience and safety in handling and shipping. Every panel, bar, post, drawer side and drawer bottom, is framed and fitted in the most perfect manner. The doors are perfect fitting, the drawers and bins slide without friction or binding. THE BINS are made entirely of wood, the bottoms of three-ply stock and laid transversely, a big improvement over metal bottoms as they will not dent or corrode and flour will not mold in them. They can be easily removed for airing and cleaning.

THE TRIMMINGS are the best quality cast brass with French lacquer to prevent tarnishing. The doors have patent spring fasteners that work without friction.

IF THERE IS ANY DOUBT IN YOUR MIND of the superior super-extra quality of these splendid kitchen cabinets, of the purity and high quality of material, the perfection of construction or the beauty of finish, **send us your order with the distinct understanding that if they are not all we claim them to be,** the best in material, the best in construction, the best in finish, the finest kitchen cabinet made, regardless of name, make or price; if, when you have received any one of them, examined, tested and compared it with any other cabinet made, you are not more than satisfied, your money will be immediately returned to you.

No. 1K530 The convenient and practical arrangement of this splendid Kitchen Cabinet will be readily recognized. It is 75 inches high. The base has a 27x44-inch top and is fitted with our patent drop bins, one to hold 60 pounds flour, the other partitioned for meal and sugar. Bins are supported by wheels attached to their sides and run on a track reducing the friction and permitting the bins to be easily moved when filled. Each bin can be readily taken out for cleaning and airing. Above bins are two roomy drawers for linen and cutlery. The two kneading and chopping boards can be easily removed and placed on top for convenience in using. Top section has a roomy china cabinet with glass paneled doors and spring fasteners. Below china compartment are two cupboards and two roomy shelves for packages, utensils and various commodities used in every kitchen. Bins, drawers and doors fitted with best quality cast brass handles. This cabinet holds in a convenient and practical way all the necessary commodities and cooking utensils used in the preparation of the meals. This splendid high grade kitchen cabinet we guarantee superior in quality of material, workmanship, finish and convenient arrangements to any kitchen cabinet generally offered by others at $20.00 to $25.00. Securely crated and shipped from factory in Grand Rapids, Michigan. Shipping weight, 300 pounds. Price **$13.25**

No 1K537 This splendid Kitchen Cabinet is 75 inches high. The varied assortment and arrangement of drawers bins, china cabinets, shelves etc., furnish a place for every utensil and commodity used in the kitchen. The base has a 27x44 inch top, a roomy cupboard for pots, pans, a large flour bin to hold 50 pounds of flour and two drawers for knives, forks spoons and other kitchen cutlery. The kneading and chopping board can be taken out and placed on top when used. The top section has a china cabinet, with glass doors and spring fasteners. Note the convenient cupboard for corn starch, oatmeal and similar packages, the tilting bins for sugar and salt and pockets on the doors for small packages, etc. Below is a broad shelf for tea, spice and coffee cans and other necessary utensils. Drawers and bins easily removed for airing and cleaning. The doors perfectly fitted, the drawers and bins when filled move without binding or friction. Roomy, convenient, sanitary, made of the best material, constructed and finished to last a lifetime, this magnificent labor saving kitchen cabinet will be fully appreciated by every housewife. A finer kitchen cabinet in every way than is generally offered by other dealers at $22.00 to $28.00. Shipped direct from factory in Grand Rapids, Mich. Shipping weight, 319 pounds. Price....... **$15.65**

No. 1K543 The wonderful utility, convenience and roominess combined in this Kitchen Cabinet will be fully appreciated in every home. Entire cabinet, 76 inches high. The base has a 27x44-inch top and contains a large bin to hold 60 pounds of flour, above which is a cutlery drawer and removable kneading and chopping board. The roomy cupboard to the left with broad shelf will hold pots, pans, etc. The inside of the door fitted with an upper rack holding four spice cans and a lower rack for packages of various kinds. The top section has a large cupboard with broad shelf for dishes, packages and various commodities used in every kitchen. Note the drop bin for sugar in the center, each side of which are two roomy drawers. The inside of door on the right has an upper rack with three spice cans, below which is a rack with coffee and tea cans. The outer side of the door has a "Daily Reminder" and a "Card Index." The door on the left is fitted with two racks for packages, bottles, etc. All drawers and bins easily removed for convenience in cleaning. Every commodity used in the modern kitchen is provided for in this magnificent kitchen cabinet. A place for everything and everything in place. Shipped direct from factory in Grand Rapids, Mich. Shipping weight, 310 pounds. Price **$17.45**

No. 1K548 This is the most complete Kitchen Cabinet ever offered by any dealer. A place is provided for every utensil and commodity used in the modern up to date kitchen. Entire cabinet is 78 inches high. Base has a 27x44-inch top. The large drawer in the base has a bread and cake compartment with hinged metal covers, above which are two drawers for linen and cutlery. The inner side of cupboard door has a rack with four cereal cans, below which is a convenient shelf for packages, etc. The kneading and chopping board can be placed on top for convenience in using. We call your special attention to the top section with the china cabinet in the center, to the left of which is a bin to hold 50 pounds flour with flour sifter beneath. On the right is a spacious cupboard and tilting sugar bin. The inside of door has a rack with tea and coffee cans, a "Daily Reminder" for recording the need of new supplies from the grocery, "A Card Index" and a rack with four spice cans. A splendid combination of drawers, shelves, bins, racks, etc. all easy of access and by their location make this kitchen cabinet a whole kitchen in itself, reducing the labor of cooking and producing sanitary and economical results. This cabinet has no equal in the superior excellence of its material, workmanship and finish, and in its compact, convenient and orderly arrangement.

Shipped direct from factory in Grand Rapids, Michigan.

Shipping weight, 325 pounds. Price **$19.85**

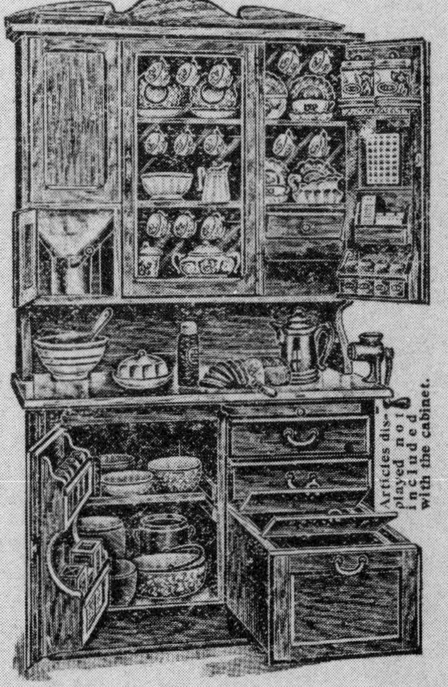

Wilson Kitchen Cabinets were Sears Roebuck's best in 1908. (Courtesy Sears, Roebuck and Company.)

The Bohn Sanitor Kitchen table was one type offered in 1917. **$45-65**

Kitchenware

Kitchen furniture. The furniture industry took the first step in the modernization of the kitchen with the introduction of the Hoosier fitted kitchen cabinet in the late 1800s. The Hoosier free-standing unit was the first major step in the evolution of the modern kitchen.

The kitchen cabinets were made of hardwood and had a natural wood finish. A kitchen cabinet that had no top was often called a baking cabinet or dough table. In the Sears Roebuck 1902 catalog, they ranged from $3.59 to $4.95 for a top-grade cabinet. The latter had swinging bins instead of the harder-to-operate sliding ones. This top-grade cabinet was said to be mouse and dust proof. The kitchen cabinets with tops ranged in price from $7.45 to $8.35.

Until 1910, most of the work surfaces on the fitted cabinets had a metal finish called Nickeloid. The introduction that year of a porcelain enameled work surface was an instant success. This led to the creation of the popular porcelain-enamel-top kitchen table. The most popular size table was 25″ × 40″, according to Earl Lifshey in *Housewares Story.*

The 1916 Sears Roebuck catalog listed oak and maple kitchen cabinets for $16.45 and other wood cabinets for $7.85 to $12.45. Kitchen tables sold for from $3.95 to $4.95. A white all-steel cabinet was relatively expensive at $24.95.

The kitchen cabinets continued to have natural wood finishes. They were said to be the most wonderful invention ever devised for the housekeeper. Their usefulness, convenience, and economy made them extremely popular. The cabinets were made of maple, oak, or walnut. The convenience was readily recognized because there were special places for flour, sugar, cutlery, linens, spices, cereals, dishes, coffee, and tea.

The kitchen cabinet did more to coordinate utensils and working processes than any other piece of kitchen equipment. It saved endless steps by grouping together supplies, utensils, and tools. It put sunshine in a housewife's day!

Sinks. Little thought is given to kitchen sinks today, but they have changed significantly in fifty years. Kitchen sinks in the early 1900s were made of wood, iron, steel, soapstone, enamel or porcelain on steel or iron, cast enamel, or stoneware.

The *Chautauqua Cookery or 20th Century Housekeeping* book said the sink should be near the range and should have a window above. A wooden sink should be kept well painted. If one was made of iron, it could be washed with kerosene once a week to keep it from rusting. The drain should be scalded after each dishwashing, and never should crumbs or grease go into it. It should be scrubbed every day with hot soapsuds and a brush, then wiped with a cloth to dry. Wiping the sink with a dishcloth was never to be tolerated.

Sinks ranged from 18″ × 30″ to 20″ × 40″. The 18″ × 30″ wall-hung steel sink complete was priced at $6.95, as compared to the $10.15 cast iron sink. The corner wall-hung sink was cast iron and sold for $11.75 to $14.40. The cast enamel sink had painted legs and the choice of oak or porcelain drainboards. The latter was more expensive. The Acme stoneware sink had a mosaic drainboard, was guaranteed for ten years against leakage, and cost $11.25 in the 18″ × 30″ size.

Accessories. Accessories have added a decorative note to the kitchen for years. These include such items as canisters, spice sets, match safes, breadboxes, and water coolers. In the early 1900s, Sears Roebuck offered decorated japanned tinware, made in Europe, that was lithographed in bright colors and designs. Japanned containers were most common in tin, but they were also available in china, stoneware, and glass.

In the 1916 Sears Roebuck catalog, a japanned "sanitary" fifty-pound flour bin and sifter sold for $1.95. The ad said it was "handy and convenient. Saves time, prevents waste, keeps out dust, insects, etc. Heavy tin,

The Sellers Kitchen Cabinet in 1917 had an unusual flour bin that made it easy to fill.

Sellers

THE BETTER KITCHEN CABINET

KITCHENEED

This Trade Mark Identifies Every "Sellers"

Can You Afford To Be Without "Sellers" *Kitcheneed* "Special" in Your Home?

Think how many footsteps to the pantry and back again, and to the cupboard and back again, you take each day in preparing your daily meals. And then with this wearying trot, trot, trot, in mind, just imagine "Sellers" *Kitcheneed* "Special" in your kitchen.

Imagine pulling down the automatic lowering flour bin just as easy as can be, filling it, and as easily pushing it back into position; then filling your sanitary glass sugar bin, your sanitary glass coffee, tea and spice jars; putting every ingredient you will use in preparing that meal and every utensil into its place in "Sellers" *Kitcheneed.* And then pull up your kitchen stool, comfortably sit down to your *Kitcheneed's* sanitary, porceliron, guaranteed, extension work table and, sitting, prepare *every* meal. And with this in mind, go to the "Sellers" agent in your city who will price *Kitcheneeds* to you from about $19.85 to about $50.00, and who sells them on easy terms of payment, and see if "you really can afford to be without "Sellers" *Kitcheneed* in your home.

G. I. SELLERS & SONS CO., 1004 THIRTEENTH ST., ELWOOD, IND.

In the meantime write for our Booklet "The Auto Bin Girl"—it tells and illustrates the complete *Kitcheneed* story, and let us tell you the name of the dealer nearby who will demonstrate "Sellers" to you.

Illustrating
"Sellers" *Kitcheneed* "Special"
With Automatic Lowering Flour Bin

Roll Rim Enameled Lavatories.

Roll Rim Enameled Lavatories are cast in one piece, have large improved patent overflow, ornamental exterior and are supplied with painted iron brackets, chain and waste plug coupling with rubber stopper. Length of back, 21 inches; size of bowl, 12x15 inches.

No. 24R7570 Price, **$6.25**

Roll Rim Enameled Corner Lavatories.

Enameled Iron Corner Lavatory, same as our No. 24R7570, only to use in a corner. Length of sides, 16 inches; size of bowl, 12x15 inches. They are furnished without brackets.

No. 24R7572 Price, **$6.00**

Sanitary Roll Rim Iron Wash Sta .ds.

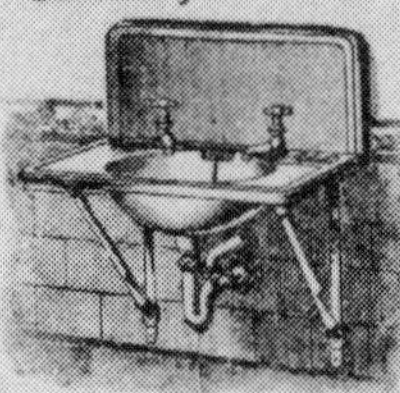

No. 24R7574 Ł oll Rim White Enameled Iron Lavatories; have the appearance of marble. All parts are accessible and carefully fitted together. All exposed surfaces are enameled or bronzed, making it a substantial and perfectly sanitary plumbing fixture, easily kept clean and bright. Wash Stand complete as shown, includes: 18x24-inch countersunk roll rim slab with soap tray and 12x15-inch oval, patent overflow basin, all cast in one piece; 10¼-inch high roll rim back; full length nickel plated brackets; compression basin cocks; overflow strainer, chain and waste plug coupling with rubber stopper, all nickel plated.

Price, each.......................................**$14.00**
Price, with nickel plated supply pipes..... 15.50

Roll Rim Iron Wash Stands.

No. 24R7576 Roll Rim White Enameled Iron Lavatories to place in corner of room. For description, sizes, etc., see No. 24R7574 above. In ordering be **sure** and state which corner of room stand is to be placed, right or left hand.

Price, each... **$15.00**
If wanted with nickel plated supply pipe, add $1.50 to the above price.

Enameled Iron Sectional Lavatories.

Enameled Iron Sectional Lavatories are especially adapted for hotel, restaurant and school house use. Size of each section, 18x24 inches. Height of back, 10½ inches. Length over all, 48 inches. Size of bowl, 12x15 inches. Furnished complete with four nickel plated compression basin cocks and two brackets, overflow, plug and chain.

In ordering, state whether right or left hand end is wanted.

No. 24R7578 Price, complete.............**$19.50**

Enameled Roll Rim Kitchen Sinks.

Enameled (Porcelain) Roll Rim Kitchen Sinks, with 12-inch back. Made of steel or cast iron, white enameled inside, painted blue outside. Makes one of the neatest, cleanest sinks ever put on the market. Furnished complete with faucets and brackets.

No. 24R7580	Steel Price, complete	Cast Iron Price, complete
Size, 18x30 inches........	$6.95	$10.15
Size, 18x36 inches........	7.80	11.00
Size, 20x36 inches........	8.15	11.75
Size, 20x40 inches........	8.85	12.65

REFER TO PAGES 7 TO 10 FOR FREIGHT AND EXPRESS RATES.
You can tell almost exactly what the freight or express will amount to on your goods without writing to us for this information.

Enameled Roll Rim Sinks for Corner.

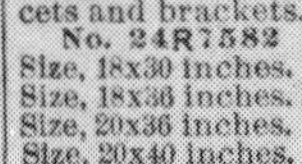

Cast Enameled Roll Rim Sinks for corner of room, with 12-inch back and sides, white enameled inside, painted blue outside. Made of high grade cast iron, free from all defects. Furnished complete with faucets and brackets.

No. 24R7582

Size, 18x30 inches.	Price, complete...........**$11.75**
Size, 18x36 inches.	Price, complete........... **12.70**
Size, 20x36 inches.	Price, complete........... **13.45**
Size, 20x40 inches.	Price, complete........... **14.40**

Cast Enameled Kitchen Sinks.

No. 24R7584 Cast Enameled Roll Rim Kitchen Sinks, with 15-inch back, with air chamber, painted iron legs and brackets, drain board and nickel plated Fuller bibbs. A high grade sink, everything first class.

Size of Sink	With 24-inch Oak Drain Board. Price, complete	With 24-inch Enameled Drain Board. Price, complete
18x30 inches........	$20.00	$22.50
18x36 inches........	22.00	....
20x36 inches........	22.40	25.00
20x40 inches........	24.00	....

Acme Stoneware Kitchen Sinks.

No. 24R7586 Our Acme Stoneware Sinks have 16-inch high backs, patent metallic rims, brass strainer and waste connection; mosaic drain board, two Fuller faucets, two 18 to 24-inch extension legs (painted), and galvanized hanging soap cup. Guaranteed against leakage for ten years.

Size of sink	Size of drain board	Total length	Price
18x30x8 inches	18x20	50 inches	$11.25
20x36x8 inches	20x20	56 inches	12.40
20x45x8 inches	20x24	64 inches	13.40

Can furnish above sinks with brass rims in place of metallic rims for $2.25 in addition to price of any of above sizes.

GRANITINE LAUNDRY TUBS.

Granitine Combination Kitchen Sink and Laundry Tubs.

No. 24R7590 With high back, soap cup, strainer and painted iron legs. In ordering please state the height of back wanted. Backs higher than 16 inches will be charged **extra.** We do not furnish faucets unless specially ordered, but 16-inch backs, and faucet holes in the backs, will be sent unless otherwise ordered. All measurements are outside.

Length, feet...........	4	4½	5
Width, feet...........	2	2	2
Depth, inches...........	16	16	16
Price, 16-inch back....	$11.00	$11.75	$12.25

Two Compartment Granitine Laundry Tubs.

With High Back and Soap Cup.

No. 24R7592 In ordering, please state the height of back wanted. We do not furnish faucets unless specially ordered. Tubs have zinc rims and 16-inch backs, and faucet holes in the high backs, will be sent unless otherwise ordered. All measurements are outside.

Length, feet...........	4	4½	5
Width, feet...........	2	2	2
Depth, inches...........	16	16	16
Price, 16-inch back....	$10.00	$10.75	$11.25

Cast Sinks.

No. 24R7600 Cast Iron Sinks. Made of high grade gray iron, painted or white enameled inside, flat rims. fitted for 1¼-inch lead pipe.

	Painted	White Enameled Inside, Painted Outside
Size, 16x24 in...	$0.82	$2.15
Size, 18x30 in...	1.10	2.45
Size, 18x36 in...	1.35	3.15
Size, 20x36 in...	1.60	3.45
Size 20x40 in...	1.85	3.85

Cast Slop Sinks.

No. 24R7604 Extra Heavy Cast Iron Slop Sinks.

Size, 16x16x10 inches. Price, each...............**$1.25**
Size, 14x20x12 inches. Price, each............... **1.65**

Cast Iron Corner Sinks.

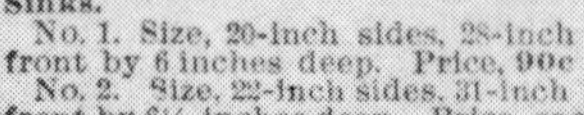

No. 24R7606 Cast Iron Corner Sinks.

No. 1. Size, 20-inch sides, 28-inch front by 6 inches deep. Price, 90c
No. 2. Size, 22-inch sides, 31-inch front by 6½ inches deep. Price, each.........**$1.00**

Steel Sinks.

Wrought Steel Kitchen Sinks. These sinks are made from one plate of steel and superior to cast iron sinks **in every particular,** being lighter, stronger and more durable; are fitted for 1¼-inch lead or 1½-inch iron pipe, and come painted or galvanized in the following sizes:

No. 24R7608 Painted.

Size	Weight, lbs.	Each	Size	Weight, lbs.	Each
16x24x6	13	$1.40	20x30x6	21¾	$1.87
18x30x6	15⅛	1.65	20x36x6	23	2.20
18x36x6	18⅛	2.00	20x40x6	25½	2.56

No. 24R7609 Galvanized.

Size	Weight, lbs.	Each	Size	Weight, lbs.	Each
16x24x6	13	$1.63	20x30x6	21¾	$2.20
18x30x6	15⅛	2.00	20x36x6	23	2.56
18x36x6	18⅛	2.34	20x40x6	25½	2.92

Seamless Wrought Steel Sinks with Turned Edges. This sink is adapted for exposed or open plumbing and has improved brass strainer couplings. They are made of one piece of steel, are finely finished and one of the strongest sinks made. Cannot crack or rust out. Fitted for 1¼-inch lead pipe or 1½-inch iron pipe. Furnished in three finishes and sizes as follows:

No. 24R7613 Painted.

Size	Weight, lbs.	Each	Size	Weight, lbs.	Each
16x24x6	13	$1.42	20x30x6	22½	$1.90
18x30x6	15⅛	1.68	20x36x6	23	2.25
18x36x6	18⅛	2.02	20x40x6	25½	2.60

No. 24R7614 Galvanized.

Size	Weight, lbs.	Each	Size	Weight, lbs.	Each
16x24x6	13½	$1.68	20x30x6	21¾	$2.25
18x30x6	18¾	2.00	20x36x6	28	2.60
18x36x6	24½	2.39	20x40x6	30	3.00

No. 24R7616 White Enameled Sinks, nicely finished; outside color blue.

Size	Weight, lbs.	Each	Size	Weight, lbs.	Each
16x24x6	14	$3.02	20x30x6	22½	$3.96
18x30x6	19¼	3.61	20x36x6	29	4.45
18x36x6	25	4.10	20x40x6	31	4.91

The 1902 Sears Roebuck catalog had Enameled Roll Rim Kitchen sinks made of steel or cast iron, white enamel inside, and painted blue outside. (Courtesy Sears, Roebuck and Company.)

japanned on outside." The price of a metal breadbox was $1.55. Tin flour and sugar canisters were also available.

In the same catalog, a twenty-three piece clear glass kitchen assortment, including coffee, salt, tea, pepper, measuring cup and pitcher, jelly glasses and molds, rolling pin and creamer, sold for $1.45. A fifteen-piece china cereal and spice set sold for $3.45.

"Dandy" yellow kitchenware was also offered in 1916. Some of the prices were: cereal jars 18¢ each; ten-pound sugar jar 32¢; fifteen-pound flour container 50¢; and butter jars from 15¢.

Cookware. Cookware, in the first two decades of the twentieth century, was made of tin, granite, porcelain-enamel cast iron speckled dark blue or gray; iron, copper, and aluminum. Aluminumware, which was introduced in 1892, did not gain any popularity until the late teens. Housewives distrusted its light weight, plus it was expensive and often of poor quality. Corning introduced glass cookware in its Pyrex ovenware line in 1915.

Enamelware in gray, blue, and white, and white porcelain-enamel steelware, aluminum, and iron were all available in 1916.

Ringed Pot Covers, IC Tin.

No. 23R5545 Hemmed edges.

Inches		8¼	9
Price, each		4c	4c
Inches	9¾	10	10½
Price, each	4c	5c	5c
Inches		11	11½
Price, each		5c	6c
Inches		12	12½
Price, each		6c	7c

Miners' Gold Pans.

No. 23R5548 Miners' Gold Pan, smooth steel, polished. Inside diameter, 16½ inches. Weight, 1½ pounds.
Price, each 20c

DECORATED JAPANNED TINWARE.

Our Decorated Japanned Tinware is of European manufacture and is beautifully lithographed in bright colors and pleasing designs. Owing to the quantities in which we import it we are able to sell it at about the same price as the ordinary japanned tinware, which it far excels in attractiveness and beauty.

No. 23R5900 Decorated Japanned Oblong Tray. Made of heavy tin and finished in bright colors. Size, 15¾x12 inches. Weight, 14 ounces.
Price, each.............29c

No. 23R5904 Decorated Japanned Spice Box. Well made, with rounded corners and decorated in colors. Has six round inside boxes labeled for various spices. Size, 7x4¾x3¼ inches. Weight, 14 ounces. Price, each......48c

No. 23R5912 Decorated Japanned Comb and Brush Case, embossed and finished in bright colors with mirror in center. Size, 10½x7¼ inches. Weight, 8 ounces.
Price, each...............25c

No. 23R5915 Decorated Japanned Comb Case, same as above but smaller and without mirror. Size, 8¾x3¼ inches. Weight, 2 ounces.
Price, each..........5c

Tea and Coffee Canisters.

Made of tin and decorated in fancy colors, with porcelain knob; well made and artistic.

No. 23R5921 Tea Canister, one-pound size. Weight, 5 ounces. Price, each....10c

No. 23R5922 Coffee Canister, one-pound size. Weight, 8 ounces.
Price, each..........10c

No. 23R5923 Tea Canister, two-pound size.
Price, each..........12c

No. 23R5924 Coffee Canister, two-pound size. Price, each..........12c

No. 23R5926 Pepper Shaker; fancy decorated tin, assorted colors. Size, 3¼x2 inches. Weight, 1 ounce. Price, each......5c

No. 23R5930 Decorated Tin Square Match Safe, embossed and finished in assorted colors. Will hold a box of parlor matches. Size, 4½x4½ inches. Weight, 2¼ ounces.
Price, each.............6c

No. 23R5932 Wall Match Safe, embossed tin, finished in bright colors with scratcher. Size, 7¼x4 inches. Weight, 1 ounce.
Price, each..........5c

No. 23R5935 Child's Decorated Tin Mug. Assorted designs, bright colors. Large size, 3x3¼ inches. Weight, 2 ounces. Price, each...6c

No. 23R5937 Child's Decorated Tin Mug. Same as above, but smaller. Just the thing for the little ones. Size, 2¾x2¾ inches. Weight, 1 ounce. Price, each..........4c

Sears Roebuck's 1902 catalog offered decorated japanned tinware. They said that, because of the quantities they imported, they were able to sell it at the same price as ordinary japanned tinware even though it was far more attractive. It was decorated with bright colors. The tea and coffee canisters have porcelain knobs. (Courtesy Sears, Roebuck and Company.)

JAPANNED WARE.

Flour Boxes.

No. 23R6000 Hinged covers, decorated.

Pounds	25	50
Weight, each, pounds	2¼	4
Inches	10x20	12x22
Price, each	54c	72c
Pounds		100
Weight, each, pounds		7
Inches		14½x28
Price, each		$1.02

Cream City Flour Bin and Sifter, IX.

No. 23R6002 Japanned and nicely ornamented. The sifter proper is protected from pressure by the flour in the bin by our **new shield** which enables the reels to work easily and smoothly, and obviates all grinding through of foreign substances. The flour is protected from coming in contact with the iron crank by an **angular tin sleeve,** and a **tin skirt** below the sifter prevents the flour from scattering all over the bottom of the bin, but instead directs it into the proper receptacle. The sifter rests on a strong ring, which extends all around the inside of the bin, holding it securely in place, and still allowing it to be easily removed for cleaning.

Pounds	25	50	100
Weight, crated, pounds	10½	16	21
Inches	10¼x23	13x27¼	15½x33¼
Price, each	$1.34	$1.67	$2.33

Square Bread Boxes.

No. 23R6005 Japanned.

Inches	9¼x9¼x13½
Weight, lbs.	2½
Price, each	46c
Inches	10¼x11½x15
Weight, lbs.	3
Price, each	54c
Inches	10⅜x12½x17
Weight, lbs.	3¾
Price, each	63c

Round Sugar Boxes.

No. 23R6009

Inches	10x10	12x12
Weight, each, pounds	2	3
Price, each	42c	60c

Knife and Fork Boxes.

No. 23R6015 Open.

Inches	2¾x8¾x13½
Weight, each, pounds	1¼
Price, each	30c

Folding Lunch Boxes.

No. 23R6019 Without flasks.

Nos.	1	2
Inches	7½x3¾x3¾	9x4x4
Weight, ea. oz.	10	11
Each	14c	17c

With flask. Weight, each, 1 pound, 9x4x4 ......41c

Round Spice Box.

No. 23R6025 Covered, round inside boxes. 7½ inches. Weight, each, 1¾ pounds. Price, each..42c

Box Graters.

No. 23R6029 2x5 inches. Weight, each, 2 ounces.
Price, each......................2c

The Improved Edgar Nutmeg Grater.

No. 23R6030 It will not clog, tear the fingers, nor drop the nutmeg. It grates the nutmeg very fine, distributes it evenly, **and grates it all up,** leaving no pieces. It is simple and durable. Weight, each, 4 oz.
Price, per dozen, 84c; each......................8c

Dinner Horns.

No. 23R6035 With improved mouthpiece.

	Plain	Japanned
Inches	9	9
Weight, ounces	3	3
Price, each	4c	5c
Per dozen	42c	51c

Large Dinner Horns.

No. 23R6038 Japanned. Improved mouthpiece. 13¼ inches. Weight, 4 ounces.
Price, per dozen, 60c; each......................5c

No. 23R6043 Comb Cases. Assorted colors, 2⅜x5½x7 inches. Weight, each, 4 oz.
Price, each...... 5c
Per dozen......54c

Dredge Boxes.

No. 23R6047 Size, 2¼x3½. Weight, each, 4 ounces.
Price, per dozen, 42c; each........4c

Pepper Boxes.

No. 23R6050	Small	Large
Inches	1½x2¾	1¾x3
Weight, each	2 oz.	3 oz.
Price, each	2c	3c
Per dozen	18c	25c

Square Match Safes.

No. 23R6052

Inches	2⅛x2½x3½
Weight, each	3 oz.
Price, each	4c
Per dozen	40c

Twin Match Safes.

No. 23R6053 Assorted colors.

Inches	4¼x5
Weight, each	3 oz.
Price, each	3c
Per dozen	36c

Match Box Holder and Safe.

No. 23R6055 Match Box Holder and Safe. Holds full box of 200 matches. Nicely finished. Weight, each, 4 ounces.
Price, each...........................8c

Match Scratcher.

No. 23R6067 Match Scratcher. This is the latest novelty in this line. It is attractive, cheap and durable. Made of tin and striking surface of best quality of emery cloth. Diameter, 5 inches. Weight, 1 ounce. Price, each..............................4c

Light Cash Boxes.

No. 23R6080 With lock.

Inches.	9½	10½	11½	13
Wgt., lbs.	1¼	1½	1¾	2½
Price, ea.	44c	49c	54c	63c

No. 23R6089 Deed Boxes. With hasp.

In.	9½	10½	11½	13
Wgt. lbs.	1	1½	1⅝	2
Each	33c	38c	44c	52c

Combination Lock Cash or Treasure Boxes.

No. 23R6090 These boxes are made from very heavy stock, finished in black enamel, striped with rich gold bronze. The dial is large and legible. The owner can set a new combination as often as may be required without taking the lock to pieces. Trays are not furnished with boxes. For trays see following number. Extreme outside measures of all boxes are ⅜ to ½ inch larger than sizes below. Knobs project ⅜ inch beyond the ribs.

Length, inside	9 in.	10½ in.	12 in.	14 in.
Width	6 in.	7 in.	8 in.	10 in.
Depth	3¾ in.	4⅛ in.	5¼ in.	6¼ in.
Boxes, price, each	$2.74	$2.90	$3.13	$3.52

No. 23R6092 Inside Partitioned Trays, to fit inside our No. 23R6090 cash box.

Size, inches	9	10½	12	14
Price, each	39c	59c	63c	$1.17

Fire Proof Cash Box.

No. 23R6094 Fire Proof Cash Box. The fire proof walls of this box are sufficiently thick to make it absolutely fire proof in any residence. It is a perfectly safe receptacle for deeds, bonds, contracts, mortgages, notes, insurance policies, tax receipts, jewelry, etc. To test this box we had one subjected to an intense heat in a furnace. Not only was the iron heated red hot, but it reached a white heat, which is the point just before iron melts. The contents of box were not even marred. No fire could ever occur out in the open air to equal the intense heat to which this box was subjected. Furnished with a first class padlock with two keys. Dimensions: Outside—13 inches long, 9 inches wide, 6½ inches deep; inside—10 inches long, 6 inches wide, 3 inches deep. Approximate weight, 50 pounds. Price, each..........................$3.95

Bill Head Boxes.

No. 23R6095

Parts...	1	2	3
Inches,	1⅛x9x6¾	2¼x9x9½	3¼x9x13
Weight..	6 oz.	12 oz.	1⅜ lbs.
Each...	22c	30c	41c

Postoffice Boxes.

No. 23R6097

Parts	Wt. ea. lbs.	Inches	Price, each
1	½	4⅛x4⅞x6	22c
2	⅝	4⅛x7⅝x6¼	30c
3	1	4½x1 x6¼	36c

Candlesticks.

No. 23R6105 Japanned Candlesticks. Weight, 2 ounces. Size, 5 inches.
Price, each......................3c
Per dozen........................35c

Cuspidors.

No. 23R6112 Cottage Cuspidors, gold band.
Weight, 6 oz. Size, 3x7 inches.
Price, each................ 8c
Per dozen.................. 85c

No. 23R6113 Cuspidors, decorated. Weight, each, 8 ounces. Size, 5½x7 inches.
Price, each $0.13
Per dozen................ 1.50

No 23R6116 Nickel Plated Cuspidors. Weight, each, 8 oz. Size, 5x7½ inches. Price, each..............22c

No. 23R6119 Cast Iron Cuspidors. White enameled inside, outside painted, assorted colors, banded. Weight, 5¼ pounds. Size, 6x8 inches.
Price, each...............45c

Spittoons.

No. 23R6125 Assorted colors. Weight, each, 10 ounces. Size, 2¼x8 inches.
Price, per dozen, $1.58; each ... 14c

Fancy Water Coolers.

No. 23R6130 Water Coolers, double wall, fitted with non-conducting material, galvanized iron reservoir, handsomely decorated in various colors, side handles, nickel plated faucets.

Gallons	2	3	4
Wt., each, crated	13	20	25
Each	$1.33	$1.67	$2.00
Gallons	6	8	10
Weight, each, crated, lbs.	30	45	55
Each	$2.33	$2.67	$3.33

Tea or Coffee Canisters.

Hinged Covers.

No. 23R6142 Coffee Canisters.
No. 23R6143 Tea Canisters.

One pound, size, 4½x4⅜ inches. Weight, 5 ounces. Price, per dozen, 90c; each..............8c

Two pounds, size, 5⅝x6 inches. Weight, 8 ounces. Price, per dozen, $1.28; each..........11c

Three pounds, size, 6¼x6¾ inches. Weight, 12 ounces. Price, per dozen, $1.66; each.. ....14c

Slop Jars and Chamber Pails.

No. 23R6155 Bailed Slop Jars. Assorted colors, banded. Weight, 1¾ pounds. Size, 9½x11 inches.
Price, each.......................27c

No. 23R6158 Chamber Pails. Assorted colors; nicely japanned, inside and out.

Quarts,....	10	12	14
Holds, qts.	9	11	13
Size	10¼x10¼	11x11¼	11¼x12¾
Weight, each, pounds	2	2¼	2⅜
Price, each	27c	30c	36c

Challenge Odorless Commode and Slop Bucket Combined.

No. 23R6162 It is impossible for the foul air to escape, even when the lid is removed, as there is inside the lid a receptacle that holds a deodorizer, and which neutralizes all gases inside the commode. The disinfectant (2 tablespoonfuls of chloride of lime), needs only to be renewed once in two weeks at a small cost. It is indispensable in the sick room, especially in cases of contagious diseases and fevers. Does not have to be emptied until filled, no matter how long it stands. Cut shows construction. Made of heavy galvanized iron, and has no paint to hold stench or disease germs. Has removable seat, etc. It needs only to be seen to convince you of its wonderful merit. Holds 9 quarts. Weight, 6¾ pounds. Price, each.... ....$1.40

Dust Pans, IC.

No. 23R6175 Japanned, round tin handles. Weight, each, 6 ounces. Size, 9x13 inches.
Price, each.................. 6c
Per dozen.....................71c

Covered Dust Pans, IC.

No. 23R6177 Japanned, round tin handles. Weight, each, 8 ounces. Size, 9x13 inches.
Price, each $0.09
Per dozen................. 1.05

Dust Pans with Brushes.

No. 23R6180 Assorted colors. Weight, 1 pound. Size, 10x12¾ inches.
Price, each 50c

The Sears Roebuck 1902 catalog shows other japanned ware that was available for the housewife. Japanned ware was made of heavy tin. (Courtesy Sears, Roebuck and Company.)

The Sears Roebuck 1908 catalog shows imported German china cereal and spice sets. The blue floral design on white was a favorite. Black japanned tin boxes were still available. (Courtesy Sears, Roebuck and Company.)

A Wagner Ware Cast Aluminum magazine advertisement in 1917. For 60¢, the 6½″ skillet pictured in the ad would be sent postpaid. A booklet was free on request.

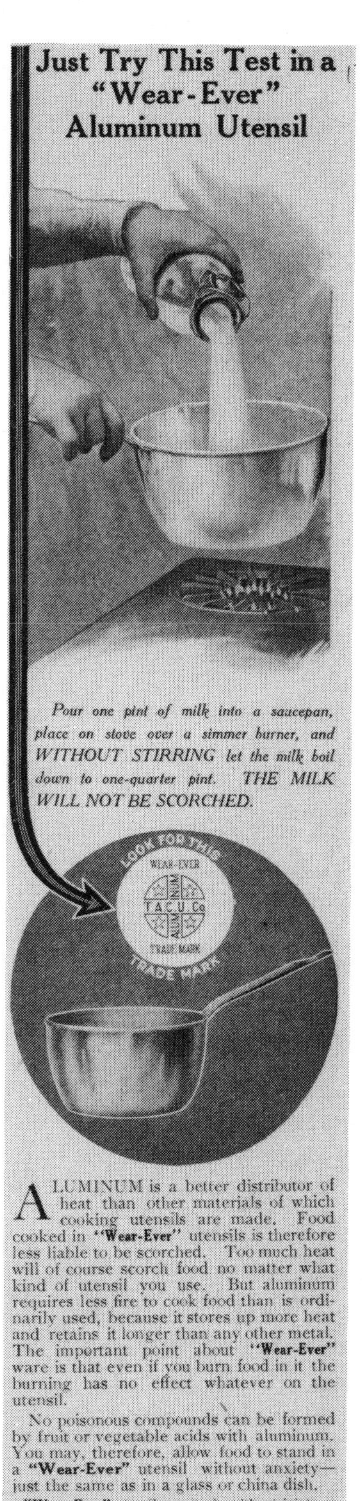

An Aluminum Cooking Utensil Company ad from 1911. The Wear-Ever test was to "pour one pint of milk into a saucepan, place on stove over a simmer burner, and without stirring let the milk boil down to one-quarter pint. THE MILK WILL NOT BE SCORCHED." The Wear-Ever trademark was adopted in 1903.

$2.73 FOR A COMPLETE OUTFIT OF PEERLESS GRAY ENAMELED WARE $2.73

PEERLESS WARE IS HIGHEST GRADE. Extra heavy, double coated enamel. Each piece carefully inspected before sending out. Peerless ware is made of heavy sheet steel, coated with pure gray enamel, two coats, baked on under an intense heat which unites the enamel to the steel body in such a manner that it cannot chip off or crack, if properly used. The enamel used on Peerless Gray Ware is absolutely pure and will not discolor or peel with age.

Price has been reduced.

YOU SAVE MONEY BY BUYING AN ASSORTMENT. We buy these sets in immense quantities and offer them to you at actual factory cost plus our one small percentage of profit. Buying from us you save at least 50 per cent on the price you would have to pay at retail and get better ware than you can get anywhere else.

PEERLESS GRAY WARE is durable and substantial, does not rust like tin or iron and is as easily cleaned as crockery. The use of good enamel ware cuts the kitchen work in half.

38,819 SETS SOLD BY US LAST YEAR

at $3.79, $3.39 and $2.95 per set. These low prices are still further reduced in this book along with over 3,000 other items of general hardware. Your saving is greater than ever.

We furnish these outfits in three different sizes, for No. 7, No. 8 and No. 9 stoves, each set containing the following articles:

1 Peerless Enameled Sauce Pan
2 Peerless Enameled Pudding Pans
1 Peerless Enameled Wash Basin
1 Peerless Enameled Windsor Pattern Dipper
4 Peerless Enameled Pie Plates, 9 inches in diameter
1 Peerless Enameled Soap Dish, to hang on the wall
1 Peerless Enameled Dish Pan
1 Peerless Enameled Soup Ladle
1 Peerless Enameled Tea Kettle
1 Peerless Enameled Coffee Pot
1 Peerless Enameled Teapot
2 Peerless Enameled Preserving Kettles

Peerless Outfit for No. 7 stove. Weight, 35 lbs. No. 9K22007 Price, complete, as illustrated and described $2.73

Peerless Outfit for No. 8 stove. Weight, 40 lbs. No. 9K22008 Price, complete, as illustrated and described $3.18

Peerless Outfit for No. 9 stove. Weight, 50 lbs. No. 9K22009 Price, complete, as illustrated and described $3.59

68-PIECE ELITE KITCHEN AND STOVE WARE ASSORTMENT ONLY $7.98

INCLUDES TINWARE, IRONWARE, WOODENWARE AND EVERYTHING NEEDED ABOUT THE KITCHEN, STOVE OR LAUNDRY AT A PRICE SO LOW YOU CAN'T AFFORD TO DO WITHOUT.

OUR ELITE ASSORTMENTS contain the very finest grades of merchandise, including a solid copper nickel plated tea kettle, solid copper coffee and teapots, complete set of Potts' sad irons, and practically every necessary article in the kitchen or laundry. Read the entire list of articles contained in this immense assortment and you will find by figuring up the retail prices, that this outfit would cost you at least 50 per cent more if the items were bought separately in your best home store. We figure only one small profit on the entire lot instead of a separate profit on each item. We sell thousands of these assortments every year, buy the goods in immense quantities and offer them to you in these wholesale assortments at wholesale prices, prices lower than the average merchant pays for the goods he buys, which will not compare with ours for quality.

Three different sizes of Elite assortments, to fit No. 7, No. 8 and No. 9 stoves, each assortment containing the following articles:

1 Heavy IX Tin Copper Bottom Wash Boiler
1 Iron Stove Kettle
1 Tin Cover to fit
1 Nickel Plated Copper Tea Kettle
1 Iron Spider
1 Fry Pan, 10 inches
1 Basting Spoon
1 Stove Shovel, heavy steel
1 Nickel Plated Copper 5-pint Coffee Pot
1 Nickel Plated Copper 4-pint Teapot
1 Retinned Preserving Kettle
1 Cover to fit
1 Retinned Sauce Pan
1 Cover to fit
1 Tin Muffin Frame, 12 cups
½ Dozen Tin Pie Plates, 9 inches
1 Extra Heavy Retinned Dish Pan, 14 quarts
1 Pieced Tin Cup, 1 pint
1 Heavy Copper Bottom Water Dipper, 2 quarts
1 Flat Handled Skimmer
1 Vegetable Fork
3 Tin Bread Pans
2 Tin Cake Pans
2 Drip Pans, 10x12 and 10x14 inches
1 Dozen Assorted Patty Pans
1 Rolling Pin
1 Cake Turner
1 Retinned Colander
1 Cake Cutter
1 Biscuit Cutter
1 Doughnut Cutter
1 Nutmeg Grater
1 Large Grater
1 Revolving Flour Sifter
1 Dover Egg Beater
1 Covered Japanned Dust Pan
1 Butcher Knife
1 Paring Knife
1 Mincing Knife
1 Bread Board
1 Wood Potato Masher
1 Oval Hardwood Chopping Tray
1 Steamer
1 Set Mrs. Potts' Sad Irons, consisting of Three Irons, Handle and Stand

Sharp reduction in prices of these sets from the low prices named in our last catalogue.

Elite Assortment for No. 7 stove. Weight, 100 pounds. No. 9K22027 Price $7.98

Elite Assortment for No. 8 stove. Weight, 105 pounds. No. 9K22028 Price $8.43

Elite Assortment for No. 9 stove. Weight, 110 pounds. No. 9K22029 Price $8.86

FORMER LOW PRICES FURTHER REDUCED.

WHITE PORCELAIN ENAMELED STEEL WARE

QUALITY HIGH AS HERETOFORE.

EVERY PIECE IS MADE SEAMLESS, of one piece of sheet steel, heavily coated inside and outside with pure white porcelain enamel and with edges or border a bright clear blue color. Every piece full size and made in the best and most practical shape. It cannot be broken, is not easily chipped and is less than one-half the weight of crockery. The enamel is not affected by acids, will not discolor and is as easily cleaned as china. We recommend White Porcelain Enameled Ware for ordinary household use, camping parties, miners and prospectors. It is more serviceable than crockery as it is unbreakable, does not chip and is light in weight. Every piece of White Porcelain Enameled Ware is guaranteed first quality and the best made regardless of price.

No. 9K24200 White Porcelain Enameled Dinner Plates. 8¾-inch is the popular size.

Diameter, inches	8	8¾	9½
Price, each	$0.09	$0.11	$0.13
Per dozen	1.04	1.27	1.50

No. 9K24202 White Porcelain Enameled Cups. 3⅛-inch is the best size.

Diameter, inches	Price, each	Per dozen
3⅛	10c	$1.12
4	12c	1.36

No. 9K24204 White Porcelain Enameled Saucers. 5⅛-inch matches 3⅛-inch cup.

Diameter, inches	Price, each	Per dozen
5⅛	8c	$0.85
6	10c	1.14

No. 9K24207 White Porcelain Enameled Bowls. 5½-inch generally used.

Diameter, inches	Price, each	Per dozen
5½	13c	$1.50
7⅛	18c	2.06

No. 9K24212 White Enameled Platters. 13⅞-inch is most used.

Diameter, inches	11⅞	13⅞	15⅞
Price, each	$0.23	$0.31	$0.40
Per dozen	2.60	3.56	4.60

$2.33 FOR THIS COMPLETE PORCELAIN ENAMEL DINNER SET.

YOU SAVE ON THE COST OF EACH ITEM WHEN YOU BUY A COMPLETE SET.

IT IS POSSIBLE for us to name a low price on this complete set by reason of selling a number of items at once. We figure one small profit on the entire lot, instead of a separate profit on each item. We give you the benefit of all the saving in selecting, handling and packing the goods. It is to your interest, therefore, to order a complete outfit at one time if you can possibly do so.

This matchless set of Porcelain Enamel Ware consists of 6 large dinner plates, 6 coffee cups, 6 saucers, 1 large oval platter, 1 large vegetable dish and 1 bowl.
No. 9K22016 Price, complete $2.33

No. 9K24209 White Porcelain Enameled Vegetable Dishes. We recommend 10¼-inch size for families.

Length, inches	9¼	10¼	11
Price, each	$0.19	$0.21	$0.24
Per dozen	2.20	2.40	2.70

No. 9K24215 White Porcelain Enameled Wash Basins. The largest size is the best for most people.

Diameter, inches	10¼	12	13¼
Price, each	$0.18	$0.24	$0.30
Per dozen	2.06	2.65	3.45

No. 9K24217 White Porcelain Enameled Ewers or Water Pitchers, drawn from one piece of steel, guaranteed seamless. We sell most of the 2-quart size.

Diam. in.	5½	6	6¾
Holds, qts.	1	1½	2
Price ea.	$0.44	$0.59	$0.70
Per doz.	5.20	6.90	8.20

No. 9K24220 White Porcelain Enameled Soap Dishes, with removable drainers. Size, 4⅞x3⅞ inches. Price, ea. 18c
Per dozen, $2.04

No. 9K24223 White Porcelain Enameled Chambers. The unbreakable kind. No. 4 is full size and best to buy.

Size, No.	2	4
Diameter, inches	8	9⅞
Price	28c	41c

No. 9K24224 White Porcelain Enameled Chamber Covers.

To fit chamber No.	2	4
Price	17c	19c

A complete economy set of gray enameled ware cost $2.73. Other sets were also offered in the 1908 Sears Roebuck catalog. Kitchen and stoveware sets ranged from $3.84 to $7.98, depending on the size of the set. (Courtesy Sears, Roebuck and Company.)

LOW PRICES BEFORE, STILL LOWER NOW ON OUR LINE OF

TRUE BLUE ENAMELED STEEL WARE

GENUINE TRUE BLUE ENAMELED WARE FINEST QUALITY WARRANTED

THE BEST ENAMELED WARE IT IS POSSIBLE TO MAKE, REGARDLESS OF COST. DO NOT THINK BECAUSE WE SELL TRUE BLUE WARE AT SUCH REMARKABLY LOW PRICES IT IS NOT AS GOOD AS OTHER BRANDS. BETTER QUALITY CANNOT BE PRODUCED.

WITH A FEW EXCEPTIONS as noted, every article in the entire line is made seamless with spun covers and knobs. True Blue Enameled Ware is made of cold drawn steel. Four coats of the finest grade of enamel are applied on both inside and outside to each article of True Blue Ware. The enamel used is guaranteed to be chemically pure, free from all poisonous or harmful ingredients, and positively will not discolor from the acids of fruits and vegetables. True Blue Enameled Ware will not peel off, is as easy to clean, but is not broken like earthenware or china; is durable but does not rust like tin or iron, will outlast any other enameled ware made and is an ornament to any kitchen. The outside blue mottled surface forms a strong contrast with the pure white inside and gives a finish which makes True Blue Enameled Ware the most beautiful kitchen ware made. We do not handle seconds, and each piece is guaranteed perfect.

BEWARE OF IMITATIONS of True Blue Enameled Ware. On account of the high quality of True Blue Ware many dealers offer for sale a blue mottled ware which bears some resemblance to the original True Blue, and they will tell you it is True Blue, or just as good. DO NOT BE DECEIVED. We are the only house offering True Blue Enameled Ware, and no one can buy a piece of it except from us.

WE GUARANTEE each piece of genuine True Blue Enameled Ware to be perfect, not to leak and to outwear any other enameled ware on the market. Order a lot of it; when it comes, examine it closely. If it is not superior to any you ever used, ship it back to us and we will refund your money and pay the transportation charges both ways. Remember, there is only one genuine True Blue Enameled Ware, and it can be had only from us.

NOTE: We guarantee every piece of True Blue Ware to hold the actual quantity we say it does. We list no "trade" sizes.

37c GENUINE TRUE BLUE ENAMELED TEAPOT, HOLDS 1 QUART.

Seamed Teapots, with covers. The 2-quart size is most popular.

No. 9K24400

Holds quarts	Price
1	37c
1¼	44c
2	49c
2½	53c
3½	59c

44c GENUINE TRUE BLUE ENAMELED COFFEE POT, HOLDS 1½ QUARTS.

Seamed Coffee Pots, with covers. The 3½-quart size is the best seller.

No. 9K24402

Holds quarts	Price
1½	44c
2	48c
2½	53c
3½	59c
4	65c

82c GENUINE TRUE BLUE ENAMELED COFFEE BOILER, HOLDS 6 QUARTS.

Seamed Bottom Coffee Boilers, with covers. No. 8 size is most popular.

No. 9K24406

For stove	Holds quarts	Price
No. 7	6	$0.82
No. 8	8	.95
No. 9	11	1.15

76c GENUINE TRUE BLUE ENAMELED TEA KETTLE, HOLDS 4½ QUARTS.

Seamed Flat Bottom Tea Kettles, with covers. Rustproof, and will not discolor the water. No. 8 size is used more than any other.

No. 9K24408

For stove	Holds quarts	Price
No. 7	4½	$0.76
No. 8	6	.87
No. 9	7½	1.03

21c GENUINE TRUE BLUE ENAMELED WASH BASIN, SMALL SIZE.

The large size is best to buy.

No. 9K24410

Size	Price
Small	21c
Medium	25c
Large	34c

54c GENUINE TRUE BLUE ENAMELED DISH PAN, HOLDS 9 QUARTS.

We recommend the 15-quart size for family use.

No. 9K24412

Holds quarts	Price
9	54c
12	63c
15	76c
18	85c

15c GENUINE TRUE BLUE ENAMELED SAUCE PAN, 1¼-QUART SIZE.

Strong Lipped Sauce Pans. The 2½ and 3¼-quart sizes are used most.

No. 9K24416

Holds quarts	Price
1¼	15c
2½	23c
3¼	30c
4¼	35c

15c

41c GENUINE TRUE BLUE ENAMELED BERLIN SAUCE PAN, 2½ QUARTS.

Berlin Sauce Pans, with covers, useful for cooking almost everything. Far more convenient than the old style. We recommend 6 or 8-quart size.

No. 9K24419

Quarts	2½	3½	6	8
Price	41c	50c	59c	74c

49c GENUINE TRUE BLUE ENAMELED BERLIN KETTLE, 3¼ QUARTS.

Covered Berlin Kettles. The 6 and 8-quart are the most popular sizes.

No. 9K24423

Holds quarts	Price
3¼	49c
6	61c
8	74c

30c GENUINE TRUE BLUE ENAMELED PRESERVING KETTLE, 3½ QUARTS.

Strong Lipped Preserving Kettles. The 7 and 9-quart are the best selling sizes.

No. 9K24426

Holds quarts	Price
3½	30c
4½	34c
5¾	39c
7	46c
9	55c
13½	79c

14c GENUINE TRUE BLUE ENAMELED PUDDING PAN, HOLDS 1 QUART.

Extra Deep Pudding Pans. The 2½ and 3¼-quart are the most popular sizes.

No. 9K24432

Holds quarts	Price
1	14c
1¾	18c
2½	20c
3¼	22c

22c GENUINE TRUE BLUE ENAMELED MILK PAN, HOLDS 2¾ QUARTS.

The 6-quart size is the most popular.

No. 9K24435

Holds quarts	Price
2¾	22c
3½	24c
4¼	27c
6	36c

66c GENUINE TRUE BLUE ENAMELED WATER PAIL, 8½ QUART SIZE.

Straight Flat Bottom Water Pails. The 11½-quart size is the one generally used.

No. 9K24438

Holds quarts	Price
8½	66c
11½	75c
14	92c

10c GENUINE TRUE BLUE ENAMELED PIE PLATE, SIZE, 8 x ⅝ INCHES.

The 9-inch is used most.

No. 9K24441

Size, inches	Price
8x⅝	10c
9x¾	12c
10x1	14c

14c GENUINE TRUE BLUE ENAMELED DINNER PLATE, REGULAR SIZE.

Size, 8½ inches; which is full size.

No. 9K24445

Price, each.... $0.14
Per dozen..... 1.55

19c GENUINE TRUE BLUE ENAMELED CUP AND SAUCER, STANDARD SIZE.

Cup is 4x2¼ inches, saucer is 5¾ inches.

No. 9K24450

Price, cups, each. $0.11
Per dozen...... 1.28
Saucers, each, 8c; per dozen...... .94

14c GENUINE TRUE BLUE ENAMELED SOUP BOWL, HOLDS 1½ PINTS.

The unbreakable kind.

No. 9K24452

Holds pints	Price
1½	14c

49c GENUINE TRUE BLUE ENAMELED WATER PITCHER, 2-QUART SIZE.

The handiest pitcher you ever used for milk.

The 3-quart size is the best seller.

No. 9K24455

Holds quarts	Price
2	49c
2½	68c

62c GENUINE TRUE BLUE EMAMELED DOUBLE BOILER, HOLDS 1¼ QTS

Milk or Rice Double Boilers with cover to both vessels. Double boilers make it impossible to burn the food. The 3-quart size is best for family use.

62c

No. 9K24458

Holds quarts	Price	Holds quarts	Price
1¼	62c	3	$1.04
1¾	82c	3½	1.26

19c GENUINE TRUE BLUE ENAMELED WINDSOR DIPPER, 1-PINT SIZE.

With strong, round handles. The 1½-pint size is most used.

19c

No. 9K24463

Holds pints	Price
1	19c
1½	22c

11c GENUINE TRUE BLUE ENAMELED SOUP LADLE, 14 INCHES LONG.

Regular size, 14 inches long.

No. 9K24468

Price.................................. 11c

10c GENUINE TRUE BLUE ENAMELED BASTING SPOON, 14 INCHES LONG.

Threaded Basting Spoons. The 16-inch is worth the difference.

No. 9K24471

Size, inches	14	16
Price	10c	12c

17c GENUINE TRUE BLUE ENAMELED WALL SOAP DISH, FULL SIZE.

Wall Soap Dishes, with grates. Regular size, 6½x4x1½ inches.

No. 9K24477

Price............ 17c

33c GENUINE TRUE BLUE ENAMELED CHAMBER, SMALL SIZE.

The large size is generally used.

No. 9K24485

Size	Small	Med.	Large
Price	33c	40c	48c

14c GENUINE TRUE BLUE ENAMELED CHAMBER COVER, SMALL SIZE.

No. 9K24486

Size	Small	Med.	Large
Price	14c	17c	21c

$4.58 COMPLETE OUTFIT OF TRUE BLUE ENAMELED WARE $4.58

YOU SAVE ON THE COST OF EACH ITEM WHEN YOU BUY A COMPLETE OUTFIT

WE SELECT THE ARTICLES in these outfits from our regular stock, they are the same high grade as those listed above and are covered by the same broad guarantee. True Blue Enameled Ware is made of sheet steel, quadruple coated inside and out, full weight and full size, is strong, durable, perfect in manufacture and finish and will not break. No other ware made will give you the same service as our True Blue. We furnish three assortments suitable for stoves Nos. 7, 8 or 9 containing the following articles:

1 Tea Kettle.	1 Double Boiler.
1 Coffee Pot.	1 Dish Pan.
1 Teapot.	1 Soap Dish.
1 Berlin Kettle.	1 Basting Spoon.
1 Sauce Pan.	2 Pie Plates.
1 Pudding Pan.	1 Windsor Dipper
1 Wash Basin.	1 Soup Ladle.

YOU SAVE STILL MORE.

The low prices in our last catalogue have been still further reduced in this book on over 3,000 hardware items alone.

By selling a complete set of True Blue Enameled Ware at one time, on a single order, we are enabled to quote a much lower price than if we sold each piece separately. True Blue is the highest grade made, each piece, covered by our GUARANTEE OF SATISFACTION OR YOUR MONEY BACK.

True Blue Outfit for No. 7 Stove. Shipping weight 43 pounds, as illustrated and described.
No. 9K22012 Price............... $4.58

True Blue Outfit for No. 8 Stove. Shipping weight, 50 pounds, as illustrated and described.
No. 9K22013 Price............... $5.19

True Blue Outfit for No. 9 Stove. Shipping weight 56 pounds, as illustrated and described.
No. 9K22014 Price............... $5.79

Blue enameled steelware was a popular item. (Courtesy Sears, Roebuck and Company.)

6c REFINED SMOOTH PLANISHED STEEL DRIPPING PANS, SIZE 7x10 INCHES.

Made of heavy sheet, have wired edges and are nicely finished. State size wanted. 10x14 is the most popular size.

No. 9K23815

Size, in.	7x10	8x12	10x14	11x16	14x17
Price	6c	9c	12c	14c	17c

37c ACME COVERED ROASTING PAN, STRONGEST AND BEST, 9x13 IN.

37c

Bakes both top and bottom at the same time. The bottom is stengthened by two ribs. Has a heavy rack which keeps the meat out of the gravy. It is made of a fine grade of smooth steel. Try the pan for baking bread and you will never use anything else. Sold by agents at more than twice our price.

No. 9K23820

Number	1	2	3	4
Width, inches	9	10	11	13
Length, inches	13	15	16	18
Height, inches	7½	7½	8½	9½
Price	37c	46c	54c	64c

25c FOR 12 ASSORTED ANIMAL CAKE CUTTERS.

Just the thing for the children. Made of best IC tin.

No. 9K25038 Price, per dozen, assorted........25c

21c FOR 6 BEST GRADE TIN PASTRY CUTTERS.

Consists of two biscuit, two doughnut and two cooky cutters. Well made, nicely finished.

No. 9K25043 Price, per set of six, 21c

9c PER SET CARD PARTY CAKE CUTTERS.

For cakes resembling the different denominations of cards, hearts, diamonds, clubs, spades.

No. 9K25050 Price, per set of four cutters........9c

8c FOR AN AUTOMATIC NUTMEG GRATER, SIMPLE, DURABLE AND ECONOMICAL.

It will not clog, tear the fingers, nor drop the nutmeg. It grates very fine, and grates it all up, leaving no pieces.

No. 9K25119 Price. 8c

18c FOR A DOUBLE STEEL KNIFE COMBINED GRATER AND SLAW CUTTER.

The slicer sheet is detachable. Two knives made of best quality of steel and can be resharpened.

No. 9K25126 Price........18c

52c ONE-PIECE SOLID CAST ALUMINUM HIGHLY POLISHED SOUP LADLE.

52c

Strong, light and attractive. Will not tarnish, rust or corrode, no plating to wear off. Equal to solid silver in appearance. Is not so heavy and will not tarnish or become dull. Length, 12 inches.

No. 9K24646 Price........52c

8c FOR A SINGLE LOAF IDEAL BREAD PAN, MADE OF PLANISHED STEEL.

Makes a crisp, moist and wholesome loaf a certainty. It bakes evenly through and through. There is no danger of burning, and no special care is required. The crust is thin, smooth and even, and the loaf of beautiful shape, the bread is more nutritious, more tasty and more digestible.

		Size	Price
No. 9K25324	Double,	13⅛x10...	18c
No. 9K25326	Single,	13⅛x 5...	8c

10c FOR AN 8-CUP SOLID FRAME HEAVY TIN MUFFIN PAN

Size of cups, 3¼x1 inches.

No. 9K25396

Cups	8	12
Price	10c	16c

7c EXTRA HEAVY POLISHED TIN SANITARY BREAD PAN, No. 6.

All corners and edges are rounded, no grease, dirt or dough can become embedded in them as in ordinary pans. Full wired. Guaranteed not to leak.

No. 9K25314	No. 6	No. 7
Size, inches	8½x4½x2¾	9½x4½x3½
Price, each	7c	9c
Per dozen	75c	90c
	No. 8	No. 9
Size, inches	10¼x6¼x2¾	11¼x7¼x2¾
Price, each	9c	$0.11
Per dozen	92c	1.15

7c FOR 12 ENAMELED COVER KNOBS, COMPLETE.

With washers and nuts. Anyone can apply. When ordering, state if wanted for tea kettle or coffee pot. Made of wood with tin flanges.

No. 9K25150

Price, per 100, 55c; per doz. 7c

17c EXTRA HEAVY IXXX POLISHED TIN GRADUATED QUART MEASURE.

Made of the highest grade material heavily retinned. The best measure it is possible to produce. Will outlast a dozen of the light cheap kind. Especially recommended for dairymen, marketmen and family use. Warranted accurate.

No. 9K25163 • Price........17c

$4.89 PRINCESS STOVE AND KITCHEN OUTFIT, 66 USEFUL ARTICLES $4.89

THIS COMPLETE ASSORTMENT CONTAINS MORE KITCHEN WARE THAN YOU CAN BUY IN A RETAIL STORE FOR DOUBLE OUR PRICE, AND THE PRICE IS EVEN LOWER THAN WE QUOTED IN OUR LAST CATALOGUE.

No inferior goods or seconds are included. Every article in this assortment is strictly high grade, and we guarantee the quality and size. Read the list of articles we furnish, note the copper bottom wash boiler, copper bottom tea kettle, coffee pot and tea pot, and the other large pieces, every one of the highest grade.

WE ARE ABLE TO OFFER these Princess assortments at the remarkably low prices we do because we sell thousands of them every year and are content to figure our profit on each outfit extremely low.

WE GUARANTEE EACH ITEM in the Princess outfit to be strictly high grade, full size and entirely satisfactory. Send us your order for one of these assortments, and if you are not entirely satisfied with it, ship it back to us and we will refund your money. The greatest value outfit of kitchen ware ever offered.

Three sizes, to fit No. 7, No. 8 and No. 9 stoves.

Each outfit contains:

1 IX Tin Wash Boiler, with flat copper bottom
1 IX Tin Tea Kettle, with flat copper bottom
1 IX Tin Coffee Pot, with copper bowl bottom and enameled wood handle
1 IX Tin Tea Pot, with copper bowl bottom and enameled wood handle
1 Retinned Wash Basin. 1 IX Tin Dipper, with heavy copper bottom
2 Heavily Retinned Preserving Kettles
1 Heavily Retinned Sauce Pan
2 Retinned Pudding Pans. 1 IC Tin Colander
1 Heavily Retinned Dishpan
1 IC Tin Steamer, with rimmed cover
4 Tin Pie Plates, 9 inches in diameter
3 Tin Bread Pans
1 Tin Oblong Pan
1 Deep Oblong Pan
1 Tin Measure, 1-quart size, graduated by one-half pints. 1 Tin Funnel
1 Tin Grater, with enameled wood handle
1 Retinned Soup Ladle, with enameled wood handle
1 Tin Gravy Strainer
10 Assorted Cake, Cooky, Biscuit and Doughnut Cutters.
1 Nutmeg Grater
1 Retinned Flat Handle Skimmer
1 Cake Turner with enameled wood handle
12 Assorted Tin Patty Pans
1 Patent Rotary Flour Sifter
1 Covered Japanned Dust Pan
2 Retinned Threaded Basting Spoons
1 Tinned Kitchen Fork, 3 prongs, length, 12½ inches
1 Dover Egg Beater
3 Assorted Tin Pot Covers, to fit kettles and saucepans.
1 Square Japanned Match Box
1 Polished Lipped Frying Pan, with always cool handle
2 Sheet Iron Dripping or Roasting Pans

Princess Stove and Kitchen Outfit for No. 7 Stove. Weight, 55 pounds.
No. 9K22037 Price, complete, as illustrated and described........**$4.89**

Princess Stove and Kitchen Outfit for No. 8 Stove. Weight, 60 pounds.
No. 9K22038 Price, complete, as illustrated and described........**$5.47**

Princess Stove and Kitchen Outfit for No. 9 Stove. Weight, 65 pounds
No. 9K22039 Price, complete, as illustrated and described........**$5.97**

9c SET OF 4 FULL SIZE BEST TIN PIE PLATES.

Made of good quality tin. Not the cheap light weight, easy to rust kind. 9 inches diameter, ¾ inches deep, the popular size and the right kind to buy.

No. 9K25465 Price, per set of 4....9c

6c SET OF 6 BEST TIN TART OR PATTY PANS.

Not toys but practical pans. A set consists of one of each pattern shown in illustration; can also be used as individual jelly moulds.

No. 9K25494 Price, per set of 6....6c

24c FOR 6 POT COVERS AND GALVANIZED RACK.

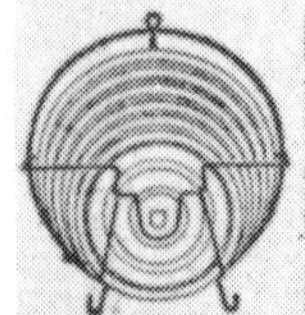

Handy outfit of one heavy galvanized wire holder and six pot covers. A cover to fit every size pot. Covers make food cook quicker and soon pay for themselves in saving of fuel. Good quality tin; one each 9, 9½, 10, 10½, 11, 11½-inch.

No. 9K25546 Price, per set, 6 covers and holder........24c

9c IXX TIN PLATE OLD RELIABLE HUNTER'S FLOUR SIFTER.

The genuine Hunter's flour sifter. Made of heavy tin plate. Also used as a scoop, measure or strainer.

No. 9K25529 Price..9c

19c THE FAVORITE SIFTER, HEAVILY NICKEL PLATED AND POLISHED.

Well worth the slight difference in price we are compelled to charge. Has fancy enameled wood handle, extra strong and durable. Will outlast half a dozen cheap, light sifters.

No. 9K25533 Price. 19c

3c FOR THIS STEEL BLADE ENAMELED WOOD HANDLE CAKE TURNER.

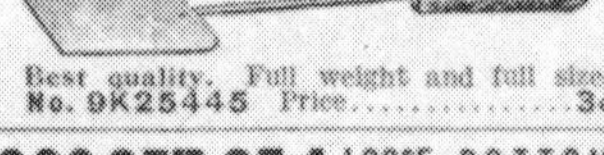

Best quality. Full weight and full size.

No. 9K25445 Price........3c

23c SET OF 4 LOOSE BOTTOM IXX CAKE PANS.

Made of good quality tin. 9 inches diameter, 1 inch deep. Prevents sticking and require no greasing.

No. 9K25505 Price, per set of 4........23c

18c FOR THIS JAPANNED EXTRA HEAVY IXX TIN SHARP EDGE DUST PAN

Rustproof handle well put on, can be hung on a nail when not in use. The best dust pan on the market. Built for wear, and will stand rough usage.

No. 9K26179 Price........18c

31c NICKEL PLATED CRUMB TRAY AND SCRAPER, POLISHED AND ETCHED.

These trays and scrapers have the appearance of the finest silver. They are highly nickel plated and polished, are decorated in handsome designs and guaranteed satisfactory.

No. 9K26198 Price, for crumb tray and scraper...31c

11c FOR A JAPANNED OVAL TEA TRAY, 14 INCHES LONG.

Has fancy scroll border decorated by hand, and is greatly superior in service to the light weight trays ordinarily sold. Well made of good material and nicely finished.

Length, inches	14	18	22
No. 9K26212 Price.	11c	16c	24c

8c RAT PROOF, MOUSE PROOF, AND DAMP PROOF METAL MATCH BOX HOLDER.

Holds full box of 200 matches. Made of heavy IXX tin plate. Nicely finished. Has sand paper to strike them on. Order one of these holders, put it up in a convenient place and stop groping around in the dark for a match.

No. 9K26055 Price, each........8c

6c RETINNED STEEL SLOTTED MIXING SPOON OR CAKE BEATER.

One piece. Smooth and easily cleaned. Length, 11½ inches.

No. 9K26552 Price........6c

17c HANDY KITCHEN SET, CONSISTING OF FORK, SPOON AND CAKE TURNER.

Consisting of one wood handle steel flesh fork, 11 inches long; one retinned wood handle basting spoon, 10¾ inches long, and one nickel plated perforated cake turner, 14½ inches long, mounted on card.

No. 9K26567 Price, per set.... 17c

A variety of kitchen utensils and cookware from the 1908 Sears Roebuck catalog. (Courtesy Sears, Roebuck and Company.)

The Compact, Sanitary Kitchen, 1920 to 1930

Mechanization invaded the household after World War I. The 1920s saw eager acceptance by the housewife of any labor-saving devices and witnessed the rise of huge businesses to supply her electrical and mechanical needs.

As the kitchen gradually became more efficient, it also became smaller and more compact. The all-white "sanitary" kitchen of the early 1920s was smaller. Christine Frederick, author of *Household Engineering*, told housewives that an efficient kitchen must be small and compact with a place for food preparation only; all unrelated work should be kept out. Kitchen efficiency could be achieved with a step-saving arrangement of the equipment required in preparing food and clearing dishes. Food preparation involved collecting materials, preparing, cooking, and serving. Clearing involved removal, scraping, washing, and putting away. Utensils were to be stored at the place where they were used.

In order to be sanitary, the walls had to be nonporous and as easy to clean as possible. Usually they had a wainscoating of tile with an oilcloth fabric or painted wood surface above. It was recommended that linoleum or a similar particle floor covering be used, because a wood floor could collect dirt between the boards.

The room contained separate furnishings — a sink made of iron, slate, soapstone, or "modern" white enameled iron; a stove on legs; a movable kitchen cabinet with a worktop of wood or a sanitary top that was impervious to grease (of porcelain or metal); a wood or enamel table; and an icebox.

The kitchen of the 1920s was smaller, designed to fit into bungalows, apartments, and small houses where the housewife did her own work.

For the large kitchen, a good work center could be provided by a table in the center of the room. The tabletop could be of zinc, enamel, porcelain, or any other material that was impervious to grease.

By the mid-1920s, housewives were told they should have some color in the kitchen to make it a more cheerful place to work. Color did not mean that cleanliness had to be sacrificed. The sterile white food laboratory could be changed to a kitchen with an inviting atmosphere. The introduction of color met with overwhelming acceptance by homemakers who realized it would be much more enjoyable to work in colorful surroundings.

Christine Frederick, in her 1925 book *Efficient Housekeeping*, said that equipment should be bought on the basis of the number of times used, not on initial cost. The equipment should be comfortable to use, well finished with good construction, and be easy to care for and clean. For example: if it does rapid work but requires six to eight minutes to wash, dry, and reassemble, then the same *total* time is consumed. No device should take longer to clean and adjust than the time it saves by its increased efficiency.

The major equipment and work processes involved should be arranged in working sequence. The refrigerator and cabinet were used for storage and supplies. The preparation of raw food involved the work surface of the cabinet and sink; cooking involved the stove. A dish cupboard, wheel tray, and serving table were helpful for serving, and the wheel tray, sink, and dish cupboard handled the "clean up." The efficiency of the kitchen depended on having suitable equipment arranged in a motion-saving and time-saving sequence.

The kitchen in the 1920s became smaller and more efficient. What had started the decade with the white "sanitary" look, had become a more colorful and cheerful room in which to work. One way of changing color in the kitchen was to paint over linoleum with enamel or deck paint. Some homemakers painted the floor either beige or green and, for a decorative affect, applied a different color paint with a sponge. The kitchen's efficiency was further enhanced by the introduction of color in the mid 1920s.

Gadgets

In the 1920s, kitchen tools and gadgets were catering more to the housewife's needs. After 1921, stainless steel, which required no scouring, was being used for some kitchen utensils. By the late 1920s, there were easy-to-use can openers that did not leave a jagged edge, and knife sharpeners that required little skill to operate.

In 1921, Armstrong advertised that their linoleum rugs were for the kitchen or dining room because they were sanitary, easily cleaned, and attractive. They came in a variety of patterns and colors and would lie flat without fastening. Notice the hardwood floor showing around the rug and the interesting work surface on either side of the sink. (Courtesy Armstrong World Industries, Inc.)

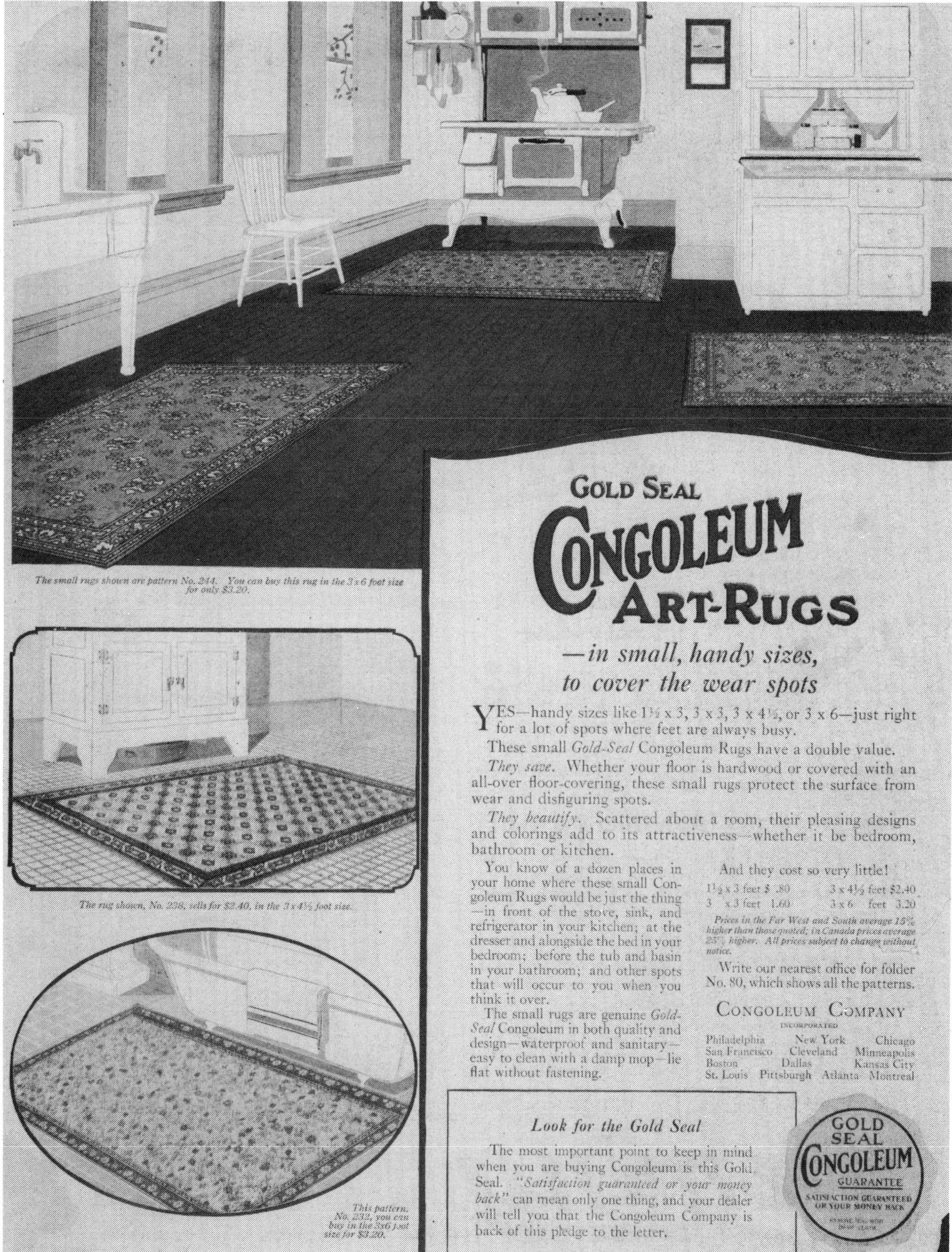

A 1921 advertisement for Congoleum Art-Rugs. The rugs ranged in size from 1½′ × 3′ at 80¢ to 3′ × 6′ at $3.20. (Courtesy The Congoleum Corporation.)

© 1924 The Hoosier Manufacturing Co.

HOW TO EQUIP THE MODERN KITCHEN

—making it well ordered and attractive at little cost

By Lois M. Wyse, Director Hoosier Test Kitchens

No longer do women believe that running water and a gas range make a *modern* kitchen. They know that even with these conveniences, it can still be a cheerless drudgery room.

The really modern kitchen must meet two great requirements. First, it must be attractive—an inviting, restful place to work. For *where* we work has so much to do with *how* we work! You know that dismal depression that engulfs you in a cluttered, unsightly kitchen. But in an orderly, cheerful room—how much more happily we work and therefore more easily!

Second, the kitchen must be convenient; *fully, completely furnished!* Of all rooms in the house, the one where you spend the most and hardest working hours, should be *planned* to the last detail. You need adequate equipment to route your work and save much fruitless effort and countless steps.

Now for the new-day kitchen —with Hoosier Kitchen Equipment!

And now you can have such a kitchen—fresh, inviting and efficient—with surprising ease and economy. In the test kitchens of the Hoosier Manufacturing Company at Newcastle, Indiana, domestic science experts have designed equipment that really furnishes your kitchen as completely and attractively as any other room in the house.

The first need to be filled, is what no modern kitchen can be without—a working center! To serve this important purpose the Hoosier Kitchen Cabinet is designed. Planned with scientific regard in every exclusive detail, the Hoosier provides a completeness not possible in any other working center that may be devised.

Hoosier Double Cabinet Unit—*Provides extra storage space which every kitchen needs for utensils, dishes and food supplies. Very convenient for a bathroom cupboard. Also furnished as a single unit*

With the Hoosier Cabinet as the central unit, other Hoosier units are designed to complete the equipment. Every kitchen, of course, needs ample cupboard space in addition to that afforded in the cabinet itself. This added space, once supplied by the old inconvenient butler's pantry, Hoosier now provides in modern movable units, single or double size.

These units may be used in connection with the cabinet on either side or placed in other suitable spaces in the room. With any arrangement you have a complete kitchen suite, matching in finish and design—as uniform as if made to your own special order.

Another attractive Hoosier convenience is the Breakfast Set of table and chairs. Daintily finished in white enamel and decorated in bright colors, the table has a fine porceliron top and the chairs have cane seats.

To modernize old kitchens; to make the new complete

Perhaps you are worrying along with an old unsightly, inconvenient kitchen. You have refurnished the other rooms—now it is the kitchen's turn! Here Hoosier equipment ideally answers your needs, with no fuss or expense of remodeling. It is simply "out with the old; in with the new"—handsome and efficient!

If you are planning a new house, of course you want your kitchen in keeping with your other rooms. You can make it so, more completely, more easily and inexpensively with Hoosier Kitchen Equipment than with any of your own devising and building.

Hoosier Single Cabinet Unit—*Fitted to hold brooms, mops, vacuum, brushes and a score of little cleaning day necessities. May also be had in a double unit—with the cupboard unit*

Ask your architect to figure on the Hoosier size and style for your kitchen.

Free to you!—A new book on modern kitchens

We have just published a new book on modern kitchens giving many plans and ideas which you can apply to your own kitchen. This book is free to every woman who is interested in making a better home for her family. We hope you will send for it and also visit the Hoosier store in your town to see the complete Hoosier equipment. Fill out the coupon and we will mail the booklet at once.

The Hoosier Manufacturing Company
324 Leslie Street, Newcastle, Indiana

The Hoosier Manufacturing Co.,
324 Leslie Street, Newcastle, Indiana.
British Address: Ideal Furniture Equipment,
No. 9 Preston St., Liverpool.
Please send me, free, your new booklet: "Planning the Modern Kitchen."

Name __________

Address __________

City __________ *State* __________

"How To Equip The Modern Kitchen — making it well ordered and attractive at little cost." This 1924 Hoosier Manufacturing Company's advertisement said women no longer believed that running water and a gas range made a modern kitchen. The kitchen had to be an inviting, attractive room that was furnished with efficient equipment.

From 1924, "An Attractive Kitchen Makes Cooking A Pleasure!...Drudgery? No, indeed. For getting up a dinner is a pleasure, especially when the kitchen is bright, cheerful — and spotlessly clean." Blue-and-white Congoleum rug pictured, filled the requirements. (Courtesy Congoleum Corporation.)

A step-saving kitchen combination. Notice the china cupboard conveniently placed next to the sink. From a 1924 *The Home* supplement.

The center table was a labor saver in the large kitchen. From a 1924 *The Home* supplement.

"A breakfast room in blue and tan. The enameled furniture can be easily cleaned and the cretonne curtains give the feeling of sunshine even on a gray day." From a 1924 *The Home* supplement.

The 1927 Armstrong ad said "Gaiety in home decoration — if there's one place that needs it, it is the kitchen. But gay colors need a background to blend them, to hold them together. With a linoleum floor of a neutral tone...any number of color combinations can be used. In this instance cream and red worked out happily, emphasizing the unusual treatment of the cupboards and the novel wood plate shelf above the door. . . ." (Courtesy Armstrong World Industries, Inc.)

This 1929 Armstrong ad showed a sample home kitchen featuring a green and cream linoleum floor. The advertisement says it has gray enamel with touches of green for the furniture, woodwork, and electrical equipment, spotless white sink and drainboards, and dainty ruffled Swiss curtains. Notice the built-in sink and electric refrigerator. (Courtesy Armstrong World Industries, Inc.)

Many hand beaters were invented in the 1920s. Left to right:

"A. & J. Big Bingo No. 71 Pat. APL'D For." Black wooden handle, c. 1922.

"Ladd Beater No. 90; July 7, 1908; Oct. 18; other Patents Pending; U.S.A.; United Royalties Corp." White wooden handle.

"Pat. Nov. 28, 1916; Aug. 2, 1921; Pat. Pending; Made in U.S.A.; Blue Whirl. (Turner & Seymour)." Blue wooden handle. This was used for beating in a glass.

"BEATS-ALL; Patent Applied For; Mfg. By The Washburn Co. Chicago U.S.A." Green wooden handle with white tip. This beater probably preceded the beater pictured on page 78 of *Kitchens and Gadgets.* The four wings would have made it difficult to clean. The Washburn Company name was used in Chicago after 1922. **$5-9**

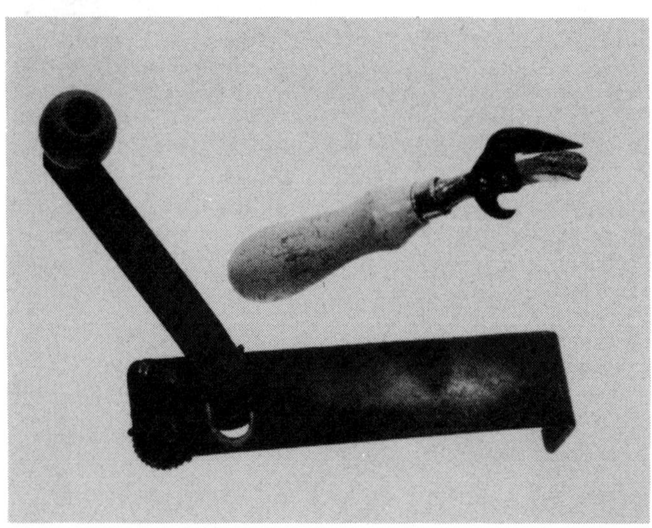

Not until the late 1920s could homemakers buy a can opener that would open the can and leave a smooth edge.

"Blue Streak; U.S.Patents Oct. 11-21, Aug. 10-23, Pat. In foreign countries; Turner & Seymour Mfg. Co. Torrington, Conn." Wall can opener with green wooden knob.

G.M.T. and Company hand can opener with white wooden handle.

Hand: $2-3.50

Wall: $3.50-7

Central States Manufacturing Company of St. Louis, Missouri, advertised that their can opener "Works Like Magic! This revolutionary invention in only a few short months has banished old can openers from over 100,000 kitchens... lifetime device that holds the can and cuts out the top leaving can rim slick, smooth and clean." A plea was made for men and women to become agents. Using a free outfit and test offers, they could earn $6 to $12 an hour.

Unmarked, unusual corn popper; made of aluminum and tin with a green wooden knob. As the corn popped, the center portion, attached to the bracket, rose, allowing room for the popping corn to expand. The knob turned a rod that was used to stir the kernels of corn to keep them from burning as they cooked. **$7.50-12**

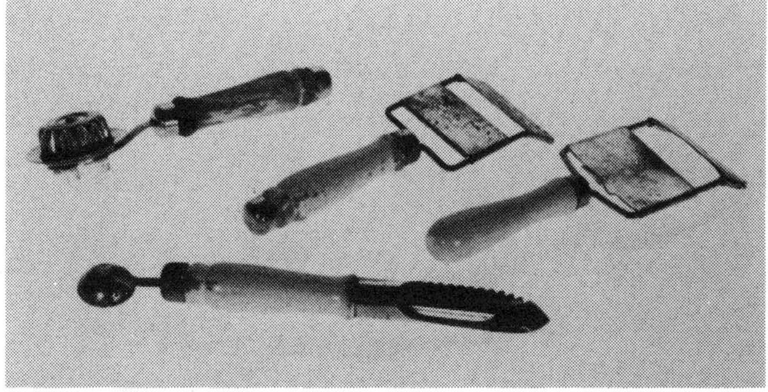

A variety of cutting tools offered in the 1920s. All have white wooden handles. Left to right:

"Dandy; Pat. Apld. For." Pie crust crimper and sealer.

"Dandy; Pat. Apl'd For." Vegetable and cheese slicer.

Unmarked vegetable and cheese slicer.

Unmarked apple corer-parer and baller. **$3-5**

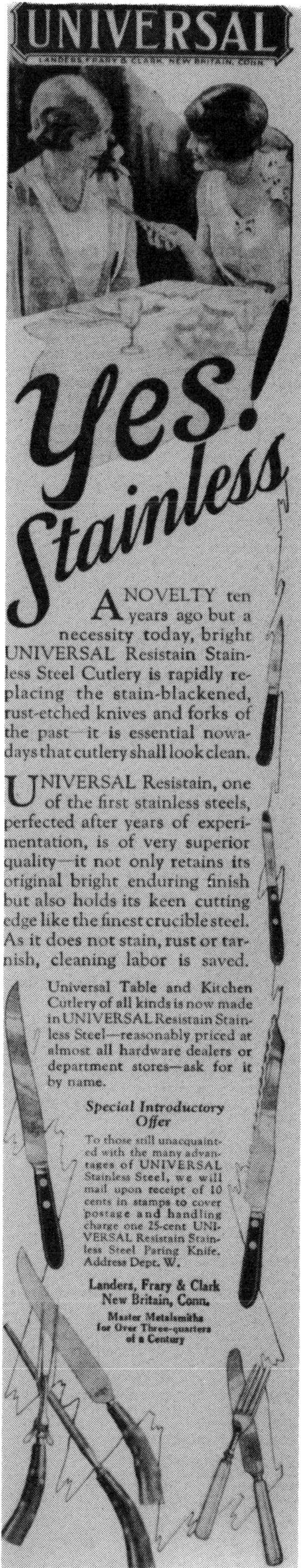

In 1929, Landers, Frary and Clark advertised their Table and Kitchen cutlery.

The Hamilton Metal Products Company, Hamilton, Ohio, advertised Climax, a perfect grater and slicer combination in 1929. The Climax could be used without danger of cutting fingers. An exclusive feature was the sanitary glass block plunger. If not available from a dealer, it could be ordered for $2 postpaid or $2.35 west of the Rockies. **$8-15**

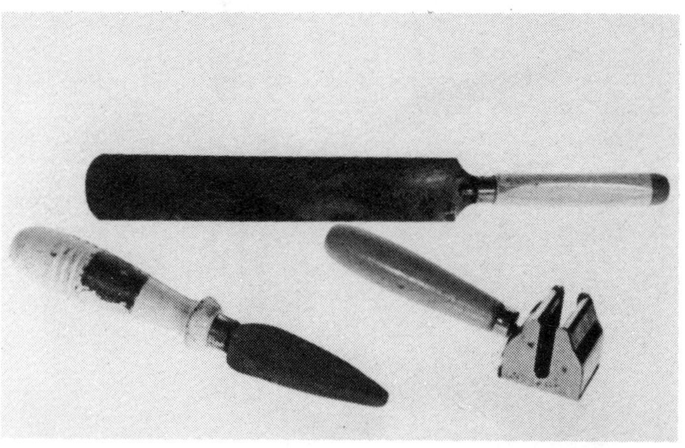

Top to bottom:

Cocomalt-Davis Baking Powder spatula with white wooden handle and green tip. **$2-3.50**

"Monarch Pat. 1,468,611 Turner & Seymour, Torr. Ct." This knife sharpener has a blue wooden handle. It was patented in 1923 and would have taken less skill to use than a sharpening stone. **$2-10**

"Norton Abrasives-Crystolon Knife Sharpener No. 273A Reg. U.S. Pat. Office" White wooden handle. (Note: Many people sharpened knives on the unglazed edge of a crock.) **$2-10**

A. & J. four-blade chopper and bowl with a white wooden handle with blue tip. **$6-9**

"Victor; Made in U.S.A.; National Manufacturing Company Worcester, Mass." Black wooden knob.

"Watkins Baking Powder Spices Extracts Triple Sifter Pat. Apld. For." Black wooden knob. **$4-12**

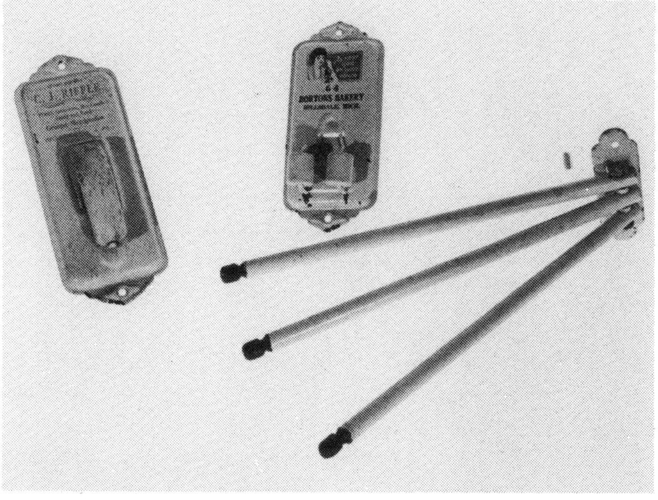

Left to right:

"Compliments C. J. Riffle Fruits, Groceries, Dry Goods, Flour & Feed General Merchandise Hillside…Pa." White towel holder. **$3.50-6**

As near as your phone was 64 Bortons Bakery, Hillsdale, Michigan. This white metal broomholder came in a box that said: "The New Queen Broom Holder Patented. The most practical and convenient household article ever invented. Put it up now and you'll never want to be without it. Keeps the broom straight. Broom will last forever & sweep cleaner. The hard maple rollers grip firmly — every time — without scratching or marring the handle. Will hold any size broom. Manufactured by C. F. Erickson Company Inc. Des Moines, Iowa." **$3.50-6**

Unmarked towel rack has a white metal holder with three wooden poles painted white with green tips. **$2-3.50**

The four-way electric outlet above solves the problem of using several electric appliances at once. It may be used on the table, or the top part may be separated from the bottom and inserted in a wall or base outlet ready to take care of lamp, radio, fan, etc. It has a six-foot cord and comes in a variety of colors.

New Kitchen Conveniences

Practical tested devices to lighten work in the home
Reviewed by Lily Haxworth Wallace

IN THE steel wool holder illustrated at the top of the page the disadvantage of having the small particles of wire find their way into one's skin is eliminated, for this is an invention for keeping the hands away from the metal. The steel wool itself has been specially treated to resist rust, then compressed into parallel or "brush" form and stitched so as to hold it in place. Each unit is, under ordinary conditions, sufficient to last for a year. As it becomes used up or worn down, gradually pull it farther out of its holder, which is made of extra heavy red rubber. Refills can be secured to put into the holder, which certainly seems strong enough to last for years. Just wet the metal in hot water and use as a cleaner for aluminum or other utensils. If soaps and cleaners containing a strong free alkali are used, be sure to rinse the appliance thoroughly before putting it away to keep the holder in good condition.

Special Cord Set: The connecting cord is usually the first part of any electric appliance to wear out and this is hardly to be wondered at when one considers the tug and pull to which such cords are commonly subjected when removing them from any piece of equipment to which they are attached. Shown just below is a cord set with a convenient pull which releases all strain on the cord itself. It is made to fit all standard electric appliances and is remarkably easy to plug in or out. The "pull" never gets hot. It may be secured either with or without an "on and off" switch.

Special Electric Cord Set

Percolator Top Holders: Below is shown a percolator top with a safety belt arrangement which prevents its falling off—a circle of lightweight aluminum which fits over the knob and under the metal of the percolator lid, holding the cap firmly in place. It cannot slip and yet it may be removed easily if desired. These tops are made of unbreakable glass.

Rubber Bottle Caps: The cap really looks like a miniature cap—peak and all. It is made of pure Para rubber (amber color) and may be boiled for sterilization. The peak with its little indentation gives a good purchase for the removal of the cap at feeding time, to be replaced by an anticolic nipple. The cap not only protects the contents of the baby's bottle from all possible contamination but also the lip of the bottle itself. A similar cap of the same Para rubber fits a regulation size milk bottle and has the same peak feature. These caps are leak-proof and air-tight.

Handled Pans: Pie plates and cake pans with handles facilitate their removal from a hot oven. Many of us have good cause to know the difficulties attending the transfer of a scalding hot juicy berry pie from oven to table, especially if it should be in the back of the oven with another pan in front. The handles are raised above the level of the plate itself.

Left—Percolator Top Holder
Right—Rubber Bottle Caps

Handled Pans

"New Kitchen Conveniences" were described in the October, 1929, issue of *Women's World* magazine.

New electrical food mixer **SPEEDS UP** *cooking and baking*

MAKES A *DIFFERENT* ELECTRICAL GIFT

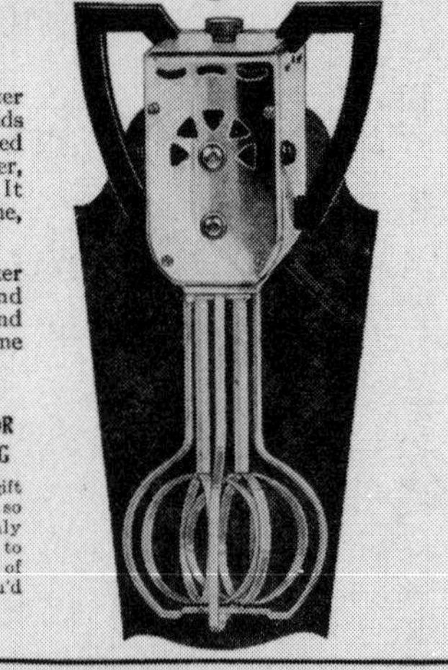

The Dormeyer Electric is an all-purpose mixer handling perfectly all requirements from liquids to heavy cake batters or large batches of mashed potatoes — and making everything smoother, lighter, more appetizing, by its thoroughness. It stirs, whips, mixes, beats foods in 1/10 the time, without aching wrists and tired arms.

The new Improved Dormeyer Electric Food Mixer has wide range of speed, stands by itself and operates alone in the bowl—it's powerful and absolutely tireless. Not only saves untold time and work but makes ingredients go further.

Because it mixes so thoroughly you'll enjoy lighter and closer grained cakes; smoother mayonnaise; more tender griddle cakes; fluffier whipped cream; better omelets, custards, puddings, etc. Write today for full information.

KEEP IN MIND FOR CHRISTMAS GIVING

Makes a marvelous gift because so handsome, so useful, so thoroughly well made. Suggest to the other members of the family that you'd like a Dormeyer.

The Dormeyer is built for a lifetime's service. Chromium plated. Guaranteed electrically and mechanically. If your electrical store can't supply, write us.

A. F. DORMEYER MFG. CO., Dept. B-3
2640 Greenview Ave., Chicago

Please send folder and prices of the new Dormeyer.

Name__________

Address__________

City__________ State__________

The New Improved **Dormeyer** Electric Food Mixer

A 1929 Christmas advertisement for a Dormeyer Electric Food Mixer. It "makes a marvelous gift because so handsome, so useful, so thoroughly well made. Suggest to other members of the family you'd like a Dormeyer."

ANNOUNCING

The New UNIVERSAL *Automatic* TOASTER

TRY the latest and most highly perfected way of making delicious toast—***without watching—without burning***—in the UNIVERSAL Automatic Toaster.

—Place bread in toaster rack and slide into oven.

—Press down timing lever and forget that you are making toast.

—When toast is done to your liking (usual time about a minute), toaster rack automatically slides out with the kind of toast that arouses appetites—hot, crisp and evenly browned on both sides at once, the kind that melts away in one hungry crunch.

The Exclusive UNIVERSAL "Sliding Rack" Method of delivering toast free of oven allows current to remain on continuously, resulting in an evenly heated oven which toasts exceptionally fast and always with beautiful uniformity.

Visit your nearest UNIVERSAL Dealer and try the UNIVERSAL Automatic Toaster for yourself. You will discover not only a very superior way of toasting bread but also a classically designed piece of tableware of exquisite beauty.

To assure yourself of the best in electric appliances for the home, always insist upon UNIVERSAL—the standard of fine household equipment and the choice of discerning home managers for over 75 years.

A 1927 advertisement for the new Universal automatic toaster.

Westinghouse Turnover Toaster. Marked: CAT #TF3110V; 550W Pat. 1-28-14, 8-25-14; Westinghouse Electric & Manufacturing Company, Mansfield Works, Mansfield, Ohio USA. Removable cord. **$10-18**

Small Appliances

Irons. Westinghouse introduced the first automatic (non-adjustable) iron — never too hot and never too cold. The first adjustable-temperature automatic iron was introduced by Liberty Gauge and Instrument Company of Cleveland (which became part of Proctor-Silex in 1929).

In 1929, General Electric was the first to facilitate ironing around buttons with their Button Nook. Chrome plating was also introduced in 1929.

Heel rests were introduced by G.E. and Westinghouse.

Mixers. The first mixer to be mounted on its own stand was the 1920 KitchenAid manufactured by Hobart. The Dormeyer electric food mixer was introduced in 1927. It had its own stand and could operate alone in a bowl. Its advertisement said it was powerful and absolutely tireless and that it saved untold time. "It stirs, whips, mixes, beats food in 1/10 the time, without aching wrists and tired arms."

Toasters. During the 1920s, considerable progress was made in improving the electric toaster. The first "flip-flop" toaster, which turned the bread when a side panel was lowered, made its appearance sometime in the 1920s. These electric toasters, apart from having open sides and no pop-up facility, used the same basic heating element as their modern counterpart. Bread could be held against either side of the toaster by spring-loaded sides. When opened, the bread slid down, positioning the untoasted side toward the heating element so it could be toasted.

The Estate Stove Company of Hamilton, Ohio, introduced the first four-slice toaster in 1922. This ingeniously designed device was capable of manually reversing all four slices of bread at once. The same year, Edison Electric Appliance introduced "The newest turnover toaster — a Hotpoint servant."

Toastmaster, the first commercially successful automatic toaster, was introduced in 1926 by the Waters Bentry Company. The company was acquired that same year by McGraw Electric Company.

A 1927 Toastmaster ad claimed that their new toaster would make perfect toast every time "without watching, without turning and without burning. The toaster times the slices, pops them up when ready and shuts off the current."

Large Appliances

Dishwashers. The kitchen equipped with an electric dishwasher made the housewife's work much easier. Everything except silverware and glasses could be sorted, washed, rinsed, and dried.

A woman's magazine in 1926 discussed a hypothetical choice of an oriental rug or an electric dishwasher. The writer opted for the dishwasher because she couldn't have both. After looking at her needs and budget, she saw that the dishwasher would create happiness, simplicity, hospitality, privacy, and comfort. The oriental rug was set aside for the future.

Although electric dishwashers were offered as early as 1924, they still were not widely accepted by the public twenty years later. Many women doubted that dishwashers were necessary. In contrast, the electric refrigerator was quickly accepted because it was a real necessity.

The electric dishwashing machine had an enameled top that served as a convenient table. Notice that the dishwasher is near the sink and storage cupboards to save steps.

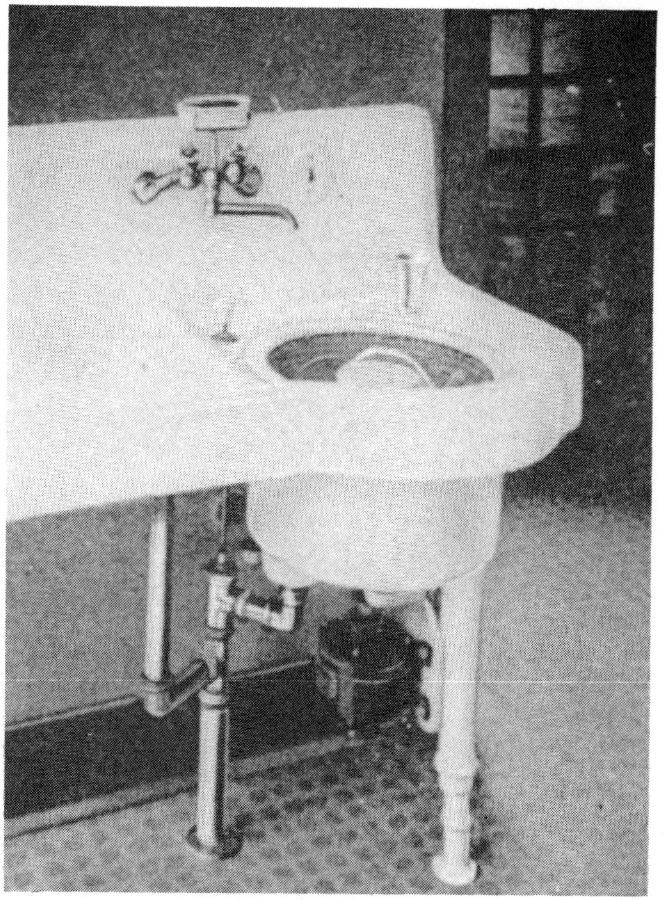

A built-in dishwasher was an innovation in 1924.

WHITE HOUSE GAS RANGES

OUR FINEST GAS RANGE
FULL PORCELAIN ENAMELED TRIM
RIGHT OR LEFT HAND OVEN

$68.25 **Rotary Flame Star Burners. Cast Iron Frame and Legs.**

THE WHITE PORCELAIN enameled parts will not discolor, crack or chip from heat. As easily cleaned as a china disk. Just wipe them off with a damp cloth. Besides the white enameled parts shown in the illustration, the drip pan and broiler pan are also white enameled. All self-indicating valve handles are of white porcelain.

OVEN is large in size and guaranteed to do the finest baking. Constructed to use all of the heat without waste. A good gas saver. Aluminum finished inside. Two adjustable wire racks enable you to use both upper and lower parts at the same time. **Broiler** is also aluminum finished inside. Extra large, accommodating everything you might wish to broil.

BURNERS—The cooking surface has one giant and three regular cast iron cored and drilled, one-piece Star rotary-flame burners which produce the most efficient heat for the gas consumed of any stove manufactured. **The oven and broiler** have three tubular cored and drilled burners, controlled by a self-indicating lever handle at front.

BODY is made throughout of a good grade steel with a strong cast iron frame and legs. Nickel trimmings. **The cooking top** is made in two anti-warping sections equipped with four sectional lids. Note the convenient shelf below the cooking surface.

DIMENSIONS—Size oven 18½x14 in., broiler 18½x10 in. Size of cooking top 25x22 in., height from floor 30 in. Extreme height 52 in. Requires 6 in. stove pipe, and has ¾ in. gas pipe connection.

9J-1423S GAS RANGE—Oven right or left hand side. Ship. wt., about 250 lbs. Price **$68.25**

REQUIRES ONLY 38 IN. OF FLOOR SPACE

$49.00 **With Right or Left Hand Oven**

This compact, space-saving range, with its oven at convenient working height; its liberal shelf spaces; its extending canopy over cooking top; its smooth, easy-to-keep-clean castings, nickel plating and porcelain enameled doors, is the delight of every woman.

THE BAKING OVEN does perfect, even work with no waste of heat or fuel. Removable bottom. A **double tubular drilled burner** furnishes heat for both oven and broiler. Has safety pilot lighter and front peep hole to see size of flame. **The broiler** has deep tray and wire rack adjustable to several positions. Also flue connection for carrying off odors.

COOKING TOP is cast iron in sections. Just right height. Four 2-section lids and two skeleton lids.

BURNERS—One giant and 3 standard size star burners, cored and drilled. Burn with rotary flame. One piece, easily removed for cleaning. **Simmering burner** at center that also acts as a safety pilot lighter for other burners. All levers at front.

CONSTRUCTION—Cast iron frame, black enameled steel body, polished nickel trim. White porcelain enameled doors. Removable, galvanized tray beneath burners. Aluminized oven linings and racks. **Extension canopy** over cooking top with flue connection to carry off odor.

DIMENSIONS—Width 38 in., height 58 in. over all. Cooking top, less shelf, 21x21 in. Oven 14x19x14 in. Broiler 14x19x10 in. Takes 6 in. stove pipe. Has ¾ in. gas connection. Ship. wt., 220 lbs.

9J-1412 WHITE HOUSE GAS RANGE—Oven on right or left side. Choice.......... **$49.00**

9J-1412S—As above with white splasher back. Each........ **$60.85**

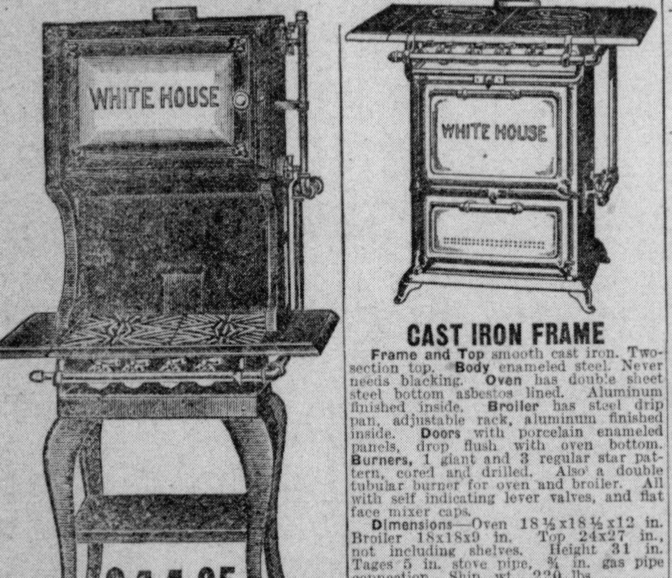

$44.35

The elevated oven has a one-piece cored and drilled cast iron **double tubular** burner at bottom, for baking, and a single burner of ...e style at top for broiling, toasting or roasting. Heavy steel broiling pan with san...y wire-rack, two strong adjustable wire shelves. **Oven bottom** double sheet steel, ...sbestos lined and easily removable. **Oven door** has white porcelain enameled panel. **Top** has four No. 8 two-section lids, and two skeleton lids. **Four rotary flame burners,** one piece, cored and drilled cast iron. One giant burner, 3 regular size. A removable galvanized steel pan catches any drip from cooking. **Frame and legs** smooth cast iron, strong and rigid. **Enameled steel body** easily kept clean.

DIMENSIONS—The combination oven and broiler measures 18½x16x12 in. Cooking top, less shelves, 22x24 in., height cooking top 30 in., extreme height 58 in. Flue ...ection 5 in. gas pipe connection ¾ in. Ship. wt., 190 lbs.

...—**Each**........ **$44.35**

CAST IRON FRAME

Frame and Top smooth cast iron. Two-section top. **Body** enameled steel. Never needs blacking. **Oven** has double sheet steel bottom asbestos lined. Aluminum finished inside. **Broiler** has steel drip pan, adjustable rack, aluminum finished inside. **Doors** with porcelain enameled panels, drop flush with oven bottom. **Burners,** 1 giant and 3 regular star pattern, cored and drilled. Also a double tubular burner for oven and broiler. All with self indicating lever valves, and flat face mixer caps.

Dimensions—Oven 18½x18½x12 in. Broiler 18x18x9 in. Top 24x27 in., not including shelves. Height 31 in. Tages 5 in. stove pipe, ¾ in. gas pipe connection. Ship. wt., 220 lbs.

9J-1118 Gas Range—Each.................. **$45.70**

PRESSED STEEL FRAME

Body high grade steel, enameled finish. **Frame** unbreakable pressed steel. **Top** 2-piece cast iron with four 2-section lids and two skeleton lids. **Burners,** 1 giant, 3 regular in cooking top, and a double tubular burner for oven and broiler. All burners 1-piece cast iron, cored and drilled. Self-indicating lever handles, and flat face mixer caps. **Oven bottom double** sheet steel asbestos lined, easily removable. **Broiling oven** has pressed steel pan with sanitary wire rack. **Both doors** pure white porcelain enameled.

DIMENSIONS — Oven 16x16x12 in. Broiler 16x16x8 in. Top 24x22 in., not including shelves. Height 34 in. Takes 5 in. stove pipe, ½ in. gas pipe connections. Ship. wt., 175 lbs.

9J-813 Gas Range—Each... **$30.45**

WITH OVEN ONLY

Has heavy sheet steel body. **The ov...** is a good baker. Has double sheet ste... bottom asbestos lined, deflecting the he... arount sides, giving an even temperatu... in the whole oven. Bottom easily remove... **Top** two-piece cast iron with four section... lids and two skeleton lids. **Burners** unde... oven, two tubular cast iron cored an... drilled. Cooking top has one giant and ... regular burners, all star pattern, one piec... cored and drilled.

DIMENSIONS—Oven 16½x16 in., 1... in. high. Top 22x24 in., not includin... shelves. Height 31 in. Takes 5 inc... stove pipe and ½ inch gas pipe conne... tion. Ship. wt., 145 lbs.

9J-716 Gas Range—Each.... **$27.60**

White House Gas Ranges from the 1921 Cussins and Fearn catalog. The finest gas range sold for $68.25. It had full white porcelain-enamel trim. An all-black compact range sold for $49.

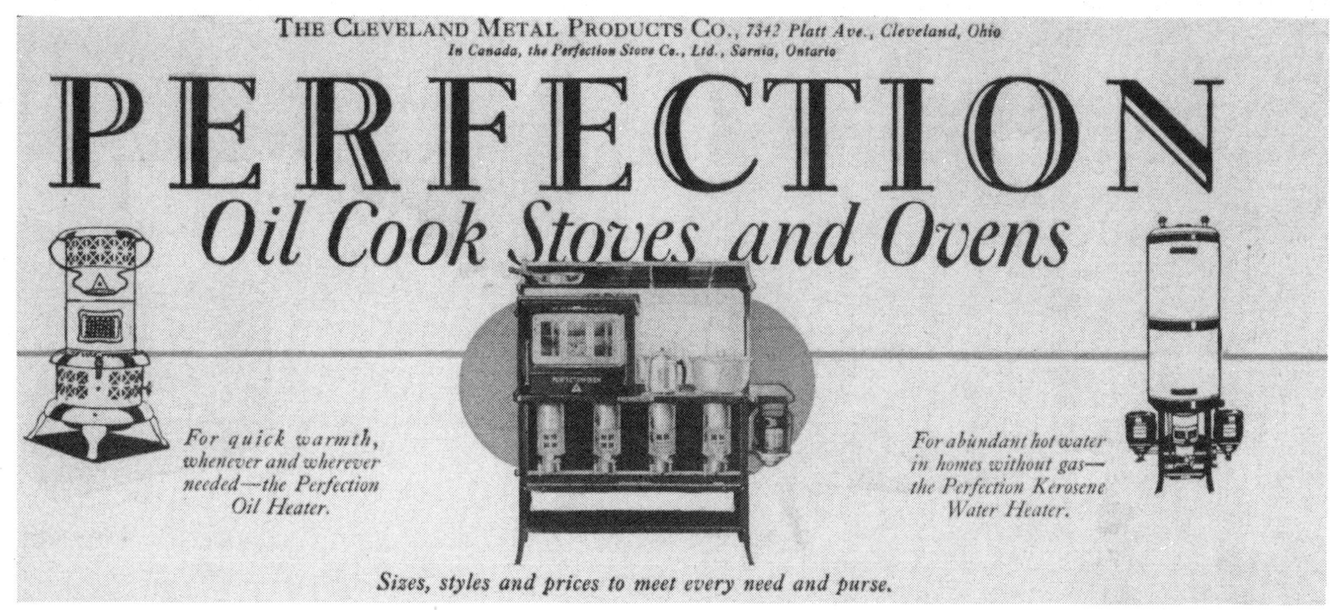

In 1925, the Cleveland Metal Products Company offered their Perfection Oil Cook Stoves and Ovens. "They let Mother come out of the kitchen earlier and less tired." They also had a Perfect Kerosene Water Heater.

Ranges. The gas range changed little until the 1920s, when gas companies that had lost a lot of lighting revenue to electric companies put a greater emphasis on improving their ranges.

In 1923, gas stoves were fitted with Regulo, a thermostatic control. Also, the oven was made easier to clean, and the stove was made lighter and more efficient, economical, and time-saving. By the late 1920s, ranges had improved broilers, which emitted little smoke.

It wasn't until the 1920s that many improvements were made on electric ranges, including enclosed-type surface units, thermostatic oven control, and enamel exterior finishes, which were a joy to look at and easy to clean.

In 1926, Westinghouse made the first porcelain-enamel range, which came in black and white. That same year Westinghouse brought out a cabinet range (with no legs). By 1927, they were offering ranges in a rainbow of colors, including red.

Refrigerators. Adequate refrigerator space is economical and necessary as a health safeguard. There were two things necessary for use of an icebox: convenience in icing and care of waste water. City and suburban families were able to have frequent ice deliveries. If the icebox were located near the door or built into the outside wall, one could avoid the annoyance and dirt of having cakes of ice carried into the kitchen.

It was essential to have proper drainage for the water. If there was a drain pan underneath to catch the water, the housewife had to be alert, or else the pan overflowed. This could be prevented by having a drainpipe leading to the outside through the wall or by having a pipe connected to the kitchen sink.

The William Campbell Company of Alliance, Ohio, had a cabinet-type electric range model in 1928. This company called their ranges Electric Fireless Cooker Ranges. They worked off a home lighting circuit through an outlet and "cooked as fast as gas."

In 1929, the William Campbell Company advertised their range on legs for one-third off the factory price. It worked from any lighting plug, and they offered a thirty-day trial.

An ice saver in the cold weather. This was an oblong box with a screen at the back to admit outside air. The box fit into an oblong sheet of metal at the back, which could be adjusted to the width of the window. This was available for use during appropriate months of the year.

This 1929 Monarch Electric Range was manufactured by the Malleable Iron Range Company, Beaver Dam, Wisconsin. It had a built-in kitchen heater, controlled heat, and automatic time-temperature oven control. Homemakers could choose a Monarch to fit any kitchen color scheme: pure white, Sunshine yellow, or Nile-Green.

The California refrigerator was raised to place food in it or to have access to the food.

There were several other cooling devices used between seasons or as an auxiliary to the icechest or box. One of these was the window cooling box.

The California-type iceless refrigerator was a cooling box built on the principle of a dumbwaiter. A cool cellar was necessary for this type of iceless refrigeration.

Electric refrigerators were available in the 1920s. Some of them manufactured their own ice, while others cooled the air of the interior air chambers to the desired temperature. These refrigerators were expensive, but they did not require visits from the iceman. Servel produced the first gas refrigerator in 1926. By the mid-1920s, gas and electric mechanical refrigerators had become popular, resulting in lower prices. They no longer looked like the old iceboxes, which had dark wood exteriors, and they were becoming self-contained.

General Electric presented the first all-steel refrigerator with the Monitor on top on March 22, 1929. It was priced at $215—much more affordable than refrigerators a decade before. (Courtesy General Electric Corporation.)

The California refrigerator dropped below the level of the floor so its top was covered with the same material as the floor.

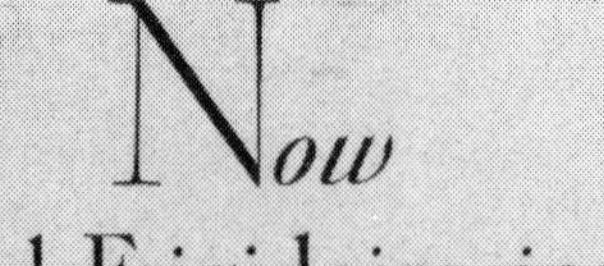
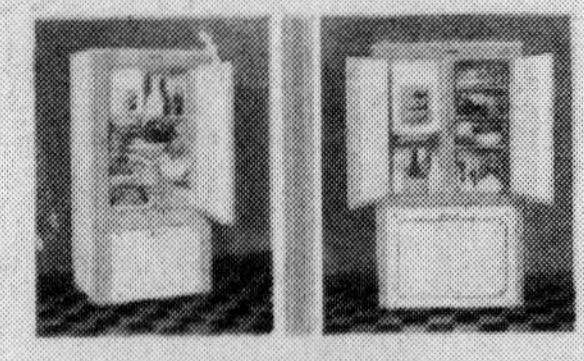

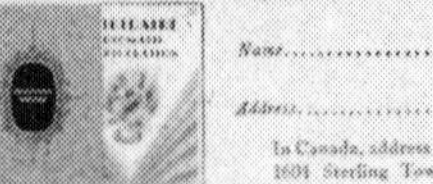

Frigidaire had both a one-door and a two-door refrigerator in 1929.

Buying Household Articles

Household items large and small could be purchased in the late 1920s. Some were plain and others colorful — all were useful.

The list of items costing less than a dollar was long, including stainless steel cutlery — knives, forks, pie servers, and spatulas and, of course, the "indispensable" knife sharpener. Also on the list were egg beaters with plain or colored handles; bread knives with serrated edges that cut thin, even slices; pastry jaggers and crimpers; and vegetable and fruit ball cutters. Wooden pounders, small chopper and bowl sets, self-pulling corkscrews, and much more were available in this price range.

Among the articles priced between $1 and $2.50 were cooking thermometers, can openers that clamped on the table or fastened on the wall, and metal wastebaskets. Here, too, were attractive sets of refrigerator dishes in heat-resistant glass or colorful enamel, and many enameled cooking utensils.

On the $5 to $10 list was a variety of high-grade electrical equipment, such as grills, waffle irons, percolators, and toasters. Irons had automatic heat controls and colored handles. A colorful kitchen alarm clock reminded a homemaker when it was time to take a cake from the oven or put on the vegetables or meat. Also in this price range were colorful painted metal articles — a garbage receptacle with foot control, paper towel holder, and a vegetable storage bin with several well-ventilated compartments.

For $10 to $25, a homemaker could buy more elaborate and useful items, such as electric waffle irons, automatic toasters, grills, percolators, and coffee urns. For cleaning, there was a small floor polisher and a hand vacuum cleaner that was useful on automobile and furniture upholstery and draperies. Electric eggbeaters, which would beat cream, eggs, light batter, and mayonnaise with little effort, were also on this list.

A few articles priced from $25 to $50 were full-size vacuum cleaners (said to be a good value for the money), floor polishers of moderate size, a portable ironing machine, and a small washing machine for washbowls.

For $50 to $75, a housewife could buy better quality vacuum cleaners and floor polishers. This was also the price for high-grade ice refrigerators, fitted kitchen cabinets, and wall outlet ranges for cooking for one or two.

To purchase good quality washing machines, portable electric dishwashers, vacuum cleaners with all the attachments, ironers (called ironing machines), and better grade ice refrigerators (iceboxes), the price was between $75 and $150.

Climbing upward in the price group, $150 to $200 bought a first-quality washing machine, a variety of ironers, an electric range, a gas stove, or an electric mixer.

Automatic refrigerators, plumbed-in electric dishwasher sinks, and kitchen units to fit almost any need were the ultimate in kitchen equipment, costing approximately $200 to $300.

Kitchen Furniture

Kitchen cabinets. The kitchen cabinet saved endless trips from the kitchen to the pantry and from table to cupboard. Some had a tilting flour bin, while others had a lowering flour bin (forty- to fifty-pound capacity) with a sifter. Tea and coffee jars, spice jars, a rolling-pin rack, cake and bread drawers, a wire rack for pans, and drawers for cutlery were all features of many kitchen cabinets. The roll curtain front was featured in the 1920s. It would pull down or slide up out of the way with a gentle touch. It allowed the cabinet to be opened without disturbing anything that might be on the work top. When closed, it kept out dust and dirt.

Breakfast nooks. Breakfast nooks were becoming popular. They were usually planned as an alcove off the

$28.80 UP TO $32.10 WITH ROLL CURTAIN

WHITE HOUSE KITCHEN CABINETS

It's a pleasure to cook when you have a White House Kitchen cabinet. It extracts the drudgery from kitchen work, shortens the hours in the kitchen, leaving more time for other pleasant duties. It adds joy to the cooking, and makes the preparation of each meal a pleasure to be anticipated. It is a step-saving, ever-ready "silent servant," which, once used, you do not understand how you could ever do without.

WHITE HOUSE "SPECIAL" $47.90 AND UP

FURNISHED WITH NICKELOID OR PURE WHITE PORCELAIN IRON TOP.

Porcelain Iron Work Top

Roll Curtain on Top Section.

THIS ROLL CURTAIN CABINET has a pure **white enameled** interior top section, equipped with swinging glass sugar jar, glass tea and coffee jar, and metal rack for glass spice jars. **The Roll Curtain** that pulls down or slides up out of the way with a gentle touch, is a feature usually found only with much higher priced cabinets.

THE TILTING FLOUR BIN holds 50 lbs. Easily removed **for cleaning.** Has sifter bottom, and plenty of room below to set utensil.

THE TOP is furnished two ways—with pure white **Porcelain Iron** work-surface as shown, or with the standard **Nickeloid** top. Both styles are the **sliding type** and when pulled out measure 25x41 inches.

THE BASE is standard arrangement with sanitary wire rack on door and wood shelf that slides forward. Two regular drawers and a sanitary metal bread box.

THE CONSTRUCTION is the knocked-down type. Made of thoroughly seasoned hardwood with an attractive Golden Oak varnished finish. **Shipped from** Columbus, Ohio. Ship. wt., 185 lbs.

13K-931 Cabinet—Porcelain Iron Top, F. O. B. Columbus........**$32.10**
13K-934 Cabinet—Nickeloid Top, F. O. B. Columbus............ **28.80**

THE TOP SECTION on this cabinet represents the best in labor saving conveniences. The **Flour Bin** on left, lowers to make filling easier. A small glass panel shows instantly amount of flour on hand.

THE COMPARTMENTS are pure white enameled, easy to keep clean. The lower one is equipped with swinging glass sugar jar, and glass tea, coffee and spice jars.

THE ROLL CURTAIN is a decided improvement. It slides up out of sight at a slight push, allowing you to open the cabinet without disturbing anything on work top. When closed it keeps out all dust and dirt.

THE SLIDING TOP glides on roller bearings. When open it gives a working surface 41½x24 in. Closed it is 13½ in. deep. Furnished two ways. With the famous indestructible, pure white **Porcelain iron** top; or with the standard, sanitary **Nickeloid** top. A small groove in back of the latter, prevents water running into the cupboard part of cabinet below.

COMBINE YOUR PANTRY cupboard and work table into a single piece of furniture and save thousands of steps. Do it with this White House "Special" Roll Curtain Cabinet. Order it w[ith] the Porceliron top. After using it you [will] be glad you paid the slight extra cost.

THE BASE has a dust proof constr[uc]tion. On the left is a large two-shelf c[om]partment with sliding tray, for hold[ing] cooking utensils. Rack on the door [for] holding lids, etc. A bread board is [just] beneath the top. On the right are [two] drawers for kitchen cutlery and linen, [one] partitioned. Also a large all-metal br[ead] box with an oak front, and a sliding m[etal] top keeps the bread fresh until all u[sed]. **Made throughout of oak** with a rich gol[den] oak, varnished exterior finish. Cop[per] plated trim.

Prices F. O. B. Columbus, Ohio.

13K-840—With Nickeloid Top. Price .... **$47.9[0]**
13K-841—With Porceliron top. Price .... **$51.[illegible]**

Shipping weight, about 250 pounds.

Roll Curtain CABINET $29.90

THE CURTAINS on this cabinet divide at center and slide back, exposing interior of cabinet without disturbing any of your work on the top.

THE INTERIOR of top section is pure white enameled, easy to keep clean. Fitted with swinging glass sugar jar, also glass tea and coffee jar.

THE FLOUR BIN tilts forward for filling. Easily removed for cleaning. Has patent dispenser bottom.

WORK TOP is furnished with **Nickeloid** top as shown. Extension type, giving a working surface 25x36 inches when open.

BASE has wire rack on door and sliding wood shelf in cupboard. Two roomy drawers at right, and an all-metal bread bin with sliding metal top.

SHIPPED FROM COLUMBUS

CONSTRUCTION is the knocked-down type, strictly dependable. **Front** is genuine oak, ends of seasoned hardwood and back of 3-ply veneer. Golden oak varnished finish. Height 72 in., width 36 in., depth 26 in.

13K-932 Cabinet — Roll curtain model with standard Nickeloid top. Shipped promptly from Columbus stock. No long waits. Ship. wt., 185 lbs. Each **$29.90**

KITCHEN BASE

Has a 24x44 in. **White Wood Top** that is easily kept clean and sanitary. There is a **Sliding Bread and Chopping Board** 17½ in. square. **Two large Drawers** for cutlery and linen, and **Two Easy Sliding Bins** for flour or meal that hold 50 lbs. each. The heavy 2¼ in. square legs are securely bolted, giving a strong and durable construction. All drawers and bins are removable and easily cleaned. The cabinet is 28¾ in. high and made of oak with a neatly v[ar]nished natural wood finish. Shipped from Columbus

$10.40

13K-817 Base—Ship. wt., 80 lbs. Each................ **$10.4[0]**

KITCHEN TABLE

13K-819 Kitchen Table—26x40 in. white sanded finish, wood top. Deep box rim, drawe[r], heavy square legs varnished G[olden] Oak finish. Bolted constru[ction]. Very strong and substantial. S[hipped] knocked down from Columbus, Ship. wt., about 50 lbs. Each .... **$4[.55]**

$4.55 Bolted Construction

$14.55 For This

KITCHEN CUPBOARD

Extra Large and Roomy

With solid oak front and hardwood ends, finished in golden oak gloss. Top has two removable shelves made of three ply, cross banded stock to prevent warping. The big cupboard below has a removable shelf of same construction. Two drawers at center for cutlery and linen. Double doors in top have clear glass panels. Cupboard has knocked down construction to save freight charges. Anyone can set it up easily. Height 78 in., width 40 in., depth 16 in. outside measure. A cupboard of this size offers an abundance of conveniently arranged storage space, and is a special value at the low price. Weight crated about 140 lbs. Shipped from Columbus, Ohio.

13K-818—F. O. B. Columbus, Ohio. Price **$14.55**

The White House kitchen cabinets featured a "roll curtain." All the kitchen furniture in this page from the 1938 Cussins and Fearn Co. catalog was made of oak.

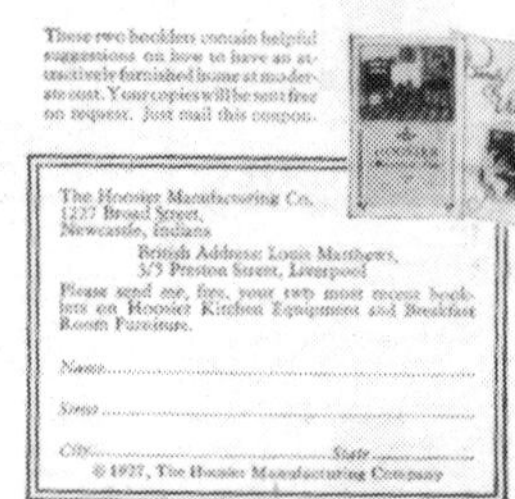

A 1927 Hoosier ad showing their kitchen cabinet, breakfast set, and Welsh cupboard. Hoosier stated that their superiority as an efficient time-saving work center was proven daily in more than two million American homes. The Welsh cupboard and breakfast set had an "Italian" two-tone finish of soft yellow and blue trim.

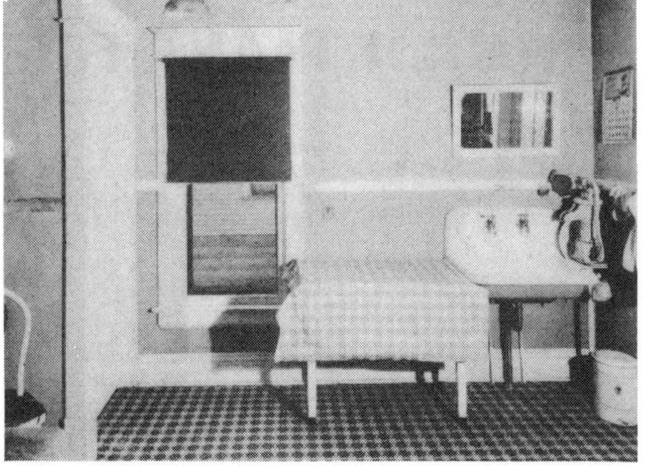

It must have been difficult to use this sink, with no drainboards and cupboards close by. C. early 1920s.

A built-in breakfast nook illustrated in a 1924 *The Home* supplement. This type of breakfast nook was designed to economize space.

kitchen, near enough to be in easy reach of the stove and cupboards, yet separated to give the feeling of an independent room. They had either built-in tables and seats or were furnished with a painted table and chairs.

Porcelain-enamel kitchen cabinets, cupboards, and tables were popular with many housewives. The furniture industry took the second major step in modernizing the kitchen with the introduction of standardized free-standing broom and utility cabinets. At first they were made of wood, but soon they were followed by the more popular steel cabinets.

The pantry disappeared from the home in the 1920s. Fitted kitchen cabinets and shelves were thought to be more efficient because the storage was where it was needed most.

Sinks. Sinks were made of various materials: iron, slate, soapstone, and the popular white porcelain-enamel cast iron, available with single or double drainboards. Drain surfaces were porcelain, zinc, or copper, all of which were practical and sanitary.

To those who were accustomed to an abundance of hot and cold water, a sink with a good water supply was essential in the modern kitchen. This didn't apply, however, to the many people in the 1920s who still lived in outlying, isolated areas and had to provide a water supply at their own expense. They could install excellent equipment that used power for a complete water supply, or a pitcher pump to be hand-operated at a sink that had some sanitary drainage for waste water.

The height of the sink was important in preventing unnecessary fatigue. Modern sinks were installed a

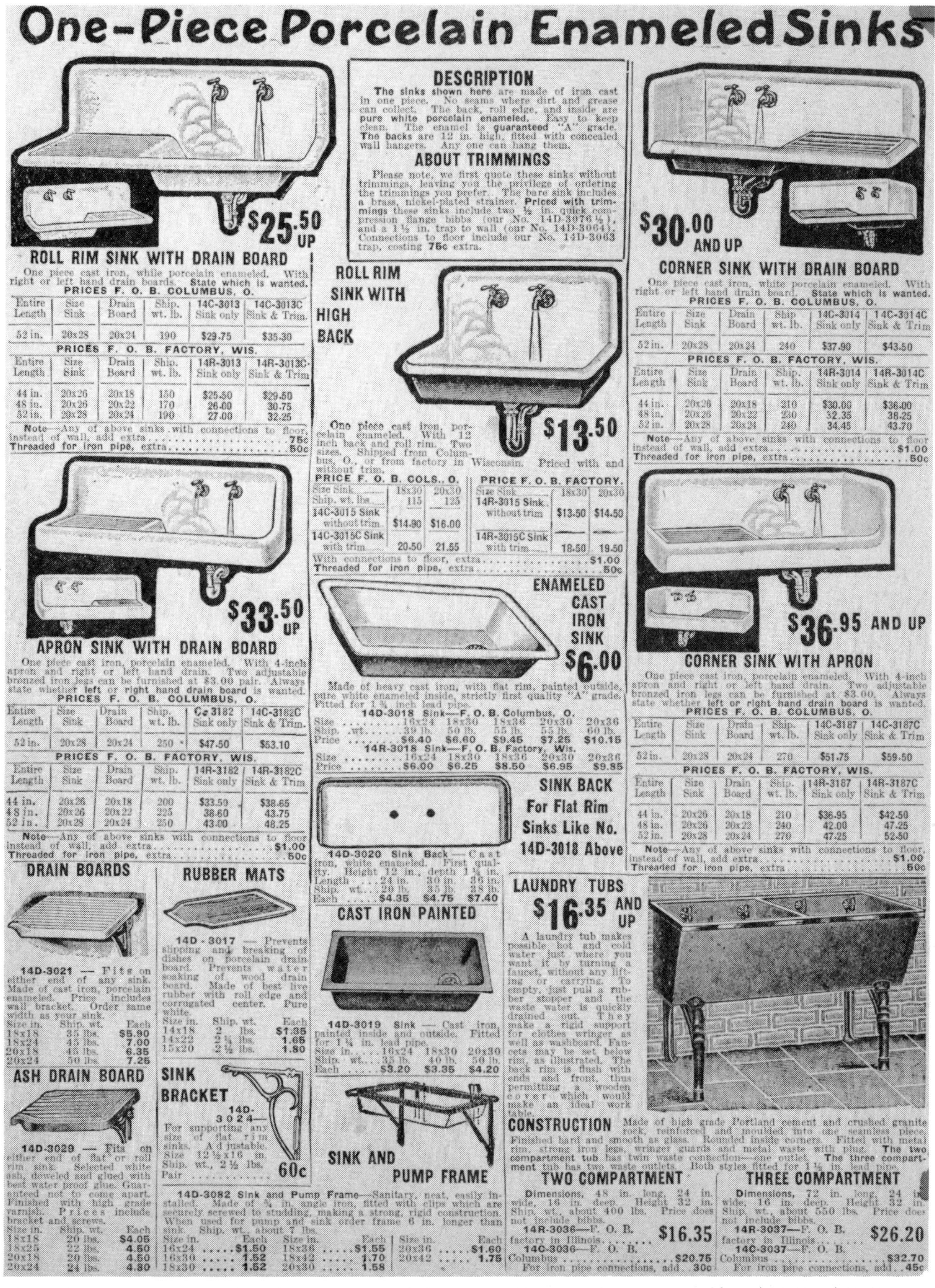

One-Piece Porcelain Enameled Sinks

DESCRIPTION

The sinks shown here are made of iron cast in one piece. No seams where dirt and grease can collect. The back, roll edge, and inside are **pure white porcelain enameled.** Easy to keep clean. The enamel is **guaranteed** "A" grade. **The backs** are 12 in. high, fitted with concealed wall hangers. Any one can hang them.

ABOUT TRIMMINGS

Please note, we first quote these sinks without trimmings, leaving you the privilege of ordering the trimmings you prefer. The bare sink includes a brass, nickel-plated strainer. **Priced with trimmings** these sinks include two ½ in. quick compression flange bibbs (our No. 14D-3076½), and a 1½ in. trap to wall (our No. 14D-3064). Connections to floor include our No. 14D-3063 trap, costing **75c** extra.

$25.50 UP — ROLL RIM SINK WITH DRAIN BOARD

One piece cast iron, while porcelain enameled. With right or left hand drain boards. **State which is wanted.**

PRICES F. O. B. COLUMBUS, O.

Entire Length	Size Sink	Drain Board	Ship. wt. lb.	14C-3013 Sink only	14C-3013C Sink & Trim.
52 in.	20x28	20x24	190	$29.75	$35.30

PRICES F. O. B. FACTORY, WIS.

Entire Length	Size Sink	Drain Board	Ship. wt. lb.	14R-3013 Sink only	14R-3013C Sink & Trim
44 in.	20x26	20x18	150	$25.50	$29.50
48 in.	20x26	20x22	170	26.00	30.75
52 in.	20x28	20x24	190	27.00	32.25

Note—Any of above sinks with connections to floor, instead of wall, add extra **75c**
Threaded for iron pipe, extra **50c**

ROLL RIM SINK WITH HIGH BACK — $13.50

One piece cast iron, porcelain enameled. With 12 inch back and roll rim. Two sizes. Shipped from Columbus, O., or from factory in Wisconsin. Priced with and without trim.

PRICE F. O. B. COLS., O.

Size Sink	18x30	20x30
Ship. wt. lbs.	115	125
14C-3015 Sink without trim	$14.90	$16.00
14C-3015C Sink with trim	20.50	21.55

PRICE F. O. B. FACTORY.

Size Sink	18x30	20x30
14R-3015 Sink without trim	$13.50	$14.50
14R-3015C Sink with trim	18.50	19.50

With connections to floor, extra **$1.00**
Threaded for iron pipe, extra **50c**

$30.00 AND UP — CORNER SINK WITH DRAIN BOARD

One piece cast iron, white porcelain enameled. With right or left hand drain board. **State which is wanted.**

PRICES F. O. B. COLUMBUS, O.

Entire Length	Size Sink	Drain Board	Ship wt. lb.	14C-3014 Sink only	14C-3014C Sink & Trim
52 in.	20x28	20x24	240	$37.90	$43.50

PRICES F. O. B. FACTORY, WIS.

Entire Length	Size Sink	Drain Board	Ship. wt. lb.	14R-3014 Sink only	14R-3014C Sink & Trim
44 in.	20x26	20x18	210	$30.00	$36.00
48 in.	20x26	20x22	230	32.35	38.25
52 in.	20x28	20x24	240	34.45	43.70

Note—Any of above sinks with connections to floor instead of wall, add extra **$1.00**
Threaded for iron pipe, extra **50c**

$33.50 UP — APRON SINK WITH DRAIN BOARD

One piece cast iron, porcelain enameled. With 4-inch apron and right or left hand drain. Two adjustable bronzed iron legs can be furnished at $3.00 pair. Always state whether **left** or **right hand drain board** is wanted.

PRICES F. O. B. COLUMBUS, O.

Entire Length	Size Sink	Drain Board	Ship. wt. lb.	C-3182 Sink only	14C-3182C Sink & Trim.
52 in.	20x28	20x24	250	$47.50	$53.10

PRICES F. O. B. FACTORY, WIS.

Entire Length	Size Sink	Drain Board	Ship. wt. lb.	14R-3182 Sink only	14R-3182C Sink & Trim
44 in.	20x26	20x18	200	$33.50	$38.65
48 in.	20x26	20x22	225	38.60	43.75
52 in.	20x28	20x24	250	43.00	48.25

Note—Any of above sinks with connections to floor instead of wall, add extra **$1.00**
Threaded for iron pipe, extra **50c**

ENAMELED CAST IRON SINK $6.00

Made of heavy cast iron, with flat rim, painted outside, pure white enameled inside, strictly first quality "A" grade. Fitted for 1¾ inch lead pipe.

14D-3018 Sink—F. O. B. Columbus, O.

Size	16x24	18x30	18x36	20x30	20x36
Ship. wt.	39 lb.	50 lb.	55 lb.	55 lb.	60 lb.
Price	$6.40	$6.60	$9.45	$7.25	$10.15

14R-3018 Sink—F. O. B. Factory, Wis.

Size	16x24	18x30	18x36	20x30	20x36
Price	$6.00	$6.25	$8.50	$6.95	$9.85

$36.95 AND UP — CORNER SINK WITH APRON

One piece cast iron, porcelain enameled. With 4-inch apron and right or left hand drain. Two adjustable bronzed iron legs can be furnished at $3.00. Always state whether **left or right hand drain board** is wanted.

PRICES F. O. B. COLUMBUS, O.

Entire Length	Size Sink	Drain Board	Ship. wt. lb.	14C-3187 Sink only	14C-3187C Sink & Trim
52 in.	20x28	20x24	270	$51.75	$59.50

PRICES F. O. B. FACTORY, WIS.

Entire Length	Size Sink	Drain Board	Ship. wt. lb.	14R-3187 Sink only	14R-3187C Sink & Trim
44 in.	20x26	20x18	210	$36.95	$42.50
48 in.	20x26	20x22	240	42.00	47.25
52 in.	20x28	20x24	270	47.25	52.50

Note—Any of above sinks with connections to floor, instead of wall, add extra **$1.00**
Threaded for iron pipe, extra **50c**

SINK BACK For Flat Rim Sinks Like No. 14D-3018 Above

14D-3020 Sink Back — Cast iron, white enameled. First quality. Height 12 in., depth 1¼ in.

Length	24 in.	30 in.	36 in.
Ship. wt.	20 lb.	35 lb.	28 lb.
Each	$4.35	$4.75	$7.40

DRAIN BOARDS

14D-3021 — Fits on either end of any sink. Made of cast iron, porcelain enameled. Price includes wall bracket. Order same width as your sink.

Size in.	Ship. wt.	Each
18x18	35 lbs.	$5.90
18x24	45 lbs.	7.00
20x18	45 lbs.	6.35
20x24	50 lbs.	7.25

RUBBER MATS

14D-3017 — Prevents slipping and breaking of dishes on porcelain drain board. Prevents water soaking of wood drain board. Made of best live rubber with roll edge and corrugated center. Pure white.

Size in.	Ship. wt.	Each
14x18	2 lbs.	$1.35
14x22	2¼ lbs.	1.65
15x20	2½ lbs.	1.80

CAST IRON PAINTED

14D-3019 Sink — Cast iron, painted inside and outside. Fitted for 1¼ in. lead pipe.

Size in.	16x24	18x30	20x30
Ship. wt.	35 lb.	40 lb.	50 lb.
Each	$3.20	$3.35	$4.20

ASH DRAIN BOARD

14D-3029 — Fits on either end of flat or roll rim sink. Selected white ash, doweled and glued with best water proof glue. Guaranteed not to come apart. Finished with high grade varnish. Prices include bracket and screws.

Size in.	Ship. wt.	Each
18x18	20 lbs.	$4.05
18x25	22 lbs.	4.50
20x18	20 lbs.	4.50
20x24	24 lbs.	4.80

SINK BRACKET

14D-3024—For supporting any size of flat rim sinks. Adjustable. Size 12½x16 in. Ship. wt., 2½ lbs. Pair **60c**

SINK AND PUMP FRAME

14D-3082 Sink and Pump Frame—Sanitary, neat, easily installed. Made of ¾ in. angle iron, fitted with clips which are securely screwed to studding, making a strong, rigid construction. When used for pump and sink order frame 6 in. longer than sink. Ship. wt., about 7 lbs.

Size in.	Each	Size in.	Each	Size in.	Each
16x24	$1.50	18x36	$1.55	20x36	$1.60
16x30	1.52	18x42	1.70	20x42	1.75
18x30	1.52	20x30	1.58		

LAUNDRY TUBS $16.35 AND UP

A laundry tub makes possible hot and cold water just where you want it by turning a faucet, without any lifting or carrying. To empty, just pull a rubber stopper and the waste water is quickly drained out. They make a rigid support for clothes wringer as well as washboard. Faucets may be set below rim, as illustrated. The back rim is flush with ends and front, thus permitting a wooden cover which would make an ideal work table.

CONSTRUCTION Made of high grade Portland cement and crushed granite rock, reinforced and moulded into one seamless piece. Finished hard and smooth as glass. Rounded inside corners. Fitted with metal rim, strong iron legs, wringer guards and metal waste with plug. **The two compartment tub** has twin waste connection—one outlet. **The three compartment** tub has two waste outlets. Both styles fitted for 1½ in. lead pipe.

TWO COMPARTMENT

Dimensions, 48 in. long, 24 in. wide, 16 in. deep. Height 32 in. Ship. wt., about 400 lbs. Price does not include bibbs.
14R-3036—F. O. B. factory in Illinois **$16.35**
14C-3036—F. O. B. Columbus **$20.75**
For iron pipe connections, add .. **30c**

THREE COMPARTMENT

Dimensions, 72 in. long, 24 in. wide, 16 in. deep. Height 32 in. Ship. wt., about 550 lbs. Price does not include bibbs.
14R-3037—F. O. B. factory in Illinois **$26.20**
14C-3037—F. O. B. Columbus **$32.70**
For iron pipe connections, add .. **45c**

The sink advertisement in the 1921 Cussins and Fearn catalog shows a variety of kitchen sinks. They were white porcelain-enamel, wall hung, and had single drainboards. The prices that year ranged from $25.50 to $52.50; sizes from 20″ × 26″ to 20″ × 28″ for the sinks; and entire lengths from 44″ to 48″.

The white-porcelain sink with two drainboards provided a place for soiled dishes on one side and clean dishes on the other. The legs appear to be metal. The Standard sink in 1928 was "complete." The features included an 8″ low back, an 8″ deep sink, and an 8″ deep front. A swinging spout faucet that would not tarnish or corrode and a directly attached garbage container with removable receptacle on a folding bracket were two other features.

comfortable 36″ from the floor. Previously, little attention had been paid to the height of the sink, which had been up to each builder's discretion. A flexible rubber hose attached to the sink's hot water faucet was convenient for rinsing dishes.

Accessories. Color came to the kitchen in the late 1920s, when a colorful array of kitchen utensils and accessories was introduced. They were an instant success with housewives who welcomed color as a relief from their all-white kitchens. The accessories, which included canisters; bread, cake, and cookie boxes; clothes reels; breadboards; knife boxes; wastebaskets; and stools, came in a variety of colors.

Cookware. Cookware available in the early 1920s was much the same as in earlier years. Aluminumware was becoming more popular. Stainess steel cookware was introduced in the late 1920s.

The Club Aluminum Company manufactured Club Aluminum Utensils. The company said their utensils promoted good health because they retained essential food nutrients to aid good digestion. The products were efficient, as the heat was distributed evenly and was retained twice as long as in iron utensils. The utensils were economical because they lowered utility bills, and they lasted a lifetime since they were rivetless, seamless, and free from rust or corrosion.

GIFTS, PRACTICAL AND FRIVOLOUS

The 1926 Marshall Field's Christmas catalog offered a sixteen-piece cereal set of white china with colored floral design for $17.50. They said it was a space saver, a time saver, and an addition to any kitchen wall. The rack for the set was $3.75.
Complete set $75-145

Canisters, matchbox holder, and salt and pepper shakers were decorated in the Hollyhock design in 1929. Other sets were decorated with yellow roses.
Canisters $18-28

Match holder $7.50-15

Salt and pepper shakers, $5-7.50.

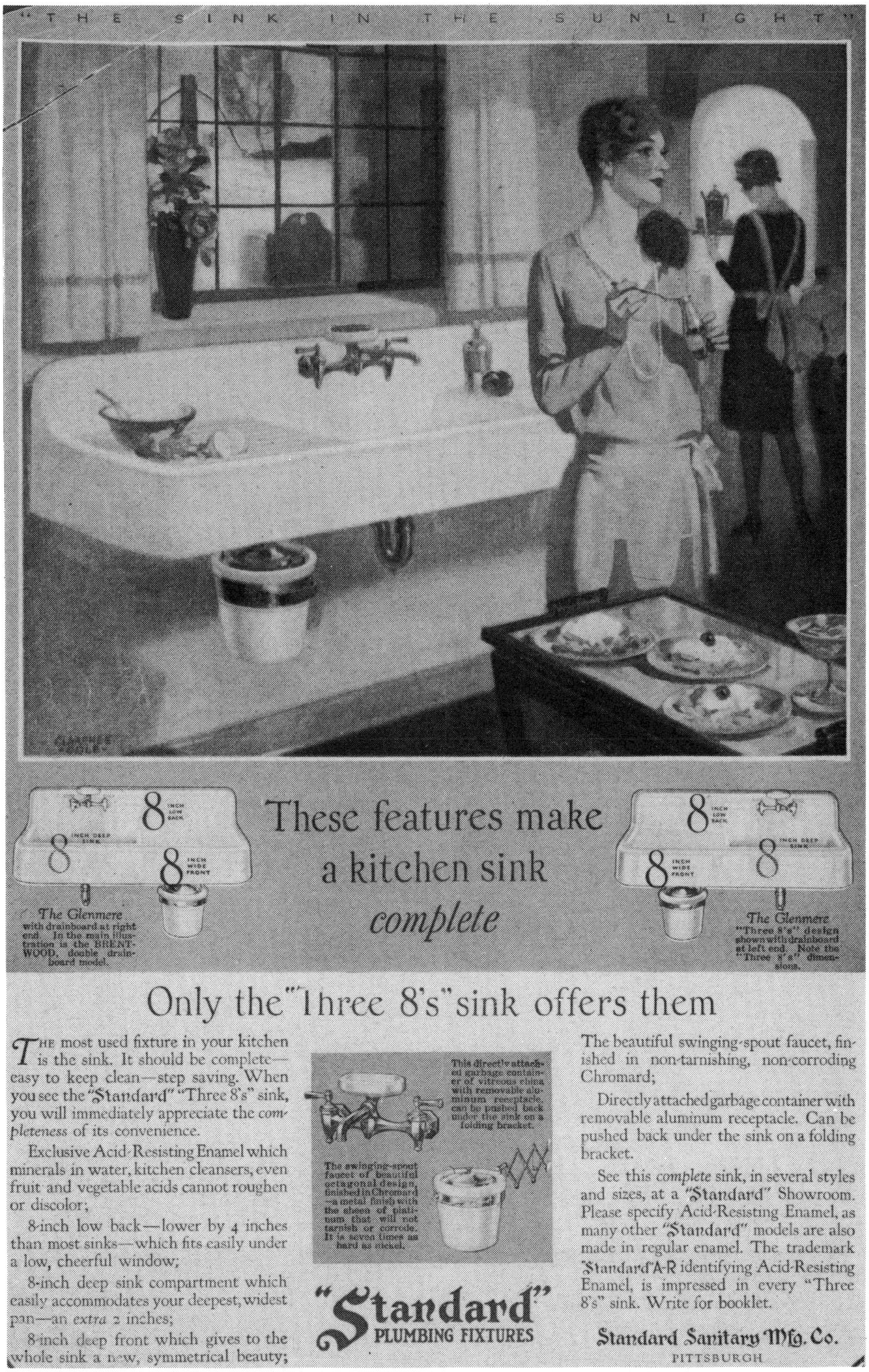

"THE SINK IN THE SUNLIGHT"

The Glenmere with drainboard at right end. In the main illustration is the BRENTWOOD, double drainboard model.

These features make a kitchen sink *complete*

The Glenmere "Three 8's" design shown with drainboard at left end. Note the "Three 8's" dimensions.

Only the "Three 8's" sink offers them

THE most used fixture in your kitchen is the sink. It should be complete—easy to keep clean—step saving. When you see the "Standard" "Three 8's" sink, you will immediately appreciate the *completeness* of its convenience.

Exclusive Acid-Resisting Enamel which minerals in water, kitchen cleansers, even fruit and vegetable acids cannot roughen or discolor;

8-inch low back—lower by 4 inches than most sinks—which fits easily under a low, cheerful window;

8-inch deep sink compartment which easily accommodates your deepest, widest pan—an *extra* 2 inches;

8-inch deep front which gives to the whole sink a new, symmetrical beauty;

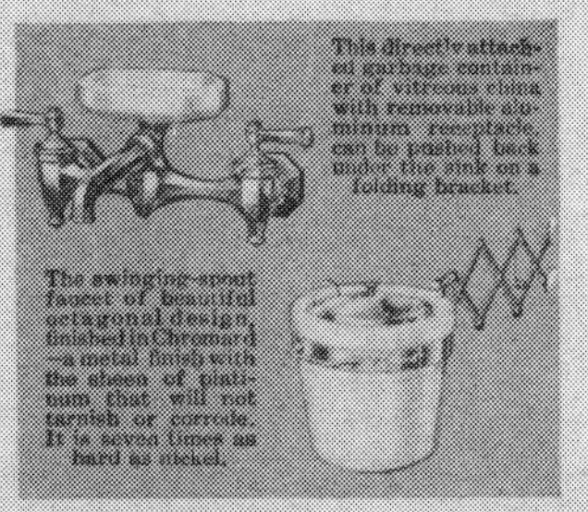

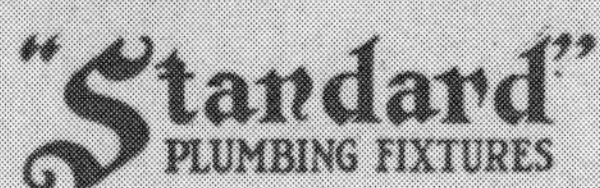

The beautiful swinging-spout faucet, finished in non-tarnishing, non-corroding Chromard;

Directly attached garbage container with removable aluminum receptacle. Can be pushed back under the sink on a folding bracket.

See this *complete* sink, in several styles and sizes, at a "Standard" Showroom. Please specify Acid-Resisting Enamel, as many other "Standard" models are also made in regular enamel. The trademark "Standard" A-R identifying Acid-Resisting Enamel, is impressed in every "Three 8's" sink. Write for booklet.

Standard Sanitary Mfg. Co.
PITTSBURGH

The Standard sink in 1928 was "complete." The features included an 8″ low back, an 8″ deep sink, and an 8″ deep front. There were also a swinging-spout faucet that wouldn't tarnish or corrode and a directly attached garbage container, with removable receptacle, that was on a folding bracket.

ALUMINUM TEA KETTLE

$4.00

LARGE TOP AND SPOUT

9B-74 — Can be filled from a faucet **through th spout** — no danger of burning fingers from steam, or of breaking off spout. The spout is securely welded on body and will support weight of kettle filled with water. **Top opening** is extra large for holding a rice boiler, thus making a double boiler out of this tea kettle—a time and fuel saver. **Body** made of heavy seamless sheet aluminum. Flat bottom. **Capacity** 7 quarts. Ship. wt., about 4½ lbs. Each.......... **$4.00**

SKILLET

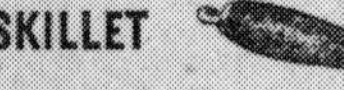

9B-1034 — Extra heavy aluminum, seamless, with always-cold handle. Diam. 9¼ in., depth 2¼ in. Ship. wt., 3 lbs. Price.......... **$1.45**

CAKE PAN

9B-835 — Seamless aluminum. Diam. 8 in. at top, 6½ in. at bottom. Depth 3 in. Ship. wt., 8 oz. Each.......... **$1.15**

PIE PAN

9B-72—Seamless aluminum. Diam. 9 in., depth 1 in. Ship. wt., 3 oz. Each.......... **38c**

PUDDING PANS

SEAMLESS ALUMINUM

No.	Size	Wt.	Ea.
9B-142	1 qt.	4 oz.	39c
9B-144	2 qt.	6 oz.	55c

JELLY CAKE PAN

9B-52—Seamless aluminum. Diam. 9⅜ in., depth 1 in. Very popular with good cooks. Ship. wt., 4 oz. Each.......... **39c**

ROUND ROASTER

9B-78 — Seamless aluminum. Self basting cover with large metal knob. Sliding vent in cover to release steam. **Bottom** 10½ in. diam., 4¼ in. deep. **Cover** 2¼ in. deep. Ship. wt., 2½ lbs. Each.......... **$1.75**

POPULAR ROASTER

9B-895—Seamless aluminum. With perforated inset which prevents meat sticking to bottom and allows basting at either end. Vent to release steam and produce the desired browning. Length 15 in., width 10¼ in., depth each half 4 in., inside measurements. Ship. wt., 4½ lbs. Price.......... **$5.65**

ALUMINUM TEA KETTLE

9B-638 — Pure aluminum, 18 gauge with cast aluminum spout lock-nutted to body. Breast double seamed to body. Wire bail, ebonized handle. Patented ear prevents bail touching side of kettle. Size 8, capacity 14 pints. Ship. wt., 4 lbs. Each.......... **$4.35**

COPPER-NICKLE PLATED

Family Size

$2.35

A well made, beautifully finished Tea Kettle. The heavy copper body is nickel-plated and polished — rust proof. Solid wire bail with always cold wood handle. Flat bottom adapted for use on any stove.

No.	Size	Capacity	Ship. wt.	Each
9B-183	8	7 quarts	4 lbs.	$2.35
9B-189	9	8 quarts	4½ lbs.	2.55

ALUMINUM WARE

Every piece stamped out of a solid sheet—no joints, seams or hollow beads. No solder to melt. Nothing to chip, scale or dissolve—the safest ware for cooking purposes. Does not easily burn, bend, break or dent. Intense heat does not affect its shape. Saves fuel, saves time in cooking.

ALUMINUM PERCOLATOR

$3.55

The perfect coffee Percolator. A special **spreader** distributes water evenly over coffee grounds insuring perfect percolation of all the coffee. **Hot well** in base brings water within 1-16 inch of the flame, starting percolation almost instantly. **The valve** at bottom of spout automatically pumps the hot water up the spout making percolation continuous and even. Made of finest aluminum beautifully finished. Wide base, with plate for use on gas or oil stoves.

9B-41 Percolator—6 cup size. Ship. wt., about 3½ lbs. Price.......... **$3.55**

9B-42 Percolator—9-cup size. Ship. wt., about 4 lbs. Price.......... **$5.75**

COFFEE POTS

Seamless **Alminum** with welded spouts and special always cold handle. Ship. wt., about 1¾ lbs.

No.	Size	Each
9B-882	2 quarts	$2.15
9B-883	3 quarts	2.35

TEA POTS

Seamless aluminum. Extra strong welded spout. Beautifully finished. Special always cold handle. Ship. wt., about 1½ lbs.

No.	Size	Each
9B-872	2 quarts	$2.55

CASSEROLES

Receivers are made of special carbonated steel, brightly finished and heavily nickel plated. Popular ornamental designs. **Insets** are fine quality earthenware, brown outside, white lined. **Diameter** 8 inches. Ship. wt., about 6 lbs.

No.	Shape	Capacity	Ea.
9B-69	Round	3 pt.	2.85
9B-94	Oval	2¼ pt.	3.05
9B-68	Round	4½ pt.	3.15
9B-93	Oval	2¼ pt.	3.45

WITH PYREX INSERTS

Receiver made of best quality brass, brightly polished and heavily nickel-plated. **Inset** is Pyrex, the most lasting baking ware made. Never chips, flakes or crazes. Size 8 in. Ship. wt., about 6 lbs.

No	Shape	Capacity	Ea.
9B-168	Round	3 pt.	6.00
9B-193	Oval	2¼ pt.	6.25

9B-169—Chafing dish style. High footed metal frame made of highly carbonated steel, brightly polished and heavily nickel plated. **The Pyrex** inset is 7½ in., diameter 2⅞ in. deep, capacity 3 pints. It is the most durable and sanitary baking ware made. Never chips, flakes or crazes. Ship. wt., 6 lbs. Price.......... **$5.20**

NON-STICK GEM PANS

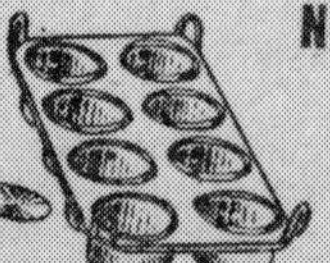

9B-8—No greasing, no sticking. Approved by Good Housekeeping Institute. **Removable metal disks** in bottom of cups solve the sticking problem. Made of heavy composition metal with heavy wire frame, terminating in legs at each corner, for pan to rest upon when inverted. A gentle pressure on discs through small hole in bottom of each cup, removes the cakes, perfectly whole. Muffins and gems may be removed while hot. Ship. wt., 1½ lbs. Set.......... **$1.00**

KITCHEN FORK

9B-415—For meat and vegetables. Retinned 10 gauge wire, enameled handle, eye for hanging up. Length over all 15 in. Ship. wt., 6 oz. Each.......... **10c**

ALUMINUM PRESERVING KETTLE

4 Qt. For

$1.30

Maximum Service and Satisfaction is to be had in these kettles.

No.	Capacity	Ship. wt.	Each
9B-22	4 quarts	1 lb.	$1.30
9B-23	6 quarts	1¼ lb.	1.65
9B-24	8 quarts	1½ lb.	2.05

CONVEX KETTLE

Seamless Aluminum, with perfect fitting lid, always cold handle.

No.	Size	Wt.	Each
9B-32	4 qt.	1¼ lb.	$1.65
9B-34	8 qt.	1¾ lb.	2.45
9B-35	10 qt.	2 lb.	2.90

DOUBLE BOILER

$1.55

Seamless Aluminum. Inset of 2 qt., fits in top of our 9B-74 Tea Kettle.

No.	Size	Wt.	Each
9B-91	1½ qt.	1¼ lb.	$1.55
9B-92	2 qt.	1½ lb.	2.00

SAUCE PAN

2 Qt.

83c

SEAMLESS ALUMINUM

No.	Size	Wt.	Each
9B-12	2 qt.	10 oz.	$0.83
9B-13	3qt.	12 oz.	0.98
9B-14	4 qt.	16 oz.	1.08

DIPPER

45c

9B-81—Rubberoid handle riveted on solid cast aluminum socket. Capacity 1 pt. Ship. wt., 5 oz. Each.......... **45c**

DRINKING CUP

9B-94 — With handle. Holds 1 pt. Ship. wt., 2 oz. Each.......... **35c**

HANDY KITCHEN SUPPLIES

STRAINERS

For straining fruit

9B-7 — Heavy tin plate. Bowl 5⅝ in diameter, 2¼ in. deep, with hook on side and riveted handle. Fine mesh wire bottom. Ship. wt., 10 oz. Each.......... **12c**

9B-716 Strainer—For tea and coffee. Bowl 5 in. diam., 2¼ in. deep, 16 mesh wire cloth. Black enameled handle, eye for hanging up. Ship. wt., 5 oz. Each.......... **12c**

9B-17 Potato Masher—Retinned wire, 11 gauge frame, 14 gauge ribs. Base 3x3¾ in. Enameled handle. Ship. wt., 8 oz. Each.......... **10c**

9B-35 Can Opener — Adjustable to any size can. Regular end knife, and hook for removing crown caps on bottles. Nickel-plated, with enameled wood handle. Ship. wt., 5 oz. Each.......... **12c**

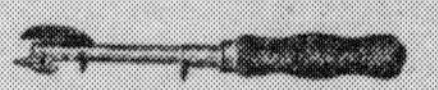

9B-168 Cake Turner—Steel, nickel-plated, with ebonoid wood handle. Blade 3¼x4¾ in. Length over all 15½ in. Ship. wt., about 5 oz. Each.......... **10c**

Jelly Strainer

9B-95—Fits on chair back or hooks over nail in wall. Extra heavy wire frame with steel bracket. Good muslin bag, with 6 in. mouth, 11 in. deep, easily removed from frame for washing. Ship. wt., 1 lb. Each.......... **25c**

DOVER EGG BEATER

Best Made

9B-75 — Also used for whipping cream. Family size, length 9½ inches. Bronzed finished castings, polished blades. Ship. wt., ½ lb. Price.......... **15c**

SINK STRAINER

9B-10—Hook for fastening in corner of wood frame sink. Also wire stand for setting in all porcelain enameled sinks. Made of heavy sheet steel, blue enameled. Size 8x19 inch across top. Ship. wt., 12 oz. Each.......... **15c**

USE WOOD LACQUER ON KITCHEN FLOORS

A complete set of Club Aluminum Utensils from 1926 were given a Certificate of Merit by the Illinois State Medical Society in July, 1925, that stated Club Aluminum Utensils enabled the housewife to prepare food without loss of food elements, which might be lost if water were used in the cooking.

◀
A variety of aluminumware was carried by Fearn and Cussins in 1921. They said every piece was stamped out of a solid sheet and had no joints, seams, or solder to melt. It would not easily burn, bend, break, or dent. It was the safest cookware and saved fuel and cooking time.

Children Need KITCHEN CRAFT *Health Cooking*

Active, growing, young bodies and busy brains, need all the health-producing mineral salts and vitamines that foods can give.

The Kitchen Craft Waterless Cooker is your assurance that these mineral salts and vitamines will be left in the foods—not drained away as in ordinary cooking. It is your guarantee of the most healthful, most tasty, and most flavorful meal possible to prepare.

The Kitchen Craft Waterless Cooker is indispensable to every family. It is so simple to use—needing no watching or attention—is so efficient and so economical of both fuel and foods—that every family should have, and can afford one.

Leading dietetic specialists including Milo Hastings—Physical Culture Food Director—endorse the Kitchen Craft Waterless Cooker as essential to the health-equipment of every household.

KITCHEN CRAFT *Waterless Cooker*

1 , 2

A complete meal of vegetables and meat or vegetables alone can be prepared over one burner without danger of mixing flavors.

Made of Aluminum in 5 sizes $7.50 and up

[*Slightly higher prices west of Rocky Mountains and in Canada*]

Kitchen Craft Waterless Cookers are sold only direct to the home by specially trained, authorized representatives identified by the Kitchen Craft Lapel button.

KITCHEN CRAFT

THE KITCHEN CRAFT CO.
Health Hill
West Bend Wis.

Please send me "Better Cooking," the booklet which describes the Kitchen Craft Waterless Way of preparing more healthful meals.

Name ....

Address ....

City ....

County.............State............

Let Us Send You This Free Book

In 1926, the Kitchen Craft Company, Health Hill, West Bend, Wisconsin, said children needed Kitchen Craft Health. This Aluminum Waterless Cooker gave the assurance that vitamins and minerals were not washed away. It was simple to use, economical, and needed no watching. The cooker came in five sizes for $7.50 and up.

The Colorful, Streamlined Kitchen, 1930 to 1940

In 1930, the Brooklyn Borough Gas Company asked Lillian Galbraith, an efficiency engineer, to study the kitchen. She approached it as an industrial production problem, using motion studies to investigate the kitchen organization problem. Motions used by the worker in performing a task were analyzed, then a systematic attempt was made to eliminate unnecessary motions and arrange the remaining motions in the most efficient sequence.

Galbraith studied making a cake and found that the cook completed fifty operations and walked 143 feet. She was able to reduce the operations to twenty-four and the distance walked to twenty-four feet.

The conclusion was that the modern kitchen, although it possessed many attractive appliances and appeared to be efficient, was far from approaching the efficiency that prevailed in the best industrial plants.

Gas, electric, appliance, and furniture companies all

One of the complete Electric Kitchens that the General Electric Institute featured in the 1933 edition of *The New Art*. Notice that the range still has the oven on top. (Courtesy General Electric Corporation.)

studied the kitchen to make it the most efficient room it could be. Never before had so much emphasis been put on the kitchen — no longer was it the "stepchild" of the house. The results of all the research were basic planning principles, three work centers, and the "streamlined" kitchen.

The three work centers established in 1935 were the refrigerator and preparation center, range and serving center, and sink and dishwashing center. All of these centers needed to be planned so that the equipment was conveniently located within the shortest distance possible. Good planning and proper arrangement of equipment provided a minimum of walking, bending, and stretching.

In the mid-1930s, many objects were redesigned as a result of the Depression, mass production, the need to stimulate sales, and "streamlining." When units were designed to be integrated around the work centers, the result was the streamlined kitchen. "Streamlined" originally meant a reduction of wing resistance. Since the mid-1930s, the word has implied a graceful design and has been used interchangeably with the word modern.

The stoves were well insulated by the 1930s, and proper ventilation was available. The modern kitchens of the time could be as cool as any other room in the house. Proper ventilation was essential. Windows for cross-ventilation and ventilating fans were desirable.

In 1933, Monel Metal was featured on the tabletop, sink, cabinet tops, and range. Monel Metal resembled silver, never rusted, chipped, or cracked, and was easy to clean. The range is the same height as the sink and work surfaces. The oven has been placed below so there is a continuous work surface.

Fans were no longer a luxury, and a great variety of them was available. They were easy to install and usually were reversible so that odors could be exhausted, or fresh, clean air could be brought into the room.

The "open plan" was introduced in the 1930s. This called for a "dining area" to be an extension of the living room, usually an L-shaped room. This was economical and made the living room look larger. But some homemakers objected to the lack of privacy and the "mess" in the living room.

In the 1930s, large businesses were tending to the housewives' aesthetic and physical comforts by making attractive household equipment.

BEFORE . . . The old-fashioned kitchen full of work, crossed and re-crossed with countless steps. The scene of hundreds of lost hours loaded with routine drudgery . . . the result is lost youth and beauty, and impaired health.

AFTER . . . The modern General Electric Kitchen—a lifetime investment that pays for itself. Easily one-by-one, each unit can be added one at a time, and each helps pay for the next through actual savings effected. The G-E Kitchen Institute, through the G-E representative in your community, will show you how to attain this desirable goal. There is no obligation to you.

(Courtesy General Electric Corporation.)

"If your heart is set on having a colorful kitchen... Green holds sway in many kitchens today!" A 1933 advertisement for Congoleum Rugs. (Courtesy Congoleum Corporation.)

In 1935, the *Delineator* magazine featured this kitchen. They noted that the generous proportions of the kitchen made it a place of ease and good cheer and that it was light and airy with plentiful work surfaces and closet space. (Courtesy the Butterick Company.)

DRAWINGS BY ROBERT SCHROYER

Here, step by step, is how to transform the old kitchen (pictured left; plan above) to the model kitchen shown below

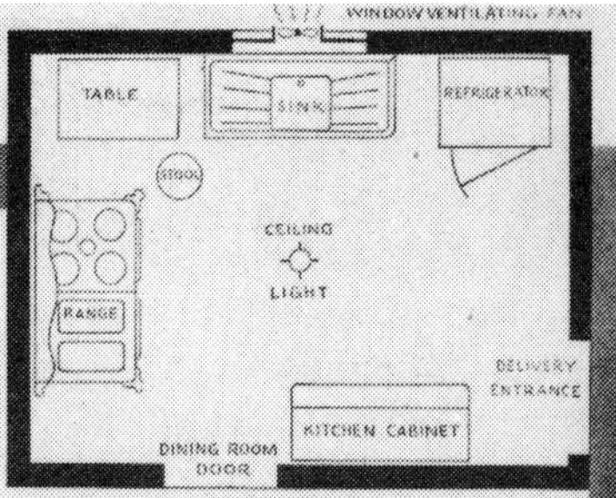

Move sink to window; switch range and refrigerator for more convenient arrangement. Add a ventilating fan

A modern refrigerator. A brand-new range. Lights over both range and sink. Getting better and better!

New Kitchens

by **ALTHEA LEPPER**

NO, THIS isn't just another of those articles on picture-book kitchens. This piece is going to be different, for it concerns *your* kitchen.

Of course, if you are building a new home, or if you have a fat pocketbook, you probably won't need our help. But if your budget can't stand a big dent right now, and if you are feeling pretty discouraged about your old kitchen, read on.

To begin with, remember that successful kitchen remodeling need not be done all at one time. You *can* modernize *your* kitchen, and spread both work and expense over several years.

The quickest way to find out what is wrong with your particular kitchen is to sit down quietly, and give it a careful once-over. Then get out your pencil, and check off its bad points on the following list: Inconvenient arrangement; inadequate lighting; bad ventilation; worn-out refrigerator; old-fashioned range; unsightly sink; insufficient cupboard space; dingy walls; hard-to-clean floors.

Now let's see what can be done, gradually and economically, to correct these faults, so that your kitchen will be a pleasant, convenient, efficient workroom. Here are the remedies—and what they will cost:

KITCHEN ARRANGEMENT: Experts agree that the sink should be placed under a window, if possible, and between refrigerator and range, with the refrigerator nearest the back door, and the range nearest the door to the dining room. This plan, in U or L shape, saves most steps and most energy. How does *your* kitchen line up with this arrangement? If it is U- or L-shaped, your task of arrangement is fairly simple. If, however, it is of odd shape, broken by doors and windows, you'll profit by consulting carpenter and plumber. Moving a window, changing plumbing pipes, current lines or fuel lines so that the most efficient arrangement of equipment is possible, is worth serious consideration.

Costs for such structural changes range from $5.00 to $75.00.

ADEQUATE LIGHTING: The average medium-sized kitchen needs more light than a central fixture affords. A good light over the sink, and a 40- to 60-watt light over the range will make you wonder how you ever got along without them. While wiring is being done, provide duplex outlets for the small electric appliances.

Costs for light outlets and fixtures will range from $5.00 to $15.00.

GOOD VENTILATION: To provide cross ventilation, and to clear your kitchen of cooking odors, install an electric ventilating fan of adequate size.

Costs for fan and installation $25.00 to $65.00.

REFRIGERATION: For a family of five, you should have at least a six-cubic-foot refrigerator. An ice refrigerator this size will cost about $75.00. An automatic refrigerator the same size about $175.00

The electric type will plug right into an ordinary wall outlet. For a gas- or kerosene-operated box, you may have to figure on a small installation charge.

Cost of refrigerator from $75.00 to $175.00 and up.

RANGES: Gas ranges, with automatic oven heat control, easy-to-clean burners and good insulation, average from $125.00 to $225.00.

Electric ranges average from $100.00 to $500.00, depending on size and the kind of heating elements you want.

Oil and combination coal and wood or gas ranges average from $75.00 to $100.00 when equipped with heat controls or thermometers.

Installation charges for gas ranges are small. Electric ranges require special wiring.

Inquire about installation costs from your electrician or utility company.

Consider your own height when you select a range, and experiment with models on the sales floor. If you are tall, or if a bad knee prevents stooping, you may find the raised oven types more convenient than table top models.

Cost of new range from $75.00 to $500.00.

SINKS: A sink of average size (experts recommend one 60 inches wide across the front, 25 inches from front to back and about 36 inches high) will range from $50.00 to $250.00. Sinks with built-in dishwashers and metal tops cost from $180.00 to $450.00, (*Turn to page 57*)

Shipshape, convenient and step-saving, this picture-book kitchen can be yours if you want it—and you can modernize gradually or rapidly, as your budget allows

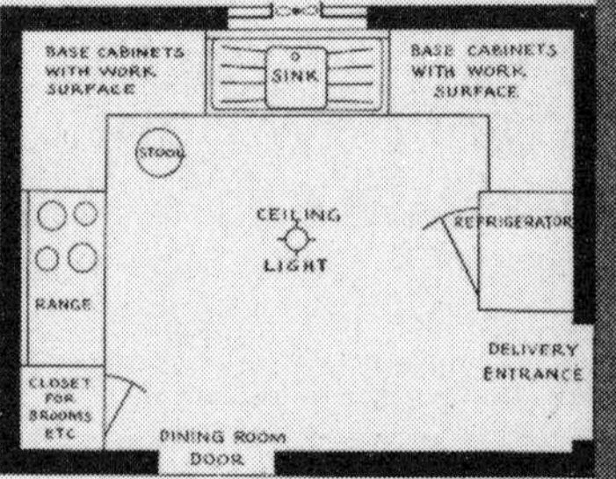

Out goes the old cabinet. In come the base cabinets with broad work surfaces. We have a new sink, too

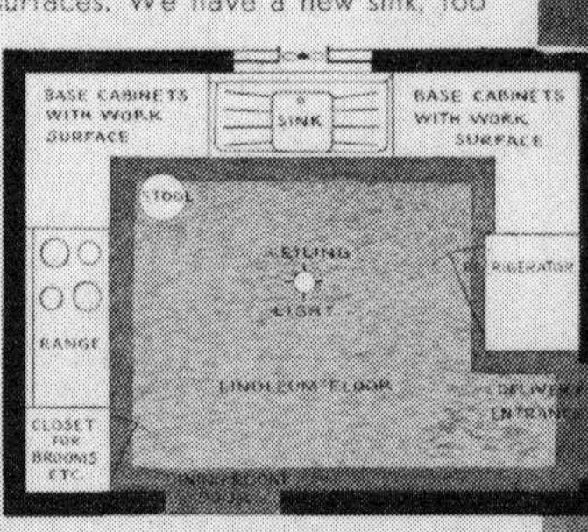

Fresh wall surfaces. Easy-to-clean linoleum. Wall cabinets. An easy, gradual, but complete transformation

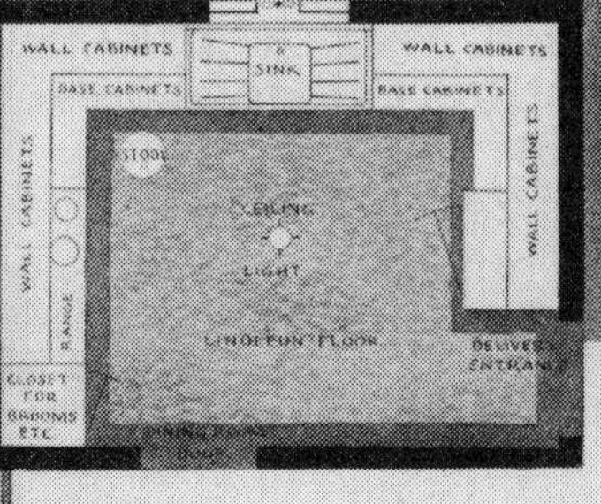

"New Kitchens" article from the November, 1936, *Delineator* magazine. (Courtesy the Butterick Company.

The 1937 Whitehead Kitchens had inviting work surfaces of silvery Monel. Notice the hood over the range, which was also Monel. Whitehead Metal Products Company of New York offered forty-two different sizes of steel wall and base cabinets and fifty-seven different models of sinks. Wall cabinets started at $14.50 and Monel sinks at $41.

A contemporary kitchen was featured in this 1937 advertisement. (Courtesy Congoleum Corporation.)

The 1939 Crane advertisement for "The family planned" kitchen. It was a kitchen scientifically arranged for efficiency, with kitchen conveniences that speeded up kitchen tasks. It was also "family planned" for play — just right for a cheery breakfast, after school treats, a game of bridge, or a midnight snack. (Courtesy Crane Company.)

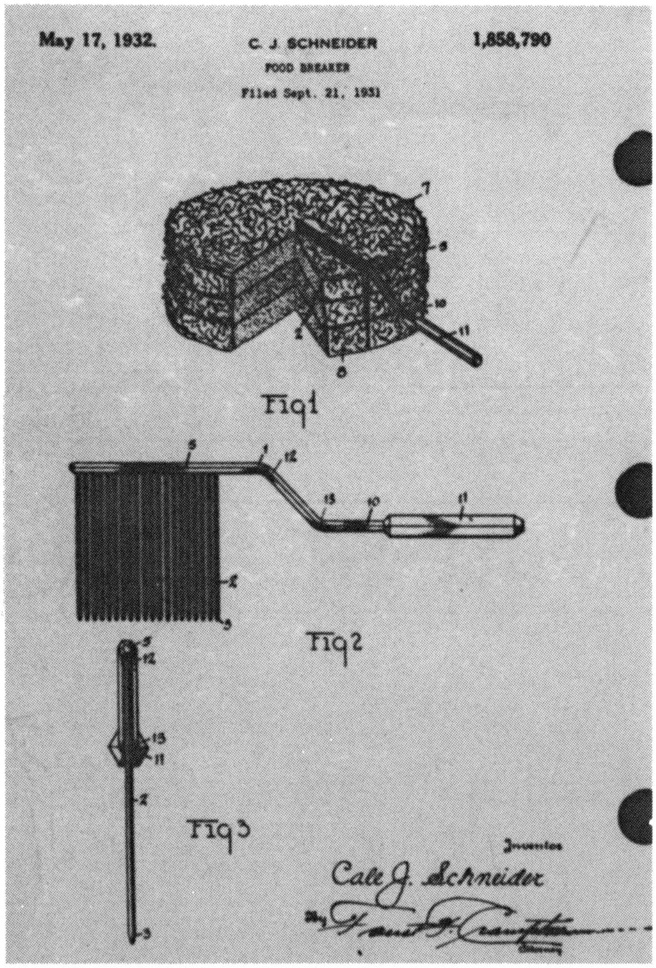

Patent picture shows the food breaker, which was invented by C. J. Schneider and patented in 1931.

Catalin Tools and Gadgets

In 1931, the Sta-Brite Company introduced catalin, the first type of plastic used for cutlery handles. It was also used for handles of utensils, tools, and gadgets. Catalin was said not to chip or break, to be non-inflammable and permanently beautiful. However, this was not the case. It soon dulled and it often cracked, but it did have great appeal because of its color and novelty. Catalin was replaced when plastics were made more durable and heat resistant. Later the Ekco Housewares Company acquired the Sta-Brite Company. Ekco called their colors burgundy red and green.

The Washburn Company called its ANDROCK line with catalin handles Jewel Kitchenware because of its jewel-like handles of jade green and red.

This came in an unmarked box with an instruction sheet inside that said: "Maid Of Honor Hostess Cake Slicer. Press prongs down through the cake and turn

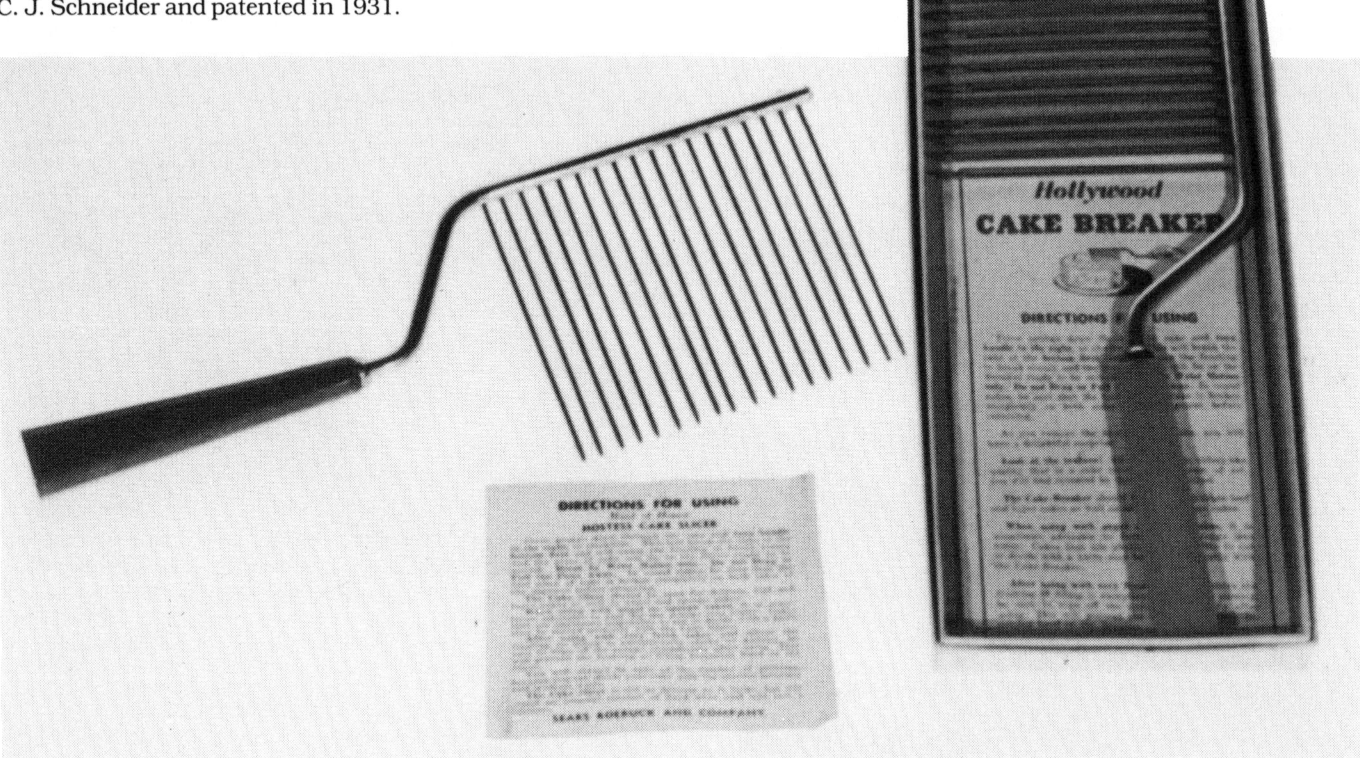

Schneider Toledo #1,858,790. Cake slicer with red or green handles.

Unmarked slicer. This came in a Hollywood Cake Breaker box. It has a gold catalin handle. **$2.50-4.50**

handle to the right, or clockwise. This will break the cake at the bottom first and will cause the frosting to break evenly and the piece of cake will lie on the Slicer ready to be served. Break by Wrist Motion only. Do not Drag or Pull the Piece Away. In round cakes, be sure that the first piece of cake is broken completely on both sides of the segment before removing...." (Courtesy Sears, Roebuck and Company.)

Hollywood Cake Breaker box was marked: "HOSTESS CAKE BREAKER. Cut cake this smart 'no crumble' way. You'll Love the way it breaks cake into perfect portions. NO MESSY CRUMBLING of FROSTING or FILLING. Both frame and prongs have non-rusting chrome finish to last a lifetime. Made In U.S.A. by Langner Mfg. Co. N.Y."

The lower part of the two-piece grapefruit corer (in center of illustration) was a "whatsit" in *Kitchens and Gadgets*. The other "whatsit" in that book turned out to be a butter curler.

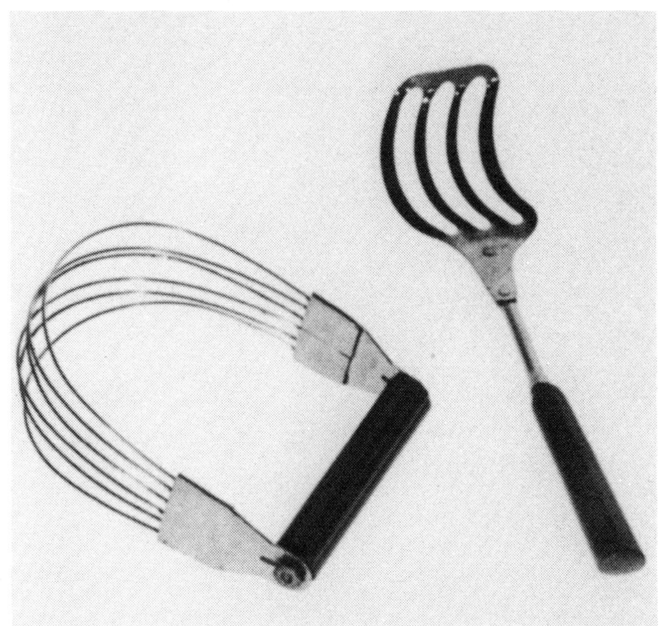

A dough blender, with its easy-to-grip handle, can be used for a variety of things. It cuts shortening through flour for a flakier crust, is good for mincing eggs, crushing berries, mixing hamburger for meatloaf, and mixing dips. Left to right:

Pat. No. 1,735236, Made In U.S.A.; Androck Stainless Steel. Red handle. **$3.50-7.50**

"A. & J. Pat. Apl'd For, Made In U.S.A." Brown handle. **$3.50-$7.50**

Corers and garnisher with red catalin handles. Left to right:

"Stainless Steel Grapefruit Corer Pat. #1,568,008."

Wizard Pat. Pending Stainless Steel. "This is a two-piece grapefruit sectioner and corer. Manufactured by the Acme Metal Manufacturing Goods Company, Newark, New Jersey.

Stainless steel garnisher. **$4-10**

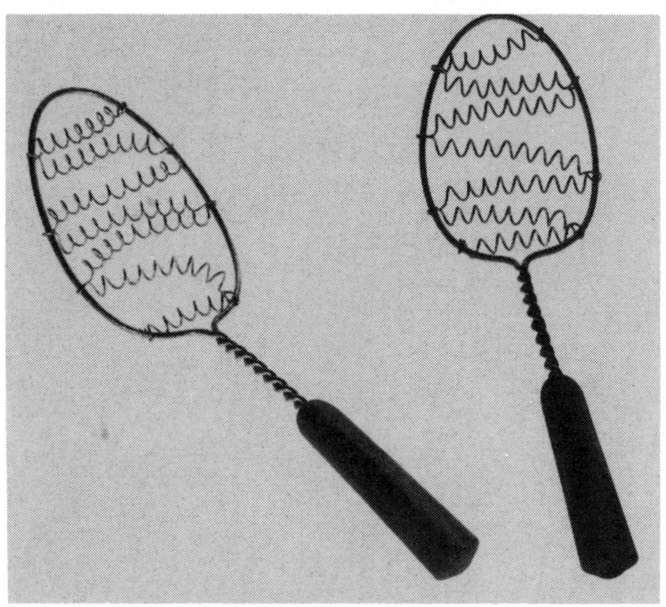

Beaters and whips can be used for beating or mixing anything from pancakes to egg whites.

Unmarked whip with green handle, unmarked whip with variegated color handle. **$2-3.50**

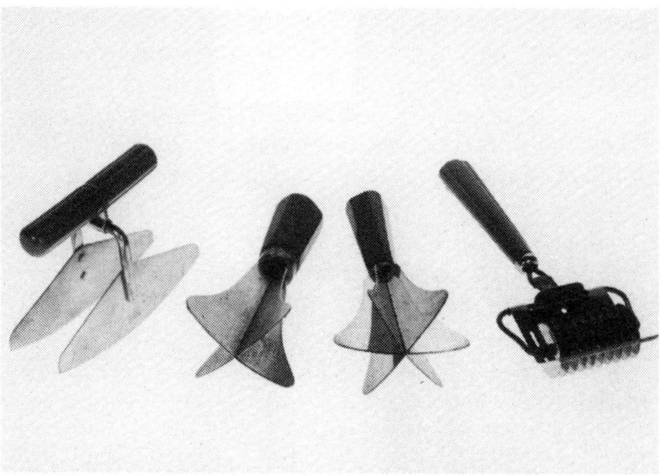

The choppers and mincers illustrated all had red catalin handles except the Androck mincer, which had a green handle. Left to right:

"Androck Stainless Steel." Two-blade chopper.

"Corona Quality St. Steel." Four-blade mincer.

"Androck Stainless." Six-blade mincer.

"Stainless; Made In U.S.A.; Press thumb here." Rotary mincer. **$3-10**

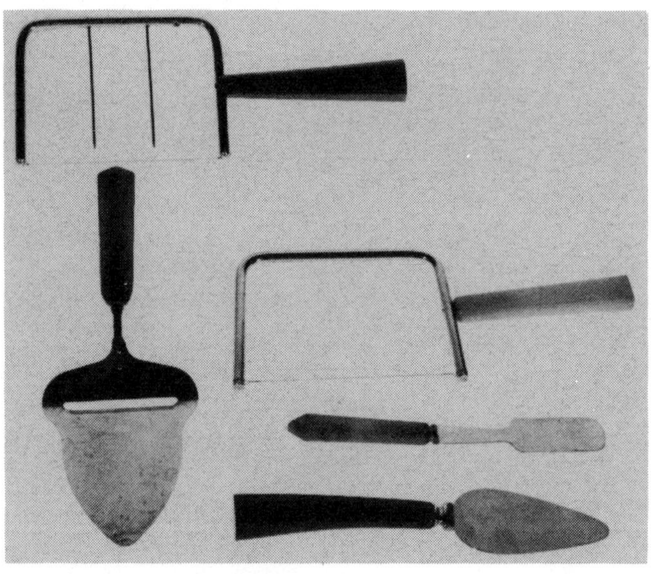

Cheese slicers and spreaders. Top to bottom, left to right:

Vaughan Pat. Apl'd For Chicago U.S.A. Red handle.

Schneider Pat. #1,961,172. Also available in smaller size. Red or green catalin handles. The patent #1,961,172 was a food slicer invented by Cale J. Schneider of Toledo, Ohio. The patent was applied for April 28, 1933, and granted June 5, 1934. "Utensil for severing or dividing...cheese, butter, cooked eggs and the like...."

Unmarked wire slicer with gold catalin handle.

Valley Forge stainless steel with gold catalin handle.

Stainless steel cheese spreader with brown handle. **$2.50-4.50**

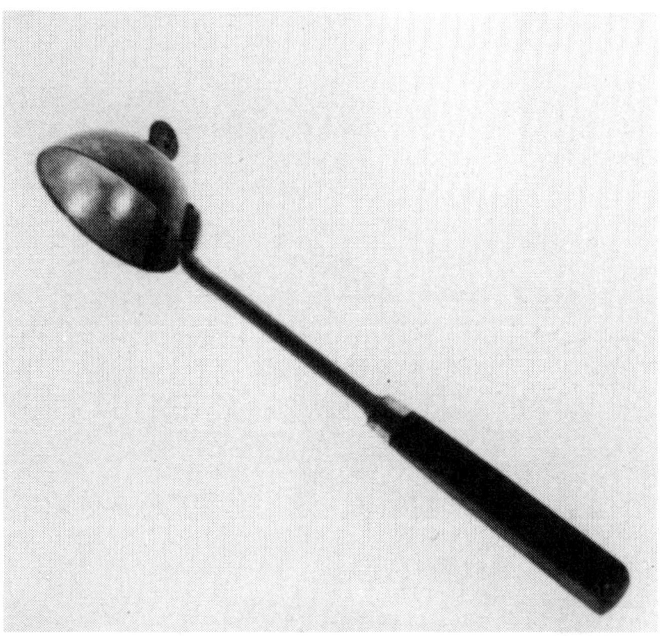

Unmarked ice cream scoop with green catalin handle. The blade is rotated by turning the wing nut. **$10-15**

A variety of knives with catalin handles. Left to right:

Stainless steel cake knife with gold handle.

Quikut stainless cleaver with red handle. A cleaver is a cross between a knife and a hatchet. It is a heavy duty tool that is useful for cutting joints in poultry and meat and for cracking soup bones.

"Marvel Stainless Steel Made In U.S.A." Fruit knife with variegated green-yellow handle.

Henry's stainless knife with serrated edge and gold or red handles. Sometimes called a tomato knife.

"Androck Stainless Made in U.S.A." Green teardrop handle. **$1.50-3**

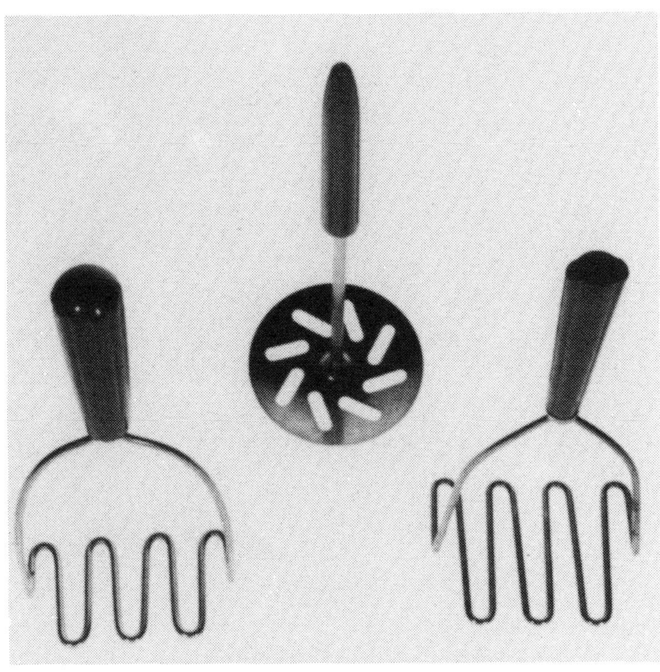

Stainless steel mashers with red catalin handles.

MAKES **CANNING** EASY

The

Foley Food Mill

Juices Bushel of Tomatoes
in 15 minutes

Converts bushel of apples into sauce in 30 minutes. Wonderful for preparing jellies, jams, preserves. Mashes and strains potatoes, carrots, squash, spinach, etc. Fine for straining infants' and invalids' foods. You'll use it daily. 30-day Money-Back Guarantee. Order by mail or send for circular.

Tested and Approved 3210 Good Housekeeping Institute Conducted by Good Housekeeping Magazine

1½ qt. Family Size, $1.50
1 qt. Junior Size, $1.25

FOLEY MFG. CO.
51 Main St., N. E., Minneapolis, Minn.

"Foley Food Mill Juices Bushel of Tomatoes in 15 minutes and converts bushel of apples into sauce in 30 minutes..." says this 1937 advertisement. The food mill mashed and strained and was available in 1½-quart Family Size for $1.50 and 1-quart Junior Size for $1.25. The Foley Manufacturing Company was located at 51 Main Street, Northeast Minneapolis, Minnesota. **$3.50-8.50**

COOKS
DELICIOUS DISHES—
WARMS BABY'S MILK
Quickly . . . Anywhere!

"SUCH a handy little stove," say women everywhere. It *quickly* boils, broils and fries everything from eggs to steaks. Makes scores of tempting dishes, too. Makes delicious toast—boils coffee—heats water for shaving—heats curling irons, pressing irons—warms baby's milk—makes candy. Good for a hundred uses.

Sterno Stove folds flat, compact. Use at home, in hotels, at the office, school, on trips. Fine for camping—cooks hot meals on the trail. Sterno Canned Heat provides the fuel. It's absolutely *safe*. No smoke, sparks, cinders. See the full line of Sterno Utensils at your local dealer's. And send 10¢ (Canada, 10c) TODAY for Introductory Sterno Cook Stove and new STERNO COOK BOOK! Dept. A-4. Sterno Corp. (Est. 1887), 9 East 37th St., New York City.

Your Own Recipe Book

STERNO
Reg. U. S. Pat. Off.
CANNED HEAT

Licensed by U. S. Government for use only as a fuel

Sterno offered a cook stove for only 10¢ in 1929. They said this handy little stove could be used to quickly boil, broil, and fry anything from eggs to steak. It could also be used to make toast, boil water or coffee, heat curling irons and warm baby's milk.

Collapsible stand marked on the bottom: "Sterno Canned Heat. S. Sternau & Co. N.Y. Sterno Stove #5003 Pat. App'd For." On extinguisher: "Sterno Flame Extinguisher Sterno Corp. N.Y. Sterno Canned Heat." On metal pans that have black removable handles: "For use with Sterno Canned Heat. S. Sternau Inc. New York."

"Green collapsible stand marked: "For use with Sterno Canned Heat. Sterno Corporation, New York Patent Applied For." **$4-7.50**

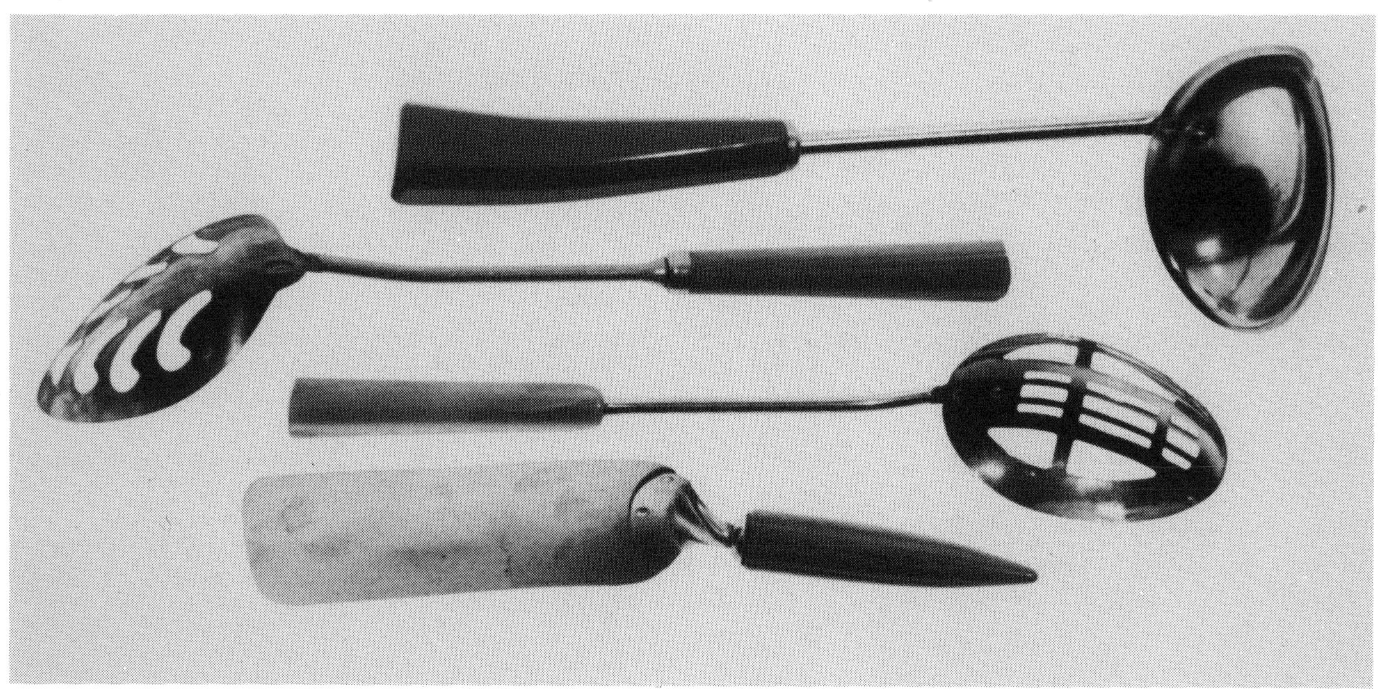

Top to bottom:

Corona Quality stainless steel pouring ladle with red catalin handle.

Stainless steel slotted spoon with red catalin handle.

Unmarked slotted spoon with green catalin handle.

"Androck Stainless Steel Made In U.S.A. Pat. #2,064,136." Turner with red catalin handle. This household utensil was invented by Stover C. Winger of Los Angeles, California, and assigned to Guy H. Hall. It was patented December 15, 1936. "Invention relates to a flexible utensil or spatula...can be used as a pie or cake server, or as a pan scraper or knife...." **$2-5**

Left to right, top to bottom:

Sta-Brite stainless fork with red catalin handle.

Sta-Brite stainless steel knife with red catalin handle.

Sta-Brite stainless steel spoon with red catalin handle.

Unmarked pickle fork with green catalin handle.

"Pat. #1,884,840; Others Pending Made In U.S.A." Syrup jar with green catalin handle, probably from Federal Tool Company.

"Robinson Knife Co. Stainless Steel; Made In U.S.A." Gold catalin knife and fork.

Unmarked lightweight green wooden handles on knife and fork, possibly from a picnic set.

Nasco Stainpruf knife and fork with marbelized wooden handles. **$.50-1.50 each**

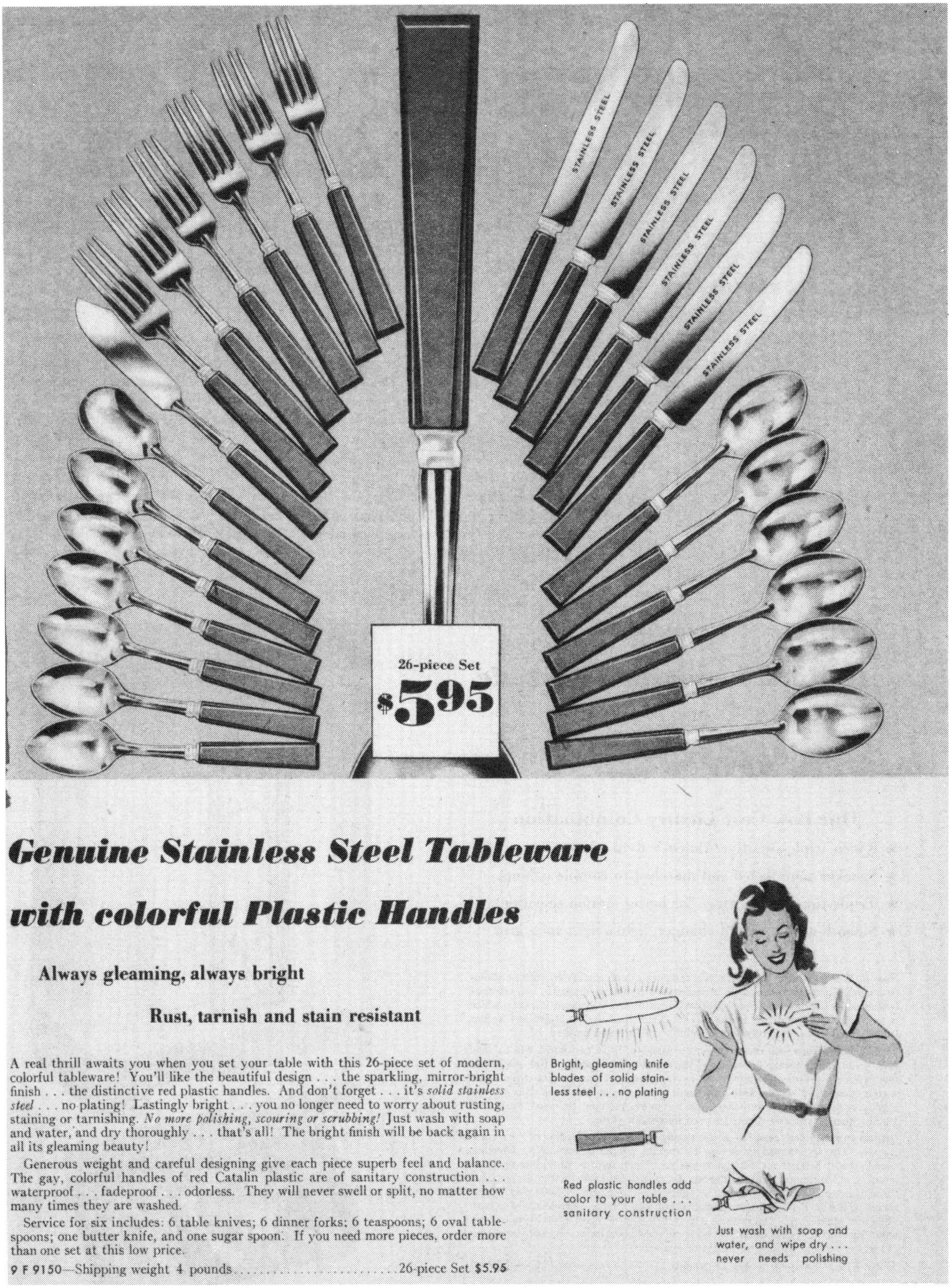

26-piece Set

$5.95

Genuine Stainless Steel Tableware with colorful Plastic Handles

Always gleaming, always bright

Rust, tarnish and stain resistant

A real thrill awaits you when you set your table with this 26-piece set of modern, colorful tableware! You'll like the beautiful design . . . the sparkling, mirror-bright finish . . . the distinctive red plastic handles. And don't forget . . . it's *solid stainless steel* . . . no plating! Lastingly bright . . . you no longer need to worry about rusting, staining or tarnishing. *No more polishing, scouring or scrubbing!* Just wash with soap and water, and dry thoroughly . . . that's all! The bright finish will be back again in all its gleaming beauty!

Generous weight and careful designing give each piece superb feel and balance. The gay, colorful handles of red Catalin plastic are of sanitary construction . . . waterproof . . . fadeproof . . . odorless. They will never swell or split, no matter how many times they are washed.

Service for six includes: 6 table knives; 6 dinner forks; 6 teaspoons; 6 oval tablespoons; one butter knife, and one sugar spoon. If you need more pieces, order more than one set at this low price.

9 F 9150—Shipping weight 4 pounds. . . . . .26-piece Set **$5.95**

Bright, gleaming knife blades of solid stainless steel . . . no plating

Red plastic handles add color to your table . . . sanitary construction

Just wash with soap and water, and wipe dry . . . never needs polishing

Sears Roebuck's 1946 catalog offered a twenty-six-piece set of stainless steel tableware with red catalin plastic handles for $5.95. (Courtesy Sears, Roebuck and Company.)

Average Shipping Weight, 10 Ounces Each

- (A) 11 F 5031—Two Aluminum Jelly Molds.....8c
- (B) 11 F 5290—8-oz. Aluminum Funnel.....8c
- (C) 11 F 5075—Aluminum Egg Slicer.....8c
- (D) 11 F 5297—13-oz. Aluminum Cup.....8c
- (E) 11 F 5016—Aluminum Doughnut Cutter.....8c
- (F) 11 F 5100—8-oz. Aluminum Graduated Cup..8c
- (G) 11 F 5295—Two Aluminum Egg Separators..8c
- (H) 11 F 5300—Pair Small Aluminum Shakers.....8c
- (J) 11 F 5249—Percolator Handle.....8c
- (K) 11 F 3259—Aluminum Egg Poacher.....8c
- (L) 11 F 5270—3 Aluminum Clothes Sprinklers.....8c
- (M) 11 F 5252—Two Glass Percolator Tops.....8c
- (N) 11 F 5321—9x9-Inch Flat Toaster.....8c
- (P) 11 F 5256—Aluminum Tea Ball.....8c
- (R) 11 F 5255—6-cup, Alum. Coffee Ball.....8c
- (S) 11 F 5190—Steel Sink Strainer.....8c
- (T) 11 F 5320—4-sided, Pyramid Toaster.....8c
- (U) 11 F 5110—4 Aluminum Measuring Spoons.8c

Green Handles • Ivory Trimmed • SMART MATCHED

CHOICE 9c EACH

Average Shipping Weight, 9 Ounces Each

- (A) 11 F 5047—11-in. Lipped Pouring Ladle.....9c
- (B) 11 F 5045—11½-inch. Basting Spoon.....9c
- (C) 11 F 5111—Graduated Mixing Spoon.....9c
- (D) 11 F 5265—11-inch long, Round Ladle.....9c
- (E) 11 F 5285—Easy Grip Potato Masher.....9c
- (F) 11 F 5269—Rubber Head Plate Scraper.....9c
- (G) 11 F 5037—½-cup Sugar and Flour Scoop.....9c
- (H) 11 F 5035—11¼-inch Flexible Spatula.....9c
- (J) 11 F 5036—13-inch Cake Turners. 4 slots.....9c
- (K) 11 F 5266—Trowel Shaped Cake Turner.....9c
- (L) 11 F 5261—Long Handle 2-Tine Fork.....9c
- (M) 11 F 5042—11-inch Slotted Spoon.....9c

EVERYDAY KITCHEN TOOLS

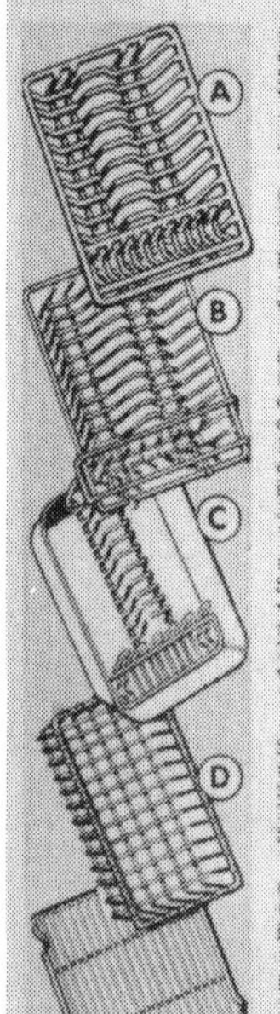

(A) Rubber Covered Dish Drainer Saves breakage. With cutlery tray. 16x12½ in. Shpg. wt., 3 lbs. 4 oz. **11 F 5344. 89c**

(B) Dish Drainer Retinned steel wire. Hinged silverware basket. Size, 16½x12¼x3¾ in. Shpg. wt., 2 lbs. 8 oz. **11 F 5330 23c**

(C) Aluminum Pan Dish Drainer. Special space for plates, dishes, silverware, 16x11x2¼ in. Pan can be used for baking. Shipping weight, 3 lbs. 10 oz. **11 F 5331..98c**

(D) Fruit Basket. Stores fruit and vegetables. Heavily tinned wire. Size, 7x14x3½ in. Shpg. wt., 2 lbs. **11 F 5131..19c**

Egg Basket. Strong heavily tinned wire basket. Securely welded. Size, 7x7 in. 3¼ in. deep. Shpg. wt., 1 lb. **11 F 5130..10c**

(E) Square Cake Cooler. Size, 11x11 in. Shpg. wt., 1 lb. 6 oz. **11 F 5125..19c**

Round Cake Cooler 10-in. diameter Shpg. wt., 1 lb. **11 F 5127...10c**

The Finest Can Opener Ever Made

Fully automatic. Opens any can with speed and neatness. No jagged edges. No spilling. No levers. Put can in place and turn handle. Can is held until handle is reversed. Features of $7.00 commercial openers. Rustless white metal. Hardened steel cutters will remain sharp for years. Shpg. wt., 1 lb. 2 oz. Pat. appl'd for. **11 F 2055..........$1.49**

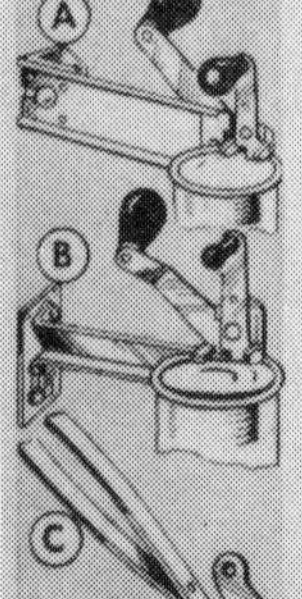

Wall Can Opener (A) Leaves no jagged edges. Steel blade. Nickel plated steel frame. **11 F 5314** Shipping wt., 1 lb. 2 oz.....**65c**

Bargain Opener (B) Holds can securely until released. Similar to 11 F 5314 but lighter. **11 F 5313..** Shpg. wt., 1 lb.....**24c**

Star Can Opener (C) Cuts off top of can. Opens all sizes. Tool steel cutter; green with black trim. 6½ in. long. **11 F 5310** Shpg. wt., 6 oz. **23c**

49c Ball Bearing Egg Beater

Price Was 65c

Made with 8 stainless steel beater wings. Equals beaters sold elsewhere for 79c or more. Strong. Easy running. Quick beating. Will last for years and beat faster and better than any egg beater you have ever used. Made with easy running ball bearings. Handle is enameled in green. Shipping weight, 1 pound 12 ounces. **11 F 5278...49c**

(A) Egg Beater High speed center drive. 8-wing. D-shaped green wood handle. Works quickly and efficiently. Shipping weight, 1 lb. 6 oz. **11 F 2045...29c**

(B) Egg Beater. As above but smaller size. Center drive. 8-wing. Shpg. wt., 1 lb. 2 oz. **11 F 5274...19c**

(C) Bowl and Beater. White opaque stippled glass bowl, graduated. 8-wing beater and cover **chromium plated.** With Black and White enameled wood handle. Shipping wt., 4 lbs. 4 oz. 1-qt. Cap. **11 F 5288..65c**

(D) 1-qt. Bowl and Beater. Clear glass graduated bowl, nickel-plated 4-wing beater. Shipping wt., 4 lbs. 6 oz. **11 F 5271..35c**

1-pt. cap. Shpg. wt., 3 lbs. 2 oz. **11 F 5272...27c**

(E) Noodle Cutter and Mincer. Shpg. wt., 8 oz. **11 F 5073..18c**

(F) Steak Maul. Metal head. Shpg. wt., 1 lb. 12 oz. **11 F 5049..12c**

(G) Serving Fork. Length, 10¼ in. Shpg. wt., 8 oz. **11 F 5260..14c**

(H) Knife Sharpener. Pull knife across steel sharpening discs. Shipping weight, 1 pound. **11 F 5088** Standard quality..**14c**

(J) Table Shakers. Modern design. Alum. Salt and Pepper shakers with black bakelite screw-on base. Shpg. wt., 6 oz. **11 F 2004** Pair..........**19c**

FINEST QUALITY WOODENWARE

Butter Molds

Hard maple. 1-oz. size is individual mold. **State which is wanted.**

11 F 5245

Shape	Cap.	Shpg. Wt.	Each
Round	1 oz.	4 oz.	8c
Round	1 lb.	1 lb. 4 oz.	34c
Oblong	1 lb.	1 lb. 4 oz.	39c

Chopping Bowls

Selected first quality hardwood. **Waxed and polished.**

11 F 5215—State Size.

Diam.	Shpg. Wt.	Each
9 in.	2 lbs.	15c
11 in.	2 lbs. 4 oz.	33c
13 in.	3 lbs. 9 oz.	63c
15 in.	5 lbs. 8 oz.	85c

Knife and Fork Box

Keeps silverware in orderly fashion. Smooth wood with clear lacquer finish. Securely glued.

11 F 5210—State size. **3-compartment.** Shpg. wt., 1 lb. 4 oz.....**18c**

4-compartment. Shipping weight, 1 lb. 12 oz......**27c**

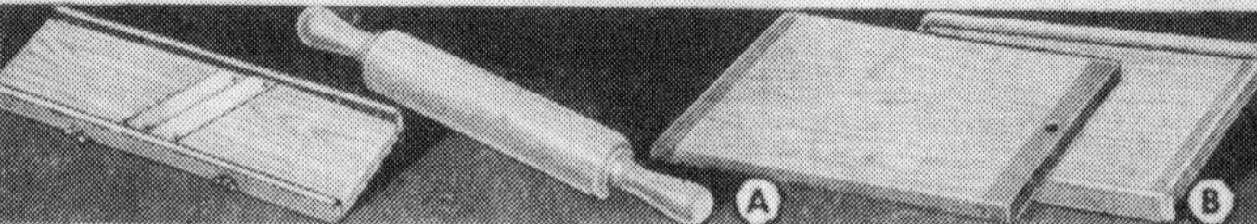

Vegetable Cutter

Selected hardwood frame with two tempered steel knives. Operates quickly... slices evenly. Adjustable. Size, 5⅛x18 in. long.

11 F 5070 Shpg. wt., 2 lbs. 7 oz....**38c**

Rolling Pins

Solid one-piece rolling pin, of hard maple, smoothly sanded, waxed, polished. Diam., 2⅛ in.; length, 19⅜ in. Approved by Good Housekeeping.

11 F 5229—Shpg. wt., 1 lb. 11 oz. **39c**

Same as above but 2½ in. dia. and 17 in. long with **revolving handle.**

11 F 5226—Shpg. wt., 1 lb. 11 oz. ..**23c**

Similar to above but 1⅞x15½ in.

11 F 5224—Shpg. wt., 1 lb. 8 oz.....**9c**

Pastry-Noodle Board

(A) **11 F 5203—Pastry board.** Won't warp. **State size Wanted.**

Size	Shpg. Wt.	Each
14x20 in.	3 lbs. 8 oz.	49c
18x24 in.	5 lbs. 6 oz.	69c

(B) **11 F 5202—Noodle board** with side cleats. Size, 20x27in. Shpg wt., 7lbs. 8oz. **$1.00**

Salad Set

Fork and spoon. Cherry wood, sanded finish. Made in France. Shipping wt., 1 lb. **11 F 5237..23c**

Wood Steak Maul

Hard **white wood.** 12¾-in. length. Head, 49 points. 2⅜ in. square. Made in Germany. Shpg. wt., 1 lb. **11 F 5222....19c**

Potato Masher

Hard white wood. Made in Germany. **11 F 5220** Shipping wt., 14 ounces....**19c**

Meat Board

11 F 5201 Size, 15x7½ in. Shpg. wt., 1 lb. 12 oz. **23c**

Mincing Knife

Double Blade. Stainless steel. 5-inch blades. **11 F 5081** Shpg. wt., 14 oz. **43c**

Single Blade. Stainless steel. 5-inch blade. **11 F 5080** Shpg. wt., 12 oz. **18c**

Plain Wood Spoons

Finest quality **white** wood. Made in Germany.

11 F 5233—State size.
12 in. Shpg. wt., 7 oz.....5c
14 in. Shpg. wt., 8 oz.....8c
16 in. Shpg. wt., 10 oz.....9c

Slotted Wood Spoon

11 F 5230—State size.
12 in. Shpg. wt., 7 oz.....8c
16 in. Shpg. wt., 10 oz.....9c

Butter Paddle

11 F 5246—Hard maple, well shaped and polished. Shipping weight, 12 ounces.....**8c**

Pie Crimper

11 F 5240—White wood. Made in Germany. Shpg. wt., 8 oz.....**15c**

Handy Slicer

11 F 5071—Hardwood frame, fluted steel knife. For fruits and vegetables. Size, 4½x11½ in. Shpg. wt., 1 lb.....**35c**

(F) 11 F 5218—Salt Box Pieced wood box, hinged lid. Made in Germany. Shpg. wt., 1 lb. 8 oz. **39c**

Accurate Dial THERMOMETERS for Every Need

For the Oven. Porcelain enameled base. Baking chart on dial. Shipping weight, 11 ounces. **11 F 5199. 33c**

For the Room. Walnut base. Porcelain enamel dial. Accurate and easy to read. Modern style. Shpg. wt., 10 oz. **11 F 8040.....89c**

For the Refrigerator White enamel with dial of porcelain enamel. Hook for hanging. Shpg. wt., 11 oz. **11 F 5198.. 24c**

For the Bath. It floats. Finished in blue and pink. Non-rusting. Shipping wt., 8 oz. **11 F 8039...33c**

Rubber Mat

For drainboard of sink. Saves breakage. **Either white or green.** 20x14-in. Shpg. wt., 1 lb. 8 oz. **11 F 5333...29c**

Soapstone Griddles

Metal bound with handles.

11 F 7966	Shpg. Wt.	Each
12 in. Round	7 lbs. 8 oz.	$1.29
9x18 in. Oval	8 lbs. 6 oz.	1.45
10¼x20¼ Oval	12 lbs. 8 oz.	1.69

PAGE 490 ☆ SEARS

You'll find chinaware to fit any purse, any taste, among Sears 27 patterns

Sears Roebuck's 1936-1937 catalog shows prices asked for

KITCHEN TOOLS • Green Handles • Ivory Trimming

Average Shipping Weight, 8 Ounces Each

(A) 11 F 6426—Handy Window Squeegee............9c
(B) 11 F 5282—10¾-inch. Batter Whips............9c
(C) 11 F 5279—10½-in. long. Wire Egg Whip............9c
(D) 11 F 2027—10½-in. long. Flesh Fork............9c
(E) 11 F 5309—Anchor Type Can Opener............9c
(F) 11 F 5085—Stainless steel, Parer-Corer............9c
(G) 11 F 5086—Stainless steel Paring Knife............9c
(H) 11 F 5040—Wire Pastry Blender............9c
(J) 11 F 5178—2½-inch. Tea Strainer............9c
(K) 11 F 5181—3⅛-inch. Flat Bottom Tea Strainer............9c
(L) 11 F 5170—3⅛-inch. Round Bottom Tea Strainer............9c
(M) 11 F 5172—Large, 5-inch. Strainers............9c

CHOICE 9c EACH

Average Shipping Weight, 8 Ounces Each

(A) 11 F 5381—Copper Scouring Ball............9c
(B) 11 F 5050—Plier Type Can Opener............9c
(C) 11 F 5397—Copper Scouring Mop............9c
(D) 11 F 5338—4-Wing Egg Beater............9c
(E) 11 F 5284—9-inch. Potato Masher............9c
(F) 11 F 5312—Handy Can Opener............9c
(G) 11 F 5390—Copper Scouring Knob............9c
(H) 11 F 5287—Six Nut Picks............9c
(J) 11 F 5382—Skour Pak Steel Wool............9c
(K) 11 F 5383—Six Steel Wool Balls............9c
(L) 11 F 5286—5-inch. Nut Cracker............9c
(M) 11 F 5046—10-inch. Basting Spoon............9c
(N) 11 F 7818—Two Asbestos Stove Mats............9c
(P) 11 F 5195—Ten Pot Cover Knobs............9c
(R) 11 F 5089—Stone Knife Sharpener............9c
(S) 11 F 6804—Wire Soap Dish............9c
(T) 11 F 6805—18-inch. Towel Bar............9c
(U) 11 F 6800—Wire Tumbler Holder............9c

EXTRA HEAVYWEIGHT RETINNED WARE

Bread Raisers
Extra heavy retinned steel. Seamless footed body. Ventilated cover. Strong handles will last for years.

11 F 4520	Shpg. Wt.	State size
13-Qt.	5 lbs. 10 oz.	$1.09
17-Qt.	8 lbs. 4 oz.	1.25
21-Qt.	9 lbs. 2 oz.	1.45

Dish Pans
Extra heavy retinned steel—seamless. Wide flat rims.

11 F 4523	Shpg. Wt.	State size
13-Qt.	5 lbs. 12 oz.	$0.95
17-Qt.	6 lbs. 4 oz.	1.00
19-Qt.	7 lbs. 11 oz.	1.15

11 F 4524—14-qt. standard quality. Shpg. wt., 4 lbs...79c

Bread Mixers
Kneads and mixes at the same time. Heavy weight.

Bread Making Instructions Included

11 F 04315	Shpg. Wt.	State size.
12-Qt.	10 lbs.	$2.59
20-Qt.	13 lbs.	3.45

(A) 3-Piece Tin Shredder Set. Shreds—Slices—Grates. Heavy tin. Shpg. wt., 1lb. 12oz. 11 F 4356 22c

(B) Tin Grater-Slicer. 4 sides, 7½ in. high. Shpg. wt., 1 lb. 2 oz. 11 F 4357....9c

(C) Covered Tin Pails. State size. 11 F 4359

Cap.	Shpg. Wt.	Ea.
2-Qt.	1 lb. 12 oz.	10c
3-Qt.	2 lbs. 4 oz.	15c

(D) Tin Drinking Cup. About 1-pint cap. Shpg. wt., 12 oz. 11 F 4308....4c

(E) Tin Graduated Measures. State size. 11 F 4400

Cap.	Shpg. Wt.	Price
1 qt.	1 lb.	9c
2 qt.	1 lb. 6 oz.	18c

(F) Heavy Tin Dipper. 1½-Pt. Shipping wt., 1 lb. 4 oz. 11 F 4479.... 13c

(G) 6 Tin Covers and Rack. 9, 9½, 10, 10½, 11, 11½-in. Shipping weight, 2 lbs. 8 oz. 11 F 4307....33c

(H) Tin Pot Covers. 11 F 4304—State size.

Size In.	Shpg. Wt.	Ea.
10 or 11	1 lb.	5c
12 or 13	1 lb. 8 oz.	8c

PRISMATIC PANS—INSURES EVEN BROWNING

11F4433—Biscuit Pans. Wired rims. State size.

Size In.	Shpg. Wt.	Ea.
11x7½x1½	1lb. 4oz.	9c
14x9 x1½	1lb.12oz.	13c

11 F 4424—Cake Pans with cutter. State size.

Size In.	Shpg. Wt.	Ea.
9x1	1 lb.	8c
10x1⅝	1 lb. 2 oz.	10c

11 F 4423—Cake Pans. Plain type. Order 2 or more. Size, 9x1 in. Shpg. wt., 1 lb. ea..4c

11F4431—Cookie Sheets

Size In.	Shpg. Wt.	Ea.
10x14	1 lb. 10 oz.	9c
11x16	1 lb. 14 oz.	13c
12x18	2 lbs. 4 oz.	17c

PRISMATIC PANS—POCKETS GREASE—PREVENTS STICKING

11 F 4425—Jelly Cake Pans. State size.

Size	Shpg. Wt.	Price
9x 9x1½	1 lb. 4 oz.	8c
10x10x2	1 lb. 6 oz.	9c

11 F 4420—Pie Plates—State size.

Diam.	Shpg. wt.	
6x1¼	8 oz....	3c
9x1½	14 oz....	4c
10x1⁷⁄₁₆	1 lb.....	5c

Pie Plate with cutter for removing pies. Size 10x 1⅜ in. Shipping weight, 1 lb. 11 F 4422..8c

11 F 4432—Bread Pans

State size, In.	Shpg. Wt.	Each
9 x5 x2¾	1 lb. 2 oz.	8c
11½x6 x3	1 lb. 4 oz.	9c
13 x4½x2½	1 lb. 8 oz.	10c

4-Piece Spring Cake Pan. With solid bottom, tube bottom, side and clip. Diameter, 9-inch. 3-inch deep. Shipping weight, 1 lb. 11 oz. 11 F 4413....34c

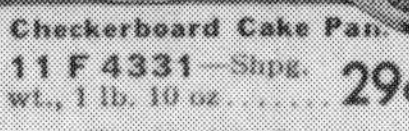

Checkerboard Cake Pan. 11 F 4331—Shpg. wt., 1 lb. 10 oz. 29c

Tin Muffin Pans. 11 F 4428—State size.
6-Cup—Shpg. wt., 1 lb...9c
8-Cup—Shpg. wt., 1 lb..14c
12-Cup—Shpg. wt., 2 lb..19c

Plain Tin Sieve Diam., 12¼-in. 11 F 4355 Shipping weight, 1 lb. 10 oz..14c

Plain Tin Fruit Jar Funnel 11 F 4311 Shipping weight, 10 oz..........5c

6-Pc. Combination Tin Funnel strainer or dipper. 11 F 4313 Shpg. wt., 1 lb..... 13c

Tin Funnels. State size.

11 F 4309	Shpg. Wt.	Ea.
¼-½-1-pt.	10 oz.	5c
1-2-4-qt.	1 lb. 12 oz.	9c

Jelly Molds
Aluminum. 2 each of 6 popular designs. For desserts, jellies, etc. Shpg. wt., 1 lb. 11 F 5019 Set of 12....... 45c

Set of 4 Cups
Measuring cup Set. Standard U.S. sizes. ¼, ⅓, ½ and 1-cup. Rustproof white metal. Shpg. wt., 11 oz. 11 F 5105 4 cups..... 15c

KITCHEN TIME SAVERS

Jiffy Nut Meat Chopper 39c
Attractively enameled top with dainty decoration. Quick action chops cupful in a few seconds. Just the thing for holiday cakes and puddings. Makes easy the usually tedious task of chopping nuts, etc. Glass jar base. State choice of Ivory, Green or Red top. Shpg. wt., 1 lb. 6 oz.
11 F 5025—Complete. 39c

(A) Top Stove Oven. Steel asbestos lined hood with heat indicator. Uses single burner. Has heat equalizer. Size, 12x12x10-in. Shpg. wt., 10 lbs. 11 F 04515....$2.49

(B) Round Oven-ette. Aluminum cover 5¾-in. high. 10 in. steel base. Wire rack included. For top of stove baking. Uses ¾ less fuel than oven. Shipping weight, 4 lbs. 4 oz. 11 F 4516....$1.09

(C) New! Syrup Jug. For table service. Glass base, colored catalin handle. Spring slide operated by thumb, controls flow and positively prevents any dripping. Cap., ½-pt. Shpg. wt., 1 lb. 4 oz. 11 F 2000.....85c

(D) Protector. Green rubber protector keeps tables from being chipped or marred by kitchen clamping devices. Fits all table or shelf tops. Shpg. wt., 4 oz. 11 F 5083.....15c

(E) Coffee Mill Grind your own coffee and be sure it's fresh. New, modern design, easily adjusted to any desired fineness. Glass hopper holds about 1 lb. Black enameled cast iron body. Graduated glass receiver. Ht., 15⅝-in. Shpg. wt., 8 lbs. 14 oz. 11 F 2060....$2.10

(F) Coffee Mill Grinds quickly, easy to adjust. Air tight cover, glass hopper holds about 1-lb. Graduated glass receiver. Ht., 16-in. Shpg. wt., 7 lbs. 11 F 5316.....$1.39

(A) New 3-in-1 Sifter. Three screens—sifts 3 times in one operation. 4-cup size. No gears. 11 F 5022 Shpg. wt., 2 lbs. 79c

(B) Improved Sifter. Operated, with one hand—easy squeezing motion. 2 fine mesh screens. 5-cup size. 11 F 5030 Shpg. wt., 1 lb. 10 oz....69c

(C) Extra Heavy Tin Flour Sifter. Enameled handle and knob. 5-cup size. 11 F 5028 Shipping weight, 1 lb. 10 oz...23c

Bargain Sifter. Made of heavy tin. 1-cup size. 11 F 5029 Shpg. wt., 10 oz. 8c

(D) Bargain Cookie Press. Complete with 4 discs for making cookies of various designs. Tinned body with plunger. 11 F 5044 Shpg. wt., 14 oz. 19c

Stainless Steel Syphon NEW!
Soda water at less than per qt.! Use plain hydrant water and one charge bulb, then screw the top down and you're ready to make delicious sodas and drinks. 11 F 5728—Shipping wt., 2 lbs..........$2.87
11 F 5729—Ten Recharging Bulbs. 1 bulb makes 1-quart. Shpg. wt., 1 lb...54c

(A) Nutcracker Cracks any size nut, leaves nut meats unbroken. Thumb screw for fastening to table. Nickel finish. 11 F 2005 Shpg. wt., 2 lbs. 14 oz. $1.15

(B) Corn Popper Fine wire mesh on heavy frame. Long wire handle and sliding cover. 7x9x2½-in. 11 F 5325 Shpg. wt., 2 lbs. 3 oz..........20c

(C) Round Corn Popper Polished steel. Long handle with sliding cover. Capacity 4 qts. 11 F 5332 Shipping weight, 3 lbs. 6 oz...29c

SEARS ☆ PAGE 491

kitchen tools. (Courtesy Sears, Roebuck and Company.)

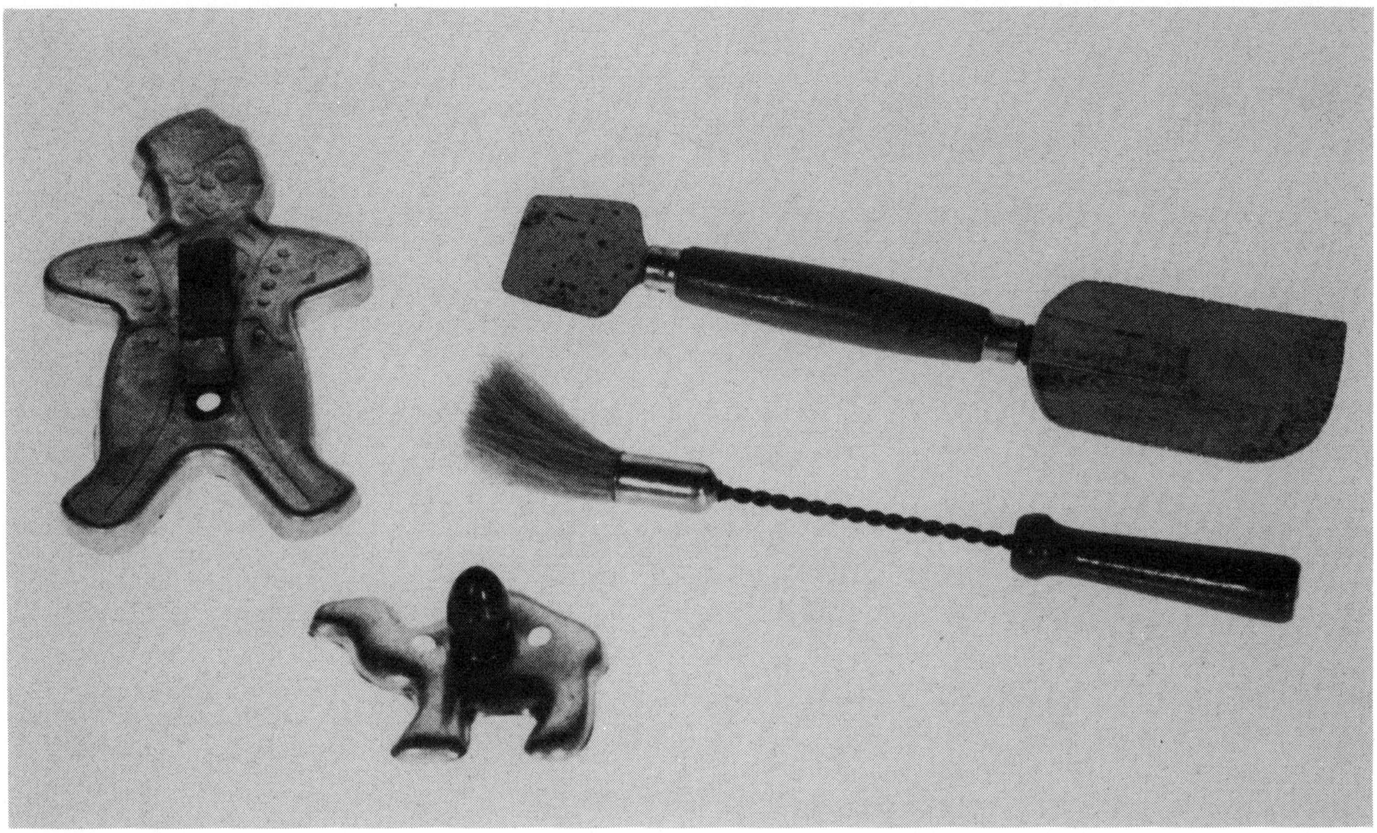

Cookie cutters, brush, and scraper were common gadgets in the kitchen.

Unmarked camel cookie cutter with green wooden handle.

Unmarked man cookie cutter with green metal handle.

Unmarked pastry brush with green wooden handle.

"Kitchen King Bowl & Plate Scraper" marked on rubber end. "Pan Scraper Pat. Pend." on metal end. Green wooden handle. **$1.50-4**

Kraft Sandwich Cutter Set. Bridge playing was an extremely popular pastime in the 1930s. This novelty set has green enameled wooden handles. **$6.50-9 with box**

Colored Enameled Handled Tools and Gadgets

Baking tools. "Kraft Sandwich Cutter Set Takes The Trick At Card Party Luncheons" (on each side).

On back of box: Kraft Sandwich Recipes for dainty luncheons.

> Open Face Sandwiches — Slice white bread thin; cut with Kraft cutters. Spread clubs with Kraft Cream Cheese Relish, garnish with a slice of stuffed olive. Spread hearts with Kraft Pimento Cream Spread, garnish with pimento. Spread diamonds with Kraft Pineapple Cream Spread, garnish with maraschino cherry. Spread spades with Kraft Roquefort Spread, garnish with a tiny sprig of parsley.
>
> Hot Pineapple Cream Dainties — Roll baking powder biscuit dough ¼ inch thick; cut with Kraft cutters; bake in a hot oven 425 degrees. Split each biscuit, add a filling of Kraft Pineapple Cream Spread, put together again and serve hot.
>
> Roquefort Crispies — Slice rye bread thin, cut with Kraft Cutters; toast on one side. Spread untoasted side with Kraft Roquefort Cream Spread. Serve immediately. Home Economics Department. Kraft-Phenix Cheese Corporation, Chicago.

A Taylor advertisement said: "Cook By Temperature say all modern cook books....Cook By Taylor say all modern cooks. For success every time, don't guess — know that the temperature of your oven is exactly right...." Taylor Instruments also made candy and deep fat thermometers.

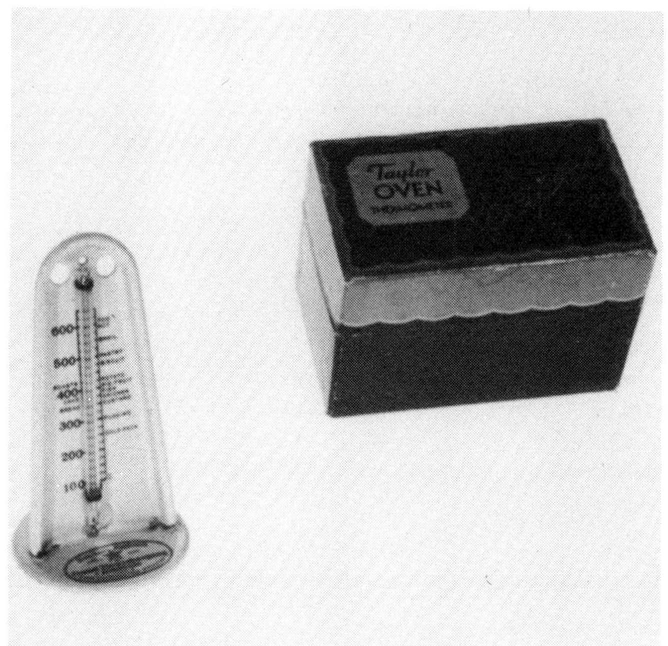

The easy-to-read Taylor oven thermometer and recipe file box sold for $2 in 1937. **$1.50-3.50**

Beaters and whippers. Beaters are one of the few pieces of small equipment that have constant and varied use. They are used to mix ingredients for batters and sauces, to whip cream, and to beat egg whites. There was a variety of beaters, whisks, and whips sold during the 1930s.

The instruction sheet for the Aero-Whip said it was fast and easy to clean. It gave directions for whipping cream; mixing dry flour with water or milk for gravies, etc.; beating eggs; mixing batter for French toast; mixing formulas for babies; and mixing health drinks and ice drinks. It was one of the most useful tools in the kitchen.

Can openers. On box:

Vaughan's "Drop-A-Way" Pat. 2,173,159.

Vaughan's Safety Roll Jr. No. 25 Wall Model Can Opener opens round, square & oval cans with standard rims....

(1) Place rim of can over gear wheel.

(2) Pull solid metal handle upward forcing shearing blade through top of can just inside top rim.

(3) Turn long handle forward until top of can is completely removed. To release can, push down all-metal handle.

Vaughan Novelty Mfg. Co. Inc.
3211-25 Carroll Ave.
Chicago, U.S.A.

On box:

The Sealer that Seals! SEAL KING U.S. Pat. No. 1943470. (Directions): Screw on cap. Adjust device over cap, hooking plate under lip of jar. Engage clip with top of cap. Pull lever toward handle bar, placing wheel on edge of cap. Bear down lightly on handle,

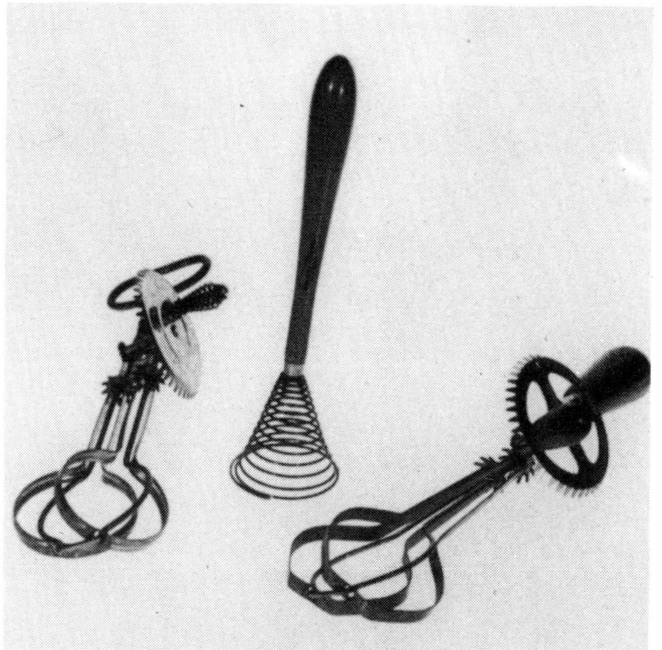

Left to right:

A. & J. rotary beater with green metal handle.

Fluffy Beater whisk with green wooden handle. **$2-7.50**

"Automatic Wire Goods Mfg. Co. Inc. U.S.A." Rotary beater with red wooden handle.

Aero-Whip, box, and instructions. On lablel: "Aero-Whip — Patent Applied For. It's spatter proof. Cream Whipper. The Fletcher, Terry Company Forrestville, Conn. U.S.A." Cream-colored plastic with a red plastic top. Marked on the top: "Fletcher — Terry Co. Pat. Appl'd For — Aero-Whip #50; Forrestville, Conn. U.S.A." **$2-4.50**

pull toward you and go completely around edge of cup.

A Valuable Canning Maid.

Aurora Precision Devices P.O. Box 365 Aurora, Illinois.

No Leaks and Spoilage!

No Loosely Sealed Jars!

No More Throwing Away Old Covers!

No More Rough Edges!

Let SEAL KING Protect Your Canned Goods.

Inventor Walter Fabrick of Elgin, Illinois, claimed his invention was "Inexpensive to manufacture, easy to handle and manipulate, thoroughly efficient and reliable...." The application was filed in February, 1932, and patent was granted January 16, 1943. It has a green wooden handle.

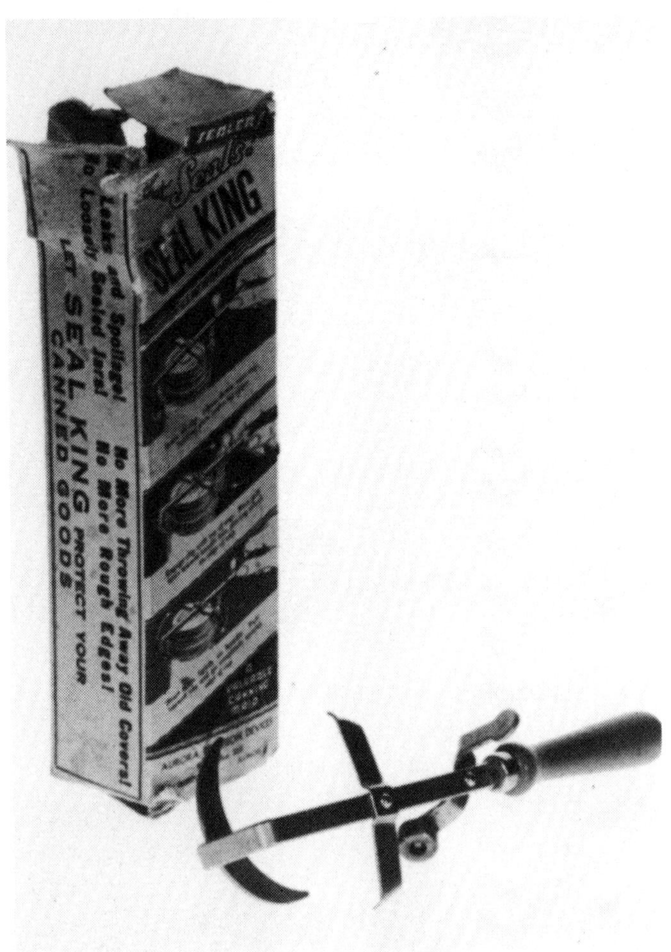

Jar sealer and tightener, box. Marked on sealer: "W. J. Fabrick Elgin, Ill. U.S.A. Pat. **$3.50-6.50 with box**

Can openers with vacuum cap removers. This type of can opener is durable, but it does leave a sharp, rough edge. Left to right:

Unmarked, with green wooden handle.

"Allaround Line; Made In U.S.A." Green wooden handle.

Kut-Ezy Pat. Pend. Lamont N.Y.C. "Red wooden handle.

"Super-Tric Pat. Pend." Bottle and can opener and knife sharpener with green wooden handle.

Androck. Green with two white bands on handle. **$1-3**

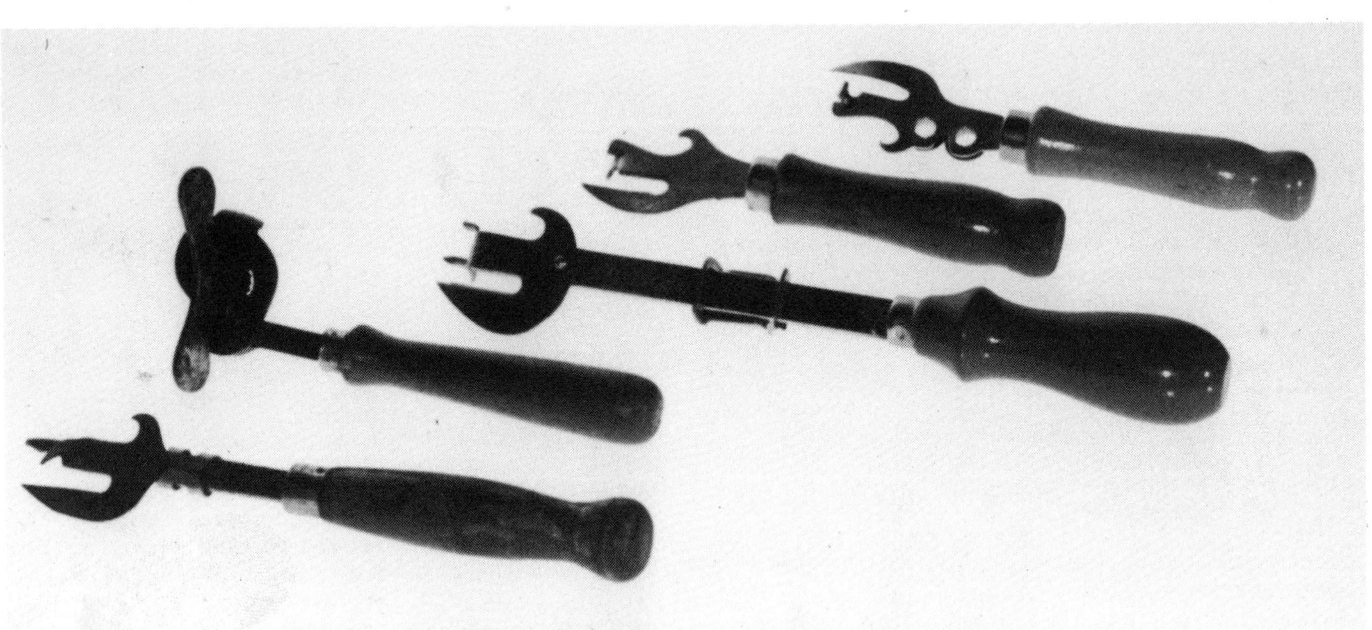

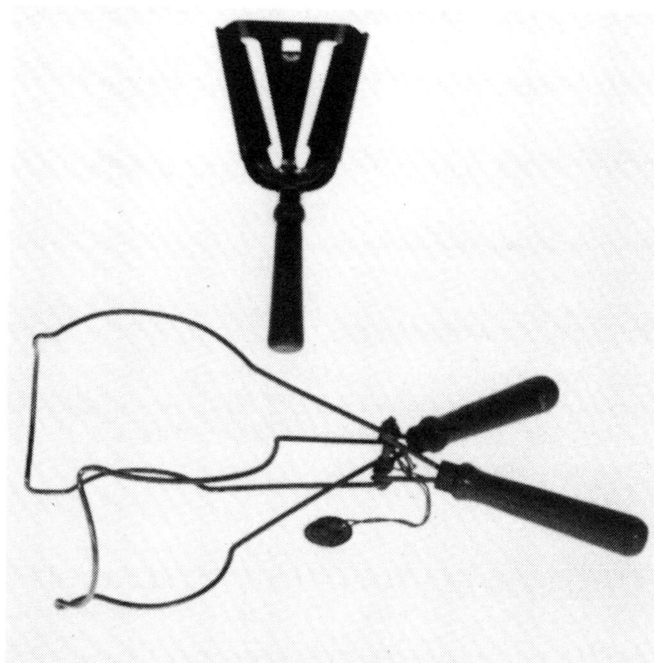

"Everedy Cap-Master; Frederick, Md. U.S.A." This is a jar opener and wrench with a green wooden handle.

"Pat. Pend. For pints and quarts." This jar opener with green wooden handle has a pricetag attached that says "Van Camp." **$3-7.50**

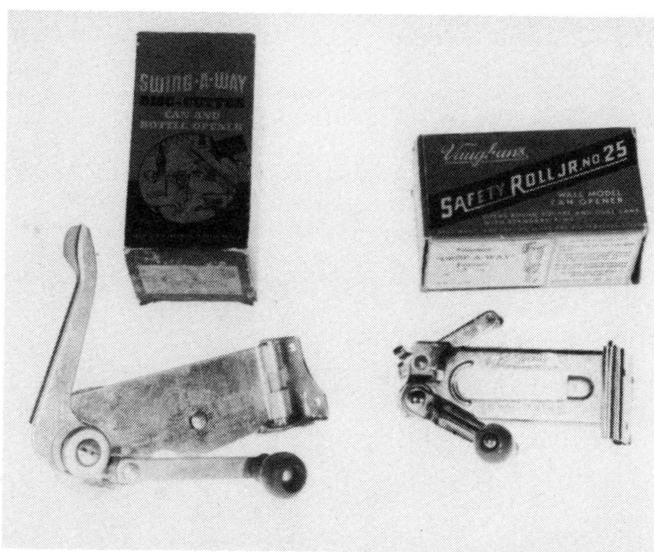

Left to right:

Marked on can opener: "Vaughan's Safety Roll No. 25 wall model can opener. Pat. No. 1,834,277 others Pend." This can opener was patented in 1939 and has a red wooden enameled handle.

Marked on can opener: "Swing-A-Way Can Opener Pat. 2,102,174 Steel Products Mfg. Co. St. Louis, Mo. U.S.A."

On front of box: "Swing-A-Way Disc Cutter Can and Bottle Opener. Swings back flat against the wall. Do it the safe easy way with Swing-A-Way." The patent was granted in 1937. The can opener has a red wooden handle. **$3.50-6.50**

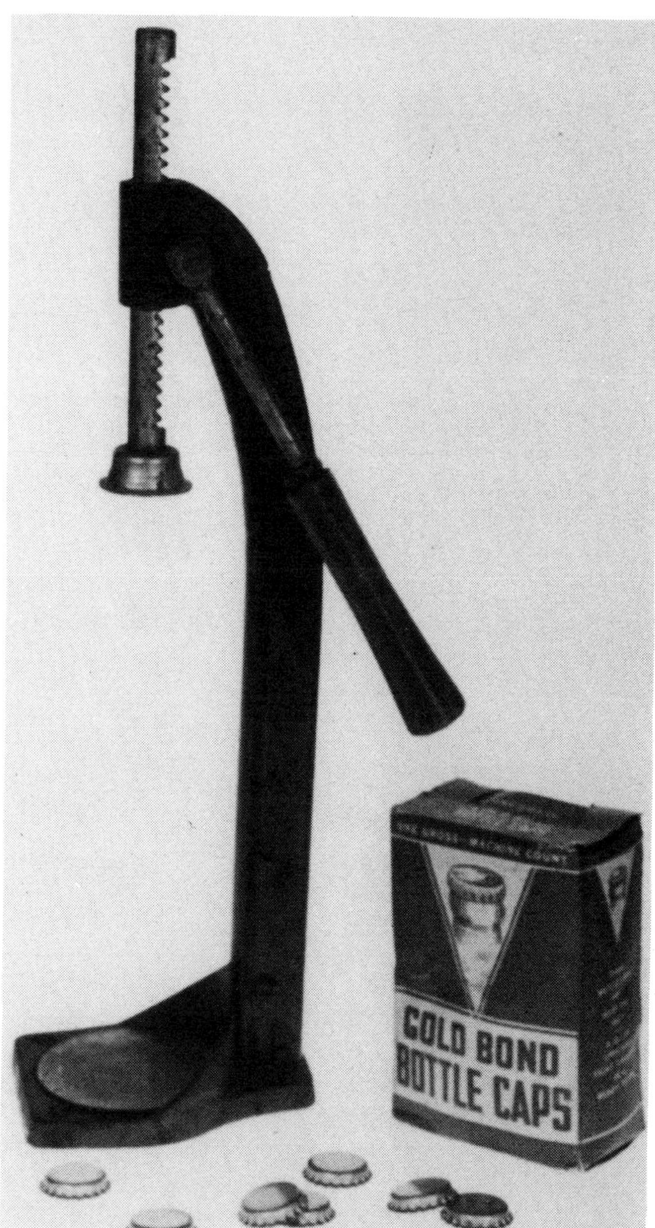

The bottle capper is marked: "E (in a diamond); Made In U.S.A." The original price, $2.79 is still on it. It was made by the Everedy Company of red metal. **$5-9**

Left to right: Seeco stainless steel single-blade chopper with blue wooden handle.

"Samson Stainless Steel Made In U.S.A." Double-blade chopper with green wooden handle. **$2-8.50**

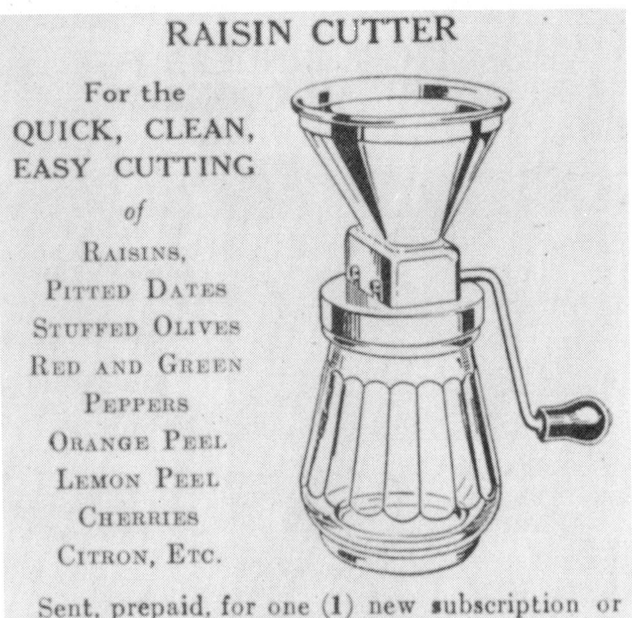

A rotary raisin cutter could be also used for cutting pitted dates, stuffed olives, red and green peppers, orange and lemon peel, cherries, citron, etc. This cutter would have been sent prepaid for one new subscription to the *Boston Cooking School* magazine, or for 75¢. **$6-10**

The METCO Food Grater was a new grater, complete with self-contained bowl, in 1936. **$3.25-10**

The box is marked on top: "Vaughan's Improved Pea Huller & Bean Slicer #550. A Kitchen Aid To Every Housewife. Hulls Lima Beans Perfectly."

On side: "Speedy & Easy! Perfect Kitchen Aid For Shelling & Slicing! Now, you can serve vegetables in a delightfully different shape...slice beets, carrots, apples, potatoes and whole vegetable kingdom. Marvelous shoestring potatoes. For shelling lima beans, peas, etc., you merely change a small roller. So simple a child can use it. Make canning easy with this time saver." It has a black wooden handle.

Juicers. Exerpts from the Knapp Orange Juicer booklet:

> Knapp's Orange Juicer fills a long felt need. It gets all the juice out of oranges, lemons and limes — to the last drop.
>
> It extracts about 15% to 25% extra juice out of each orange, or about as much juice from five oranges as can be obtained from six oranges with old methods....
>
> Knapp's Orange Juicer is easily operated by hand and does its work better than devices that cost several times as much.
>
> It is made of aluminum — metal on which citric acid has no effect — the metal which is easiest of all to clean...
>
> Knapp's Orange Juicer is both efficient and economical. It is sanitary — your hands do not touch the juice; and it is always ready because it is so simple that it can't get out of order.
>
> ...is a necessity for the home, the party or picnic.

Turners. Often referred to as spatulas today, have many uses. These include removing cookies from baking sheets, turning hamburgers and pancakes. The perforated turners are good for lifting foods that need to be drained.

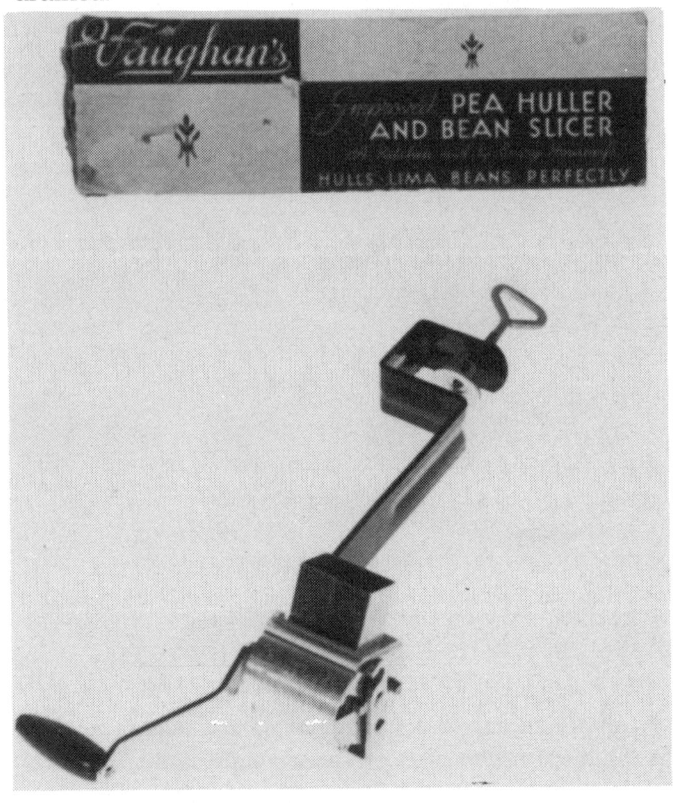

"Vaughan's Improved Pea Huller and Bean Slicer. Pat. Pend. Vaughan's, Chicago." (Refer to pages 41 and 55 of *Kitchens and Gadgets* for the history of the manufacturer.) **$10-28 complete**

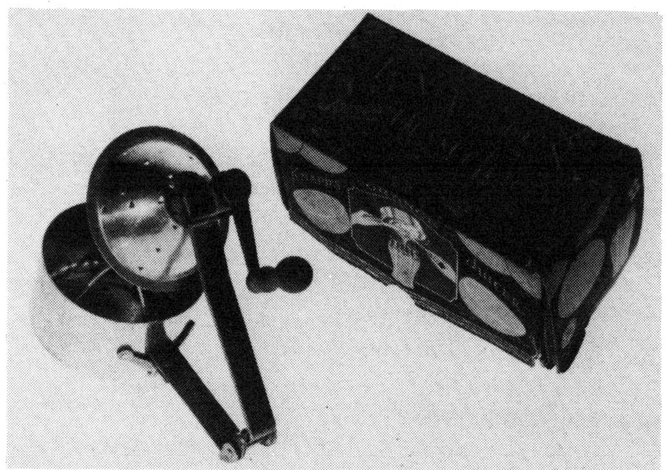

"Knapp's Orange Juicer Pat. Pend. Do Not Press Here" (on natural wooden handle). On the box on top: "KNAPP'S Famous Orange Juicer Pat. Pend. Knapp-Monarch Co., Inc. Saint Louis — U.S.A." **$3.50-9**

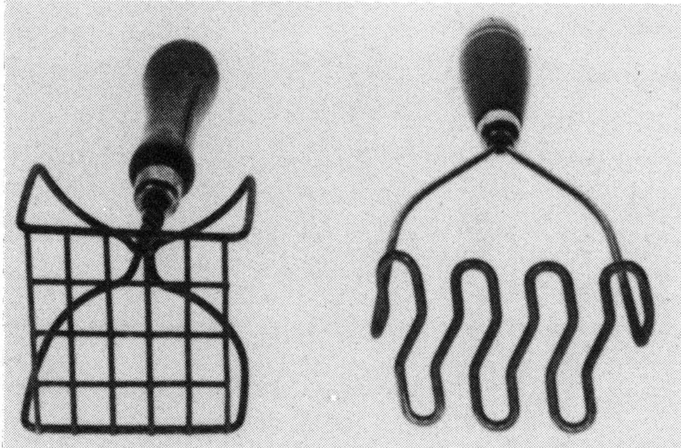

The most common type of potato masher has the zigzag wire attached to the handle. The other masher with the twisted wire base may mash well, but it is hard to clean. Left to right:

Unmarked, but probably A. & J. Has green wooden handle with ivory bands.

Unmarked, with green wooden handle and blue tip. **$2.50-4**

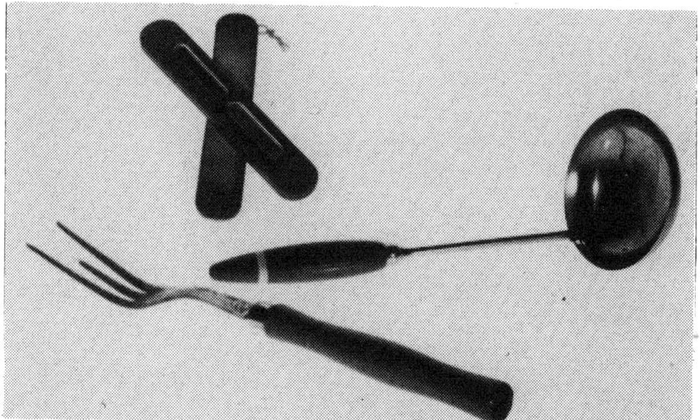

GMT. Company, Germany. Five-minute timer of green wood.

Vaughan, Chicago. Fork has green wooden handle.

A. & J. Ladle has blue wooden handle with white band. **$3-5**

Metal wire lifter and slotted spoons with green wooden handles were useful for lifting and draining foods and vegetables. Left to right:

Samson stainless steel.

Androck.

Unmarked.

Unmarked. Could be used to lift spaghetti. **$3-6**

The first three turners from the left are A. & J. with green wooden handles. The fourth is from Rumford, The Wholesome Baking Powder. **$3-5**

Heavy foods in hot weather steal your pep
New food-drink supplies needed nourishment

WHEN you eat heavy foods in hot weather, do you feel uncomfortable, drowsy, no ambition for work or play? Take Nature's hint. Give your stomach a rest.

TODDY, a remarkable food-drink, makes this possible. No waiting for heavy foods to digest. Takes but a minute to make and drink. Digests almost instantly—so that you can go right out and play golf, tennis, baseball, with renewed vigor and vim—and with no distressing effects.

Most people regard milk as nature's most perfect food; the most nourishing; the most digestible. A comparison of TODDY with milk discloses startling facts. Not only is TODDY easier to digest than milk, but it provides practically twice as much nourishment.

One glass of TODDY has three times as many carbohydrates as a glass of milk. It contains 60% more protein (tissue-builder), 70% more calories, 65% more mineral matter (needed for nerve, bone, and blood), and is richer in vitamines—those mysterious elements so essential to good health.

A glass of TODDY has more food value in calories than big 8-ounce servings of oatmeal and cream, or beef stew.

Induces Refreshing Sleep

TODDY quickly nourishes tired nerves. That's why a cup of hot TODDY before retiring brings restful sleep. While you sleep, TODDY continues its restorative work. You awaken refreshed; eager to tackle your daily duties.

Doctors recognize Barley Malt Extract, the base of TODDY, as one of the best body-building foods. It is *very rapidly* absorbed, feeding nerves and muscles *quickly*. TODDY brings it to you in a delicious drink—equally good hot or cold. Thousands prefer it to tea or coffee, not only because the latter have no food value and contain an alkaloid that affects the nerves, but because *they like TODDY better*.

Not only are my children enthused with TODDY as their regular morning and evening drink, but I have found a vast difference in their increase in weight.
H. A. Bell
1649 Cumberland Rd.
Cleveland Heights, O.

Physicians Recommend TODDY

TODDY is not a medicine but a delicious and healthful food-drink for everybody every day. Hospitals and sanitariums serve it. TODDY is especially beneficial for nursing mothers, anemic children, convalescents, the aged, and for all run-down, tired, and nervous conditions.

Try TODDY Today

—and you'll feel like a new person in a few days. Mail the coupon for generous sample, *free*.

Grocers and Druggists sell TODDY

Maltop, Inc., 1205 Broadway, Buffalo, N. Y.
Please send me generous sample of TODDY free:
Name..........
Street..........
Town.......... State..........

A 1926 advertisement for Toddy's "A Meal in a Glass" has illustrated "Toddy" with a golf club. Toddy was a food drink that could be served hot or cold. It could be made in a minute, digested almost instantly, and it even induced restful sleep. It was made by Maltop, Inc., Buffalo, New York.

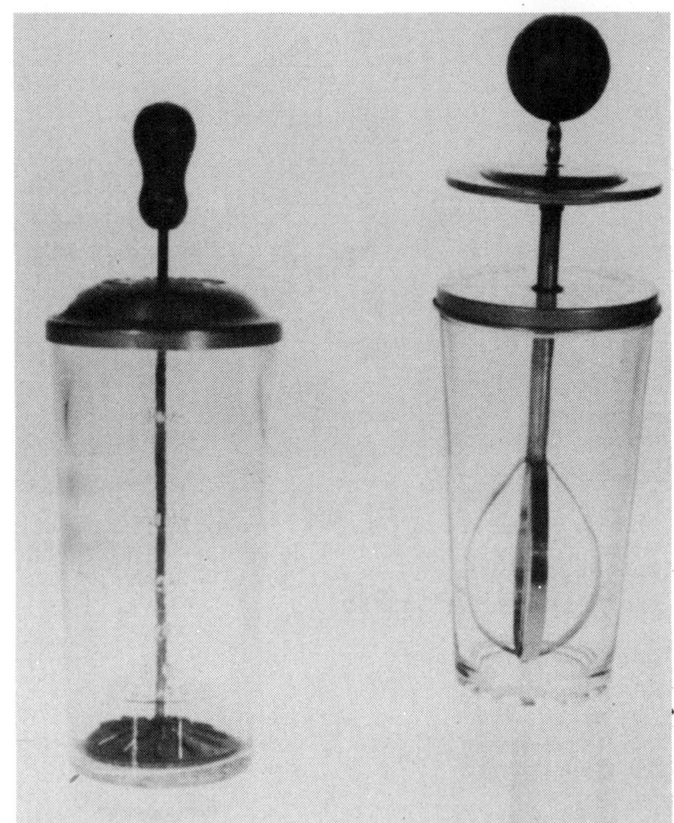

Left to right:

The lid says: "Toddy mixer takes ten seconds." The bottom says: "A meal in a glass." It has a green wooden knob.

"Jiffy-Mixer Made In U.S.A. Pat. No. 2,181,833." This mechanical action mixer, patented in 1939, has a red wooden knob. **$2.50-5**

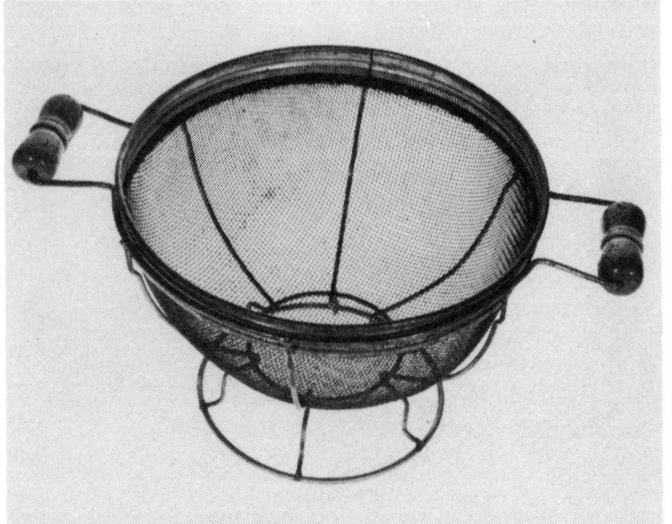

Unmarked colander strainer with green wooden handles and three ivory bands. "Speedier and more efficient than the ordinary colanders. Can be used for steaming rice, macaroni, etc. Detachable bowl. Strainer easily cleaned...." The George Worthington Company, 1936. **$6-10**

Unmarked rotating brush for a container larger than a quart milk bottle; green wooden handle. It has been suggested that this brush would have worked well to clean bedsprings.

Unmarked dishmop with green wooden handle.

Regal United trademark, "Reg. Made In U.S.A." on other side: "U.S. Mfg. Corp. Decator, Ill." The fly swatter is wire mesh with a blue wooden handle. Refer to pages 41 and 54 in *Kitchens and Gadgets*. **$2-6**

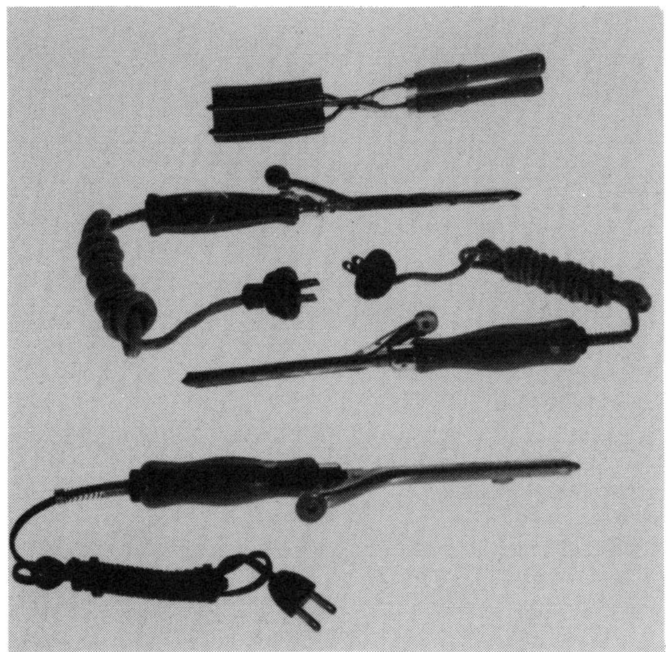

Curling irons, with green handles, were an important part of a lady's grooming. It's interesting that they have gained popularity once again. Top to bottom:

Unmarked non-electric crimper with two handles.

"Electrex-United Drug Co. Boston, Mass. Cat. No. C18." The curling iron has an on-off switch, plastic cool button, and cloth cord.

"110V. & 15W." On paper label: "Duro."

On label: "U.S. Pat. #2,094,858 Made In U.S.A.; Penco 371a series 12 W or 110 volts AC only; U.L. seal."

Warren H. Stansberry assigned his "Process Of Making A Curling Iron" to the Peerless Novelty Company, Grand Haven, Michigan. It was patented October 5, 1937. **$2-10**

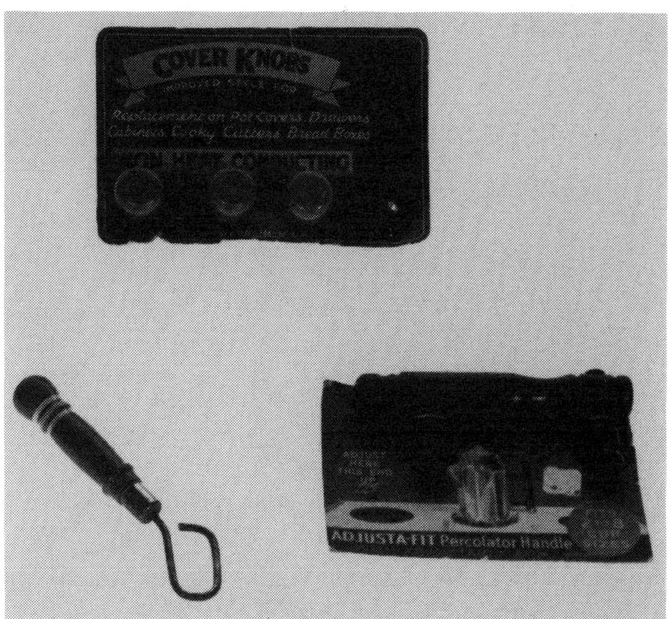

Pot or lid lifter with unmarked green wooden handle. It was used for pots that had bale handles and lids with rings for lifting instead of heat-resistant knobs.

Unmarked green wooden pot knobs. The card the knobs are on is marked: "COVER KNOBS/Improved Style For Replacement on/Pot Covers, Drawers, Cabinets, Cooky Cutters, Bread Boxes./Non Heat Conducting Rust Resistant/Made In U.S.A."

Unmarked black wooden percolator handle. On card: "Adjusta-Fit Percolator Handle With Adjustable Arm Fits 2 to 8 cup sizes." **$1-3.50**

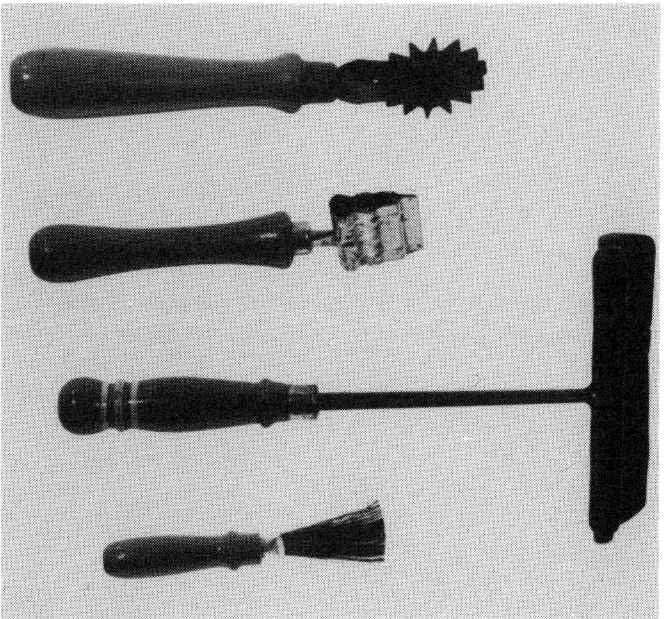

Top to bottom:

Unmarked green-handled leather working tool, often thought to be a kitchen tool.

"W. Munro Mfg. Cam. N.J. Pat. Apd. U.S.A." This holds a razor and is used to scrape windows. It has a green wooden handle.

Unmarked rubber squeegee with green wooden handle, used to clean windows.

Unmarked wire brush with green wooden handle used to clean hairbrushes. Often mistaken for a sink brush. **$2-4**

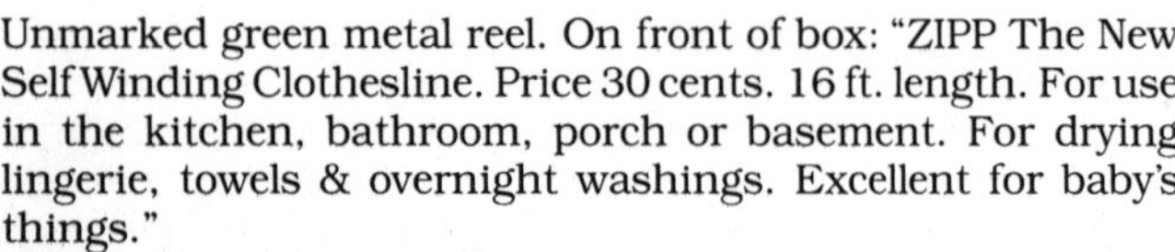
Unmarked green metal reel. On front of box: "ZIPP The New Self Winding Clothesline. Price 30 cents. 16 ft. length. For use in the kitchen, bathroom, porch or basement. For drying lingerie, towels & overnight washings. Excellent for baby's things."

On back: "Something new in a clothes line. Mfg. by Columbus Spring & Specialty Co. Columbus, Ohio U.S.A." **$3.50-6**

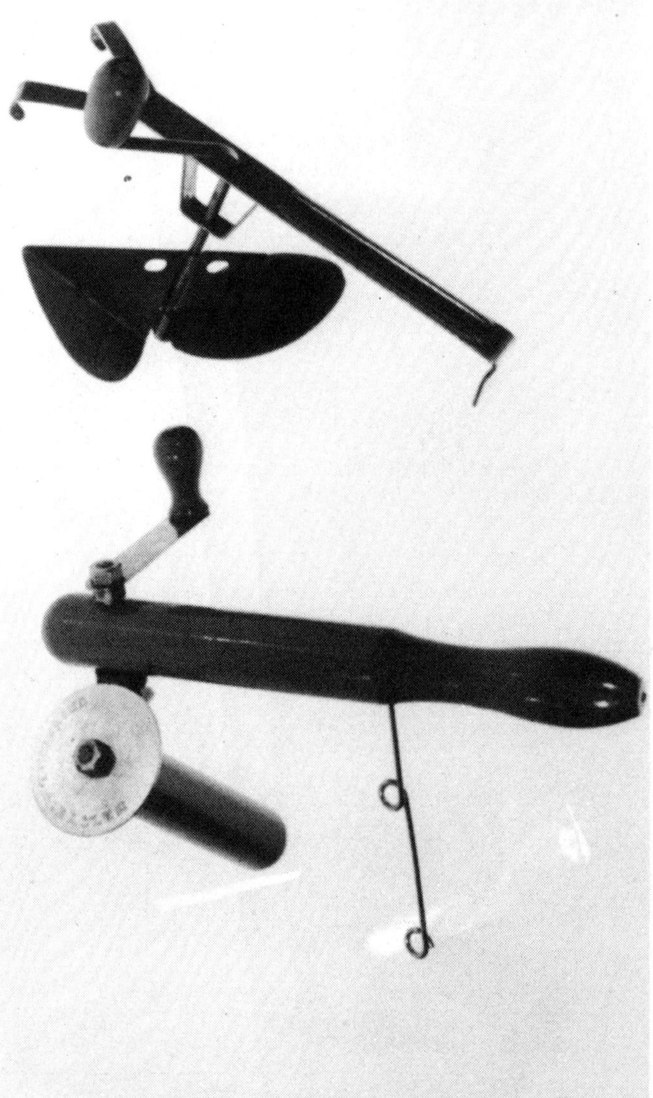

Top to bottom:

"A. & J. Made In U. S. America." This is used by clamping it on a strainer which, when complete, is called a revolving strainer. Often this type of rotator blade is seen by itself for sale at shows. **$1.50-4**

Universal baller. This is used to wind skeins of yarn. **$6-10**

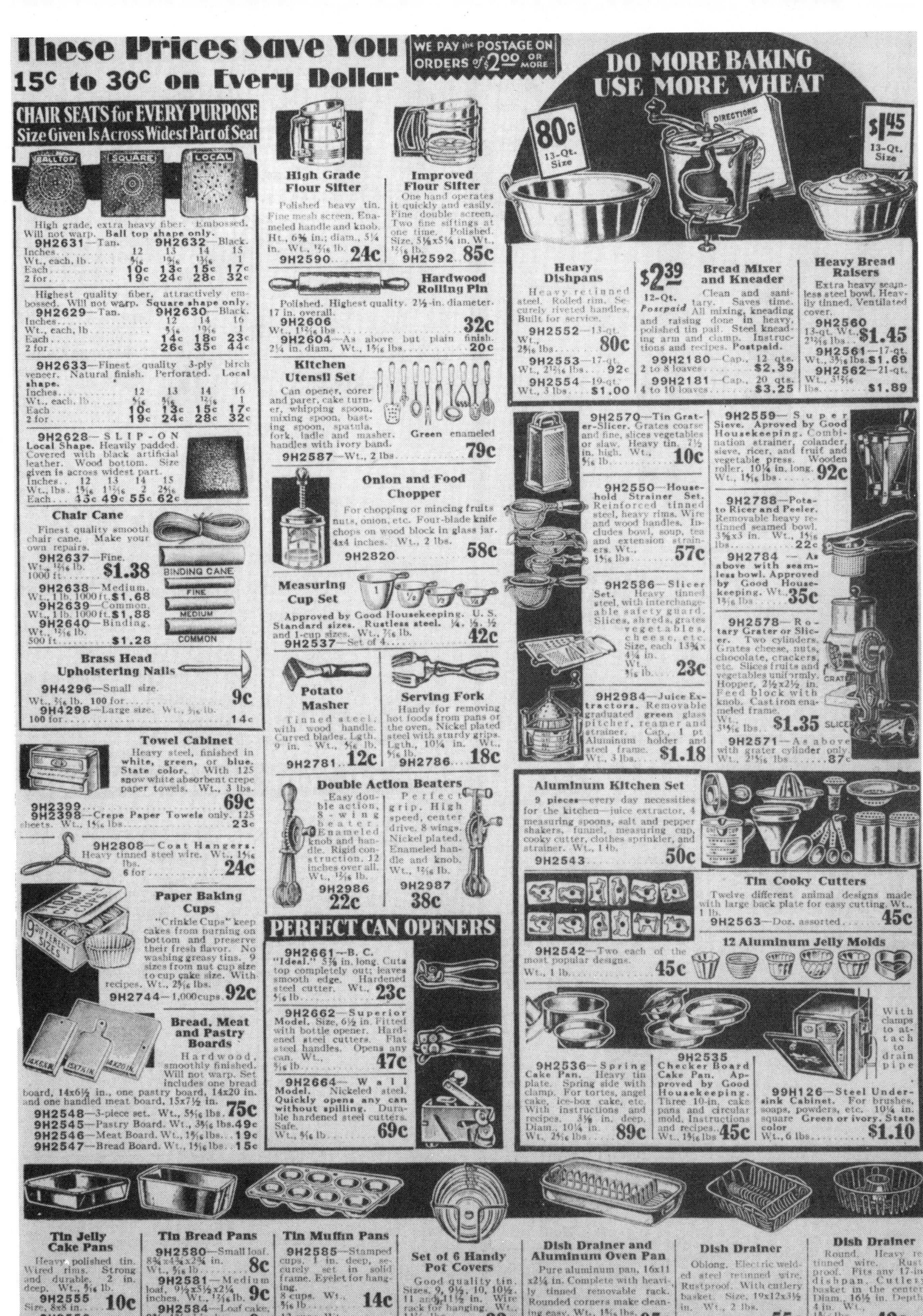

A 1932 Sears Roebuck sampling of kitchen items with hard-to-believe prices. (Courtesy Sears, Roebuck and Company.)

Ritz Kitchen Tools

Each utensil is brilliantly nickel plated and fitted with a contrasting black molded bakelite "Skyline" handle tipped with polished virgin aluminum molded permanently into the handle. The handles cannot come off—they cannot overheat, break, chip or scar with the ordinary use. There is no enamel to chip off and water cannot swell or crack them. A neat circular ridge on the handle insures a firm grip in the hand.

Scraper Spoons

Plain, squared on end and sides to scrape corners of pans. Length overall, 12 ins. One dozen in a carton; weight, 3¼ lbs.

No. **507** Scraper Spoons....per Doz. **2.40**

Scraper Spoons

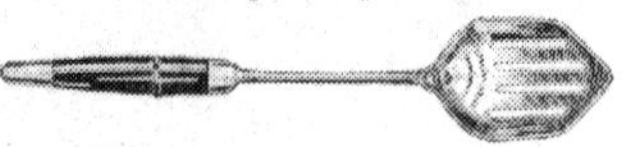

Slotted, squared on end and sides to scrape corners of pans. Length overall, 12 ins. One dozen in a carton; weight, 3¼ lbs.

No. **520** Scraper Spoons....per Doz. **2.40**

Pouring Ladles

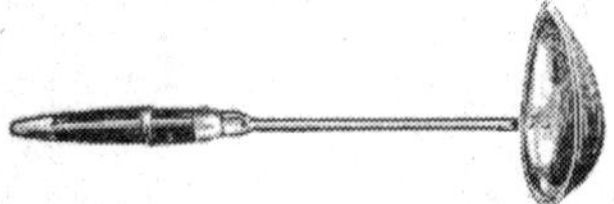

New style, egg shaped for easy pouring. Length overall, 12¾ ins. One dozen in a carton; weight, 3¾ lbs.

No. **546** Pouring Ladles....per Doz. **2.40**

Batter Whips

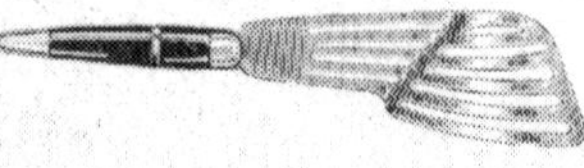

New style, curved to fit bottom of bowls. Length overall, 11¾ ins. One dozen in a carton; weight, 2¼ lbs.

No. **550** Batter Whips.....per Doz. **2.40**

Cake Turners

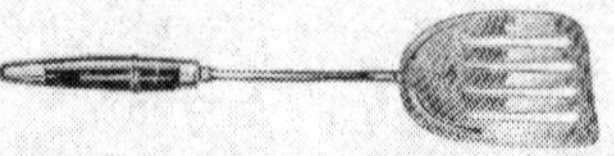

Perforated with streamline slots. Length overall, 13¾ ins. One dozen in a carton; weight, 3¼ lbs.

No. **530** Cake Turners.....per Doz. **2.40**

Kitchen Tools

Offset shank, new modernistic design. Length overall, 12½ ins. One dozen in a carton; weight, 2¾ lbs.

No. **517** Kitchen Tools.....per Doz. **2.40**

Plate Scrapers

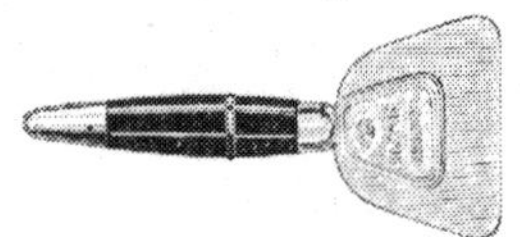

White rubber cast on metal spine. Length overall, 5½ ins. One in a cellophane envelope, one dozen in a carton; weight, 1¾ lbs.

No. **532** Plate Scraper.....per Doz. **2.40**

Two Tine Forks

Securely fastened to shank. Length, 13 ins. One dozen in a carton; weight, 2¾ lbs.

No. **538** Two Tine Forks....per Doz. **2.40**

Potato Mashers

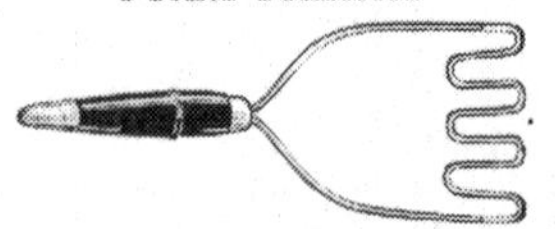

Four loops, bright finish. Heavily plated wire. Length overall, 9½ ins. One dozen in a carton; weight, 3 lbs.

No. **504** Potato Mashers..per Doz. **2.40**

Narrow Spatulas

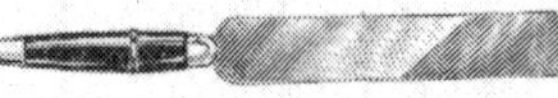

Spring steel blade, not plated. Size of blade, 6⅜x1¼ ins; length overall, 11½ ins. One dozen in a carton; weight, 2 lbs.

No. **556** Spatulas.........per Doz. **2.40**

Tea Strainers

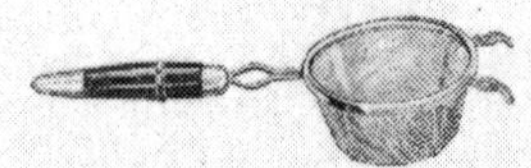

Reinforced. Fine mesh. Diameter of bowl, 3⅛ ins. One dozen in a carton; weight, 2¼ lbs.

No. **597R** Tea Strainers...per Doz. **2.40**

Bowl Strainers

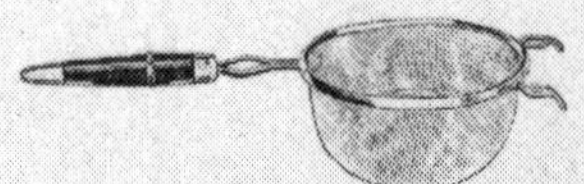

Medium mesh. Diameter of bowl, 5 ins. One dozen in a carton; weight, 4 lbs.

No. **505** Bowl Strainers....per Doz. **2.40**

No. 480 Assortment

Assortment consists of three dozen (36) pieces; one quarter dozen (3) of each of the above numbers. One assortment in a carton.

No. **480** Kitchen Tool Assortment..................................Each **7.20**

Can Openers

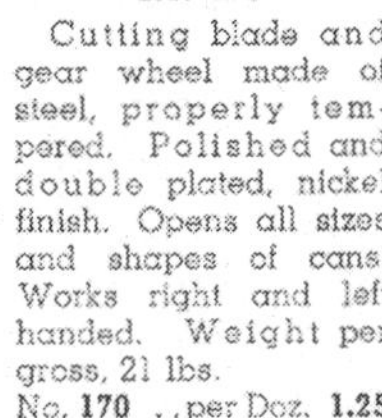

No. 170

Cutting blade and gear wheel made of steel, properly tempered. Polished and double plated, nickel finish. Opens all sizes and shapes of cans. Works right and left handed. Weight per gross, 21 lbs.

No. **170** ..per Doz. **1.25**

No. 5 Edlund Junior

Made of nickel plated steel, with green, yellow, blue or red handle. Will cut tops of round, square or oval cans cleanly leaving no jagged edge. Length overall, 6½ ins.

No. **5** ....per Doz. **6.00**

Can and Bottle Openers

No. 27

Tempered steel blade, iron handle, nickel plated all over. Length overall, 5½ ins. Weight per 100, 16⅔ lbs.

No. **27** ....per Box **1.20**

Ten in a display box.

No. 50

Can and bottle opener. Nickel plated tempered steel blade. Green handles. Easily cuts around edge at top or side or square or round cans. Positive cap remover. Length overall, 5 1/8 ins. Weight per gross, 15¼ lbs.

No. **50** ....per Doz. **1.20**

One dozen in a display box.

No. 22

Tempered steel blade, nickel plated. Polished white birch handle. Length overall, 6 ins. Weight per 100, 18⅓ lbs.

No. **22** ....per Box **1.20**

Ten in a display box.

No. 31½

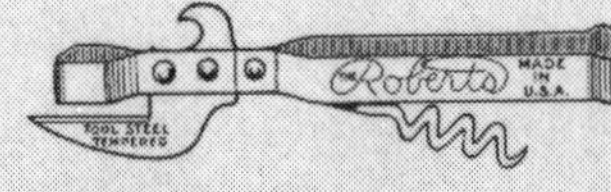

Cork puller and bottle opener. Nickel plated and burnished. Tempered tool steel blade. Weight per gross, 16 lbs.

No. **31½** ....per Doz. **.60**

One dozen in a display box.

Can Openers

No. 4 Edlund Household

No. 4-T **No. 4-W**

Opens any can, oval, square or round. Leaves a smooth rounded edge. Bracket on wall style is made in two parts so opener may be completely removed. One in a carton. Weight per dozen: table style, 28 lbs.; wall style, 32 lbs. One in a carton.

No. **4-T** Table Type...........Each **1.50**

No. **4-W** Wall Type..........Each **1.50**

Dazey DeLuxe

Carbon steel cutting wheel set at best angle for easy operation. Polished cadmium rustproof plating. Weight each, 1½ lbs.

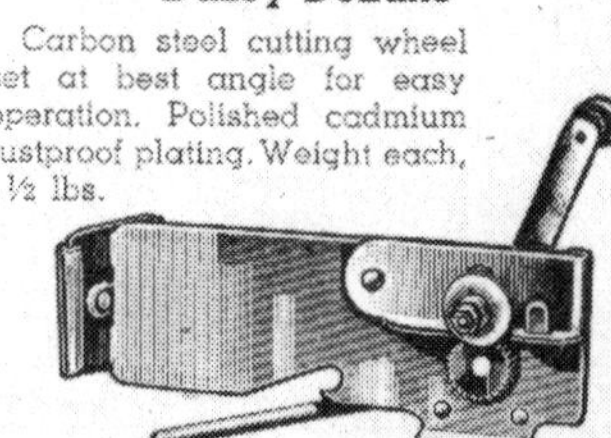

No. **169** DeLuxe Can Opener..Each **1.69**

Dazey Senior

Same as the DeLuxe but with spring action pivoted cutting wheel. Wt. each, 1½ lbs.

No. **139** Senior Can Opener..Each **1.39**

Dazey Junior

Similar to DeLuxe and Senior models. Wt. each, 1 lb.

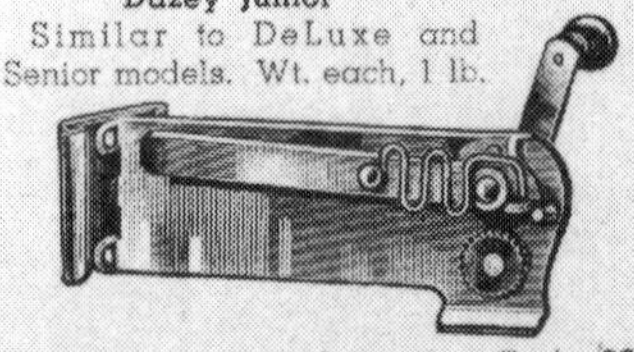

No. **69** Junior Can Opener....Each **.69**

Dazey "Heavy Duty"

Made for use in restaurants, hotels, hospitals, etc. where large sized cans are opened. Opens cans of various sizes or shapes with no change of adjustment. Clamp on bench or work table. One in a shipping carton. Weight each, 6 lbs.

No. **675** Heavy Duty Can Opener.......Each **6.75**

The George Worthington Company, in their 1936 catalog, offered Ritz kitchen tools manufactured by the Ekco Houseware Company. (Courtesy George Worthington Company.)

Here's a gift that any couple will bless you for!—the Hotpoint Coffee Maker. It makes *perfect* coffee *every* time! Makes it by a vacuum application of the drip system, scientifically proved the best. This model (the "Clermont") makes 6 cups—and is only $9.95; 8-cup size, $10.95. The "Granville" makes 6 cups and is $6.95.

"A new servant from me to you"—that's what you're giving in this amazing Hotpoint Mixer. Does all those arm-tiring tasks of whipping, beating—mixing. The motor's in the base—so no oil can drop into the bowl. Quiet, fast, compact. All manner of useful attachments come with it—and it's only $22.50!

A cook that works wonders! This Hotpoint Sandwich Grill prepares anything from a toasted sandwich to a complete, tempting meal... *right at the table!* It toasts, grills, fries—and it's handsome. You can give it—for just $11.95—and win real, old-fashioned gratitude this Christmas!

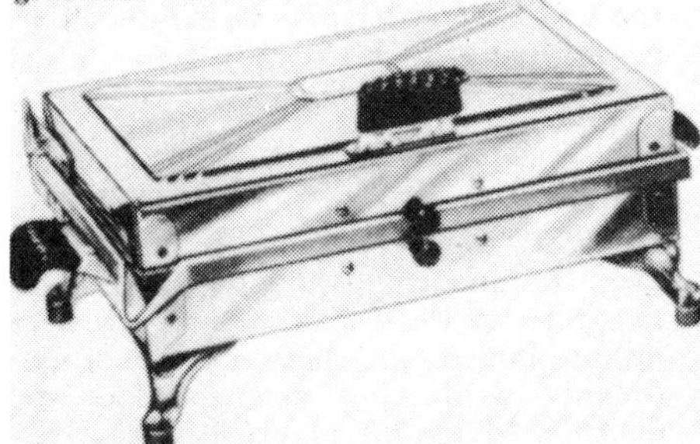

You'll be the talk of the breakfast table—if you give this Hotpoint Radio-Toggle Toaster. Toasts two slices...handy "knob" automatically turns both slices at once. $6.95. Other Hotpoint toasters: DeLuxe $5.95, and Riviera $3.95.

To make a man say "Thanks!"—depend upon this new G-E Electric Razor Blade Sharpener. Makes a single blade last longer than a whole package used to! Automatic—stops itself when blade is sharp. Only $7.50. Non-Automatic, $5.95.

To be popular with a whole family give this Hotpoint Waffle Iron (the Lancaster). It makes glorious, mouth-watering waffles in a jiffy... waffles that never "stick." $6.45. There are others to choose from too: the Ambassador, Chastleton, Lennox—from $17.50 to $8.95.

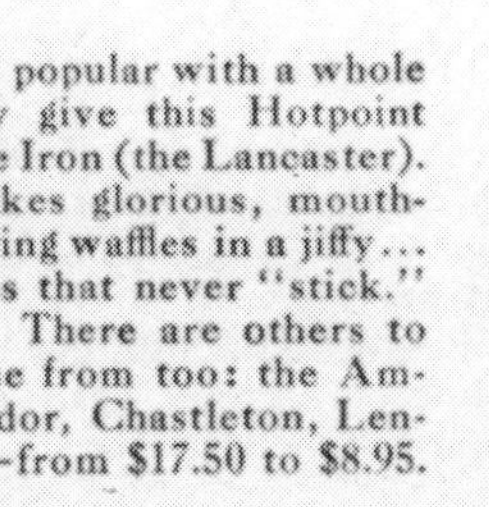

These are but a few of many General Electric Hotpoint gifts. See them all at your dealer's.

GENERAL ELECTRIC. Hotpoint

GENERAL ELECTRIC CO., MERCHANDISE DEPT., SECTION E-1712, BRIDGEPORT, CONN.

Smartly styled, small General Electric appliances in 1933.

Small Appliances

Electric coffeemakers. Electric percolators were priced from 84¢ to $4.65 in the 1936 Sears Roebuck catalog. Glass coffeemakers sold from $1.85 to $5.45 that same year.

Electric corn poppers. Sears Roebuck's electric "Challenge" corn popper was made of heavy chromed metal with a stirring handle on top and listed for $1.55 in the 1936 catalog. A blue steel model was priced at 88¢.

Electric eggs cookers. Electric egg cookers, said to be ingenious, were popular in the 1930s and 1940s. Eggs cooked in live steam were easier to digest, although they had the same nutritive value as eggs cooked in water.

FRESHLY GROUND COFFEE
Saves the Flavor for the Cup
New KitchenAid household Coffee Mill

KitchenAid offered a household electric coffee mill in 1938. **$25-40**

Sears Roebuck sold their Challenge nine-cup electric percolator for $1.29 in 1932. (Courtesy Sears, Roebuck and Company.)

Look what Santa brought me!
Now I can always serve hot coffee...for John with his steak, for Sis with her dessert, and when Bill gets home from the office, two hours later, the coffee is still hot. The Anyheet Control Silex keeps coffee any heat. All Silex glass coffee makers brew better tasting coffee in Pyrex brand glass guaranteed against heat breakage.
Anyheet Control Silex, black trim, $6.95; red trim, $7.45. Other Electric Table Models $4.95 up... Kitchen Range Models . . . $2.95 up.
DIAL YOUR HEAT
Brewing completed without removing glass from stove
THERE IS ONLY ONE
Genuine SILEX
GLASS COFFEE MAKER

The 1937 electric Silex coffeemaker had the Anyheet Control, which kept the coffee hot for hours if necessary. Table models sold for $4.95 and up. Earlier model Anyheet Control could be purchased for $1.50. **$8-18**

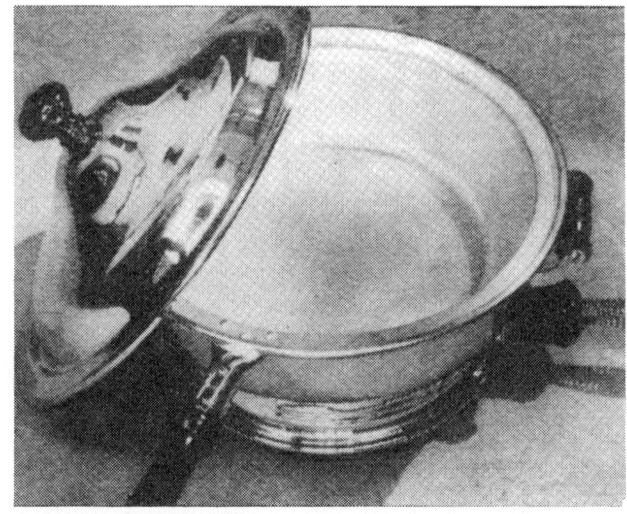

An electric chafing dish was the symbol of hospitality in the 1930s. This particular dish was available in 1933 and was considered a perfect gift for a daughter away at college and for mother at home. **$15-22**

Electric irons. Kerosene and gasoline irons were still offered in the 1930s. In 1937, Sears' safe kerosene iron sold for $4.98, with gasoline irons from $2.24 each.

By 1934, some irons had all-plastic handles for a cooler grip, and an attachable cord. The first steam iron to get U. L. approval was the Steam-O-Matic by the Steam-O-Matic Corporation of Milwaukee, in 1939.

Hankscraft Egg Cookers

115 Volts—A.C. 60-Cycle

Automatic

Is a four egg capacity cooker finished in ivory with flashing Chromium dome. Its graceful design makes it beautiful as well as practical to any breakfast table. Boils, poaches or scrambles eggs in live steam. Shuts off automatically. Amount of water in base governs cooking time. Equipped with rubber cord and rubber pull plug cap. One in a Carton.

No. **794** .... Each **1.95**

Hankscraft Egg Cooker Sets

Set consists of No. 794 Egg Cooker in ivory and chrome as shown above and attractive serving tray with four egg cups in either green, blue or ivory. One in a Carton.

No. **800-G**	Green	Each **3.95**
No. **800-B**	Blue	Each **3.95**
No. **800-I**	Ivory	Each **3.95**

The George Worthington Company's 1937 catalog had Hankscraft Egg Cookers and Egg Cooker Sets. This four-egg cooker boiled, poached or scrambled eggs in live steam and shut off automatically. (Courtesy George Worthington Company.) **$5-9**

The Coleman Lamp and Stove Company had general offices in Wichita, Kansas, and branch offices in Philadelphia, Chicago, and Los Angeles in 1931. The instant lighting and self-heating Coleman irons could be used anywhere — indoors or out. They came in colors with nickel trimming. Coleman also manufactured cook stoves, camp stoves, and lamps and lanterns. **$25-38**

A combination mixer-juice extractor and bowls were priced at $9.95 in the 1932 Sears Roebuck sale paper. Also shown is a Dormeyer mixer at $4.95. (Courtesy Sears, Roebuck and Company.)

In 1933, Hamilton Beach offered their food mixer for $18.75, with beaters and two bowls. The other attachments, juice extractor, meat grinder, slicer-shredder, coffee grinder, and potato peeler, could all be purchased separately as desired. They ranged in price from $2.75 to $8.

Electric mixers. By 1930, manufacturers were offering mixers with attachments that included lemon squeezers, dough mixers, mincers, flour sifters, cheese graters, and knife sharpeners, all for the same machine.

The Sunbeam® Mixmaster®, introduced in 1931, quickly gained public acceptance through its extensive advertising campaign and promotion. This mixer, mounted on a heavy cast base, had a turntable on which its milk glass bowls revolved, and it was equipped with a juicer attachment. The big plus was that it sold for under $20.

A magazine article in the mid-1930s said the electric mixer was one of the favorite and most valuable aids. All through the day it could be used and bring joy to the housewife. It did almost everything but cook the food. It mixed all batters, whipped cream, fluffed egg whites, beat candies, whipped potatoes, and more. Separate attachments could be used for juicing oranges, chopping vegetables, slicing and shredding foods, etc.

The mixer was a servant that was never ill or asked for more wages. Two good reasons for owning a food mixer were to save time and to reduce fatigue.

Electric mixers from the 1930s are still available and depending on the condition, are valued from $18 to $45.

This 1933 General Electric mixer was green. It could do the mixing, stirring, beating and whipping that were formerly done by hand. (Courtesy General Electric Corporation.)

The 1936 Hamilton Beach food mixer was a more streamlined model. This kitchen "swiftie" was available in ivory or white with black trim for about $21.

KitchenAid called their mixer a Complete Food Preparer in 1938.

The 1939 Automatic Sunbeam® Mixmaster® was a popular model. The Mix-Finder dial made it possible to turn the dial to the correct speed to get a job done. It was said to be easy to clean and it was simple to lift the motor and beaters off the stand for use anywhere in the kitchen. (Courtesy Sunbeam® Appliance Company.)

The 1937 Nesco ad illustrates all the roaster's uses. They claimed it was more than a master baker — an electric chef and pastry cook combined. **$10-28**

Roasters. The automatic electric roaster was a reality in the 1930s. It was considered a modern way to cook by the manufacturers because it was a complete electric range, no bigger than the size of a large roasting pan. The electric roaster could roast, broil, stew, fry, bake, grill, and toast. Plus, it could be used to cook automatically for two or a crowd and at the same time keep the kitchen cool. Sears Roebuck's Heatmaster was priced at $19.95 in 1936.

Toasters. By the 1930s, there were many improvements in the electric toaster. Proctor Electric Company replaced the tick-tock control of the 1920s toaster with silent controls. It signaled with a light or bell and automatically shut off when toast was done. This model was said to toast a uniform color.

Three different model toasters from the 1930s are valued from $10-18.

The Capitol Products turn-over toaster has solid sides and was a popular toaster in the 1930s. It was manufactured in Winsted, Connecticut.

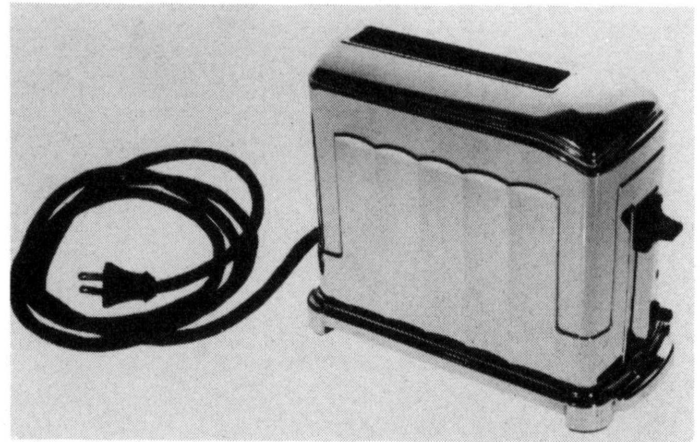

The Toastmaster automatic toaster was manufactured by the McGraw Electric Company in Minneapolis, Minnesota. It is a one-slice toaster, suggested for the smaller family, for the low price of $9.95 in 1939. An ad that year said "no watching, no turning, no burning...."

The Delta Pop-Down Automatic toaster was manufactured by the Delta Manufacturing Corporation, Philadelphia, Pennsylvania. It has streamlined markings on each side and a dark-light dial and release. This toaster works by inserting bread in the slots on top. The bread drops down into a tray in the base when toasted.

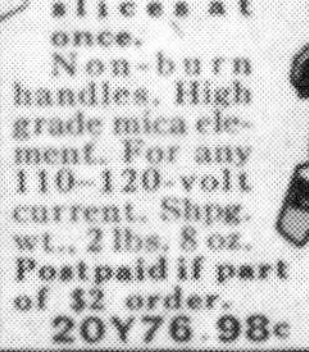

An oven-type toaster that toasted both sides of the bread at once, a two-slice toaster that toasted one side of the bread at a time, and a waffle iron with heat indicator, all shown in the 1932 Sears Roebuck sale flyer. The Heatmaster cord set cost 19¢. (Courtesy Sears, Roebuck and Company.)

"Have you a cranky old toaster-burner in your home — a treacherous finger-blisterer? If you have, you're in luck. That wretched Jonah is actually worth money — for once!..." A 1939 Toastmaster advertisement for a $2 trade-in.

Waffle irons and sandwich grills. Automatic waffle irons were not available until the 1930s. There were many innovations, such as single waffle irons, twins, or a combination waffle iron-sandwich grill that had replaceable or reversible grids for waffles. The 1932-1933 Sears Roebuck catalog showed a nonelectric waffle iron that was used on a stove and sold for the modest price of $1.25.

General Electric had a single Hotpoint waffle iron that made "glorious, mouth-watering waffles in a jiffy... waffles that never 'stick,' $6.45." Other models ranged from $7.50 to $8.95 in 1933. This same year, they offered a sandwich grill that would toast, grill, and fry at the table for just $11.95.

Waffle irons are priced anywhere from $5 to $12 today.

Toastmaster called their appliance a Waffle Baker in 1937.

The K-M Twin Waffle Iron made two delicious waffles at the same time. It cost $7.95. In this 1937 Knapp-Monarch ad, a sandwich grill is also pictured. This appliance also sold for $7.95.

80 WHERE OHIO SAVES!
The Cussins & Fearn Co., 24 Ohio Stores

ELECTRICAL APPLIANCES SAVE TIME

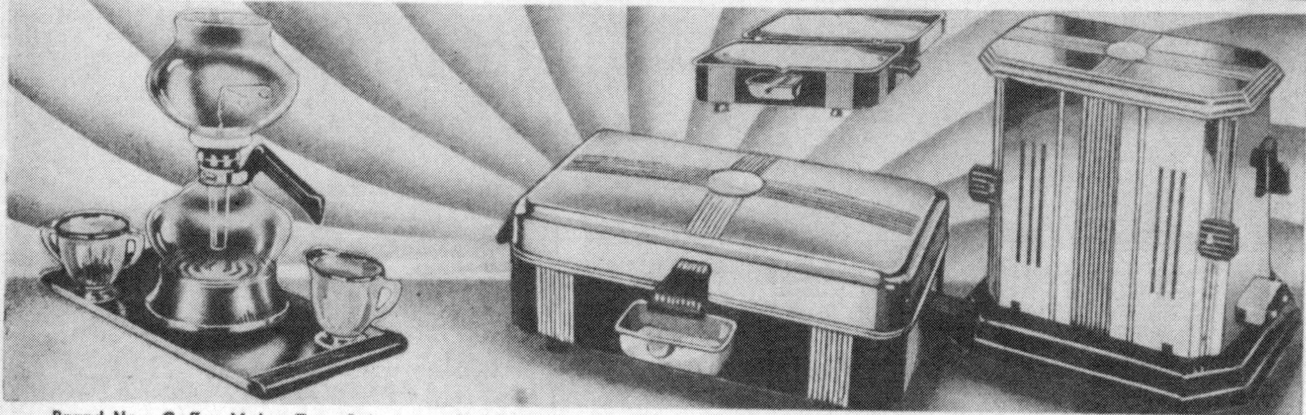

Brand New Coffee Maker Tray Set

Good coffee—delicious and clear—every cup the same—can be served piping hot at the table with this attractive Glass Coffee Maker Tray Set. Coffee brewed is the newer, better way of making coffee and this smart tray set is just the thing for table service. Set includes

- 7 Cup Electric Coffee Maker
- Satin and Lustre Finish triple-plate chrome tray.
- Chrome plated stove with ebonized handles and cord.
- Clear crystal creamer and sugar. Platinum banded
- The complete set at an amazingly low price

★4G-1492 Electric Coffee Set. $4.95

Patrician Sandwich Toaster and Double Grill

Delicious, crisp, sandwiches or sizzling hot grilled steaks, pancakes, bacon and eggs or chops, quickly and easily made, right at the table. The satin **chrome plated grids**, which are easy to keep bright and shining, are evenly heated by double **nichrome elements** in base and cover. They will give long, reliable service. A novel **sliding hinge** allows either thick or thin sandwiches to be toasted, with equal ease. A **convenient grease cup** on the front catches drippings. Cool Bakelite Handles.

★4G-1336—115 Volts, 500 Watts, 10¼ inches long, 5¾ inches wide and 4½ inches high.................................. $2.89

Bersteds Patrician Modern Electric Toaster

A brilliant new creation in black and chrome. Its generous sized, life-long heating elements wound on mica. Toast two full-sized slices of bread in a jiffy. A flip of the handle opens the doors and turns the toast without touching it. Both the side and door handles are of Bakelite.

- 115 Volts, 450 Watts. Height 7 inches, length 7¾ inches, width 6 inches.
- Complete with Underwriters's Approved Cord.
- An extraordinary value which has an abundance of quality and beauty.

★4G-1335—Electric Toaster $2.29

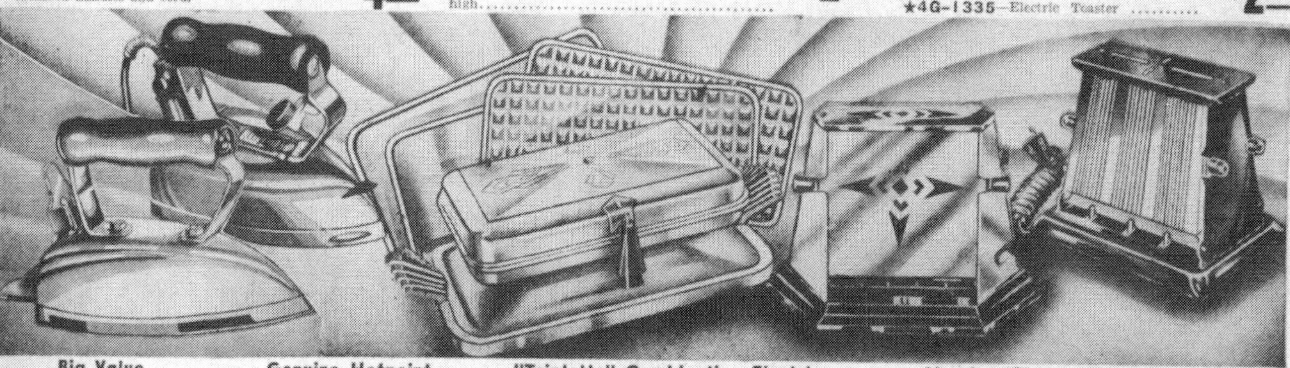

Big Value Electric Iron

Trim lines, cool black ebonized handle. **Highly polished** nickel plated shell and sole. Complete with plug guard and rest. **Element is reliable** and efficient, nichrome ribbon wound on mica. Built to give long dependable service.

4G-1153D Price Less Cord 99c

Genuine Hotpoint Electric Iron

An unusually substantial iron at a remarkable low price for an iron of nationally known quality. Guaranteed one year. Heating element wound on mica. Thumb rest for easier ironing. Comes complete with Underwriters' Approved Cord.

4G-1138D Hotpoint Iron Complete with cord.................. $2.89

"Triplette" Combination Electric

- WAFFLE MOULD
- SANDWICH TOASTER
- ELECTRIC GRILL

Three useful appliances combined in one practical, attractive unit that fills nearly every table need.

Up-to-the-minute design, brilliant in sparkling chromium plate.

A simple screw arrangement allows waffle grids to be removed quickly and easily so that chrome plated grids can be inserted. For frying steaks, chops, eggs and pancakes. Nichrome heating elements in cover and base. Waffle grids of fine cast aluminum. Handles are polished bakelite.

4G-1528D — Complete with Underwriters' Approved cord and plug......... $4.69

Massive Chrome Electric Toaster

It's a big toaster! It toasts the largest slice of bread. Attractive black baked enamel base with gleaming chrome trim. Big generous size heating element of nichrome ribbon wound on genuine mica.

A touch of the finger lowers the doors and turns the toast. Be sure to see this big new toaster at any C&F store.

4G-1548D—Complete with approved cord and plug $1.98

Sparkling Chrome Electric Toasters

Here's a toaster that's a real buy. Smooth black ebonized base with chrome trim in a modern streamlined design.

Beauty isn't all either, for it has the real inbuilt quality that you expect from C & F electrical appliances.

Toasts two slices at once, and toast turns automatically when doors are lowered.

4G-1526D—Complete with approved cord and plug 89c

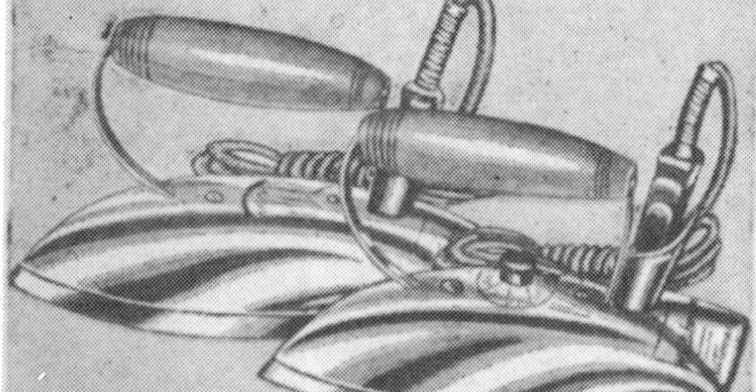

New White House Electric Irons

New type cooler handle, fully streamlined and tapered to fit the hand. Narrow, spring style, handle supports conduct less heat. Walnut handles in natural finish.

Beautifully streamlined base with easy-tilt heel rest flowing into the streamline effect. **Non-tarnishing** chrome finish. Button bevel base.

Embedded Element inserted in base under pressure. Almost indestructible. Absolutely guaranteed.

With Heat Indicator

4G-1121D—Thermostatic controlled indicator shows exact fabric temperature at all times. No guessing. Switch in cord gives complete heat control $1.98

Automatic Heat Control

4G-1122D—Ironing dial gives correct fabric heat for each kind of fabric. Instantly adjusted to desired temperature. With approved cord $3.98

Double Sandwich Toasters

★4G-1063—Trimmed with black ebonized wood handles. By laying cover back, chops, bacon, eggs and pancakes may be grilled. Less Cord.. 99c

Glass Coffee Brewer

Makes coffee the modern way—quickly—economically—better. Ever-Kool handle ebonized finish, genuine "Snap" filter Holder. Duo-Filter.

4G-1491D — With Electric Stove — Seven Cup $2.84

4G-1513D—Nine Cup ..$2.98

★4G-1514 — Less Electric Stove — Seven Cup $1.79

★4G-1515—Nine Cup ... $1.98

"DeLuxe" ELECTRIC PERCO-DRIP

Makes clear sparkling coffee in the easiest way, extracting only the desirable oils, because the coffee never boils.

- Patented heavy duy Direct Heat emersion element.
- Sixty Second percolation. Economical.
- Seamless aluminum.
- Insulated valveless pump—easy to clean.

4G-1206D—Capacity 9 cups. Priced less cord $1.79

Our Big Value PERCOLATOR

Modernistic design made of highly polished pure aluminum with monogram on sides. The heating element is guaranteed to give you satisfactory service.

4G-1202D—Price less cord. 7 Cup capacity...... $1.39

The 1938 Cussins and Fearn catalog offered an array of small appliances.

OUR PRICES SAVE YOU MONEY!

WAFFLE MOLD With Heat Indicator

Tells you when grids are ready for batter. Bakes 7¼ inch waffles in the cast aluminum, greaseless, quick heating grids. Tray protects table from heat and drippings. Efficient genuine Nichrome elements. Cord included.
★4G-1415 ..... **$3.49**

Special! WAFFLE IRON

Full chrome finish with matched front and side bakelite, ever cool handles. 7¼ inches pressed steel grids. Modern in design and appearance. Efficient in operation. A real value!
4G-1070D—Price less Cord.. **$1.98**

TWIN WAFFLE MOLD

No more waiting for more than one waffle. Bakes two plate size waffles at once. Genuine Nichrome elements, quick uniform heating. Heat indicator on top of grids. Polished chrome top mounted on convenient chrome tray with smart wood handles. Cord included.
★4G-1414 .... **$4.98**

DORMEYER, ELECTRIC MIXER, JUICER

It whips, mixes, makes salad dressings, mashes, stirs, as well as most expensive mixers! Note our low price. Large and small mixing bowls and extractor made of sparkling milk white glassware. A superior mixer in every way with three-speed tilt back motor.
4G-847 ..... **$10.95**

BUSY BEE ELECTRIC FANS

Induction type, non radio interfering motor operates on 110 volts A.C., 60 cycles only. New improved streamline base tear drop style. Four new propeller type blades. Gray finish. Approved by Underwriters.

4G-1479D— 8-inch stationary **$1.39**
4G-1480D— 8-inch oscillating..... $2.98
4G-1482D—10-inch oscillating..... 4.98

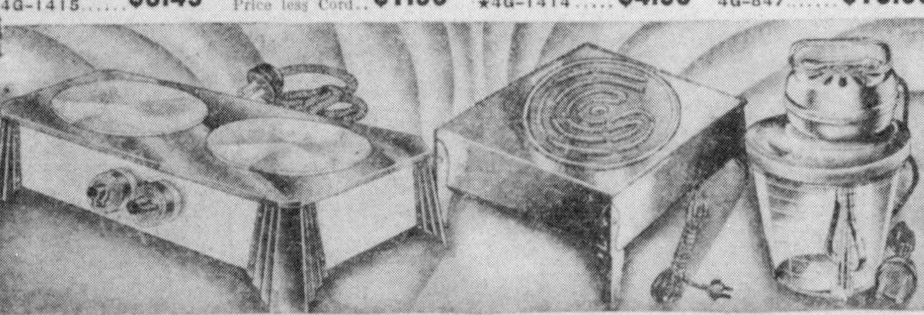

ENCLOSED TOP ELECTRIC HOT PLATE

Two units. **Three heat** selector switch. Modern **ebony, crinkled base** with attractive **chromium sides**, front and back. An efficient, attractive well made hot plate with Underwriters **Approved cord.**
4G-1328D—Two Burner, 3 Heat Hot Plate **$4.95**
4G-1327D—Hot Plate same as above but single burner. 3 Heat.................... $2.49

Big Value ELECTRIC HOT PLATE

Always ready for quick, cool cooking. Green finish. 600 watt guaranteed cooking element. Complete with cord.
4G-825D—Single Burner **74c**
4G-962D—Two burner size with two switches. 8½x17½x5¼ inches $1.89

VIDRIO ELECTROMIX

Designed as a combination whipper and mixer. **Detachable stainless beater** is easily cleaned. Portable—use anywhere. Many different uses. **Complete with bowl, motor, cord and plug.** Ready for use. A household necessity for every home.
4G-1567D—Electric Mixer **$1.00**

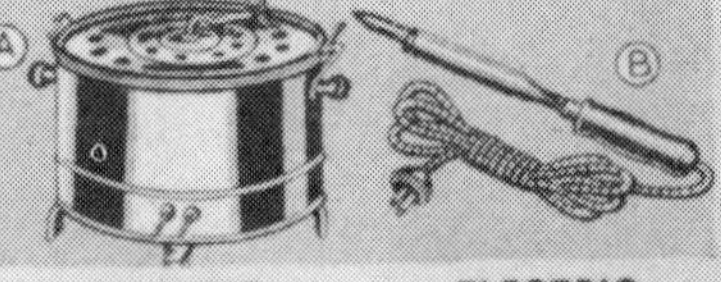

ELECTRIC CORN POPPER

Body made of sheet steel finished in pistol blue. **Bright fittings.** Perforated top. 8¾ in. diameter. Nichrome 600 watt, 105-120 volt heating element.
4G-959D—Without cord. Standard appliance cord will fit **98c**
4G-961D—Same as above but chrome plated $1.49

ELECTRIC SOLDERING IRONS

★4G-924—A 60 Watt light weight iron for Radio and electric work, each **78c**
★4G-925—A 100 Watt handy household size for any light tinkering around the house, each.. $1.19
4G-922—A 150 Watt heavy duty iron for mechanics, garages, etc. This iron is absolutely guaranteed to stand up under the heaviest kind of work, each $1.65

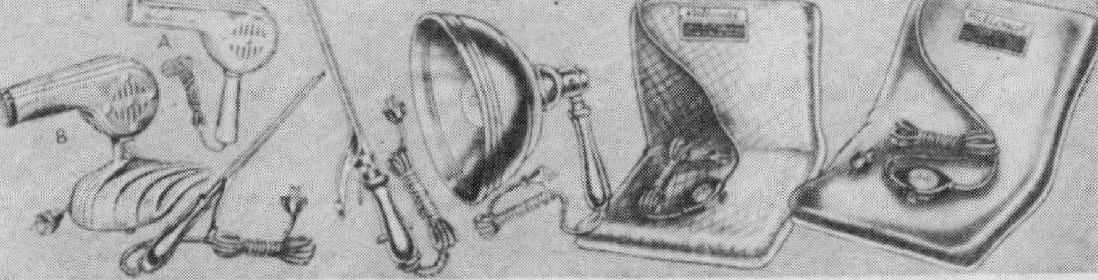

Electric HAIR DRYERS

(A) Professional style with an unusually sturdy motor. Blows strong blast of heated air.
★4G-1417—With Cord **$1.59**
(B) **De Luxe Model** with adjustable stand. Green crackle with black and ivory trim.
★4G-1598—With cord **$2.20**

Electric CURLING IRONS

(A) Nickel tube and curler clamp. Green handle. 6 foot cord.
★4G-951 ...... **36c**
(B) With switch-in handle. Detachable curler clamp.
★4G-950 .... 79c

Therapeutic Lamps

Heat that relieves pain. 6½ inch reflector. 260 watt bulb. 6 foot cord and plug.
4G-926D Hand Model.. **$1.69**
4G-929D—Replacement Bulbs. Each 54c

Electric Heating Pad

Full size 12x15". Choice of green or orchid color cover. 3-heat switch and protected by two thermostats.
4G-956D **$1.59**

Wetproof Heating Pad

Wet proof cover insures safety from spilling liquids or perspiration while in use. 4G-957D **$2.19**

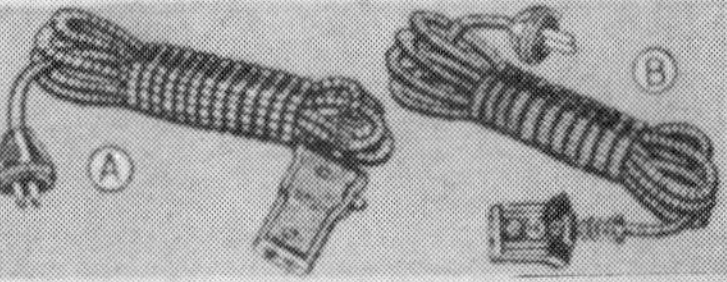

APPLIANCE CORD SET

Underwriters approved high grade 6 foot cord.
★4G-4069—Without switch in plug. Set.......... **20c**
4G-685D — With switch in plug.... 28c

SPECIAL CORD SET

Approximately 6 feet long. With bakelite plugs. An unusual value. Complete. Buy two at this low price.
4G-616D—Appliance Cord Set.. **15c**

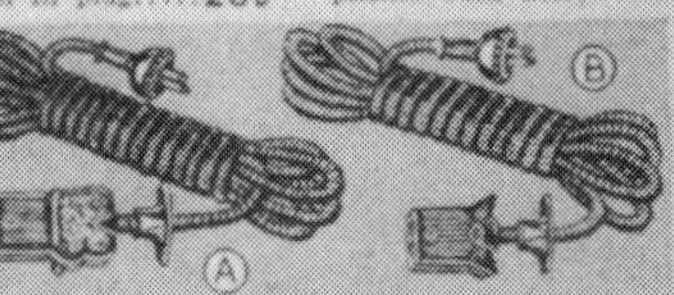

DOUBLE DUTY APPLIANCE CORD SETS

1000 Watt, 10,000 cycle, 6 ft. 2 in. cotton (gold label) heater cord, fitted with pull handle and rubber grip cap. Extra flexible and durable. Black or brown.
4G-4025D—Without Switch **35c**
4G-4026D—With Switch.. **48c**

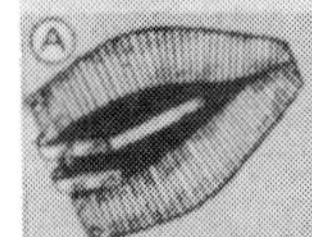

(A) Mica Heating Element

For Electric Irons. 600 watt. Fits most irons.
4G-3066D. **27c**

(B) Cone Shaped Heating Element

For Reflector Heaters. 600 watts. Edison screw base.
4G-1610... **25c**

(C) Replacement Elements

★4G-820—For three heat Hot Plate.. **59c**
★4G-821—For single heat Hot Plate. **45c**

(D) Nickel-Chrome Replacement Element

For replacing burnt out elements in hot plates, toasters, etc. 600 watt.
★4G-3002...... **10c**

(E) Round Contact Points for Electric Irons.
4G-1148—Each.............. **5c**

(F) Cloth Strainer—For glass coffee maker.
4G-858—Each ... **4c**
Doz. 44c

APPLIANCE PLUGS

(A) 4G-635D—Bakelite plug with switch.15c
(B) 4G-634D—Without Switch ..8c
(C) ★4G-1691—Armored plug without switch.....8c

Food waste disposers. In 1935, General Electric started factory production of a food waste disposer that was an electrically driven shredding machine, pumping waste down the drain. The disposer was mounted directly beneath the strainer in the sink so that waste could be flushed to the sewer system.

The food waste disposer was developed at the same time as other new appliances. The electric motor, washer, and refrigerator were originally devised for commercial use, then they entered the home. The disposer was developed for the home, then adapted for hotels, restaurants, and the U.S. Army and Navy during World War II.

A 1937 General Electric advertisement for the complete Electric Sink, featuring the Disposall and dishwasher. "Good Riddance to Bad Garbage." (Courtesy General Electric Corporation.)

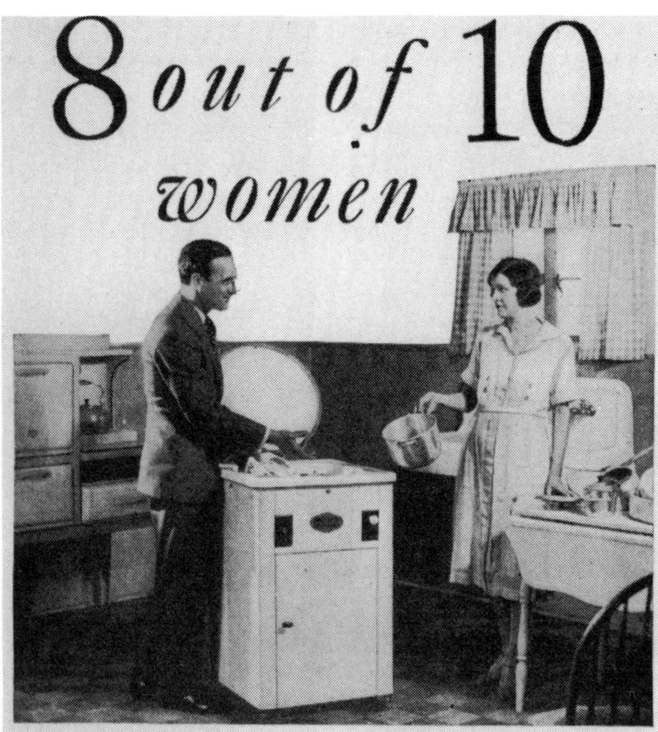

. . . asked a lot of good questions, watched the Walker answer them . . . and then decided to buy

MOST women are born skeptics. Say what we will about Walker Dishwashers, sales aren't made until the woman actually sees the machine do its job. Then eight out of every ten *buy*.

And what keen questions they ask! Here are the more important ones . . . answered very simply.

"Will it really wash, rinse and dry my dishes?" Yes, more perfectly than the most careful pair of hands . . . and in far less time.

"Will it wash pots and pans?" Yes. It will wash them perfectly. It will *not* scour or remove burned-in-food.

"Does the machine itself require cleaning?" No. The thorough water action keeps the glistening porcelain bowl clean as a china dish.

"Are my finest dishes safe in the Walker?" Yes, far more so than when they are washed by hand. The dishes remain stationary.

"Why should I have a dishwasher when I have a maid?" For sanitary reasons, to protect your family's health . . . to keep your maid contented and save her time . . . for your own use when the maid is not there.

Have *you* any further questions? If so, please use the coupon below. If not, *see* the answers to these questions, by checking No. 1 and mailing the coupon anyway. You'll bless the day!

WALKER
ELECTRIC DISHWASHERS
Sink and Cabinet Models
A few territories still open for responsible distributors

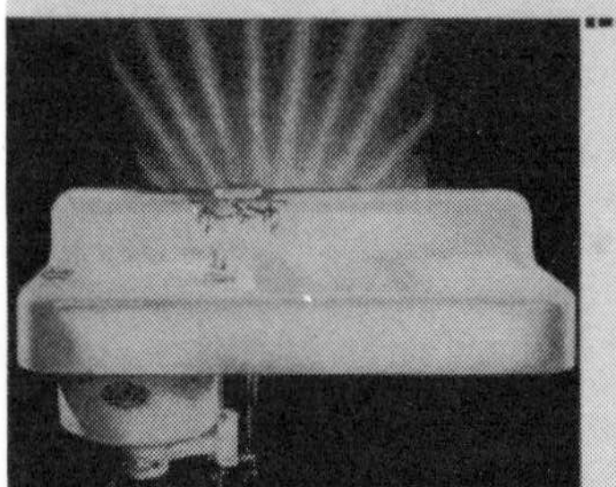

Walker Dishwasher Corporation
Syracuse, New York

☐ 1. I'd like to see a Walker work.
☐ 2. I'd like a complete booklet.
☐ 3. I'd like to improve my kitchen. Please tell me all about your Kitchen Planning Institute.

Name..
Street..
City.......................................State..........

Dishwashers. General Electric purchased the Walker Company of Syracuse, New York, manufacturer of electric dishwashers. In 1932, General Electric offered its first dishwasher. It was a square tub with single-knob control, combined with an Electric Sink. They said that their dishwasher actually washed and dried dishes, silverware, pots, and pans in five minutes. They said this eliminated the three-times-a-day job, saved extra hours for other things every day of the year, and kept hands from touching hot, greasy water.

In the 1930s, 85,000 dishwashers were purchased compared with 530,000 in the 1940s and 1,755,000 in the 1950s.

Women had many questions about the electric dishwasher. "Will it really wash, rinse, and dry my dishes?" "Will it wash pots and pans?" "Does the machine itself require cleaning?" "Why should I have a dishwasher when I have a maid?" All these questions were answered by the Walker Company.

Ranges. Tabletop ranges were first developed by the gas industry in 1930. This meant that cooking was done on top of the stove, and the oven was placed below the cooking surface. Earlier high ovens used too much cooking space and shut out light, plus manufacturers found that four-fifths of all cooking was done on top of the stove.

By the mid-1930s, gas, electric, oil and kerosene ranges with the streamlined look were brought out by numerous manufacturers. Ranges were now integrated into the modern kitchen by having the same height as other work surfaces and were proportioned to be continuous with base cabinets. The legs had disappeared on many models, and many had work surfaces between or beside burners.

Sometime in the mid-1930s, electric ranges took the lead over gas ranges. This occurred when large manufacturers of electric appliances started selling entire kitchen ensembles.

The range center needed a work surface for food preparation, cooking, and serving. Some of the equipment stored in nearby cabinets included pans, roasters, utensils used at the range for cooking, and serving dishes.

In 1930, the Walker Company offered both sink- and cabinet-type electric dishwashers. (Courtesy General Electric Corporation.)

"Flavor Zone" Lemon Pie

TIME
after
TIME
with a

Westinghouse

Flavor Zone Range

What a relief to be sure that *every* pie you make will be evenly baked, evenly browned, good beyond description! This marvelous range *always* provides even distribution of heat, and *automatic* control of time and temperature . . . enabling you to duplicate your best results again and again.

The Flavor Zone Electric Range also cooks complete dinners for you—even while you're away from home. *Fully automatic*, it turns the current on . . . then off . . . completing the cooking by retained heat, the famous old Dutch-Oven method. It's economical, too—the *only* range operating on the money-saving Flavor Zone principle.

RECIPE FOR "FLAVOR ZONE" LEMON PIE

1 Cup Sugar
1 ½ Cups Boiling Water
3 Tablespoons Corn Starch
3 Tablespoons Flour
½ Teaspoon Salt
Grated Rind 1 Lemon
¼ Cup Lemon Juice
3 Egg Yolks

Mix dry ingredients. Add boiling water. Cook in double boiler until thick. Add beaten egg yolks and cook 2 minutes longer. Add lemon juice and rind. Cool and pour into baked pie shell. Cover with meringue using 3 egg whites and 6 tablespoons of sugar.

Westinghouse Electric & Manufacturing Co., Merchandise Department, Mansfield, Ohio.
Please send copy of the Flavor Zone Book.
Name ....
Address .... BHG 4-32

Mail coupon for your copy of "Old Time Goodness for Your Modern Table."

The 1932 Westinghouse Flavor Zone Range advertisement said their automatic range would always provide even distribution of heat and automatic control of time and temperature. Their Flavor Zone method gave the best results and it was economical, too. (Courtesy White-Westinghouse Appliance Company.)

This 1933 electric range had Calrod heating units, which cost General Electric more than one million dollars to develop. It also had a "Thrift Cooker" with a five-quart kettle. It was designed for slow cooking but could be adapted for other cookery. (Courtesy General Electric Corporation.)

The 1933 Magic Chef gas range illustrates the tabletop cooking surface with oven below. Notice the backsplash board and that the legs are abbreviated compared to earlier models because the cooking surface is raised. It featured a burner that wouldn't clog, burner trays that protected burners and pipes from spattering fats and boil-overs, Red Wheel Lorain Oven regulator, a new two-piece grid-pan broiler, and automatic Time-Control clock.

This full-size cast iron coal range was permanently finished in cream and green porcelain enamel and sold for $49 in 1932. The upper closet was used for storing pans or warming foods. The compartment on the right was a thirty-two-quart-capacity hot water reservoir. It also had a Never-Fail baking oven. (Courtesy Sears, Roebuck and Company.)

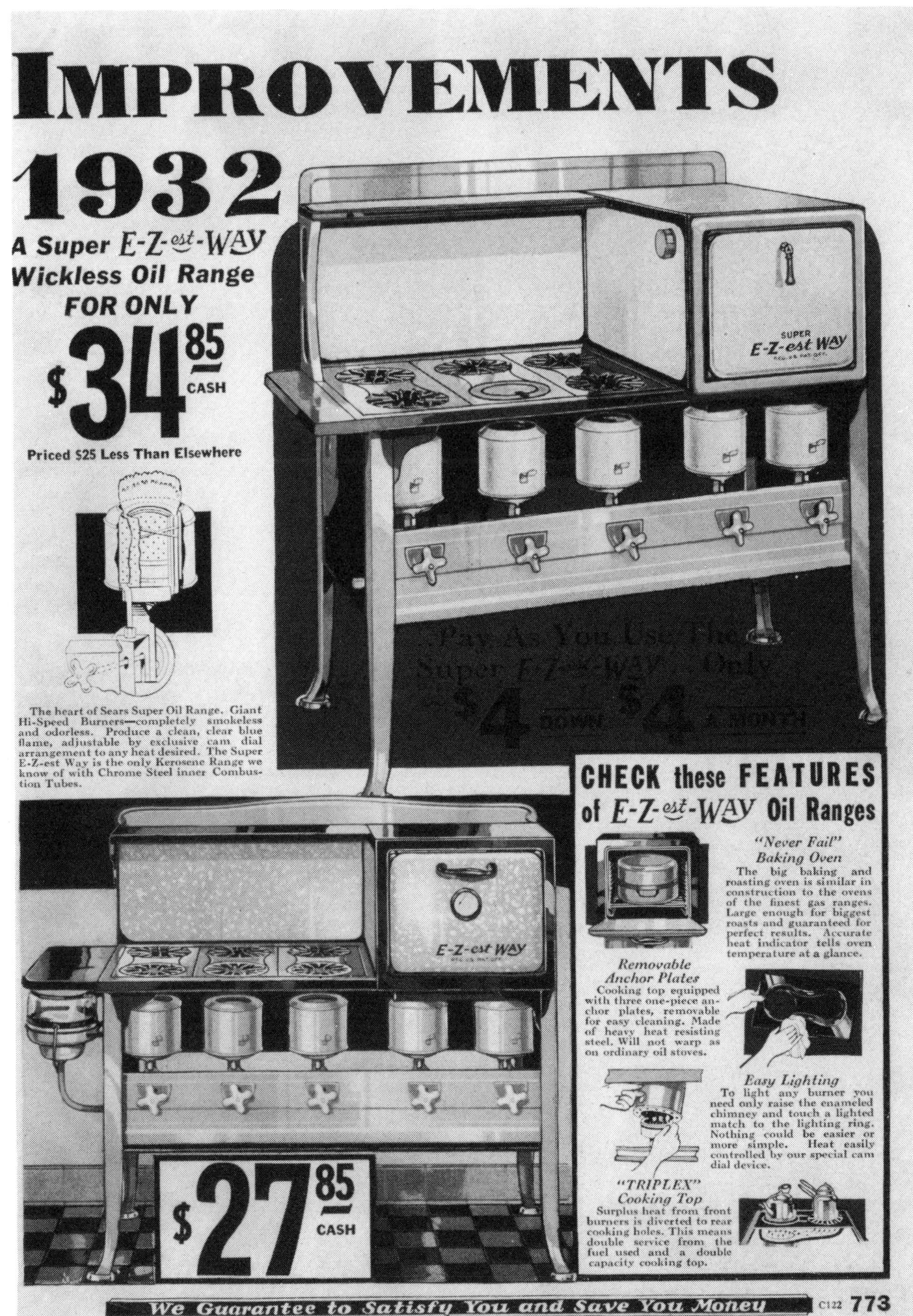

Sears also offered six-burner Wickless Oil Ranges in the 1932 catalog. Model at top was finished in cream, green, and black. Model below came in green with black trim. (Courtesy Sears, Roebuck and Company.)

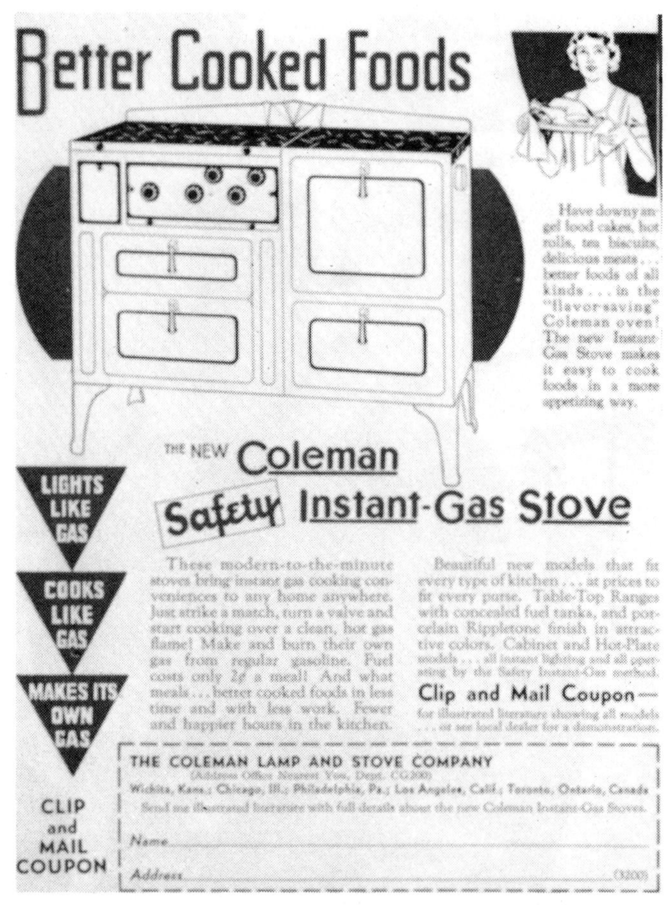

The Coleman Lamp and Stove Company had a 1933 range that "Lights like gas, Cooks like gas and Makes its Own Gas" by making and burning gas from gasoline stored in concealed fuel tanks. It came in attractive colors.

The Florence Stove Company, Garner, Massachusetts, offered ranges for every fuel — and a model for every pocketbook in 1939.

The 1939 model Tappan gas range had a Visualite Oven. This innovation let the housewife see her roast cooking without opening the door.

Refrigerators. In the course of kitchen planning in the early 1930s, it was found there was a door that was likely to open and close nearly fifty times a day — the door of one of the most important pieces of equipment, the automatic refrigerator. It was involved with more kitchen operations than any other large piece of equipment.

The placement of the refrigerator was, and is, important in a step-saving, efficient kitchen. To be most useful, it should be as near the kitchen mixing and preparation center as possible. There should be a counter beside it where food and dishes can be transferred to and from the refrigerator. Storage for the mixing and serving center should include utensils and supplies necessary for mixing, shredding, and grinding.

In the 1930s, a new principle made it possible for a refrigerator to be iced only once every four to seven days and still keep the foods at a constant temperature. This type was called *air conditioned ice refrigerator.* Only the bottom of the ice cake was exposed for refrigeration, thus giving the same constant cold temperature whether the ice chamber was full or nearly empty. The arrangement of ice rested on fins at the bottom, increasing the cooling area more than two and a half times. Below this rack was the air conditioning chamber, through which the air flowed. All the odors and gases were deposited in the water from the melting ice and carried down the drain, so only fresh, cool, conditioned air returned to the food chamber.

Manufacturers made automatic refrigerators with many convenient features. They were dependable and so indispensable that they became well established as standard equipment for the modern home in the 1930s. Gas and electric appliances were replacing the old iceboxes.

By the late 1930s, the legs had disappeared from some refrigerator models. Door storage, full-width shelves, lift-out shelves, storage drawers, and larger freezers were available. The freezer was still in the top center of the refrigerator compartment.

The 1932 Norge Rollator refrigerator. Notice that it stands on legs.

The General Electric refrigerator with the Monitor on top was still being offered in 1934. It could freeze ice faster, used less current, and operated quietly. (Courtesy General Electric Corporation.)

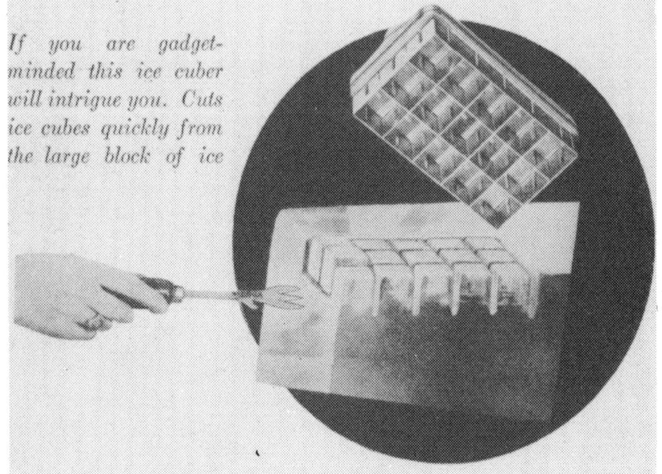

Delineator magazine said, "if you are gadget-minded this ice cuber will intrigue you. Cuts ice cubes quickly from the large block of ice."

The air conditioned ice refrigerator was new to the market in 1936. This white and chromium style ice refrigerator was no relation to the old-fashioned icebox.

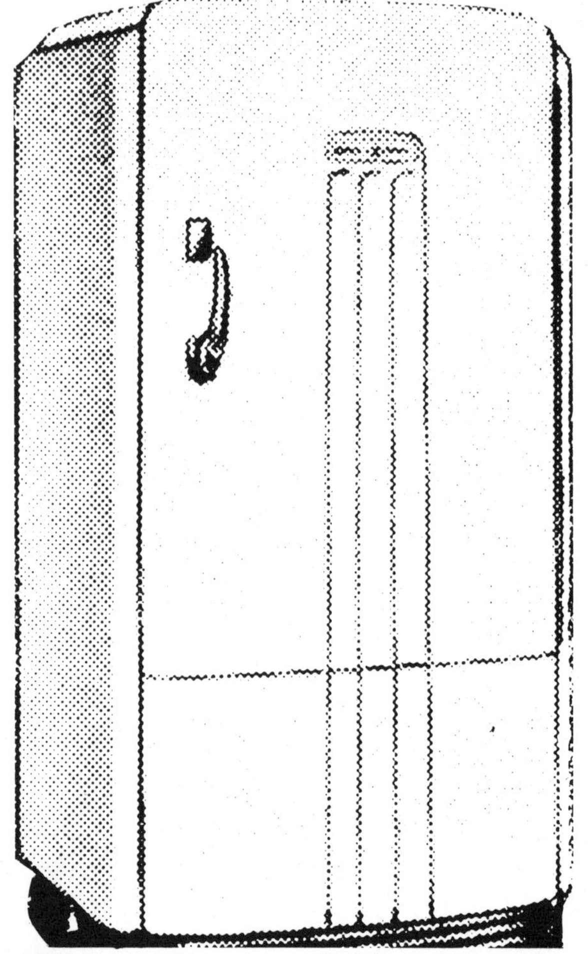

General Electric's refrigerators with Selective Air Conditions came in sizes ranging from three to sixteen cubic feet in 1939. (Courtesy General Electric Corporation.)

IT SAVES SILENTLY

BECAUSE IT FREEZES WITH **NO MOVING PARTS**

SERVEL ELECTROLUX

is winning millions with its greater comfort longer service lower costs

DIFFERENT . . . simpler . . . Servel Electrolux has *no* moving parts in its entire freezing system. A tiny gas flame circulates the refrigerant—without friction, without wear.

As a result, Servel Electrolux is permanently silent . . . brings you more years of dependable, money-saving refrigeration.

Read what these happy owners say. See the beautiful 1937 models at your gas company or neighborhood dealer's showroom. Remember, your gas company backs and services every Servel Electrolux it installs.

FOR FARM AND COUNTRY HOMES, Servel Electrolux runs on kerosene or bottled gas. Write for details to: Servel, Inc., Servel Electrolux Sales Division, Evansville, Ind. (Servel Electrolux is also sold in Canada, Central and South America.)

The Servel Electrolux gas refrigerator had three drawers for vegetables in 1937. Its simple, noisefree operation saved on upkeep (it had no moving parts) as well as food bills.

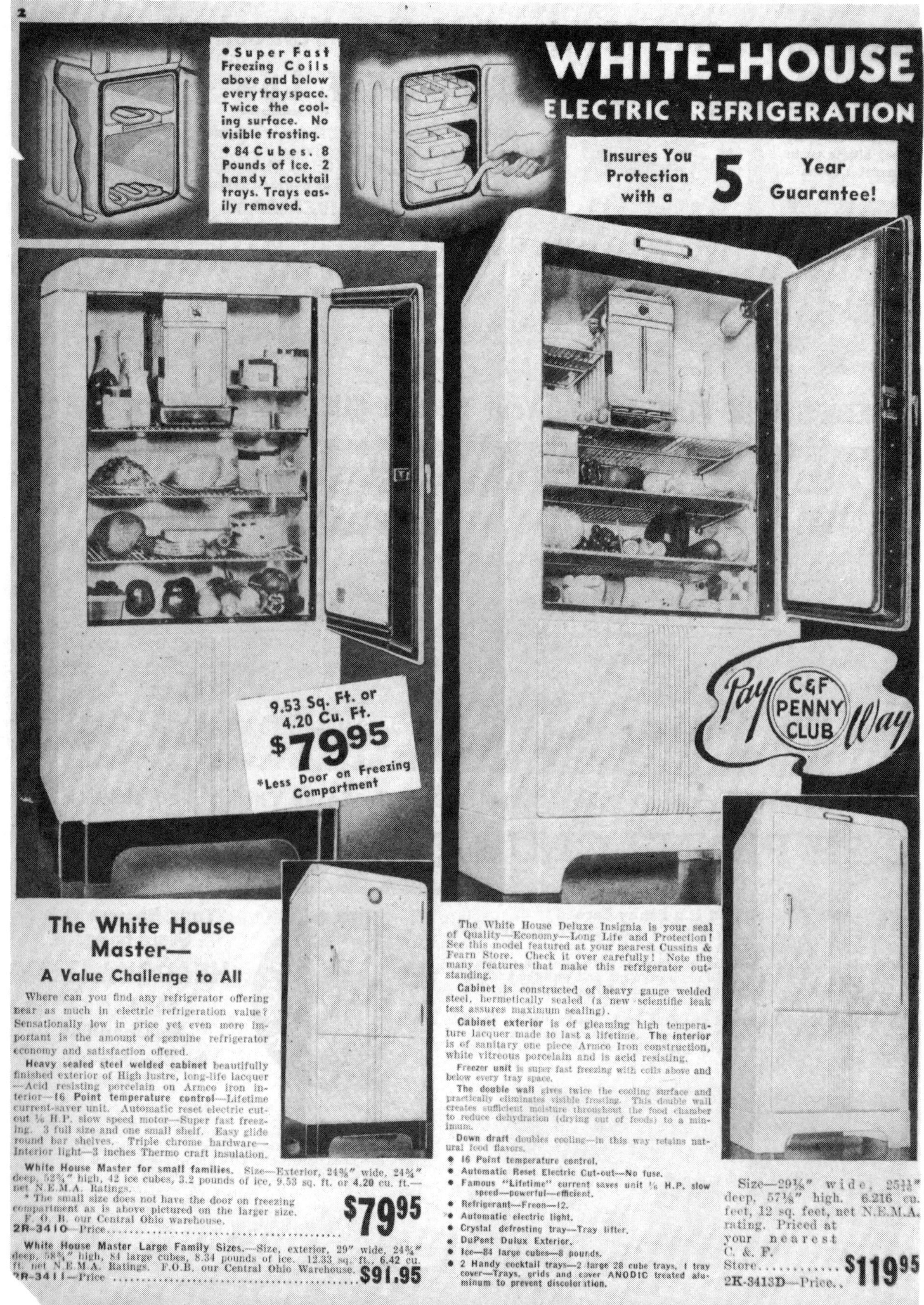

A 1938 Cussins and Fearn Company catalog advertisement for a deluxe, supreme White House refrigerator priced at $169.95.

Furniture. Food mixers were considered by some as essential electric servants for the housewife to do her work as easily and expeditiously as possible. They had a number of attachments available, which presented a storage problem.

A cabinet was made especially for this machine, providing a convenient worktable. Mixing machines could be purchased with or without cabinets and with as many attachments as were needed. They came in various sizes to meet individual needs.

Although many houses had built-in china cabinets in the 1920s, it was not until 1930 that the built-in sink design was accepted. The sink was built in with cabinets above and below and with a continuous work surface. Kitchen planning was well underway. The streamlined kitchen in 1935 was the result of years of study to make a truly efficient kitchen, with the stove, sink, and refrigerator integrated into the work process. Once the kitchen was treated as a whole, it was possible to buy components from mail order, department, and retail stores.

Porcelain-enamel tops on furniture shown in a 1930 Kompass and Stoll Company advertisement.

In 1933, mixer cabinets such as this one were the answer to finding suitable storage for the food mixer and its attachments. **$75-135**

EASY TERMS as Low as $5.00 Down See Page 106

New Queen Anne Set at Sale Prices

Sale Price $22.48 Oak 48-In. Size

Sale Price $18.25 Oak Table

$19.45 OAK

$2.60 OAK

A SALE SENSATION! Your Choice of Oak or Walnut!

Price—precedent—profit—all have been sacrificed! Savings too good to miss. Shop where you will—spend what you will, for sheer value and good looks we believe this set cannot be "topped"! Pay for it with easy monthly payments if you wish. A down payment of only $9.00 puts this set in oak, including 48-inch buffet, china cabinet, table and six chairs, in your home. See page 106 for easy terms. Tops of all pieces are genuine American walnut or quarter sawed oak 5-ply construction; fronts and ends 3-ply. Beautifully finished to a deep rich color, parts not veneered are well seasoned hardwood in matching finish. Lovely two-toned routed trimming. Buffet—with mirror, in three sizes. Mirrors are 38, 44 and 50 in. long, respectively and all 8 in. high. China Cabinet.—Top, 36x14 in. Two shelves, making three compartments for dishes. Height 61¾ in. Table—Top, 42x50 in.; extends to 70 inches. Two 10-inch leaves finished to match table top. Chairs—Solid oak or hardwood, finished in walnut, upholstered in brown Spanish grained genuine leather. Chair seat, 16x14 in.; armchair seat, 18x16 in. All pieces except chairs, shipped from factory in CENTRAL IND.; chairs shipped from our store. **Not Prepaid.**

1JM2328	Shpg. Wt.	Oak	Walnut
Buffet—48-inch	150 lbs.	$22.48	$22.68
54-inch	165 lbs.	25.48	25.68
60-inch	180 lbs.	28.48	28.68
China Cabinet	150 lbs.	19.45	19.65
Extension Table	175 lbs.	18.25	18.45
Chair	12 lbs.	2.60	2.70
Arm Chair	16 lbs.	4.60	4.70

TIME PAYMENTS SEE PAGE 106

1JM2536 1JM2517 1J2519 1JM2557

Sale Price $3.98 Drop-Leaf Table

Save—Paint Them Yourself Select Your Own Style!

Feature bargains as never before! Big reductions from former prices. Paint them aristocratic hues to suit yourself and "salt away" the saving! You'll find real pleasure in decorating them to harmonize with your own color scheme. Selected kiln dried cabinet wood, smoothly sanded and ready to paint. **Drop-leaf table** top closed, 36x21½ in. Open, 41x36 in. Two triple hinged leaves. **Extension table** closed, 42x30 in. Open, 56x30 in. Complete with two leaves. **Cathedral back chair** in two different styles; both have saddle shaped seat, artistic back rails and turned legs, stretcher braced. Act. seat, 15¼x14¼ in. Shpg. wts.: drop-leaf table, 30 lbs. Ext. table, 69 lbs.; either chair, 8 lbs. **Not Prepaid.**

1JM2517—Drop-leaf table $3.98
1J2519—Extension table 6.95
1JM2536—Panel chair 1.39
1JM2557—Spindle chair 1.39

Sale Price $1.39 Each

Regular $2.25 Value Elsewhere

Solid oak. Seven stretchers. Seat, 16½x15½ in., ht., back, 19 in. Shpg. wt., 13 lbs. **Not Prepaid.**

1JM16—Each $1.39

Unconditionally Guaranteed STAINLESS TOP
First Time at These Low SALE PRICES

$24.75 Table and Four Chairs In Ivory

A breakfast set table with an unconditionally guaranteed STAINLESS top of **porcelain** enamel. Recently offered in our General Catalog and **now for the first time at reduced prices.** Others ask as much for tables with ordinary tops. Fruit juices and vinegar do not stain this top—even boiling acid will not stain it. Laboratory tested and guaranteed stainless. And not only an improved set with a guaranteed stainless top but an improved set at a price actually one-fourth less than regular sets sell for elsewhere. Three new enamel color combinations baked-on for beauty, long life and glossy smoothness. Soft gray with deep blue trim; ivory offset with green; bright apple green with rich contrast of orange. Artistically decorated. Table: Top, 43x36 in. (36x21 in. with leaves down). Frame of select hardwood. Convenient drawer. Carefully turned legs. Shipped with legs and leaves detached; easily put together. Sturdy fiddle back chairs of select hardwood. Actual seat, 15½x14¼ in. Shpg. wt., table 76 lbs., chair, 11 lbs., set, 120 lbs. **Not Prepaid.**

1JM2515 State Finish.	Ivory with Green Trim	Gray with Blue Trim	Green with Orange Trim
Table	$14.75	$14.85	$14.95
Chair, Each	2.85	2.90	2.95
Table, 4 Chrs.	24.75	24.85	24.95

WE DO NOT PAY THE FREIGHT

Sale Closes August 31 1930

$1.69 Your Choice In Golden Oak

Solid oak. Your choice of slip seat upholstered in artificial brown grained Spanish leather or saddle shaped wood seat. Golden or fumed oak finishes. State choice. Shpg. wt., 14 lbs. **Not Prepaid.**

1JM194—Imitation leather seat, 16x14 in. Golden Oak $1.69
Fumed Oak 1.74
1JM139—Wood seat, 17½x15 in. Golden Oak $1.69
Fumed Oak 1.74

SEARS, ROEBUCK AND CO. C451 2133

Sears Roebuck had a sale in August, 1930, on unpainted extension and drop-leaf tables and stainless-top table and chair sets. The sets came in three new enamel color combinations: soft gray with blue trim, ivory offset with green, and bright apple green with a contrast of orange. (Courtesy Sears, Roebuck & Company.) **$195-295**

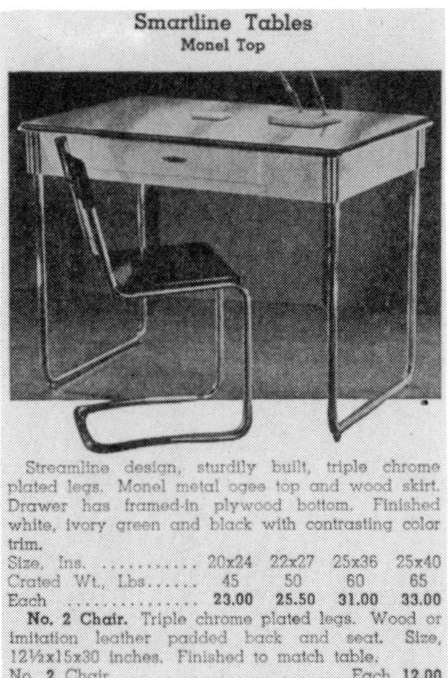

Smartline Tables
Monel Top

Streamline design, sturdily built, triple chrome plated legs. Monel metal ogee top and wood skirt. Drawer has framed-in plywood bottom. Finished white, ivory green and black with contrasting color trim.

Size, Ins.	20x24	22x27	25x36	25x40
Crated Wt., Lbs.	45	50	60	65
Each	**23.00**	**25.50**	**31.00**	**33.00**

No. 2 Chair. Triple chrome plated legs. Wood or imitation leather padded back and seat. Size, 12½x15x30 inches. Finished to match table.
No. 2 Chair ....Each **12.00**

The George Worthington Company had this Smartline table with Monel top in their 1936 catalog. Notice the streamlined design of the chrome-plated legs. It was finished with white, ivory, green, and black with a contrasting color trim. (Courtesy George Worthington Company.) **$20 - 35**

HOOSIER

book of low-cost, modern

KITCHEN EQUIPMENT

Many a family has paid more for an old-fashioned kitchen cabinet than you need now pay for Hoosier equipment that looks like it was built in, yet can be taken with you if you move. The details are in this free book. In it, too, you'll find kitchen plans, color-scheme suggestions and many other things you'll be glad to know about planning the kitchen for greater beauty and convenience —either with a portable cabinet that needs no carpenters or decorators or with Hoosier built-in equipment. Send for the book. Just address:

HOOSIER MANUFACTURING CO.
337 Bart Street, New Castle, Ind.

The Hoosier Manufacturing Company marketed their kitchen equipment in 1937 by stressing that you would need no decorators or carpenters to plan the kitchen for greater beauty and convenience if you bought their portable built-in-look cabinets.

The hinged top of this three-step, non-tipping stool makes a kitchen seat. The G.I. Sellers and Sons Company, Elwood, Indiana, offered this stepstool in white or ivory enamel, or brown or oyster white oak. It was priced at $4.95 in 1937. The Hoosier Manufacturing Company sold a similar shape stool for $4.25. This stool had a solid top for a seat, not a hinged top like the Sellers. In order to be a three-step stool, it had to be turned top to bottom. **$8-15**

The 1930 built-in sink had work surfaces on both sides of the sink. The window over the sink and the light fixture directly overhead illuminated the sink area.

This wheel table could easily be pushed to a busy kitchen spot. White enameled, its 20″ × 16″ linoleum center is red or blue. The 8″ drop leaves are natural-finish hardwood. This table, a product of the Hoosier Manufacturing Company, was priced at $12 in 1937. **$25-40**

Sinks. The development of the built-in sink was discussed in magazine articles by 1930. Detached sinks were losing favor for their wasted space, and the same was true of drainboards. The modern sink was an integral part of cabinet and cupboard installations. The sinks were sunk into the work surface with the plumbing hidden behind doors paneled with metal cane to give proper ventilation.

The sink center was one of the three centers that were part of basic planning principles established in 1935. The sink center usually had counters on each side that were used for food preparation and the stacking and draining of dishes. The base cabinets provided storage for saucepans, bowls, and utensils used daily. The wall cabinets were in easy reach for storage of dishes and glassware. Fruits and vegetables were also stored in this area.

This was a double sink with the laundry, dishwasher side 4″ deeper than the other side. A wire rack was placed in the deep side. Dishes were washed in the regular way in the shallow side, then placed in the wire rack. The dishes could then be rinsed with the spray attachment, covered with the drainboard, and left to dry.

In the 1937 catalog, Sears Roebuck offered the "Rinsink," which was a kitchen cabinet, an enameled laundry tub, and a dishwasher and dryer. (Courtesy Sears, Roebuck and Company.)

An example of white steel kitchen units that could be purchased in any combination is shown in this 1938 Cussins and Fearn Company ad. Other companies offered wooden kitchen units in colors or natural finishes.

DOES the sheer loveliness of this bright Monel corner make you blush for your own kitchen? Does its uninterrupted "flow" of silvery metal make *your* kitchen seem disorganized and inefficient?

Modernize with Monel. Only in Monel can you achieve these ultra-modern effects — with all equipment perfectly matched. For instance, only in Monel is it possible to match the latest model ranges of all leading manufacturers with a complete assortment of sinks, cabinets and work-tables.

Monel in Matched Units

This wide variety helps explain why Monel practically has a corner on model kitchens being built today by women's magazines, utility companies and equipment manufacturers. *Matched equipment* is the watchword for 1937 kitchens. And the easiest—and loveliest—way to do the matching is in Monel.

It's good psychology to Monel-ize your kitchen. The play of light over these shining surfaces makes hours in the kitchen pass cheerfully—and quickly. And with easy-to-clean Monel topping off everything, kitchen work becomes definitely easier.

A joy to work with

You'll find, also, that Monel is good for your nerves. This tactful metal is resilient. It subdues the clatter of pots and pans. And helps prevent breakage of your best china and glass.

Finally, Monel resists all attempts to destroy or mar its beauty. Acid fruit juices find that their efforts to make stains are—fruitless. It is proof against hot pots and pans . . . rust proof, chip proof, accident proof.

You can't guess the prices

Everybody guesses too high. Most people simply can't believe that Monel sinks start at $64.00. And sink-and-cabinet combinations at $94.50. In all, there are 57 different models to choose from. Cabinet sink models are available in any length from 41 to 144 inches in fractions of an inch.

For full information about Monel sinks and tanks, write to the manufacturers, Whitehead Metal Products Co. of New York, Inc., 304 Hudson St., New York, N.Y. For information about other Monel household equipment, address

THE INTERNATIONAL NICKEL CO., INC
73 Wall Street New York, N.Y.

2/3 NICKEL + 1/3 COPPER = MONEL

Monel Metal inherits from Nickel its finest qualities—strength, beauty and ability to withstand rust and corrosion. When you specify metals, remember that the addition of Nickel brings toughness, strength, beauty and extra years of service to steels, irons and non-ferrous alloys.

The Monel sink has an 8″ backsplash and crumb cup strainer. The sink is surrounded with silvery Monel work surfaces. Monel Metal looks like nickel, is almost as hard as steel, and it resists corrosion. It is crackproof, chip-proof, accident-proof, and resilient, which helps to subdue the clatter. A 1937 advertisement.

The Hoosier Manufacturing Company offered a "built-in sink," plus a variety of other kitchen units in 1936. These were to be built in, not movable as were their earlier fitted kitchen cabinets.

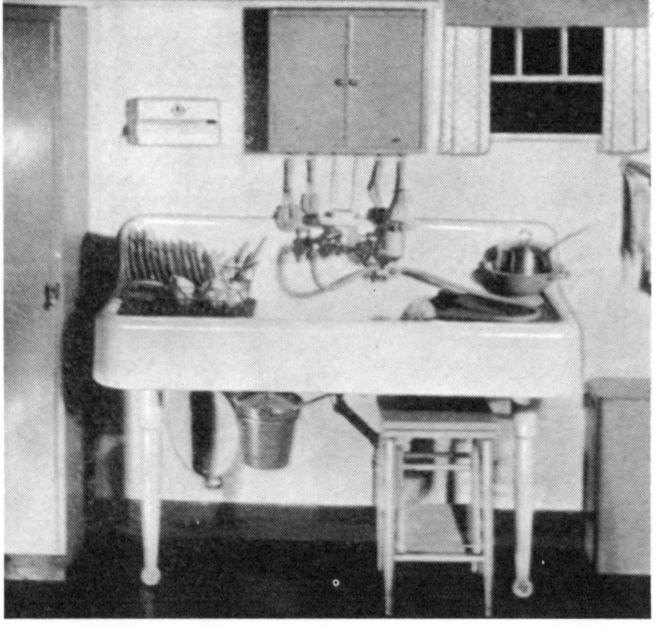

A 1932 kitchen in the Lazarus Book showed a kitchen sink that had a box of paper towels over the sink, a cabinet for supplies, and a rack for brushes. A kitchen catch-all swung at a convenient height under the sink. Another necessity was the stepstool. A dishwasher was attached to the faucet, ready for work.

Accessories. The modern kitchens of the 1930s had accessories that added a welcome dash of color. Housewives were urged to keep their kitchens compact and colorful.

Refrigerator space-savers were popular in the 1930s. They were made of a variety of materials, such as vitrified china, enamelware, pottery, or clear glass baking containers with lids. The latter did triple duty, as they made food visible and could be used for baking and saving leftovers. Refrigerator dishes saved space and kept food separated and fresh. Refrigerator dishes did away with a hit-or-miss assortment of containers, and they allowed the circulation of air necessary for cooling.

The National Enameling and Stamping Company manufactured many kitchen items under their tradename Nesco. Their Garden Girl accessories included canisters, breadbox, recipe box, soapflake box, dustpan, step-on can, and cleanser-can holder, all available in several colors in the 1930s. A few of the color combinations were white trimmed with black and red knobs, ivory trimmed with green, and white trimmed with blue.

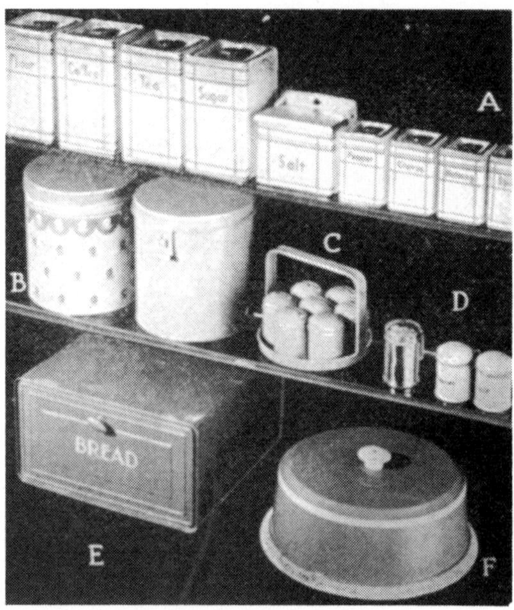

From the Lazarus 1932 cookbook:

A- Is a typical cereal set of pottery with colored stripings and clearly lettered names.

B- Canisters like this come in various sizes for tea, coffee, sugar, flour, and the flower pattern was effective in an otherwise simple kitchen. Next to it is a pastel solid-color one for conservative tastes.

C- Here's a handy little tray with tiny canisters for all your spices, in pretty painted tin.

D- Single individual salt and pepper and spice container can be had in painted tin or shining aluminum, all legibly marked.

E- You need a good breadbox — perhaps one like this, of enameled tin.

F- This is a cake board and cover — the board of wood, the cover of painted tin with handle.

The 1936-1937 Fall-Winter Sears catalog said that an inexpensive way to a smart, tidy kitchen was with matched kitchen containers. They featured the Silhouette Girl design that came in green with ivory trim or ivory with red trim. The pieces ranged from 49¢ to $1.19.

The Nesco jappaned ware was called Pantry Shelf in the 1937 Sears Roebuck catalog. The canister set sold for 50¢, drop-door breadbox $1.39, hinged breadbox 89¢, and the step-on can $1.19.

Montgomery Ward offered their containers in two designs. The moderately priced design came in a choice of white with black trim and knobs, ivory with green trim and knobs, or green with ivory trim and knobs. All had a bright floral spray. The low-priced "Floral Plaid" was finished in ivory with red plaid containers.

Nesco also had rounded Kitchen Vogue containers in white with either delphinium blue or geranium red trim in 1938.

From the Sears Roebuck 1932 sale catalog, a four-piece canister set in green and ivory. This set did not have a flour canister. (Courtesy Sears, Roebuck and Company.)

In 1933, a new refrigerator accessory was a "Lazy Susan," which provided easily accessible storage in glass jars for six different items. The jars fit together on a revolving stand, which was placed on a refrigerator shelf. A touch of a finger brought any jar to the front. The clear glass jars made the contents visible. The jars fit together with flat covers so no space was wasted.

Four Nesco Garden Girl ads. The prices in 1936 were: canister set $1.95, breadbox $2, two shakers 50¢, and cleanser-can holder 75¢.

Canister set $18-28

Breadbox $18-28

Shakers $5-7.50

Cleanser-can holder $2-7.50

Modern kitchens by NESCO featured color ensembles of enameled and jappaned ware in 1936. The Garden Girl jappaned ware was white with black trim and red knobs.

The dustpan, wastepaper basket, and clever holder for the soapflake box were available in several colors in the Country Girl pattern. **$4.50-10**

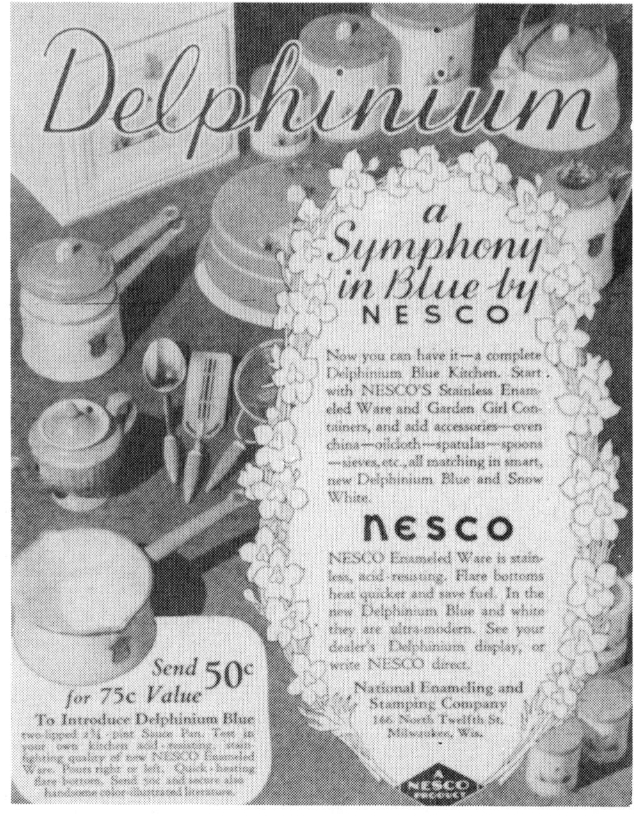

National Enameling and Stamping Company introduced their Delphinium Blue Enameled Ware and Country Girl ware with a 50¢ offer. The purchaser received a 75¢ value — a two-lipped 2¾-pint saucepan and color-illustrated literature.

Luncheon twins in the Country Girl pattern were also available in 1936. They were used to serve and store foods. The above was a jappaned ware cover and crystal tray for cake or sandwiches; below, divided relish tray; each $1.75. **$3-10**

Cake Covers and Trays
With Detachable Wire Carrier

Decorated covers with white stripe and white enameled metal trays. Tray can be used as a cake salver or service tray. Furnished in three colors, delphinium blue, red and ivory, all with white stripe and flower decoration. Diameter tray 12½ in.; height inside 4 in. One-quarter dozen of one color in a carton; weight, 8 lbs.

No. **20DB.** Delphinium Blue
No. **20R.** Red
No. **20 I.** Ivory
.......................per Doz. **15.00**

Japanned cake cover with lithographed decorations and fancy glass knobs, size 12x4½ in. Four ivory and two green covers packed in carton, with six ivory edge tin trays to match, and six detachable wire carriers. Shipping weight per assortment, 10 lbs.
No. **365** Cake Cover and Tray Ass'ts.
.......................per Ass't **4.50**
One-half dozen in a carton.

"Pic-Nic" Kit and Cake, Pie and Cooky Saver

Top is a regular Cake Cover and Tray, high enough for largest Angel Food Cake, and wide enough to hold a frosted 10-in. cake. Under this cover a large dish, pan or bowl of salad or other food can be carried to outing.

The second compartment will hold a large pie and the lower one cookies, etc. Finished in green, ivory, red and black with lithographed decorations.

Size overall 11[illegible]x9[illegible] in. Shipping weight per dozen, 48 lbs. One in a carton.

No. **5580G.** Green..........per Doz. **15.00**
No. **5580 I.** Ivory..........per Doz. **15.00**
No. **5580R.** Red..........per Doz. **15.00**
No. **5580B.** Black..........per Doz. **15.00**

Cake covers and Pic-Nics were popular in the 1930s. Nesco's Kitchen Gay ware came in white with red or green trim. (Courtesy George Worthington Company.) **$3-10**

EMPRESS JAPANNED WARE
White with Either Red or Blue Trim

Bread Box

Size 13¾x6¼x9½ inches. One-half dozen in a carton.
No. **321SR.** Red Trim ....per Doz. **8.50**
No. **321SB.** Blue Trim ....per Doz. **8.50**

Flour Canister

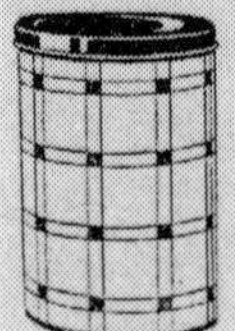

Size 7½x10 inches. One dozen in a carton.

No. **305SR.** Red Trim...per Doz. **4.25**
No. **305SB.** Blue Trim..per Doz. **4.25**

Canister Set

Four pieces as follows:
Sugar canister, coffee canister, rice canister, tea canister. One-half dozen set in a case.

No. **306SR.** Red Trim ....per Dozen Sets **8.50**
No. **306SB.** Blue Trim ....per Dozen Sets **8.50**

Range Set

Four pieces. Size of each 3¼x2⅜ inches. One and one-half dozen sets in a carton.
No. **308SR.** Red Trim ....per Dozen Sets **3.00**
No. **308SB.** Blue Trim ....per Dozen Sets **3.00**

Cake Safe

Size 10½x3¾ inches. One-half dozen in a carton.
No. **311SR.** Red Trim ....per Dozen **8.50**
No. **311SB.** Blue Trim ....per Dozen **8.50**

Cookie Box

Size 10¼x2¾ inches. One dozen in a carton.
No. **310SR.** Red Trim ....per Dozen **4.25**
No. **310SB.** Blue Trim ....per Dozen **4.25**

Step-On Can

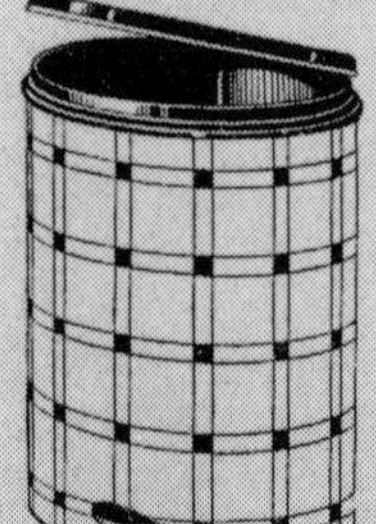

Twelve quart capacity. Size 9½x12 inches. One-half dozen in a carton.

No. **322SR.** Red Trim ....per Dozen **9.75**

No. **322SB.** Blue Trim ....per Dozen **9.75**

Oval Waste Basket

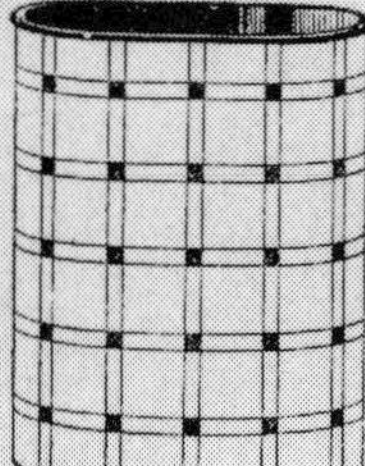

Diameter, 11x6⅝ inches; height, 12½ inches. One-half dozen in a carton.

No. **605SR.** Red Trim ....per Dozen **4.25**

No. **605SB.** Blue Trim ....per Dozen **4.25**

Serving Tray

14¼ inches in diameter, 1 inch deep. One dozen in a carton.
No. **411SR.** Red Trim ....per Dozen **4.25**
No. **411SB.** Blue Trim ....per Dozen **4.25**

Dust Pan

One dozen in a carton.
No. **319SR.** Red Trim ....per Dozen **1.75**
No. **319SB.** Blue Trim ....per Dozen **1.75**

Eight Piece Assortment

Consists of one each of the following pieces:
No. 605 Waste Basket
No. 322 Step-on Can
No. 306 Canister Set (4 pieces)
No. 319 Dust Pan
No. 321 Bread Box
No. **282SR.** Red Trim Assortment.........Each **3.00**
No. **282SB.** Blue Trim Assortment.........Each **3.00**

PI KITCHEN JAPANNED WARE
Rich Ivory with Green Stripes

Bread Box

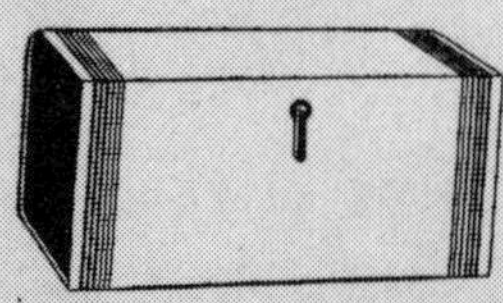

One-half dozen in a carton; weight of carton, 16 lbs.
No. **321PI** Bread Box................per Doz. **8.50**

PI KITCHEN JAPANNED WARE
Rich Ivory with Green Stripes

Canister Set

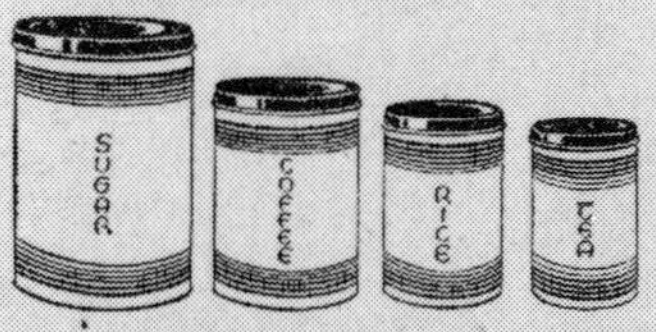

Four pieces as follows: tea canister, rice canister, coffee canister, sugar canister. One-half dozen sets in a carton, weighing 18 lbs.
No. **306PI** Canister Set.............per Dozen **8.50**

Step-On Can

One-half dozen in a carton, weighing 25 lbs.
No. **322PI** Step-on Can ....per Dozen **9.75**

Oval Waste Basket

12 quart. One-half dozen in a carton, weighing 13 lbs.
No. **605PI** Oval Waste Basket ....per Dozen **4.25**

Dust Pan

One dozen in a carton; weight, 7¾ lbs.
No. **319PI** Dust Pan ....per Dozen **1.75**

The "A" Pack

Consists of one each of all of the PI items listed (Nos. 306, 319, 321, 322, 605) each item individually wrapped and surrounded by corrugated board. Size of pack 25x14½x13¾ inches; weight, 19 lbs.
No. **282PI** "A" Pack....................per Set **3.00**

Empress ware was white with either red or blue trim, and PI jappaned ware was ivory with green stripes. (Courtesy George Worthington Company.)

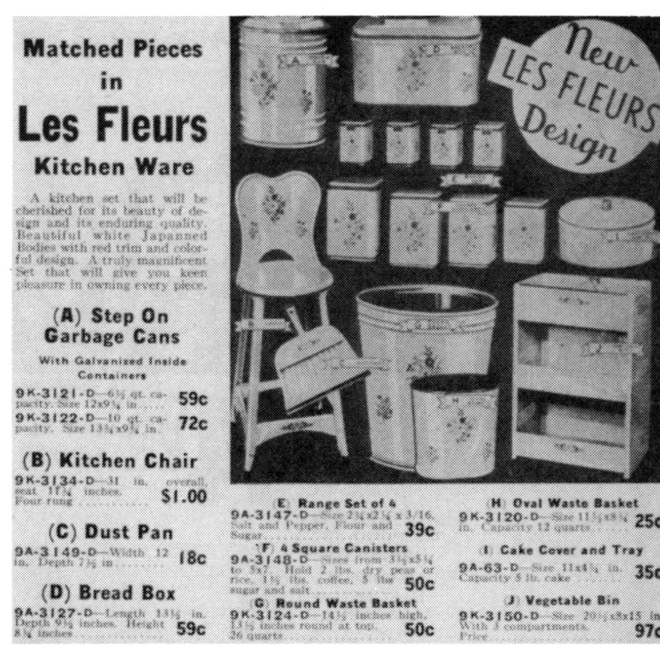

Les Fleurs kitchenware was white with red trim and colorful design, as illustrated in the 1938 Cussins and Fearn Company catalog.

Step-on can $5-10
Canisters $18-28
Chair $15-18
Vegetable bin $8-15
Wastebaskets $7.50-16

SANETTE step-on cans came in four sizes and colors and were sold for as little as $1.50 in 1939. One of the exclusive features was the rubber-cushioned, quiet-closing cover. The manufacturer was Master Metal Products, Inc., Buffalo, New York.
$5-12

Grouping of 1930 stainless steel and aluminum utensils, including a double boiler, dutch oven, waterless cooker (in center), and fry pan.

TWIN SAUCEPANS

JUSTIFY THEIR POPULARITY

Double pans save space, time and fuel

6 to 20% Fuel Savings Found in Delineator Institute Experiments

The problem of cooking four different things with only three top-stove burners available is a familiar one. Triple pans, already on the market, have solved many problems of cooking space. But the twin saucepans fill a real need, since it is more often necessary to cook two things over one burner than three.

The pans are easily cleaned because their corners are rounded and they are shallow enough for the hand to reach all parts readily. They hold about one and one-half quarts each. Where it has been necessary to wait to cook one thing after another in single pans, each requiring a whole burner, these pans are great time savers. For the one-burner kitchenette cook, they are "situation savers."

Institute tests on the new twin saucepans showed actual savings of six to twenty per cent in fuel. In most cases, the fuel savings vary with the kind of range used, and also with the variety of fuel. Their economy, added to their great convenience, proves that the twin saucepans deserve their popularity.

The 1933 *Delineator* magazine said that their new double or twin saucepans offered a 6 to 20 percent fuel savings. The pans held 1½ quarts each, were easy to clean with their rounded corners, and offered the convenience of cooking two foods at the same time on the same burner. (Courtesy the Butterick Company.)

USEFUL OVER THE RANGE

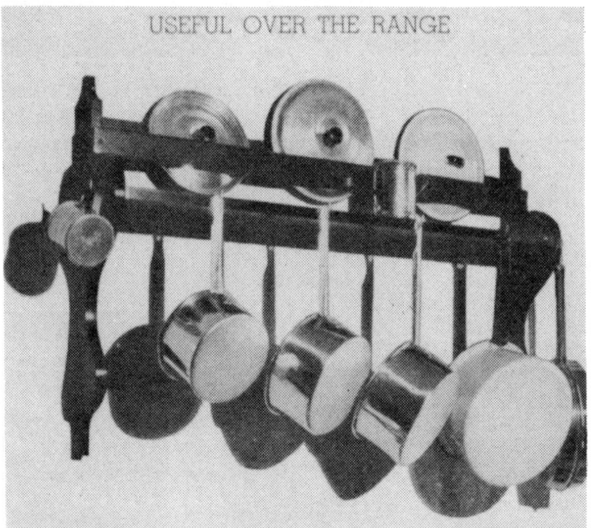

A handy place to put the pans and covers you use most frequently

Those who know the convenience of hanging pans above or near the range will appreciate a combination pan and cover rack, and small shelf. Those who haven't hung up their pans will want to try it.

This rack consists of a narrow wooden shelf with a slot above it, for pan covers, made of narrow wooden strips. This slot will hold six or more covers according to sizes.

Along the edge of the shelf are hooks for pans—saucepans, fry pans or what you will. On the shelf stand the salt and pepper shakers, the flour dredger and cans of coffee and tea if they aren't too large. This three-inch shelf keeps the pots and pans from hanging too close to the wall. It is a convenient affair and also looks well on any kitchen wall, and may also convince you that your pots and pans are so delapidated that you need new ones.

The rack was a handy place to put the pans and covers that were used most frequently. The shelf had room for salt and pepper shakers, flour dredger, and small containers of coffee and tea. The rack was attractive, convenient, and could be hung either above or near the range.

Cookware. The sheen of stainless steel and aluminum, the gleam of copper, and the colorful array of enameled cookware offered by many companies in the 1930s attracted many housewives. Also available were iron utensils and glass cookware. In 1936, the latest thing in glass was the glass pan for stove-top cooking. It was said that these saucepans would not break if they were heated or treated "rough." A wire handle clamped on and easily could be removed so the pan could be used for table service.

A 1933 Wear-Ever aluminum cooking utensil advertisement asked the question, "If your husband prepared 1095 meals a year...would *he* worry along with your present cooking tools?" The answer was, "You just know he'd discard the saucepan and frying pan whose loose wobbly handles cause them to swing in your face like windmills...replace them with "Wear-Ever" pans that have rigid, non-slipping, non-burning handles." It then went on to give other advantages of Wear-Ever products.

A Nesco Fantasy enamelware saucepan set (one, two, and three quarts) came in three colors — delphinium blue, yellow, and red for $1.69. Matching mixing-bowl sets were also available for $1.49.

The humble pots and pans took on a streamlined, smart appearance that was to make the housewife enamored with cooking and more interested in recipes. These new utensils were practical, attractive, and more efficient than older utensils.

Pyrex Ware Assortments

No. 375 Set

Set consists of the following:

Quantity	Item
1	No. 209, 9½x1½ in. Round Pie Plate
6	No. 414, 4-oz. Custard Cups
1	No. 8, Round Measuring Cup
1	No. 683, 7⅞x3 in. Round Casserole with Utility Cover

No. **375** Set, complete.................. per Set **1.95**

No. 450 Home Outfitter Set

Two 11-piece sets, retailing for $4.50, each set consisting of the following:

Quantity	Item
1	No. 683 Round Casserole with Utility Cover
1	No. 209 Round Pie Plate
1	No. 232 Oblong Utility Dish
6	No. 414 4-oz. Custard Cups
1	No. 76 Percolator

No. **450** Set, complete.................. per Set **9.00**

Packed with Free Display

No. 145 Set

An 8 piece matched set. Two new 1½ quart "Sweet and Low" casseroles and 6 of the new No. 445 thin rimless custard cups in an attractive display and gift box.

No. **145** Set, complete.................. per Set **1.45**

"Sweet and Low" Pyrex Oven Ware

No. 445 Custard Cups

Thin, rimless. Matches No. 723 Casserole and No. 123 Baking Dish. Outside dimensions, 4x1⅝ in.

No. **445** Custard Cups............... per Dozen **.90**

No. 723 Casseroles

Round, Double Duty Casseroles, Utility cover. 1½-quart. Outside dimensions, 8½x3⅛ inches.

No. **723** Casseroles....................... Each **1.00**

Twelve in a Case.

No. 123 Open Baking Dish

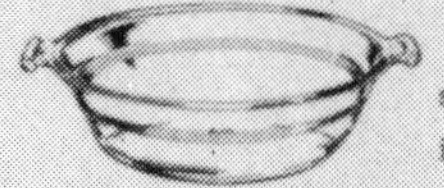

Round, 1½-quart. Outside dimensions 8½x2¾ inches.

No. **123** Open Baking Dish................ Each **.65**

Twelve in a Case.

Pyrex Top of Stove Ware

Clear transparent glass for cooking directly on the flame. Glass handles and chromium trim.

Double Boilers

No.	Cap. Qts.	Outside Body Dimensions, In. Width	Height	Each
6762	1	6 1/16	7½	**3.45**
6763	1½	6½	8¼	**3.95**

Six in a Case.

Sauce Pans

With Cover

No.	Cap. Qts.	Outside Body Dimensions, In. Width	Height	Each
6733	1½	6 1/16	5⅞	**2.00**
6734	2	6½	6 1/16	**2.35**

Six in a Case.

Without Cover

No.	Cap. Qts.	Outside Body Dimensions, In. Width	Height	Each
6713	1½	6 1/16	4 11/16	**1.65**
6714	2	6½	5⅛	**1.95**

Twelve in a Case.

Pyrex Top of Stove Ware

Clear, transparent glass for cooking directly on the flame on any type range.

Pyrex Sauce Pans

No.	Cap. Qts.	Size, Inches	Carton Lots, Dozen	Wt. Lbs.	Each
		With Plain Steel Handle			
6832	1	6⅞x2¾	1	23	**.95**
6833	1½	7⅞x3	1	28	**1.25**
		With Chrome Plated Handle			
6832C	1	6⅞x2¾	1	23	**1.10**
6833C	1½	7⅞x3	1	28	**1.40**

Pyrex Skillets

No.	Cap. Pts.	Size, Inches	Carton Lots, Dozen	Wt., Lbs.	Each
		With Plain Steel Handle			
6817	1	7x1½	1	19	**.75**
		With Chrome Plated Handle			
6817C	1	7x1½	1	19	**.90**

No. 265 Pyrex Three Piece Set with Chrome Handle

Set consists of two sauce pans—both the No. 6832—1 qt. and the No. 6833—stewing and warming up, 1½ qt. Ideal for boiling, meats, vegetables, fruits, etc. One No. 6817—7 inch skillet for fried eggs, meats, vegetables, etc. Removable chrome handle fits all three dishes. One set in a carton, six sets in a case.

No. **265** Three Piece Sets................ Each **2.65**

No. 66 Pyrex All Glass Coffee Makers

All glass filter plate. Serving bowl may be put directly on flame for reheating coffee. Dripless rolled edge—no spout to break. Easy to regulate strength of coffee. Capacity, 6 cups. One in a carton. Six in a case.

No. **66** Glass Coffee Maker.............. Each **3.50**

No. 76 Pyrex Crystal Percolators

Flame resisting. For use directly on the flame or electric heat without the need of asbestos mats. Many uses. For boiling liquids — brewing tea — serving hot or cold beverages. Modern design. Chromium mountings for novel glass handle. Lock on glass cover. Nickel plated coffee basket assembly. Capacity 6 cups. One in a carton. Twelve in a case.

No. **76** Crystal Percolators.............. Each **1.79**

No. **76B** Glass Bottoms only.............. Each **.60**

George Worthington Company 1937 catalog showing the top-of-the-stove Pyrex glass cookware. Corning introduced its Pyrex flameware in 1936, which meant glass cookware could be used on top of the stove as well as in the oven, strengthening its appeal. (Courtesy George Worthington Company.)

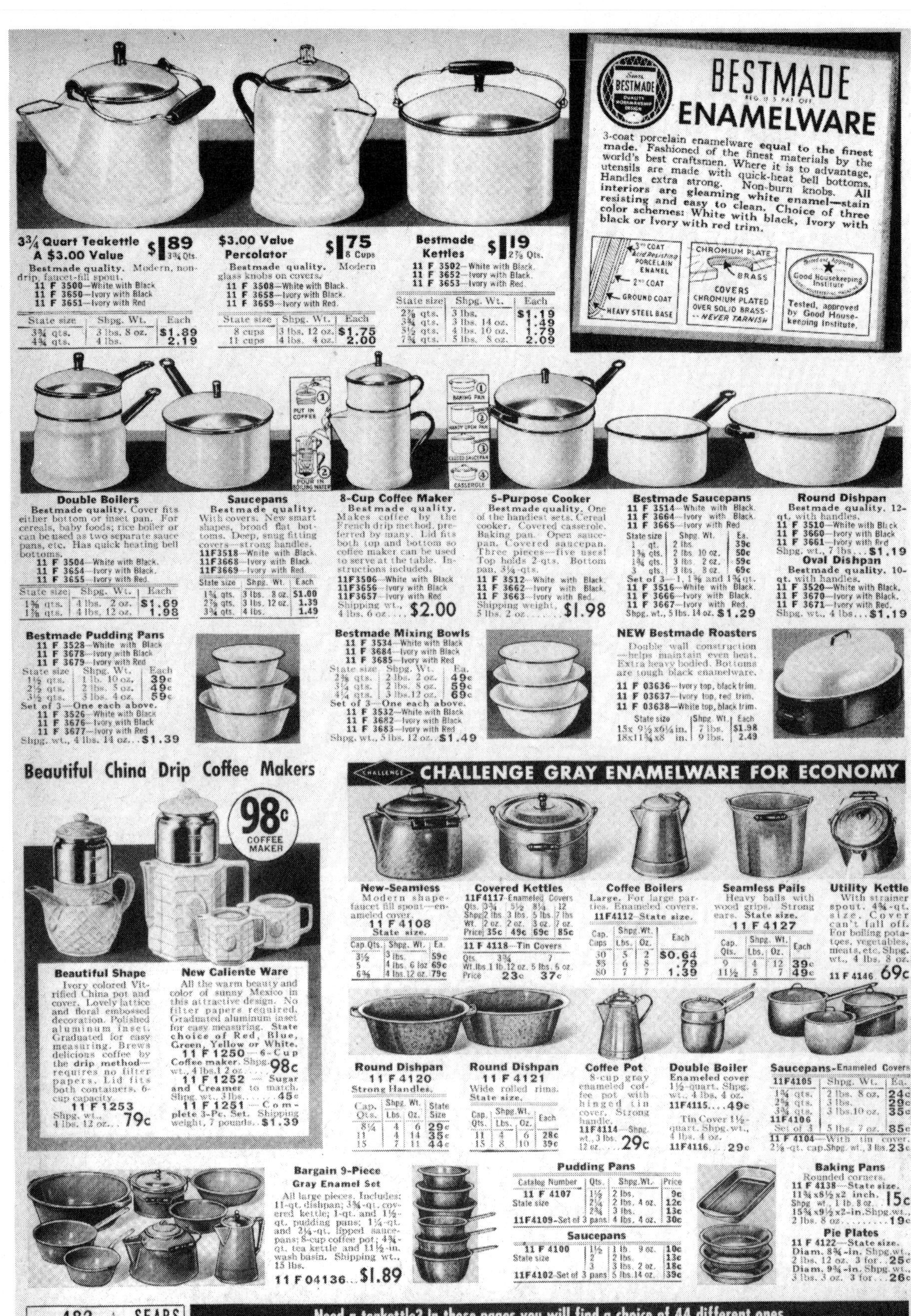

Sears Roebuck's 1937-1938 catalog offered gray enamelware and white enamelware with black, ivory with black, or ivory with red trim. China drip coffeepots were sold for from 79¢ to 98¢.

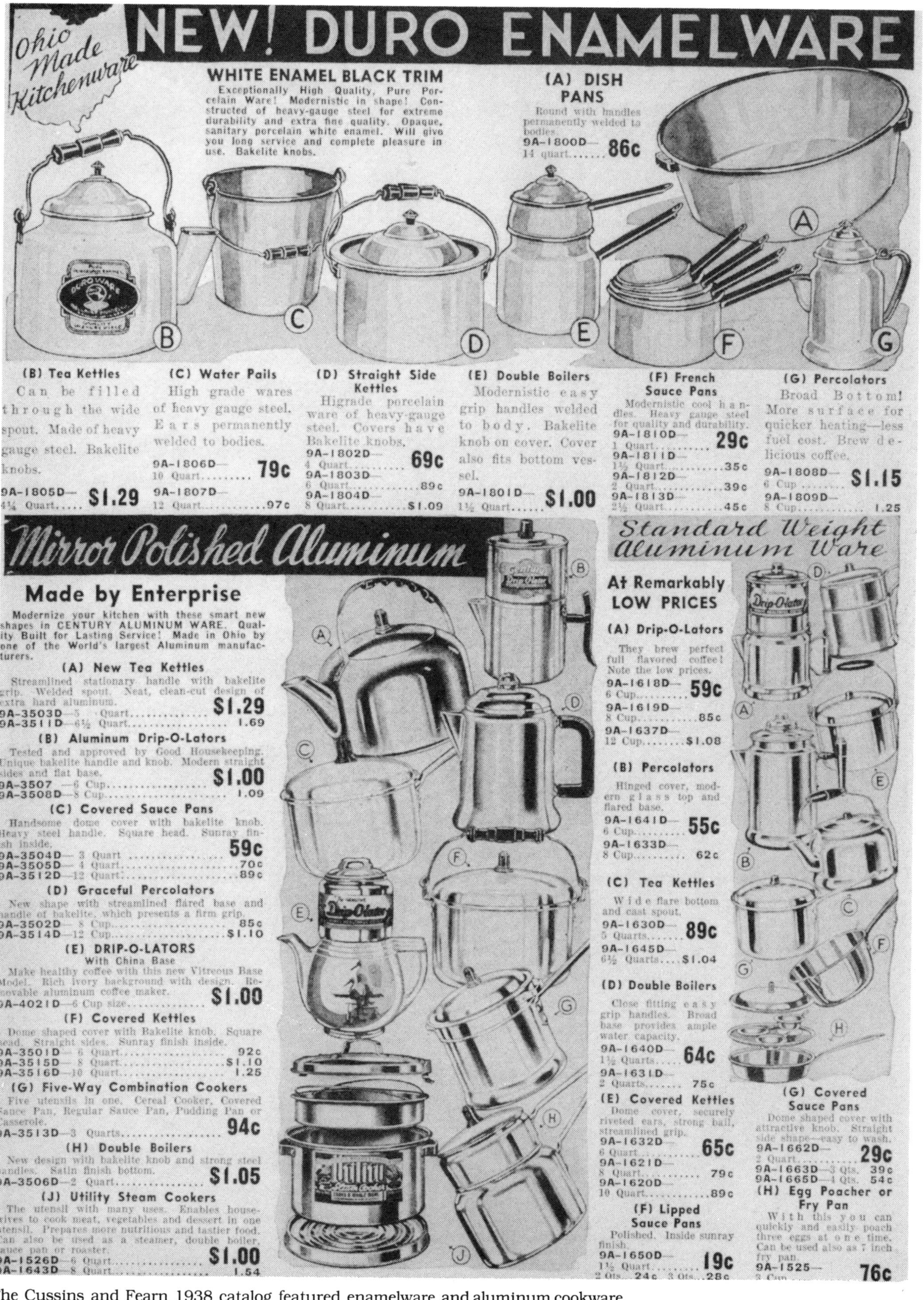

Ohio Made Kitchenware

NEW! DURO ENAMELWARE

WHITE ENAMEL BLACK TRIM

Exceptionally High Quality, Pure Porcelain Ware! Modernistic in shape! Constructed of heavy-gauge steel for extreme durability and extra fine quality. Opaque, sanitary porcelain white enamel. Will give you long service and complete pleasure in use. Bakelite knobs.

(A) DISH PANS

Round with handles permanently welded to bodies.
9A-1800D— 14 quart....... **86c**

(B) Tea Kettles

Can be filled through the wide spout. Made of heavy gauge steel. Bakelite knobs.
9A-1805D— 4¼ Quart..... **$1.29**

(C) Water Pails

High grade wares of heavy gauge steel. Ears permanently welded to bodies.
9A-1806D— 10 Quart......... **79c**
9A-1807D— 12 Quart...........97c

(D) Straight Side Kettles

Higrade porcelain ware of heavy-gauge steel. Covers have Bakelite knobs.
9A-1802D— 4 Quart.......... **69c**
9A-1803D— 6 Quart...........89c
9A-1804D— 8 Quart..........$1.09

(E) Double Boilers

Modernistic easy grip handles welded to body. Bakelite knob on cover. Cover also fits bottom vessel.
9A-1801D— 1½ Quart...... **$1.00**

(F) French Sauce Pans

Modernistic cool handles. Heavy gauge steel for quality and durability.
9A-1810D— 1 Quart......... **29c**
9A-1811D— 1½ Quart...........35c
9A-1812D— 2 Quart............39c
9A-1813D— 2½ Quart...........45c

(G) Percolators

Broad Bottom! More surface for quicker heating—less fuel cost. Brew delicious coffee.
9A-1808D— 6 Cup....... **$1.15**
9A-1809D— 8 Cup............ 1.25

Mirror Polished Aluminum

Made by Enterprise

Modernize your kitchen with these smart new shapes in CENTURY ALUMINUM WARE. Quality Built for Lasting Service! Made in Ohio by one of the World's largest Aluminum manufacturers.

(A) New Tea Kettles

Streamlined stationary handle with bakelite grip. Welded spout. Neat, clean-cut design of extra hard aluminum.
9A-3503D—5 Quart............. **$1.29**
9A-3511D—6½ Quart............. 1.69

(B) Aluminum Drip-O-Lators

Tested and approved by Good Housekeeping. Unique bakelite handle and knob. Modern straight sides and flat base.
9A-3507 —6 Cup................. **$1.00**
9A-3508D—8 Cup................. 1.09

(C) Covered Sauce Pans

Handsome dome cover with bakelite knob. Heavy steel handle. Square head. Sunray finish inside.
9A-3504D—3 Quart **59c**
9A-3505D—4 Quart.................70c
9A-3512D—12 Quart................89c

(D) Graceful Percolators

New shape with streamlined flared base and handle of bakelite, which presents a firm grip.
9A-3502D—8 Cup...................85c
9A-3514D—12 Cup.................$1.10

(E) DRIP-O-LATORS With China Base

Make healthy coffee with this new Vitreous Base Model. Rich ivory background with design. Removable aluminum coffee maker.
9A-4021D—6 Cup size............. **$1.00**

(F) Covered Kettles

Dome shaped cover with Bakelite knob. Square head. Straight sides. Sunray finish inside.
9A-3501D—6 Quart..................92c
9A-3515D—8 Quart.................$1.10
9A-3516D—10 Quart................ 1.25

(G) Five-Way Combination Cookers

Five utensils in one. Cereal Cooker, Covered Sauce Pan, Regular Sauce Pan, Pudding Pan or Casserole.
9A-3513D—3 Quarts................ **94c**

(H) Double Boilers

New design with bakelite knob and strong steel handles. Satin finish bottom.
9A-3506D—2 Quart................ **$1.05**

(J) Utility Steam Cookers

The utensil with many uses. Enables housewives to cook meat, vegetables and dessert in one utensil. Prepares more nutritious and tastier food. Can also be used as a steamer, double boiler, sauce pan or roaster.
9A-1526D—6 Quart................ **$1.00**
9A-1643D—8 Quart................. 1.54

Standard Weight Aluminum Ware

At Remarkably LOW PRICES

(A) Drip-O-Lators

They brew perfect full flavored coffee! Note the low prices.
9A-1618D— 6 Cup.......... **59c**
9A-1619D— 8 Cup...........85c
9A-1637D— 12 Cup.......$1.08

(B) Percolators

Hinged cover, modern glass top and flared base.
9A-1641D— 6 Cup.......... **55c**
9A-1633D— 8 Cup.......... 62c

(C) Tea Kettles

Wide flare bottom and cast spout.
9A-1630D— 5 Quarts...... **89c**
9A-1645D— 6½ Quarts....$1.04

(D) Double Boilers

Close fitting easy grip handles. Broad base provides ample water capacity.
9A-1640D— 1½ Quarts..... **64c**
9A-1631D— 2 Quarts...... 75c

(E) Covered Kettles

Dome cover, securely riveted ears, strong bail, streamlined grip.
9A-1632D— 6 Quart........ **65c**
9A-1621D— 8 Quart......... 79c
9A-1620D— 10 Quart...........89c

(F) Lipped Sauce Pans

Polished. Inside sunray finish.
9A-1650D— 1½ Quart........ **19c**
2 Qts....24c 3 Qts....28c

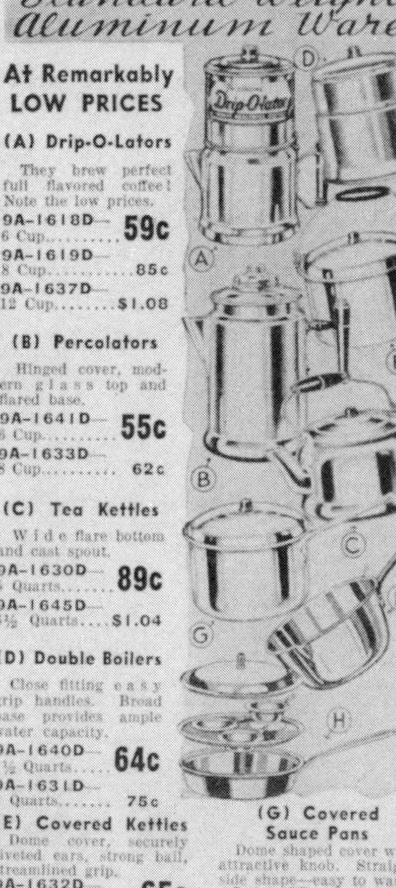

(G) Covered Sauce Pans

Dome shaped cover with attractive knob. Straight side shape—easy to wash.
9A-1662D— 2 Quart.......... **29c**
9A-1663D—3 Qts. 39c
9A-1665D—4 Qts. 54c

(H) Egg Poacher or Fry Pan

With this you can quickly and easily poach three eggs at one time. Can be used also as 7 inch fry pan.
9A-1525— 3 Cup....... **76c**

The Cussins and Fearn 1938 catalog featured enamelware and aluminum cookware.

IVORY DECORATED UNIVERSAL OVEN PROOF WARE

Beautiful ivory color with neat decorations. Guaranteed against crazing when used for baking purposes.

No. 36 Au Gratin Casseroles

Lid can be used for baking pies or making Au Gratin dishes.

No. 36—Capacity, 3½ pints; diameter, 8 in. ....per Dozen **16.80**

Mt. Vernon Casseroles

No. 43—Capacity, 2¼ pints; diameter, 7 in. ....per Dozen **14.40**

No. 56—Capacity, 4½ pints; diameter, 8 in. ....per Dozen **15.00**

No. 32 Pie Plates

Sufficiently thick to properly bake the undercrust after removed from the oven.

No. 32—Diameter, 10 inches ....per Dozen **6.00**

Pudding Dishes

No. 12 used as apple baker.

No. 12—Diameter, 6 inches ....per Dozen **2.00**

No. 65—Diameter, 8 inches ....per Dozen **6.00**

No. 37-39 Ice Box Sets

6 Piece Set

Consists of three bowls and three covers for same making 6 pieces. Can also be used for baking purposes.

Contents

1 No. 37—4 in. Bowl with cover
1 No. 38—5 in. Bowl with cover
1 No. 39—6 in. Bowl with cover

No. 37-39—Ice Box Set. . per Doz. **18.00**

No. 21 Mixing Bowl Sets

5 Piece Set

Contents

1 No. 16—5 in. 1 No. 19—8½ in.
1 No. 17—6 in. 1 No. 20—10 in.
1 No. 18—7 in.

No. 21—Mixing Bowl Set ....per Dozen **28.20**

No. 62 Covered Shallow Bowls With Covers

Set of 3

Set consists of 3 pieces, one each of 7, 8 and 9 inch diameter.

No. 62 Set..........per Doz. Sets **36.00**

No. 10 Custard Cups

No. 10—Capacity, 5 oz. ....per Dozen **1.80**

Pitchers

No. 21—Capacity, 1 Pint ....per Dozen **6.00**

No. 23—Capacity, 2 Pints ....per Dozen **8.40**

No. 25—Capacity, 3¾ Pints ....per Dozen **12.00**

No. 91 Covered Pitchers

No. 91—Capacity, 1½ Pints ....per Dozen **10.20**

No. 41 Bean Pots

No. 41—Capacity, 40 Oz. ....per Dozen **12.00**

No. 97 Salad Sets

Consists of Salad Fork, Salad Spoon and Salad Bowl which can be used for baking purposes. Diameter of bowl, 9½ inches.

No. 97—Salad Sets....per Dozen **15.00**

No. 2930 Salt and Pepper Shaker Sets

Set consists of one 4 in. salt shaker and one 4 in. pepper.

No. 2930—Salt and Pepper Shaker Sets ....per Dozen **7.20**

No. 34 Lard Bowls

Can also be used as a baking casserole.

No. 34—Diameter of bowl, 6 in. ....per Dozen **9.00**

No. 74 Canteen Jugs

Ideal for refrigerator uses.

No. 74—Capacity, 2 Pints ....per Dozen **12.00**

No. 69 Tea Pots

No. 69—Capacity, 33 ounces ....per Dozen **12.00**

Camwood Ivory Dinner Ware Sets

Camwood Ivory dinner ware, Mountain Tea decoration, plain shape in a beautiful Ivory color, artistic decoration, and guaranteed against the common fault of crazing or glaze checking.

32 Piece Sets

6 Plates, 7 in. 6 Saucers
6 Plates, 4 in. 6 Cups
6 Fruit Plates, 4 in. 1 Dish, 8 in.
1 Baker, 7 in.

No. 267—32 Pc. Set..........Each **6.50**

53 Piece Set

8 Plates, 7 in. 8 Saucers
8 Plates, 4 in. 1 Covered Sugar
8 Coupes, 6 in. 1 Creamer
8 Fruits, 4 in. 1 Baker, 7 in.
8 Cups 1 Dish, 8 in.

No. 490—53 Pc. Set.........Each **10.95**

Ivory Decorated Universal Oven Proof Ware was carried by The George Worthington Company in 1937. (Courtesy The George Worthington Company.)

Colorful Kitchens, Kitchenwares, and Toys

Linoleum, introduced in America during the 1870s, brought some color to the kitchen. Prior to 1917, linoleum, although considered sanitary, was drab and dull and was used primarily by institutions for kitchen and bathroom counters and flooring. After World War I the Armstrong Cork Company staged a massive advertising campaign to change this commercial image. Advertisements were placed in leading home magazines and salesmen carried color plates in their pattern books to promote linoleum sales.

In 1918, Frank Alvah Parsons, president of the New York School of Fine and Applied Art, New York City, wrote *The Art of Home Furnishing and Decoration*, which was published by the Armstrong Cork Company. Parsons theorized that "Man is exactly what he lives in." He wrote that color played an important part in the attractiveness of the kitchen. Patterns should be chosen for the decorative effect, making the rest of the room a plain color. Particularly good colors were white or cream and light tones of gray. In sunny and very light rooms, soft greens and blues could be used. Nothing was more important than color, and nothing expressed personality and charm more clearly. Parsons wrote this at a time when the "sanitary" (all-white) kitchen was at its height in popularity.

Cheerfulness seemed to fly out the door when efficiency was introduced into the kitchen. The "sanitary," all-white kitchens became laboratorylike — immaculate in their mechanical slickness, but sterile and very lonely looking. There was no room for the softening, homespun quality and intimate touches that had made Grandmother's kitchen so livable.

The introduction of color into the kitchen began in the 1920s. Homemakers were told that the floors and walls of their kitchens should have finishes that were attractive and restful to the eye. At the same time they should be easy to clean. The all-white kitchen was not as comfortable on the eyes as kitchens painted in soft yellows, buffs, or tans. The more restful colors relieved eyestrain and helped prevent bodily fatigue.

Green, a combination of yellow, expressing light, and blue, expressing coolness, was considered the ideal kitchen color and became very popular in home decoration.

In 1924 *The Home* advised that kitchen walls should, if possible, be finished to the wainscoating with metal tiles, which were easy to install on plaster or wooden walls. This tiling was comparatively inexpensive and, with a minimum of labor, could be kept spotlessly clean. Oilcloth wall fabric was another recommended alternative for the walls.

Painted furniture found favor again because of the cheerful effect it created in sun parlors, breakfast nooks, and other areas. Some households were forced to make-do with inexpensive, unattractive mismatched furniture gathered at various times without regard to color or finish. A set of brushes and a can of paint were a tremendous help in alleviating the problem of unmatched sets. The great advantage of paint and enamel for furniture was that it could rejuvenate dilapidated appearances from years of hard use quickly and economically. It was a joy to see how lovely colors transformed old furniture or woodwork into new beauty.

Linoleum was quite decorative. It furnished a hard, easily washed floor surface that could be purchased in almost any color or pattern desired. Solid colors, patterns, and tiled or mottled effects could be obtained that permitted magical transformations.

Color was added to appliances during the late 1920s to "make them more acceptable to feminine taste." Frigidaire marketed a refrigerator in 1925 that was hand-painted in red, black, and gold.

Color invaded the kitchen...on pots and pans, on furniture and floors...marching in a bright parade by the late 1920s. The vogue of color was truly welcomed. The kitchen became brighter, more pleasant, and a more cheerful place in which to work.

Once the mechanics of kitchen design had been worked out, attention turned to the decorative scheme. The approved kitchen in the early 1930s combined convenience and charm. It was small and compact in arrangement with a light and colorful, pleasing decor. The average woman loved to display her flair for bright, gay colors in her workshop, and manufacturers obliged by producing sets of color-trimmed utensils and kitchen accessories.

In making the color plan it was advised that the walls and ceilings were the first consideration and should be light in color to reflect light. Kitchens of the time were frequently lighted by one central ceiling fixture, so reflected light was depended upon to increase visibility in work areas.

It was possible to have as much individuality and personality in the kitchen as there was in the living room. The pleasant atmosphere of a colorful room gave a tremendous lift to one's spirits. Appliances, flooring, cabinets, counters, accessories, and wall coverings in cheerful colors went a long way toward making work less tiresome.

Color in the larger pieces of equipment was highly promoted in the first half of the thirties. This equipment included such things as stoves, sinks, refrigerators, tables, and cabinets. Since colored appliances were more expensive, many people preferred white for the major, more permanent pieces. But walls, woodwork, floors, curtains, utensils, shelving, dish towels, spice jars, and other accessories blossomed with bright color.

Color was the magic wand...when it was waved it worked miracles! It could turn a mouse of a room into a room with personality. It could put a dash of excitement into the dullest corner. A small room could have walls pushed out with light cool green, or blue, or gray. A dark room could be brightened with yellow or off-white wall color that increased light by reflection.

It was possible to make a home friendlier and more comfortable by choosing the right color combinations. A cold, cheerless room could be made to say "welcome." Warm effects could be painted into a room that faced north, and cool relief could be brought into those rooms that faced the afternoon sun. Narrow halls and stuffy rooms could be made to appear spacious and airy with the right colors.

If the kitchen happened to be one of those rare ones that was larger, it could be made cozy by painting the floor and ceiling the same color and by using warm, rosy hues and gay patterns.

Pastels and paint tints could be used to make a room look larger. White or light tones gave the room an illusion of extra height if the ceilings were too low. Bright, strong colors were good to use on extremely high ceilings, to bring them into proportion with furniture.

A few years earlier, the trend had been toward colored finishes on large kitchen equipment. Increasingly, by the late 1930s white was regaining popularity. White appliances were preferred because they didn't dominate the decorative scheme of the kitchen. A worn-out white appliance did not create the color-matching problems encountered when colored appliances had to be replaced.

Colors in the wallcovering could be repeated in canisters, chair cushions, and pottery. This had a gay and cheerful effect. Color and pattern relationships between floor coverings, walls, and curtains were desirable. Color contrasts made for liveliness, while repetition of color had a quieting effect.

A 1912 advertising postcard featuring a "step-saving, comfort saving kitchen cabinet and the very best... most sanitary and biggest ice-saving refrigerator." Notice the wall-hung sink and cast iron stove.

A partial view of the kitchen in Warren G. Harding's home in Marion, Ohio, as it looked when the Hardings left for the White House in 1921.

This 1930 advertisement with all the green kitchen equipment shows what Montgomery Ward was offering.

Accessories from the 1930s. *On ironing board:* spice rack $18 to $22, breadbox $18 to $28, matchbox holder $5 to $10, household scale $6 to $24, soapbox holder $4.50 to $10, hydrator $3.50 to $10, matchbox holder, breadbox, spice rack $10 to $18. *Ladder, top to bottom:* "Pic Nic" $3 to $10, colander, pottery, vacuum jug, dustpan $2 to $3.50. *On vegetable bin top to bottom:* hydrator, tray $1.50 to $3.50, cutlery box $1.50 to $3, cake safes $1 to $4.50.

A display of accessories from 1900 to 1930. *On top shelf:* japanned flour shaker and tea canister, decorated tinware tray, stoneware bowl, German china cereal and spice jars, tin comb and brush and match holder, decorated tin canister. *On middle shelf:* red-trimmed tin canister, yellowware bowl, stoneware butter holder, china blue willow canister set, decorated child's tin cup, jappaned flour canister. *Bottom shelf:* aluminum coffeepot, household scale, red baking powder tin, green and clear glass canisters, coffee grinder, string holder, cake carrier, bread box.

An assortment of jappaned, decorated tin, and plain and decorated glass canisters and jars from 1900 to 1950. Single canisters $3.50 to $18.

Cookware from 1900 to 1950. Iron dutch oven and biscuit pan; aluminum pots, pans, teakettle and coffeepots; enameled, covered pans and tea kettles; tin cookie sheet, cake pans and popover pan.

This 1937 Provincial kitchen is a colorful, step-saving room. The built-in corner cupboard and the bay window are unusual and attractive. (Courtesy Congoleum Corporation.)

A Provincial Designed Kitchen in General Electric Institute's 1933 edition of *The New Art.* (Courtesy General Electric Corporation.)

Before World War II, the better paint companies had made great strides in the development of paint. The paint was more durable and had become less expensive so that more people could buy it. Pre-mixed decorator colors were being offered in retail outlets.

The idea that paint saved the surface had been stressed by paint companies for years. That was only half the story because paint could be colorless. Colored paint saves the surface and lifts the morale. Old rooms and old furniture could be reclaimed with wonderful paint.

After the war, advances were made in the paint industry that were wonderful! The paints were quick-drying, easy-applying, and formulated from ingredients that made maintenance easy.

Some furniture was "painted" with stains of every hue that were rubbed into the woods. Plywood was plentiful, inexpensive, and paneled walls were very popular. These walls were pigmented in beautiful colors.

Light colors were suggested because they are airy and open and were ideal for the smaller rooms and open areas planned in so many postwar homes. Paint could make even the most modest home attractively appealing.

The plastic coverings on chairs added another color accent in the kitchen and were easy to clean. Housewives wanted an efficient work space with a cheerful atmosphere. They wanted colors that created a hominess in the room where the family could draw together.

After World War II the family was carefully considered in the planning of a kitchen or family room. "Togetherness" was the theme stressed by all of the shelter and women's magazines, at a time when families separated by war were reunited. The postwar kitchen was envisioned as a warm and wonderful place for the family to gather, truly the heart of the home, where the homemaker would spend many hours, the children would gather for an afterschool snack, and friends would always congregate. The concept of the "living kitchen" was so successful and popular, thousands of American homemakers, some with a rueful look backward, added a new color accent in their kitchens — a sign that proclaimed, "No matter where I serve my guests, it seems they like my kitchen best!"

"Gadgets for Good Cooking. Convenient aids to food preparation line up here and take a bow." Taken from the April, 1936 *Delineator* magazine. (Courtesy Butterick Corporation.)

Three kitchens featured in the 1939 *The Home Decorator and Color Guide* by Rockwell Kent. This guide was offered compliments of Sherwin-Williams Paints. (Courtesy Sherwin-Williams.)

"The Great God Pan" was title from a *Delineator* magazine article in 1935. These were newcomers to the realm of kitchenware. The copper gleamed, the aluminum had a sheen, and the enamelware came in bright greens and reds, pastels, candy stripes on ivory, and sharply contrasting black and white. (Courtesy Butterick Corporation.)

Accessories from the 1940s. The information on the gadgets shown is elsewhere in this book or in *Kitchen and Gadgets 1920 to 1950*. *Top row:* salt and pepper shakers $3 to $7.50, syrup and condiment jars 50¢ to $2.25. *On shelves:* plastic on left, center, and right with tulip decoration $2 to $8.50. *On ironing board:* $8 to $25, plastic teapot napkin holder $2, Ritz cracker tin with lid $5 to $12, teapot with thermometer and potholder hooks $2.50 to $7. *On ladder, top to bottom:* wax paper and paper towel dispenser $1.50 to $3; plastic measuring spoons and holder $2 to $4; plastic cream, sugar, salt, and pepper set 50¢ to $2.50. Tulip bowl set $7.50 to $15, single bowl $3.50 to $5, cutlery tray $1.50 to $3, enamel pot $3 to $5, glass jar with tulip lid $3 to $5, wind-up clock (works) $6. *Under ladder, back row:* Spice set (if complete) $10 to $18, tin plaid picnic box $9 to $15, PicNic (three-tray) $3 to $10. *Front row:* enamel pan $4 to $6.50, Pyrex bowl set $5 to $7.50, lunchbox $6.50 to $9.50.

Colorful catalin-handled kitchen tools and gadgets. *Left to right, top to bottom:* cake slicer, grapefruit corer, mincer-chopper, cheese slicer, spreader, pouring ladle, rotary mincer-noodle cutter, tomato knife, pickle fork, turner, spreader, ice cream scoop, fruit knife, dough blender, dough blender, slotted spoon.

A colorful 1942 streamlined kitchen. It has a continuous work surface with a range the same height as the cabinets. (Courtesy Congoleum Corporation.)

"Spin the shelves! Swing the table! It used to be colorless, inefficient, uninspiring—just an ordinary kitchen..." a 1946 ad. (Courtesy Armstrong World Industries.)

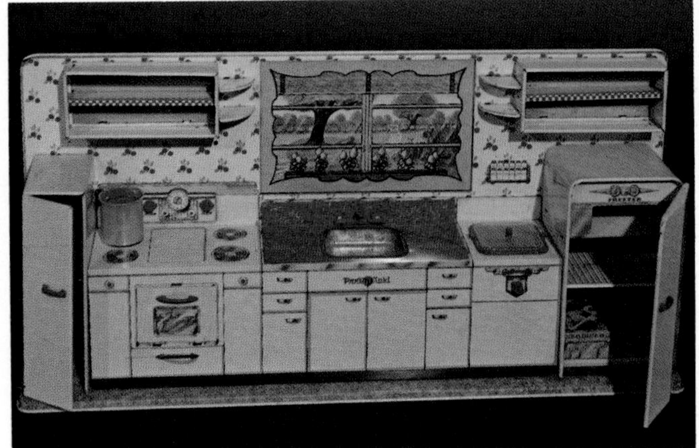

Marx Pretty Maid 1940s toy kitchen.

"Let's Have A Tea Party." Blue willow china and aluminum flatware marked Made In Germany.

"Little Homemaker's Tools." *On top shelf:* white teapot, cream and sugar, lustre cream and sugar. *On bottom shelf:* lustre teapot, cup and saucer, white cup and saucer. *Hanging:* kitchen tools with red wooden handles. *On ironing board, left to right:* Wolverine iron, muffin tin, green wooden-handle brush, blue iron, cookie jar, slotted spoon, toaster, cake pan, masher, dish rack with pots and pans, kettle. *On floor:* sweeper, refrigerator, antique iron, washing machine, tin tea set, Wolverine refrigerator, iron.

Current Values
Children's Homemaker Toys

Wooden potato masher with green wooden handle; with painted yellow knob. **$3-6.50**

Rolling pin, red wooden handles. Unmarked **$2.50-9**

Apple corer, red wood handle. Unmarked **$2.50-4**

Batter beater, red wood handle. Unmarked **$2.50-4**

Skimmer, red wood handle. Unmarked **$2.50-4**

Slotted spoon, red wood handle. Unmarked **$2.50-4**

Tea strainer, all metal. Unmarked **$2.50-4**

Juice strainer, all metal. Unmarked **$2.50-4**

Kettle, green enamel, label marked: "AMSCO TOYS; Let's Play Grown-Up; Doll-E and Kidd-E Toys." **$2.50-5**

Cookie sheet, marked: "Toy Aluminum Cookie Pan." **$1.50-2.50**

Aluminum jar, marked: "Cookies." **$1.50-3**

Saucepan with lid, unmarked, aluminum. **$1-3**

Fry pan, unmarked, aluminum. **$1-3**

Utility pan, rectangular, unmarked, aluminum. **$1-1.50**

Muffin tin, unmarked. **$2-2.50**

Square cake tin, unmarked. **$1.25-2**

Dish drainer, unmarked. **$1-6**

Blue Willow, 15-piece set, marked: "Made in Japan." **$15-25**
Blue Willow platter. **$5-12**

Teapot, cream and sugar; yellow flower on white background; marked: "Made in Japan." C. 1936 **$3.50-7**

Teapot, cream, sugar, and two cups and saucers; Lustre china with house scene; marked: "Japan." **$5-10**

Pink flower on white background, cup and saucer marked: "Made In Japan."

"Junior Miss Kitchenware; Kiddie Tea Set;" 29¢ blue and white tin, ten-piece set. **$1.25-2**

Two six-piece place settings, aluminum, marked: "Germany." **$3-6**

Four three-piece place settings, aluminum marked: "Made In U.S.A." **$2.50-5**

Carpet sweeper, brown metal, marked: "Porters Little Carpet Sweeper, Sweeps Just Like Mother's." **$8-10**

Sad iron, Mrs. Pott's style. In 1936, with stand, sold for 43¢ in Sears Roebuck catalog. **$10-16**

Iron, electric, green metal with black wooden handle, marked: "Dover Appliance Company; Dover, Ohio." **$6-12**

Iron, electric, blue metal with black plastic handle, marked: "Wolverine; Made In USA: 120V; 5W; UL Cat. No. 312." Box marked: "Wolverine #312; Electric Play Iron; Wolverine Toy Company, Pittsburgh, Pa." With box **$8-14**

Iron, electric, red wood handle, unmarked. Box marked: "It's A Honey; Mfg. by Lake Center Corporation, 2744 Nicollet, Minneapolis, Minn." With box **$8-14**

Toaster, green and white tin, marked: "Special." **$3.50-7**

Refrigerator, ice cube-freezer with turning dial, movable drawer, unmarked. **$8-14.50**

Refrigerator, marked: "Wolverine Supply and Manufacturing Company, Pittsburgh, Pa." **$8-14.50**

Washing machine with rubber roller, agitator that turns, marked: "Pet Pat. Pending; Pet Manufacturing, Inc., Dayton, Ohio." **$14-30**

Table and chairs not refinished. **$10-25**

Ironing board. **$10-14**

Marx toy kitchen, marked: "Pretty Maid." **$6.50-15**

The Postwar "Family" Kitchen, 1940 to 1950

Advertising made the streamlined kitchen the dream of the American housewife by 1940. There were numerous advertisements showing complete kitchens and many articles on decorating and planning new kitchens.

World War II interrupted and delayed the housewife's dream. Factories were retooled for the war effort, and production of kitchen cabinets and appliances was discontinued. However, manufacturers were planning for the postwar kitchen.

These plans featured modern designs, but the pleasure of the housewife was also considered. Aesthetically and physically, everything was done for the housewife's satisfaction. The kitchens were no longer clinical; colors made them cheerful. Opinion polls taken among women revealed that a picture window over the sink was a number-one priority. They wanted this so they could watch the children at play or just have a nice view while they were working. Another thing they wanted was a handy mirror in the kitchen.

This pink and black 1941 kitchen had a modern design, with the range, sink, and refrigerator all integrated into the scheme in a step-saving "L" arrangement. The kitchen was large enough to have an eating area. (Courtesy Armstrong World Industries.)

The kitchen of the 1930s, also used for dining room and office, still segregated the housewife from her family and guests when she was preparing meals. The logical answer was to incorporate the kitchen into the living room. The "open plan" by the 1940s was accepted as the means of achieving the illusion of space in the small house. Instead of being chopped into small segments and cut off by doors, the living room flowed into the dining area, often an L-shaped room. It was just a brief step into the kitchen, often separated by a room divider. Guests were present at the final stages of the meal preparation, yet not in the way, and the housewife was no longer isolated from family or guests.

After the war, the mechanization of the house and labor-saving devices replaced the need for as many servants. The servant supply was reduced because many had taken other jobs. Those who were available enjoyed higher wages. They went to work daily as at any other job, and were no longer considered "inferior" but were treated with respect.

Russell Lynes, in *Domesticated Americans*, said, "When the hostess is also the cook, class distinctions vanish; the servant and the served are one. The process of democratizing the household is complete."

According to John W. Dodds in his book *Everyday Life in Twentieth Century America*, no period in the history of the world saw such changes in everyday life as the first half of the twentieth century. Tremendous changes occurred in the kitchen, with the most dramatic taking place between World Wars I and II. Social changes had affected the kitchen, as we have seen with the final solution of the servant problem. The kitchen went from a room with no mechanized equipment in 1900 to one where automatic ranges, refrigerators, dishwashers, garbage disposers, freezers, and numerous small electric appliances were commonplace by 1950.

At the turn of the century, little consideration was given to a step-saving, efficient kitchen. But standardized kitchen equipment arranged in an efficient manner had become the rule of the day in the postwar kitchen.

All the engineering, planning, and designing of the first half century has served us well in the second half of the twentieth century. The planning principles established in the 1930s are still being used today, and most of the major appliances are basically the same. Today we can appreciate the kitchen of the 1980s when we look back at the kitchen in the past.

Modern appliances make it possible for the homemaker to spend much less time and energy to do her jobs well. Proper kitchen planning makes it easier to use these products efficiently, and it also tailors the kitchen to the family's way of life.

In 1941, Kitchen Maid offered standard unit cabinetry of "Composite Construction — wood, steel and newest compositions; each used where it serves best." They offered a free brochure, "Things To Know Before Planning a Kitchen."

READY FOR FUN without the hard work after the party's over! For this Canteen Kitchen has an Armstrong's Linoleum Floor—marbleized to hide footprints, smooth-surfaced for easy cleaning. The smart floor effect was created with three Marbelle colors—Nos. 018, 021, and 032. Wall is washable Armstrong's Linowall, Style No. 704. Counter-top, sink, and cove base are also linoleum. Send for free sketch of room plan and list of furnishings.

You're Invited
TO A STAY-AT-HOME PARTY
IN OUR
Canteen Kitchen

★☆★ **TO DO OUR PART** in the war effort, the Armstrong Cork Company has converted much of its productive capacity to the making of munitions and other vital war materials. However, your merchant can still show you Armstrong Floors that are both smart and correct. Just be sure to look for the name *Armstrong's* on the back.

BEING a stay-at-home isn't so bad these days if you can picnic right in your own kitchen. And that's easy, once you've planned your kitchen for having family fun—and for saving work, too.

That's what we did in the room above. We call it our Canteen Kitchen. In it you'll find everything for a good time at home—food, refreshments, radio, and even a phonograph for the young folks.

And in it you'll also find everything that makes Mother's job easier. The Armstrong Floor, which so cleverly gives this room its smart, modern appearance, also helps to keep this much-used kitchen tidy and neat at all times. Its marbled pattern hides spots and footprints. Its smooth surface can be wiped clean like a table top.

The walls, too, make housekeeping easier. They're Armstrong's Linowall—spatter-proof and washable, just like the linoleum floor. Linowall also covers the sides of the inexpensively built diner-counter—a smart step-saver that is also a *work-saver*, thanks to its easy-to-clean linoleum top.

Why not surprise your own family some day soon, with a room in which they can relax and have fun—and a room where you can be entirely free from heavy floor-cleaning care? Your local linoleum merchant can tell you how little it costs.

R.S.V.P. **FOR MORE ROOM IDEAS.** If you'd like a whole bookful of easy-to-do rooms, just send 10¢ for "Tomorrow's Ideas in Home Decoration" (outside U. S. A., 40¢). It's filled with full-color photographs and exciting decorating ideas. Write to Armstrong Cork Company, Floor Division, 4210 Elm St., Lancaster, Pa.

ARMSTRONG'S LINOLEUM FLOORS

for every room  *in the house*

This Canteen Kitchen was pictured in 1942. The Armstrong Cork Company did its part in the war effort; however, there were still some floorings available. (Courtesy Armstrong World Industries.)

Hustling, bustling crowds are outward signs of a busy people. But we think the real busy spot in the home is the kitchen. • The new American Kitchens are bright, cheerful, convenient, adequctely equipped with cabinet-sink and cabinet space, providing three convenient work centers for (1) Preparation, dish-washing, cleaning; (2) cooking and serving; (3) ample storage, gleaming white all-steel equipment, smartly styled, ruggedly durable, magically convenient. • Obtainable in separate units or as a complete ensemble. When? Just as soon as American Central's total war duties are brought to a victorious conclusion. Meantime — remember American.

AMERICAN CENTRAL MANUFACTURING CORPORATION • CONNERSVILLE, INDIANA

An American Kitchens ad in 1944 reminded people of the white all-steel, smartly styled, durable, and convenient kitchen, which would be available as soon as the war was won.

The 1947 Kelvinator Kitchen shows its appliance center, which included range, refrigerator, freezer, and garbage disposer. The cabinets were made of steel and had sliding glass doors.

. . . Your new kitchen need not be cold and institutional. With Kitchen Maid Cabinets of wood, it can be efficient, glamorous, yet warm and friendly too. For these cabinets combine the advantages of wood with other fine materials. Modern styling. Moderately priced. Planned especially for you by experienced specialists, with appliances of your own choice. See your dealer or send for new booklet.

The Kitchen Maid Corporation
185 Snowden St., Andrews, Indiana
Send colorful booklet with 10 beautiful kitchens and plans. I enclose 10 cents for handling.

Name ....

KITCHEN MAID
FIRST AND BEST IN
KITCHENS

The Kitchen Maid Corporation suggested you see one of their dealers, who would plan individual kitchens using appliances of the client's choice. In 1948, they offered a colorful booklet of ten beautiful kitchens and plans for 10¢.

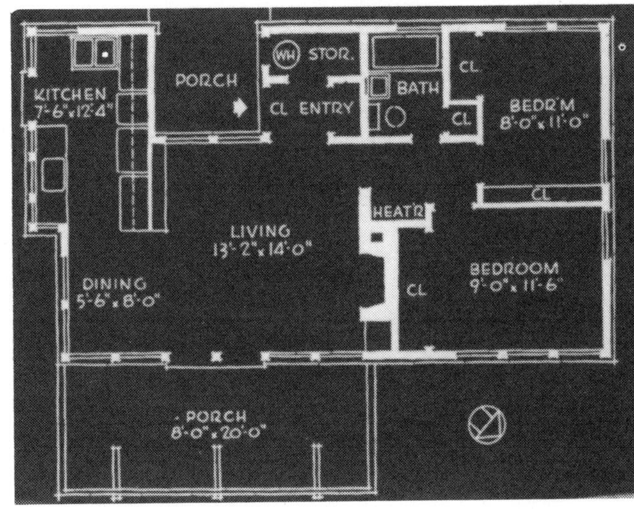

A 1948 house plan showing the open plan, with dining room off the living room and kitchen.

In 1947, American Kitchens showed how an old-fashioned kitchen could be redesigned and gradually modernized as the budget permitted.

▶
The Capitol Kitchen advertisement illustrates how an old kitchen could be modernized with 70 percent more storage space, nearly three times as much work surface, and an eating area doubled within the same four walls. This was an average-size, 10′ × 11′ kitchen.

Here's What a Capitol Kitchen Modernization Can Do!

	New Capitol Kitchen	Old Kitchen
Working Surface	42 sq. ft. (nearly 300% more)	15 sq. ft.
Storage Space	103 cu. ft. (nearly 70% more)	61 cu. ft.
Eating Area	for 4 persons (100% more)	for 2 persons

Old Kitchen

New Capitol Kitchen

PLUS beauty, convenience, efficiency

Kitchen planning, the Capitol way, can work wonders with YOUR kitchen, too. This old kitchen is now a modern Capitol Kitchen — all within the same four walls! There's nearly 70% more storage space, nearly 3 times as much working surface and eating area is doubled. This is only an average-size kitchen, too — 10 feet by 11 feet. And the U-shaped countertop is *continuous* — no cracks to collect dirt, dust or crumbs. To all this, you can add beauty, convenience and efficiency.

Have your Capitol dealer help plan your new modern kitchen within your budget. There are more than 40 types and sizes of Capitol's quality-built, heavy-gauge steel cabinets to choose from.

You'll be glad tomorrow, you bought Capitol today!

STEEL KITCHEN CABINETS AND SINKS

CAPITOL KITCHENS
ROSELLE, NEW JERSEY

Please send my local dealer's name and your Kitchen Planning Book. Enclosed is 10¢ (in coin).

Name (please print) ______________________

Street ______________________

City ______________ *State* ______________

CK-110

This 1949 kitchen has steel cabinets, an island, and corner shelves at the ends of the cabinets. The center of the island is open, making it possible to sit at it to work or to have a snack. (Courtesy Youngstown Kitchens.)

This 1950 G.E. all-electric kitchen included: an 8-cubic-foot refrigerator, dishwasher and sink, steel cabinets, range, and Disposall. (Courtesy General Electric Corporation.)

Gadgets

Baking. The instruction sheet reads:

How To Use The Sara and Aggie Cookie Press.

You will notice there are several parts to this Press. There is the Press itself, and it has a stand that can be removed; then there are four forming-plates, for making cookies in different shapes.

Now you can use this Cooky Press in two different ways. If you want to "drop" the cooky right onto the cooky pan from the Press, then you use form 8 or 6. But if you want to make a long strip of cooky dough which you will cut up with a knife so you can make rings or diamonds or "s" shaped cookies, then use the forms marked 9 or 2.

PLEASE NOTICE: First of all, wash the Cooky Press and all the parts in hot, soapy water before using the first time. AFTER using, be sure to wash out all the dough...

Beaters. Consumers Union said this was a well-constructed, easy-running beater with two speeds that easily shifted from one to the other. It had a chrominum-plated frame, stainless steel blades, was easy to clean and had a high beating efficiency.

The cardboard cylinder in which the Art Beck mechanical beater came said:

'The Art Beck Whip Beater'. WHIPS, BEATS, MIXES eggs, cream, baby's formula, hot drinks, cold drinks, gravy and sauces...with ONE HAND — perfect results in few seconds. Whips every drop. One hand operates it!

A wonderful party or bridge gift. An invaluable household aid. Easy to use....Easy to clean....So many uses....No waste....A Product of Arthur Beck Co., Chicago Copyright, 1948, by A.B. Co. Distributed by American Mdse. Dist. Chicago 2, Ill.

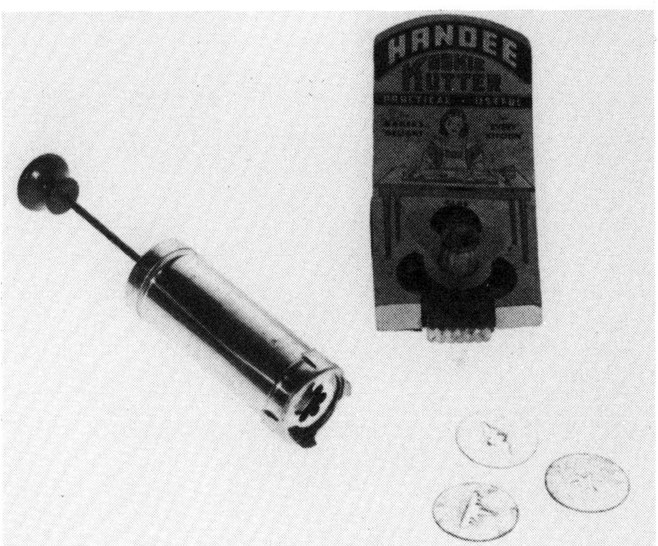

Unmarked green marbelized plastic cookie cutter. On card: "Handee Kookie–Practical–Useful. The Baker's Delight; For Every Kitchen." Original price was 20¢. **$1.50-3**

Unmarked cookie press. Forming plates are numbered 2, 6, 8, and 9. The press has a red wooden knob. **$1.50-3.50**

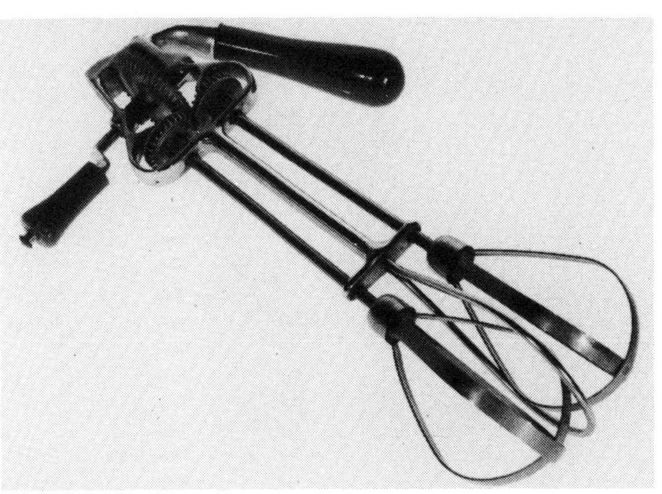

Left to right:

Unmarked mechanical beater with red wooden handle. This came in a cardboard cylinder.

"Made In England; Prov. Pat. 8135." Red wooden handle. **$2.75-5**

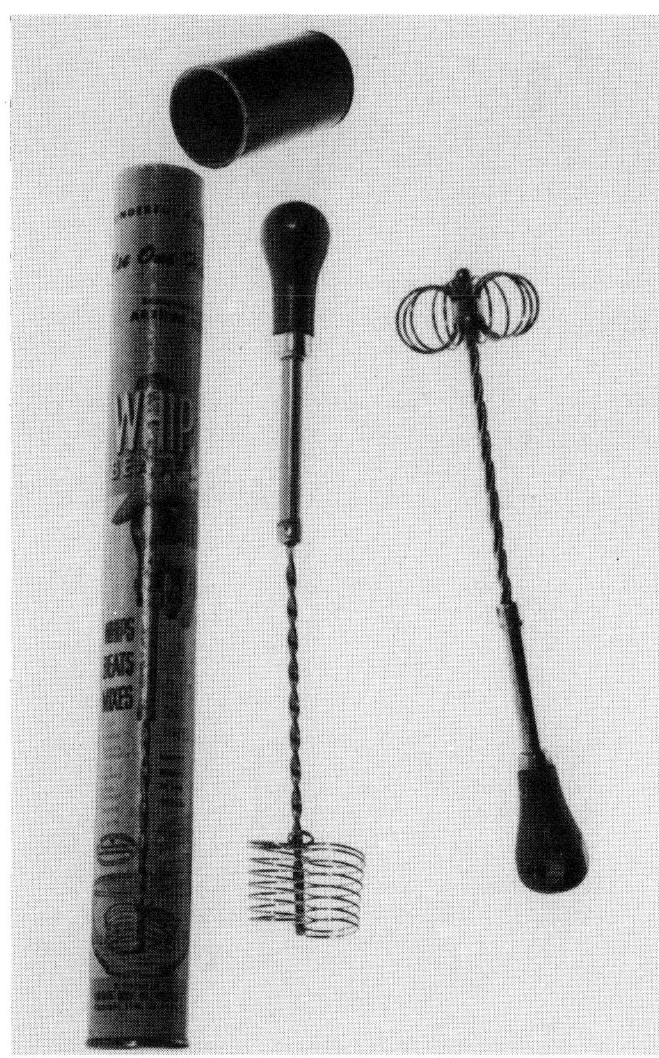

"Rotary Worlbeater; Pat. Pending; Los Angeles, Calif." A two-speed beater with red catalin handle. The Worlbeater (Na-Mac Products Company, Los Angeles) sold for $1.25. **$3.50-8**

A Na-Mac Products Corporation 1948 advertisement illustrating their products. **$1.75-8**

Can openers. Do you remember all the different size keys there were and how frustrating it was if the tear strip got snarled?

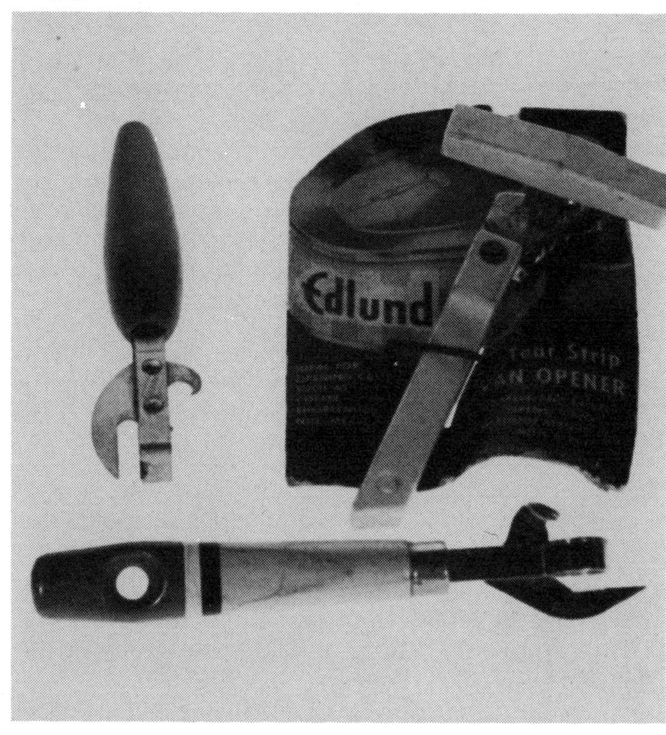

Grunert can opener. Red wooden handle.

"Tempered Tooled Steel; U.S.A. Pat. No. 2,018,083." It has a natural colored wooden handle with a red tip and white and dark red stripes.

Unmarked, with yellow plastic handle. Mounted on original card. "EDLUND TEAR STRIP CAN OPENER. Safely and Easily opens cans without struggling with a key. Ideal for opening cans such as coffee, shortening, nut, meat. Directions: Pull out starting tab on strip. Place plate of opener over rim of can so starting tab engages between rollers. Turn small handle clockwise. Tear Strip will be pulled from can, pass between rollers, and be ejected from the back of opener." **$1-3**

"Eversharp; Pat. No. 2,186,668." Green wooden handle. This can opener was patented in 1940. Wall can openers have been popular since the 1930s. **$3.50-6.50**

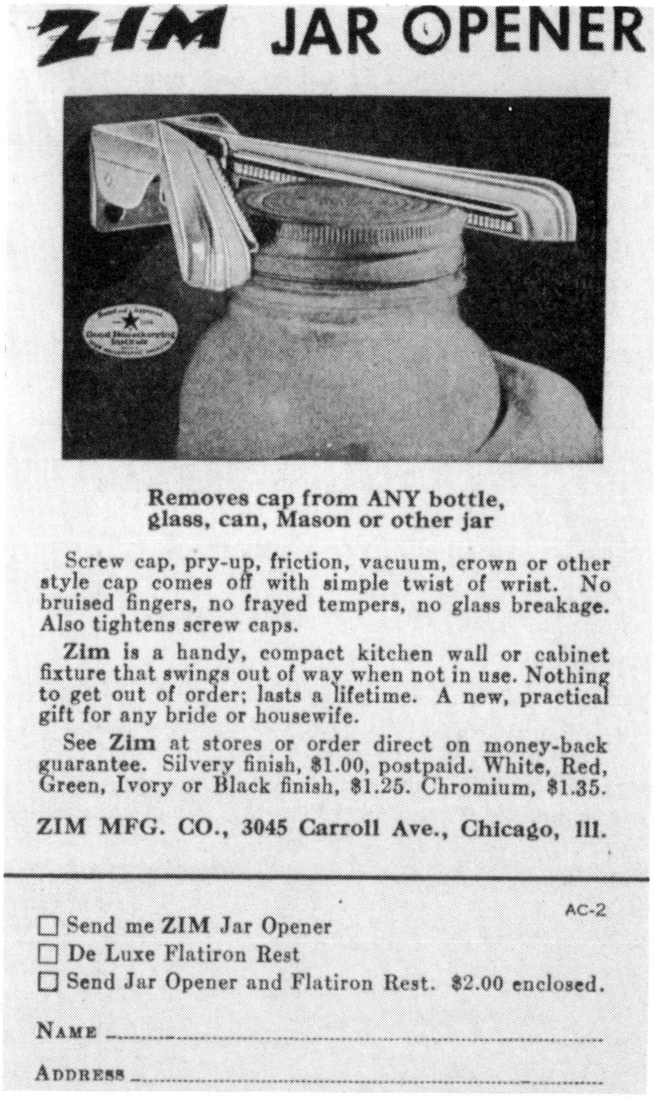

DREAM Kitchens

Dream Kitchens *always* include these familiar favorites.

*Juice-O-Mat**
T.M. Reg. U.S. Pat. Off

The Juicer that gets ALL the juice, without rind-oil, pulp or seeds.

Ice-O-Mat
Trade Mark

Easily crushes cubes or lumps, fine or coarse.

Can-O-Mat
Trade Mark

Opens cans of all shapes and sizes, leaving smooth beveled edges.

*Broil-O-Mat'**
T.M. Reg. U.S. Pat. Off.

For steaks, chops, fish or fowl. Only electric adjustable broiler made.

*Trademark Reg. U. S. Pat. Off.

Rival
MANUFACTURING COMPANY
KANSAS CITY, MISSOURI
Originalists
FIRST with a Streamlined Juicer

According to the Rival Manufacturing Company, 1944 Dream Kitchens always included these familiar favorites: "the juicer that gets All the juice... the Ice-O-Mat which crushes cubes or lumps, fine or coarse... the Can-O-Mat which opens cans of all shapes and sizes, leaving smooth beveled edges... and the Broil-O-Mat for steaks, chops, fish or fowl which is the only electric adjustable broiler made." **$5.50-14**

ZIM JAR OPENER

Removes cap from ANY bottle, glass, can, Mason or other jar

Screw cap, pry-up, friction, vacuum, crown or other style cap comes off with simple twist of wrist. No bruised fingers, no frayed tempers, no glass breakage. Also tightens screw caps.

Zim is a handy, compact kitchen wall or cabinet fixture that swings out of way when not in use. Nothing to get out of order; lasts a lifetime. A new, practical gift for any bride or housewife.

See **Zim** at stores or order direct on money-back guarantee. Silvery finish, $1.00, postpaid. White, Red, Green, Ivory or Black finish, $1.25. Chromium, $1.35.

ZIM MFG. CO., 3045 Carroll Ave., Chicago, Ill.

AC-2

☐ Send me ZIM Jar Opener
☐ De Luxe Flatiron Rest
☐ Send Jar Opener and Flatiron Rest. $2.00 enclosed.

NAME ....

ADDRESS ....

The Zim Manufacturing Company of Chicago claimed their ZIM Jar Opener would remove caps from ANY bottle, glass, can, Mason or other jar. It was a handy, compact kitchen wall or cabinet fixture that sold at stores or by ordering direct on money-back guarantee. With the silvery finish, $1 postpaid. With white, red, green, ivory, or black finish, $1.25. Chromium, $1.35. **$2.25-4.50**

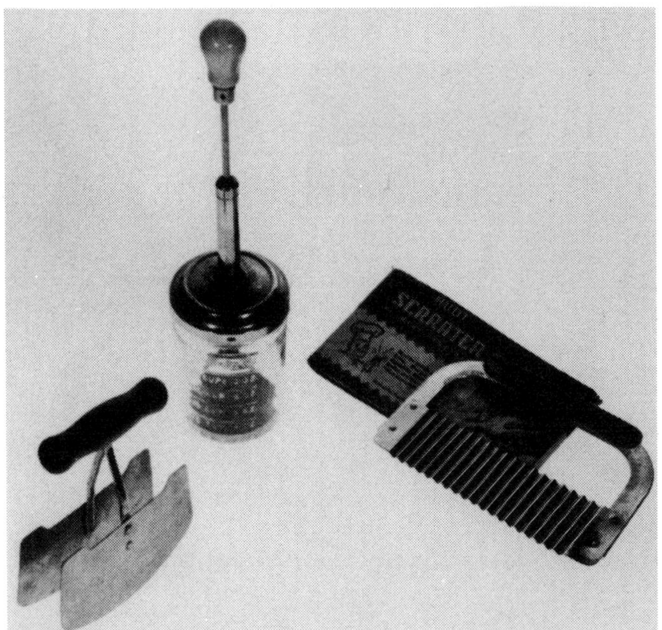

Left to right:

Stainless steel chopper with double blade, red wooden handle.

Says "Stainless" on blade. Yellow wooden knob on chopper; glass jar. Here's a tearless onion chopper that will keep you smiling through endless onion chopping. The onion is chopped inside the jar, which has a lid. This sold for $1 in 1947.

Huot St. Paul. Stainless. Red plastic handle. **$3.50-8.50**

Choppers. On package:

HUOT Serrator and Meat Tenderizer. Ideal for wrinkle edge french fries. Use on fruits and vegetables. Makes good food tastier and more attractive. Give your salads a new Zip. Perfect for tenderizing meat.

HUOT Serrates Meat & Tenderizes.

1. Cut the potato in half lengthwise with serrator.

2. Lay flat side down and cut to desired thickness, then cut into strips.

3. Lattice potatoes may be made by cutting off end of potato crossways and then turning potato ¼ turn after making each cut.

4. Serrator makes an excellent meat tenderizer. Other vegetables, fruits, pickles, cheese, etc., are turned into delicious, appetizing treats when cut with a HUOT SERRATOR. The Serrator may also be used as a bread trimmer for making canapes and party sandwiches. Easily cuts cabbage and lettuce for cole slaw and salads. HUOT Manufacturing Co. 550 N. Wheeler St., St. Paul, W 4, Minn.

Cutting tools. The Wizard grapefruit corer is mounted on a card that had a price of 29¢ on it. The card says:

Acme Grapefruit Corer and Knife. Cores; Separates; Sections. Also cores peppers-pineapples-tomatoes & apples. Directions:...place corer over center core of fruit; press and keep turning back and forth...for grapefruit....For sectioning...use blade like ordinary knife...for peppers...and tomatoes. On solid fruits such as apples, pineapples etc., press corer until it reaches desired depth; then turn one or two full turns and pull out. Acme Metal Goods Manufacturing Company.

The corer has a red wood handle; others had handles of pink or mustard color.

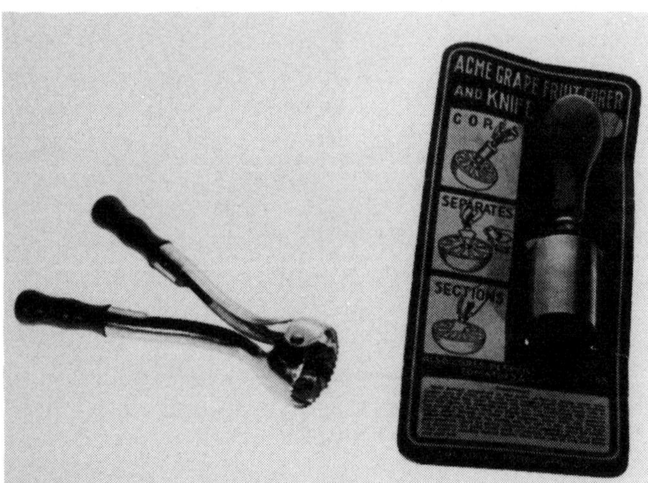

"Citra Products; Winterhaven, Fla. Stainless Steel Pat. D 50794." Red wooden handle.

"Wizard; Pat. Pend.; stainless steel" marked on outside of removable cylinder. Has red wooden handle. **$1.50-4.25**

Unmarked french fry cutter with red wooden handle. On box: "The Burns Professional Type French Fry Cutter For Home Use — Easy Cutting. Insert whole potato & press handle down. Makes 24 perfect size french fries."

Progressus — Italy. Red wooden handle. **$2.50-6**

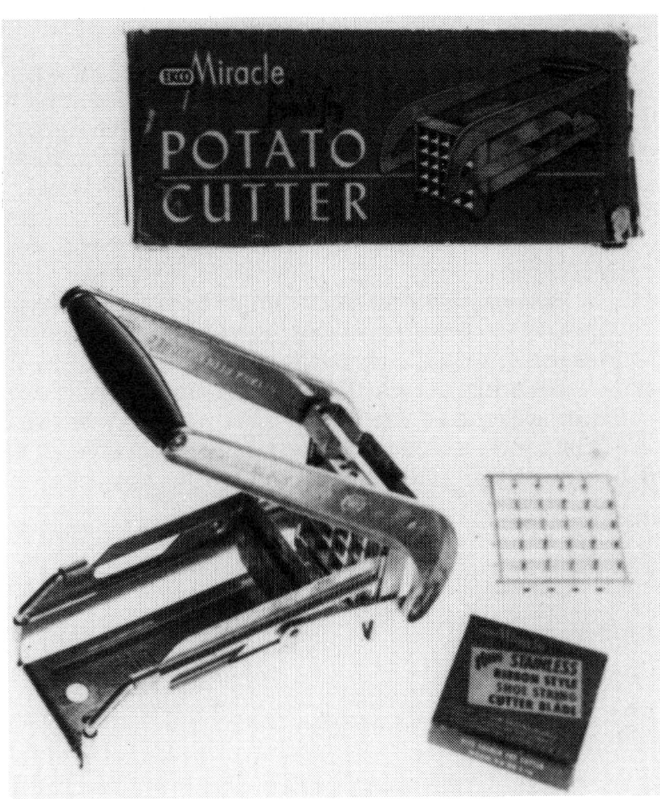

Heavily blocked, tinned; Ekco-Tomado Holland. Red wooden handle. On box: "Ekco Miracle French Fry Cutter." **$2.50-6**

On box: "Ekco Miracle New Stainless Ribbon Style Shoe String Cutter — Sharp hollow ground blades — Cuts 50 pieces at one stroke." **$1-1.50**

"Mouli Grater Made In France; U.S. Pat, 2,271,175; 2,502,867; 2,604,916; 2,587,186. Other Pat. Pend." This particular Mouli Grater was made in June, 1953, but they were made as early as 1942. Red wooden handle **$3-5**

"Mouli Shredder; Made In France, Pat's. Pend.; A Mouli Product." Red wooden handle. **$2-3.50**

Mouli Grater, on box:

Great for grating food (not your fingers): cheese, coconut, bread crumbs, crackers, chocolate, nuts, nutmeg, ginger root, hard boiled eggs, dry soap ends into chips and many other uses. Removable drum reversible for either right or left handed users. Pressure exerted on cover handle can vary the grating from coarse to fine.

Mouli Mfg. Corp., 91 Broadway, Jersey City, 6 N.J.

Mouli Shredder, direction sheet:

The set includes four rust-proof discs...slices, juliennes, and shreds...shaves ice, cannot cut hands or scratch knuckles. The rotary action is quick. The four discs are: No. 0 — fine shredding; No. 1 — medium shredding; No. 2 — julienne; No. 3 — slicing. Each can be used for potatoes, carrots, cabbage, beets, radishes and many other vegetables or solid fruits.

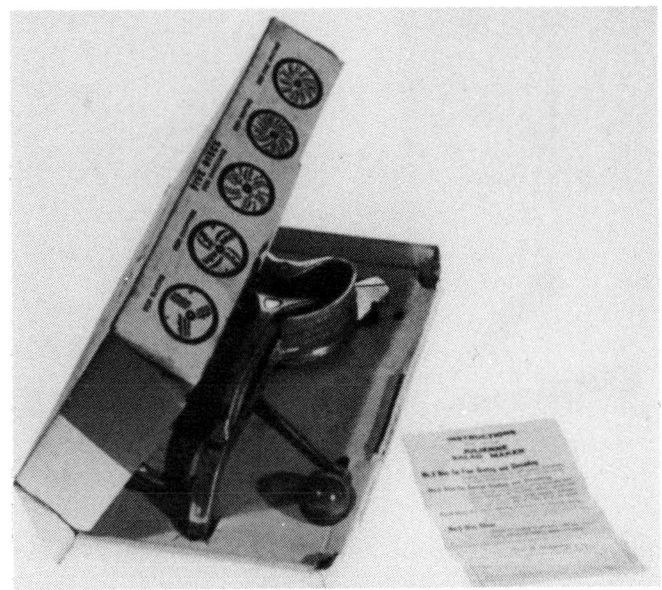

"Mouli-Julienne; Made In France; Brevete SDGD;U.S. Pat. 2,528,381; Canadian Pat. 437,082; 485,682; A 'Mouli' Product Other Pat. Pend." Red wooden handle.

The boxtop says: "Mouli Salad Maker/slices/chops/shreds/grates. Makes tasty salads easily, quickly, safely."

This set comes with five discs that can be used for slicing, chopping, shredding, grating, and fine grating. The U.S. patent was granted in 1950. **$3.50-6.50 complete**

Unmarked cheese slicer with red wooden knob. On boxtop: "CHEESE SLICER/Self-Serving/An excellent utensil for slicing eggs, soft fruit and vegetables as well as cheese. Sanitary — Clean Cutting — Polished Hardwood Base/Slice Easily As Desired."

On side: "Lorraine Novelty Mfg. Co., Inc./461 Fourth Avenue, New York, N.Y./Price 29 cents." **$3.75-5.50**

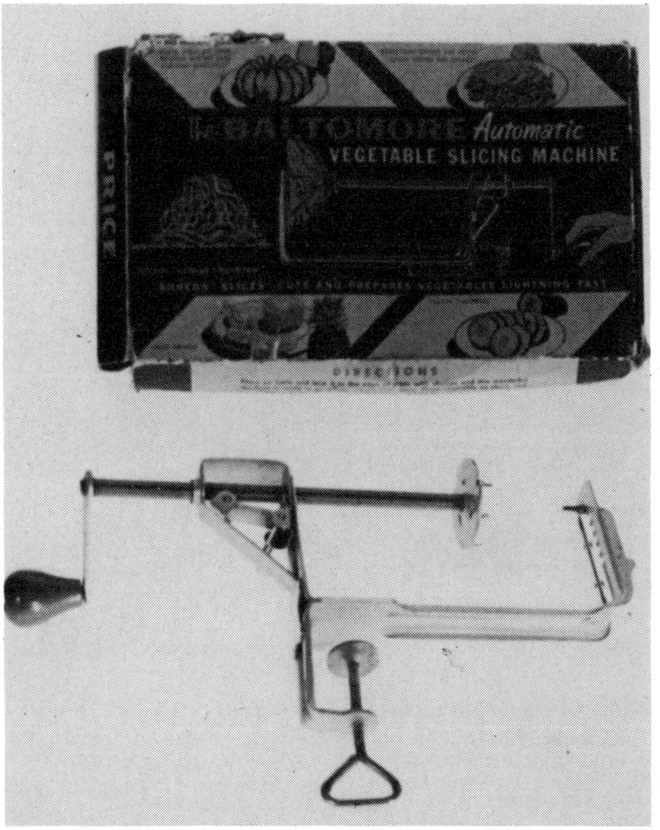

"Baltomore Slicing Machine; Pat. Pending." Red wooden handle. (Courtesy Donna Davis.) **$3.75-10**

On the box:

The BALTOMORE AUTOMATIC VEGETABLE SLICING MACHINE With Miracle Cutting Blade... "Shreds Cabbage Like Wheat", "Makes Rosettes From Potatoes And Any Hard Centered Vegetable", "Shoestring Onions For Frying", "Sliced Onions For Salads", "Sliced Pineapple", and "Sliced Cucumbers."

Directions: Place on table and lock it to edge of table. Works simply and safely. Place vegetable on chuck, rest vegetable on brass center rivet, lock lever, then turn handle for extra thin slices. For heavy cut, release lever, force rod forward and turn handle. The more force and pressure the thicker the slice.

Manufactured by the N.K. Morris Mfg. Co., Avon, N.J. For the Baltomore Corporation. Price $5.00.

Egg scales. Egg scales were important in the not-too-distant past. They were used to size eggs. Various standards were used in the early part of this century for grading the quality and size of eggs. Because there was no uniformity, buying and trading was difficult. As a result of urging by the nation's poultry industry, the United States Department of Agriculture standardized this classification. Everyone has benefited by these standards.

U.S.D.A. size weight classes are for minimum weight in ounces per dozen: jumbo, 30 ounces; extra-large, 27 ounces; large, 24 ounces; medium, 21 ounces; small, 18 ounces; peewee, 15 ounces. The quality of an egg determines the grade.

From the 1920s to 1950s, the farmer used various egg scales. After he gathered and washed the eggs, he sized or weighed them according to U.S.D.A. standards.

Norman E. Chapman of St. Paul was the inventor of the Acme Egg Grading Scale. It was patented June 24, 1924. He stated:

> To provide a device by means of which eggs may be quickly graded according to weight. In marketing eggs it is desirable to separate them into grades according to weight, so that eggs that have substantially the same weight can be placed together. A particular object of my invention is to provide a device by means of which this operation can be expeditiously performed without the trouble and time consumed in weighing the eggs on scales.

The Acme scale ranges from 18 to 26 ounces and is made of aluminum. A later model ranged from 19 to 30 ounces and sold for $2.75. By 1948, the price had risen to $5.

The Jiffy-Way jappaned scale is colorful, with its dark green base, white background, and brightly colored letters indicating the egg size and weight in ounces per dozen or per egg. This scale was invented by Benjamin Zimmer of Minneapolis, Minnesota. The application was filed April 8, 1938, and it was patented June 5, 1940. He said: "My invention provides an extremely simple and highly efficient egg weighing scale."

The Acme Egg Grading Scale was manufactured by the Specialty Manufacturing Company, St. Paul, Minnesota. **$12-20**

The Jiffy-Way egg scale is marked: "Jiffy-Way Incorporated Owatonna, Minnesota World's Largest Mfg's Egg Scales 'Jiffy Way' Patent No. 2205917 T.M. Reg. Pat. Office. Take balance at red point — Use adjustable screw for speed." **$8.50-18**

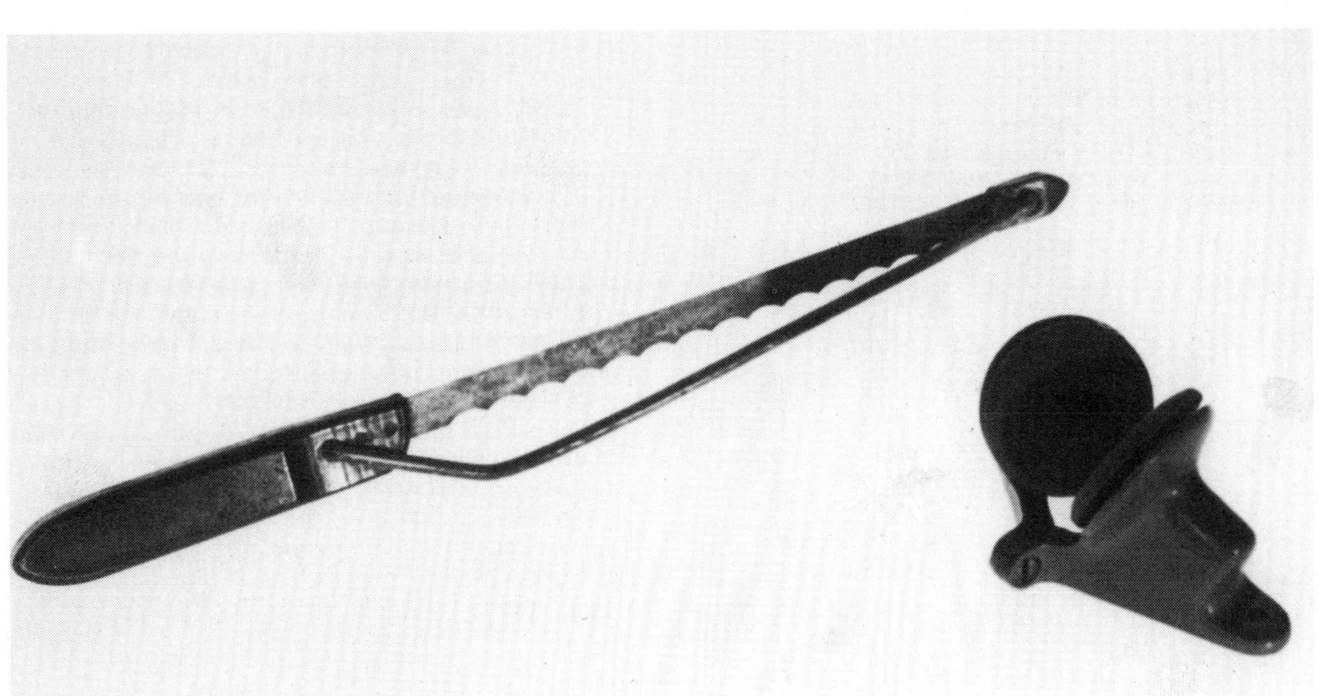

"All-Width 3 position Bread Slicer, Miller & Sons, Valley City, N.D." According to Earl Lifshey in the *Housewares Story*, the Miller's bread slicer, in 1948, delivered all widths with "plenty of housewife appeal." It sold for $1.50. **$5-8.50**

Unmarked; red cast iron. On box: "Wonder Knife Sharpener — Sharpens all types of knives. To use, merely draw blade of knife 10 or 12 times through the two abrasive stones as pictured at left." **$3-5.50**

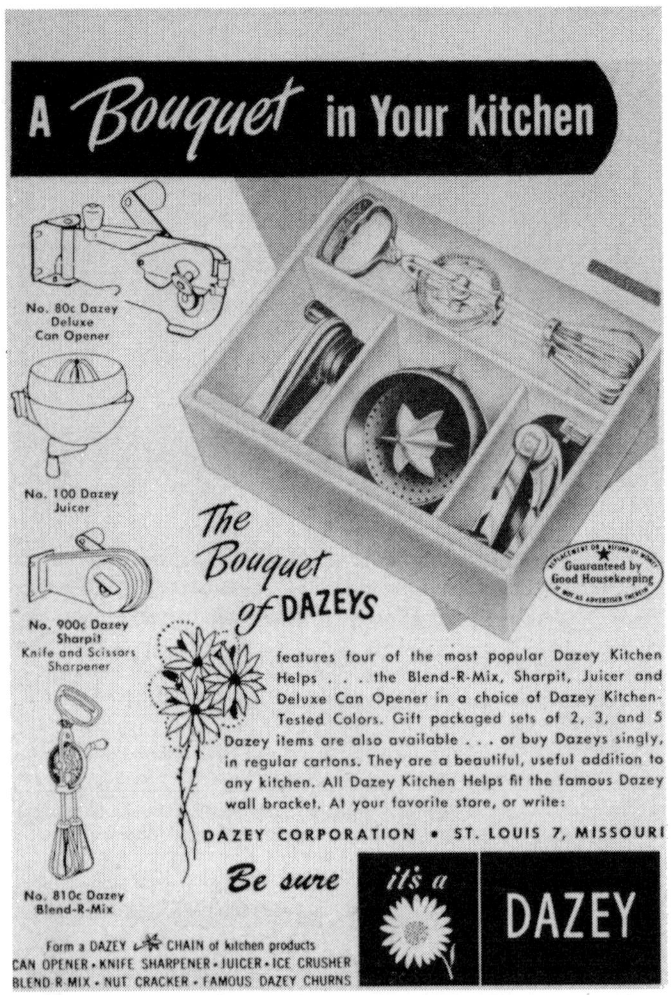

A Bouquet of Dazeys — can opener, juicer, knife and scissor sharpener and egg beater — were all products of the Dazey Corporation, St. Louis, Missouri. This 1950 ad told homemakers to form a Dazey chain of kitchen products that also included Dazey churns and nutcrackers. Their 1949 ad illustrated a Corsage of Dazeys. **$3.50-12.50**

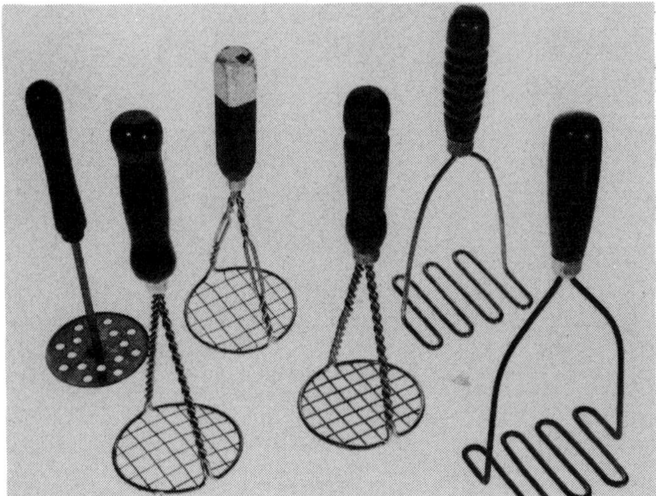

Left to right: Stainless, with red wooden handle.

Unmarked with red wooden handle and white tip.

Last four unmarked, with red wooden handles. Standard potato mashers sold for 9¢, and the best-made quality masher sold for 29¢ in the 1940 Sears Roebuck catalog. **$2-3.50**

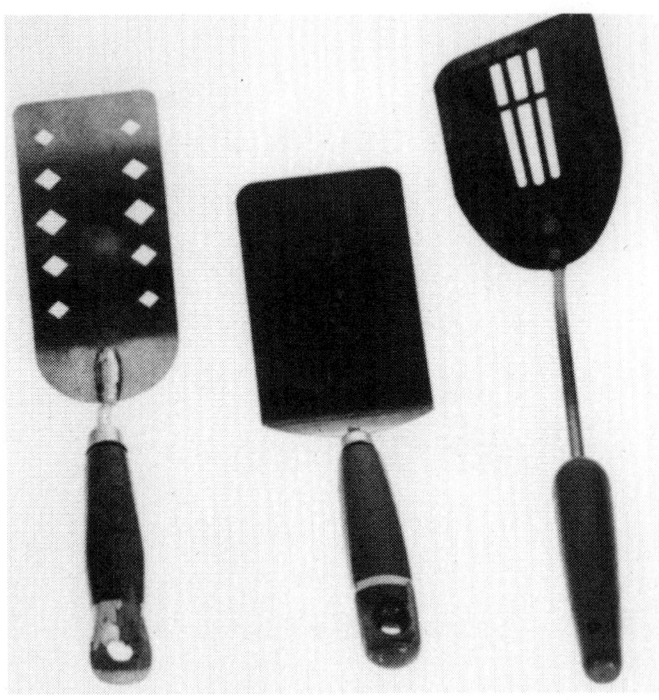

Left to right:

"Automatic Wire Goods Mfg. Co. Inc." Red wooden handle with cream tip.

"Ekco — A. & J. U.S.A." Red wooden handle with ivory.

"Androck; Made in United States Of America" Red wooden handle. **$2-3.50**

Egg cookers. Accompanying instructions:

Egg Alarm will boil your eggs *exactly* the way you want them...every time...without guesswork! Just follow these simple instructions: (1) Place up to 6 eggs in instant drain holder...then put Egg Alarm into any 2½ or 3 quart saucepan. (2) Fill saucepan with cold tap water so that water level just touches the embossed marker which describes the way you like your eggs...Each of these markers is further divided according to the number of eggs you are boiling...(3) After filling the saucepan with water, just turn the stove full up...(on electric stoves turn to "high")...and go about your business in the kitchen. When the eggs are done *exactly* the way you want them, *whistle* sounds off musically and automatically. On both gas and electric stoves use your smallest burner everytime (4) CAUTION: Eggs Are Done *Only* When Whistle Sounds Off *Steadily!* the Egg Alarm may chirp a bit when eggs are almost done, but eggs will not be ready until whistle sounds off *steadily!* Lift out by heat resistant knob. Eggs are boiled just the way you like 'em...the same way every time. No guesswork. NOTE: experiment a little. If the soft marker gives you a harder egg than you prefer, try a little less water in pan.

If it seems too soft then try a little more water. Should the whistle fail to sound, shift the pan "off center" with relation to the burner — so that heat is directly under the cone-shaped part of your Egg. EGG ALARMS MAKE WELCOME GIFTS!

The manufacturer is unknown.

Embossed lines are marked: "For medium, soft or very soft eggs varying with the number of eggs to be cooked; from 1 to 6 eggs." **$2.75-4.25**

"Androck Hand-I-Sift-Jr. Made In U.S.A." White metal with red tulips. **$2.50-6.50**

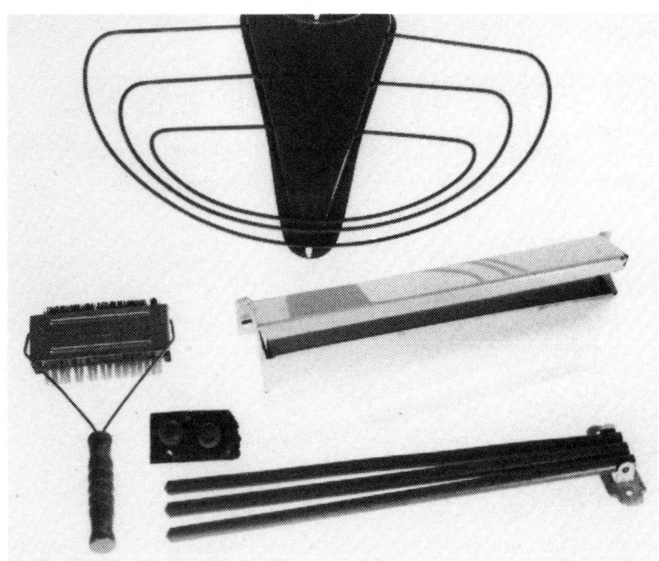

"Hi-Gene Screen Cleaner Pat. No. 2,838,777." Milton H. Schoenfield and Donald B. Schoenfield of Beverly Hills, California, filed the application for the screen cleaner March 28, 1955, and it was patented June 17, 1958. "Simple and inexpensive construction... to rapidly and effectively clean a screen of dust, insects or other foreign matter...."

"Pat. No. 2,010,293" marked on a red metal kitchen rack. This metal supporting rack was invented by Martin J. Schuiling of Grand Rapids, Michigan. It was patented August 6, 1935. The rack was used to hold dishtowels, dishcloths, or the like.

Unmarked red wooden pot cover knobs.

Unmarked red wooden towel rack with white metal bracket.

Unmarked ivory metal wax paper dispenser.

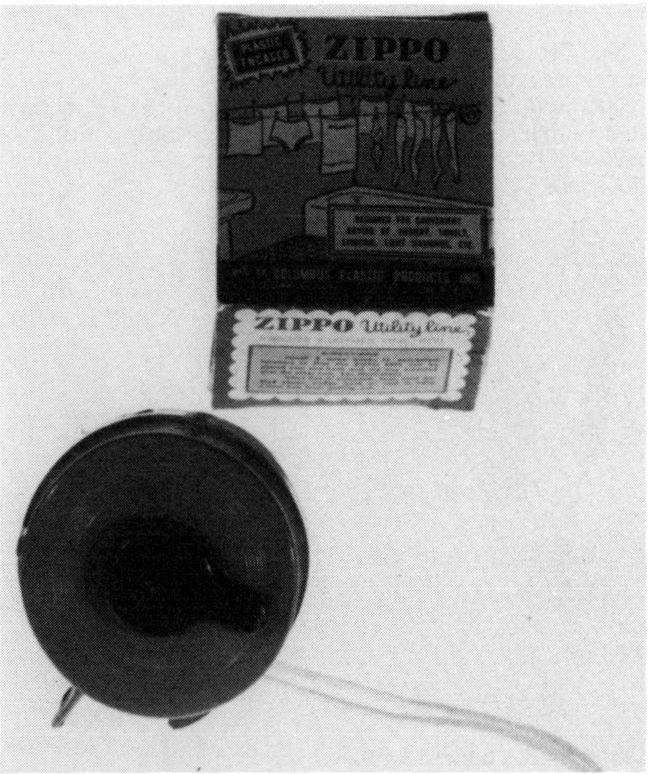

"Zippo Utility Line Columbus Plastics Inc. Cols. Ohio." On other side: "Pat. Pend. Made in U.S.A. Carlisle Furn. & Rug Co." Purple plastic case. On box: "Zippo Utility Line Indoor Clothes line reel. For kitchen — bathroom — basement — back porch."

An array of small appliances offered by the Knapp-Monarch Company for Christmas, 1940.

Small Appliances

Blenders. Although many think that the first blender was Fred Waring's, this is not so. However, the marketing efforts of the Waring Corporation did more than anything else to popularize this device. The Waring blender was introduced in the late 1930s.

The first blender was patented in 1922. Stephen J. Poplawski, the inventor, originally intended it to be used for drinks only. He designed and manufactured beverage mixers for many years. It was not until 1932 that his blender was used for blending fruits and vegetables in addition to beverages.

Knapp-Monarch called their product a "liquidizer" in 1940. It was a new and useful product for daily and party use. It mixed, chopped, and liquified fruits and vegetables and retained their natural vitamins. It was priced at $14.95.

That same year, Landers, Frary and Clark called their appliance a Mixablend. Their advertisement said it was one appliance that was never on the shelf because it had so many uses. It "blends many delicious beverages. Whips, beats, mixes, purees and chops. $19.95."

Blenders operated with an on-off switch until the 1950s, when models came out with button-type switches.

Electric corn poppers. Knapp-Monarch had a fully automatic corn popper under the brand name K-M in 1940. They called it a Tel-A-Matic corn popper. It had an ovenproof clear glass top that let a person "see every

This Knapp Monarch Corn Popper was marked on the lid and on the bottom. The metal cup, filled to the top, was the correct measure for corn kernels; filled to the line was the measure for the cooking oil. **$3-7.50**

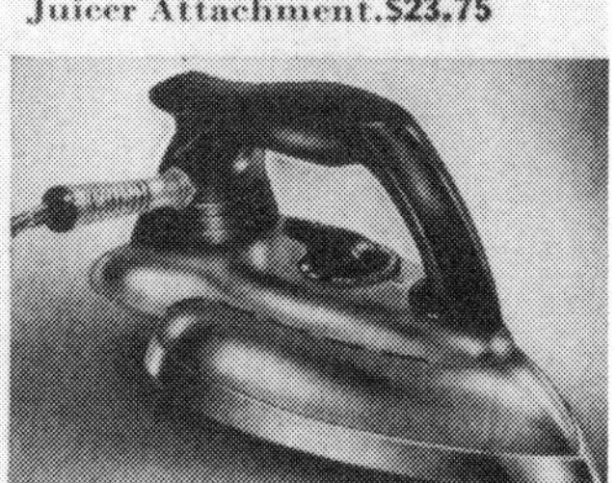

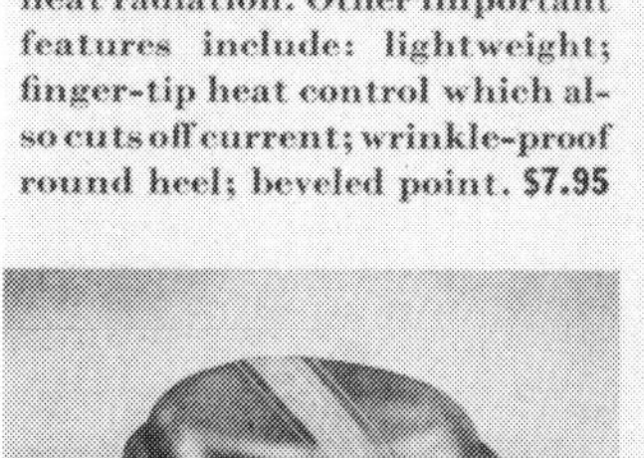

Landers, Frary and Clark's Universal brand appliances for Christmas, 1940.

The Wyndale Manufacturing Corporation, Indianapolis, Indiana, had an electric corn POPPER-PLUS. The "plus" was an electric grill under the kettle. This sold for $5.95 in 1947.

U.S. Corn Electric Popper No. 10 was manufactured by the U.S. Manufacturing Corporation, Decatur, Illinois. This three-quart model sold for $4.95 in the late 1940s.

kernal burst into huge fluffs of tender goodness."

Popcorn balls were a favorite recipe in the 1940s. The following is a Knapp-Monarch recipe:

1 cup sugar	1/4 cup butter
1/3 cup white corn syrup	3/4 teaspoon salt
1/3 cup water	3/4 teaspoon vanilla

3 quarts popped corn

Put sugar, corn syrup, water, butter and salt in a saucepan and cook, stirring until the sugar is dissolved. Continue cooking without stirring until syrup forms a brittle ball in cold water (270 degrees F). Add vanilla and stir only enough to mix it through the hot syrup. After popping the corn in your K-M Corn Popper place in a bowl large enough for mixing. Pour the syrup slowly over the popped corn and mix well. Wet hands slightly and shape corn into balls, using only enough pressure to make balls stick together. Makes 12 medium sized balls. Nuts, Candied Cherries, Gum Drops or Raisins may be added before combining with syrup, if desired.

The Fryryte was an electric deep-fryer that fried automatically. The frying could be done at the table. It was sold at department and appliance stores for $24.95 in 1950.

An ad for the sunbeam Automatic Egg Cooker read:

Set it...forget it. It's automatic...you can't miss. Now your eggs will be the SAME EVERY TIME...Three easy-to-see markings in the lid tell user how much water to use for very soft, medium, or hard-cooked eggs, or any level in between.

Handy egg poacher attachment sits on rack in Sunbeam Egg Cooker and poaches one to three eggs, in appetizing triangular shape, the same every time exactly as desired....You can cook eggs to perfection in this new Sunbeam all-automatic egg-cooker. No more of this "too soft one time" — "too hard the next" with a Sunbeam on the job. The degree of cooking depends entirely on the amount of water used. If you use the same amount every time, you'll get the same kind every time. You can't miss. The lid doubles as a measuring cup, has convenient markings at various levels. When the eggs are done the Sunbeam clicks off automatically. You can SEE IT and HEAR IT. Cooks 1 to 6 eggs even and tender throughout.

The company, originally called Chicago Flexible Shaft Company, was founded in Chicago in 1893. Sunbeam became the trade name for their appliances in 1921 and for the company in 1946.

Mixers. After World War II, mixers became lighter, smaller, and more powerful. Portable hand mixers introduced in the late 1940s, became popular in the 1950s.

Mixers from the 1940s are collectible, but not as valuable as earlier mixers.

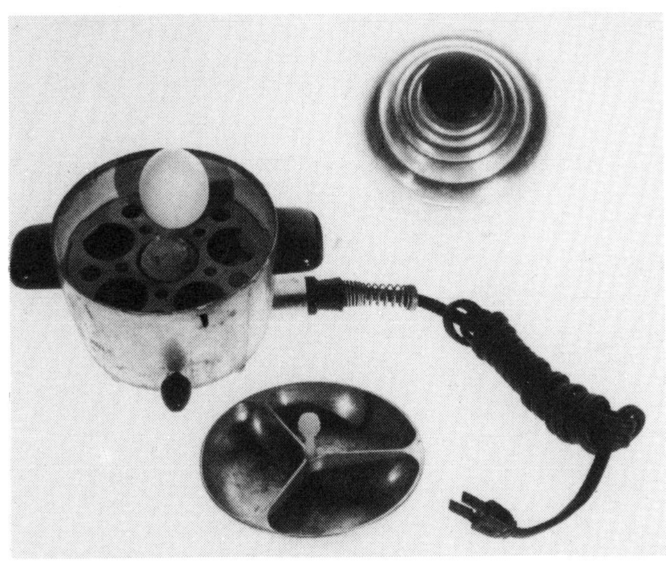

Sunbeam® automatic egg cooker from the 1940s. The heat-resistant knob is marked "SUNBEAM EGG COOKER." **$5-9**

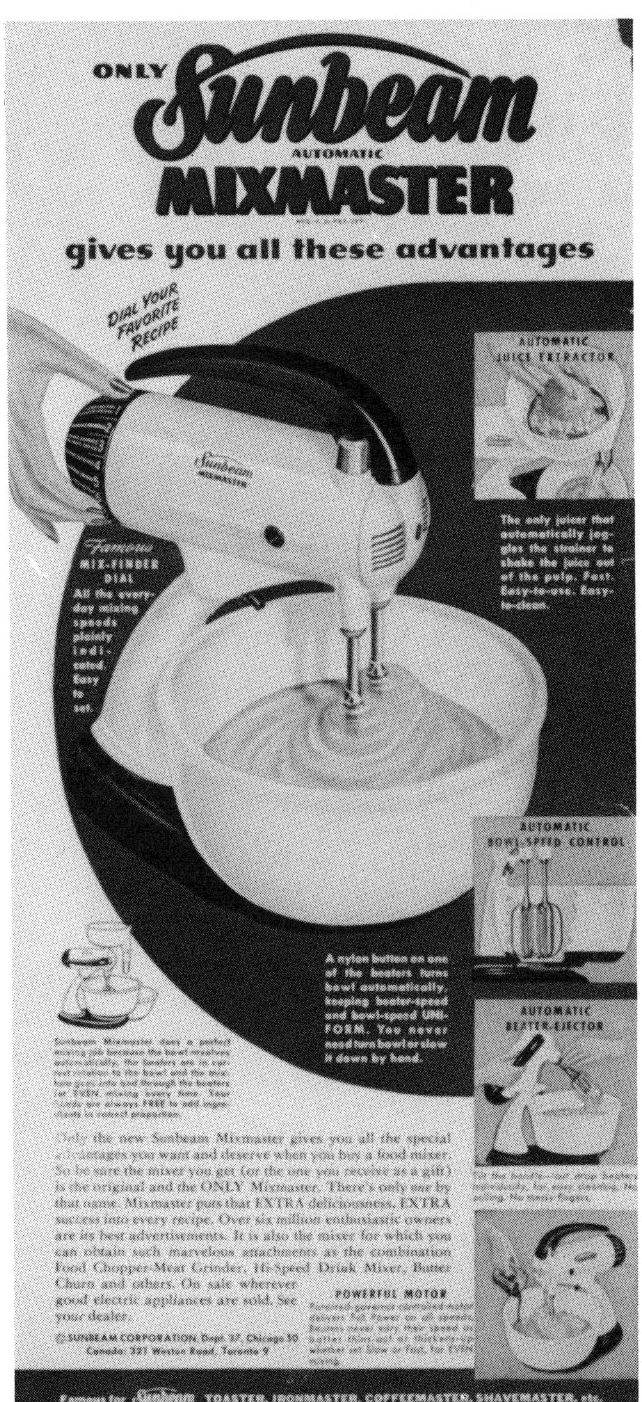

The Sunbeam® Mixmaster® in 1950 had "automatic" advantages, such as the automatic juice extractor that joggled the strainer to shake the juice out of the pulp; automatic bowl-speed control with a button on one of the beaters; automatic beater ejection by rotating the handle — no messy fingers. (Courtesy Sunbeam® Appliance Corporation.)

Electric irons. This decade saw improvements in steam irons. Waring Products introduced the first steam iron using the "flash boiler" principle in 1941. After World War II, General Electric produced this type of iron under an agreement with Waring. General Electric introduced the first front-fill steam iron in 1948.

Electric roasters. Electric roasters were still featured among the appliances in the 1940s. Magazine articles described the advantages of cooking with an electric roaster, including cooking for a picnic at home and then taking the oven with you. The insulation that kept the kitchen cool also kept the food hot while traveling to the picnic grounds. Roasters came in several different sizes, and some manufacturers also offered cabinets with storage shelves to put them on.

Toasters. It wasn't until the end of World War II that the toaster reflected many changes. In 1949, Sunbeam® offered the innovative silent, radiant-controlled toaster, which automatically lowered the bread until it was toasted.

Waffle irons and sandwich grills. Waffle irons and sandwich grills remained on the list of appliances available, just as they are today.

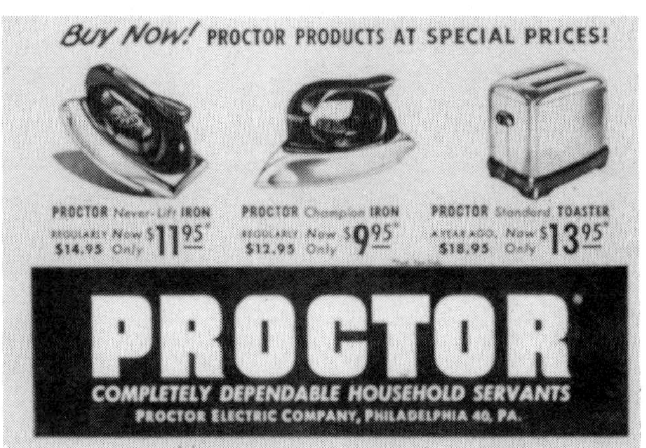

Proctor Products, manufactured by Procto Electric Company, Philadelphia, Pennsylvania, were offered at special prices in this 1950 advertisement.

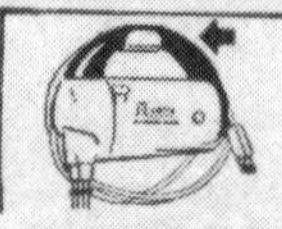

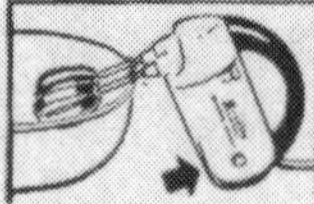

In 1949, Hamilton Beach's all purpose portable beater was called a "Mixette." It was a one-hand, three-speed mixer that left the other hand free to hold a pan or to add ingredients. It could be stored in a drawer or hung on the wall.

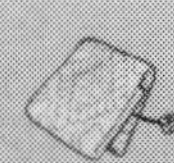

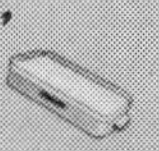

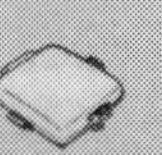

The electric Roaster-Oven was one of Westinghouse's electric appliances in 1950. (Courtesy White-Westinghouse Corporation.) **$10-18**

The Dominion Electric Corporation, of Mansfield, Ohio, featured their "pops up toast Just Right" toaster in 1948. **$7.50-12**

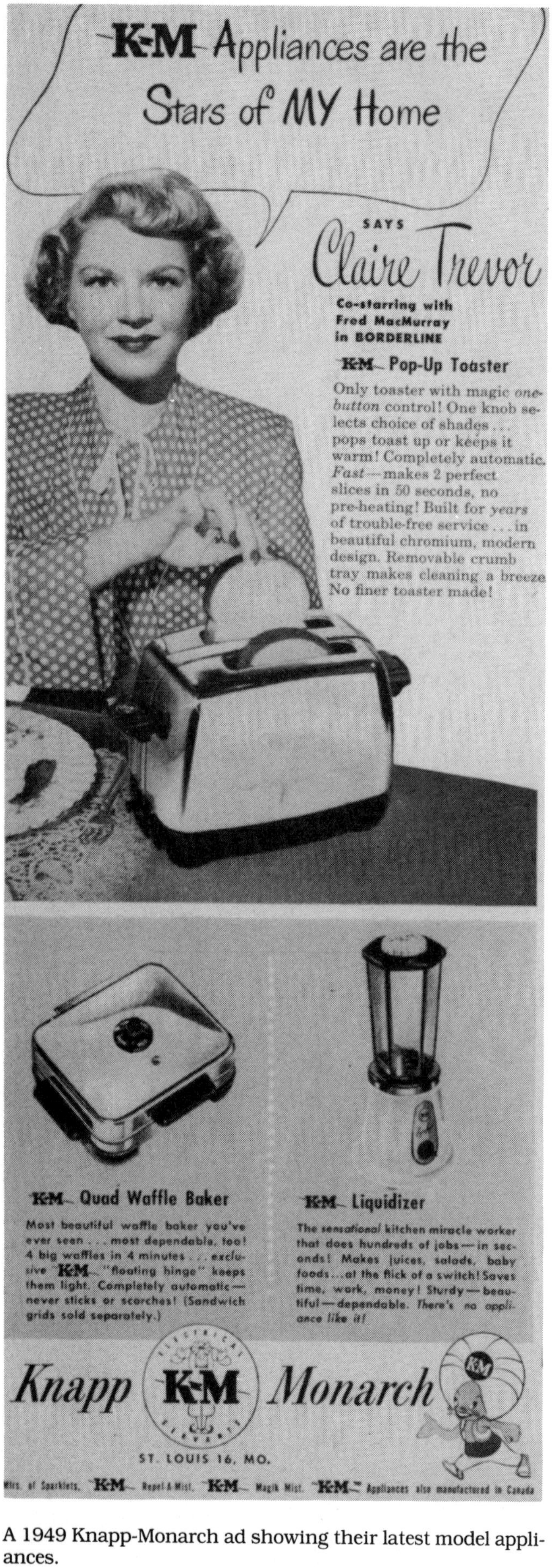

K-M Appliances are the Stars of MY Home
SAYS Claire Trevor
Co-starring with Fred MacMurray in BORDERLINE
K-M Pop-Up Toaster
Only toaster with magic one-button control! One knob selects choice of shades . . . pops toast up or keeps it warm! Completely automatic. Fast—makes 2 perfect slices in 50 seconds, no pre-heating! Built for years of trouble-free service . . . in beautiful chromium, modern design. Removable crumb tray makes cleaning a breeze. No finer toaster made!
K-M Quad Waffle Baker
Most beautiful waffle baker you've ever seen . . . most dependable, too! 4 big waffles in 4 minutes . . . exclusive K-M "floating hinge" keeps them light. Completely automatic—never sticks or scorches! (Sandwich grids sold separately.)
K-M Liquidizer
The sensational kitchen miracle worker that does hundreds of jobs—in seconds! Makes juices, salads, baby foods...at the flick of a switch! Saves time, work, money! Sturdy—beautiful—dependable. There's no appliance like it!
Knapp K-M Monarch
ST. LOUIS 16, MO.

A 1949 Knapp-Monarch ad showing their latest model appliances.

Sunbeam
RADIANT CONTROL
TOASTER
Automatic Beyond Belief!
NOW! All you do is drop in the bread
Bread lowers itself automatically, no levers to push
Toast raises itself silently, without popping or banging
PERFECT TOAST—EVERY TIME
RADIANT CONTROL automatically adjusts itself for every kind of bread . . . moist or dry, thick slices or thin.
This is the entirely new toaster that has completely changed people's conception of what an automatic toaster should do! Only after you've seen it make toast can you appreciate the sheer magic of its carefree operation. No levers to push—no popping or banging. Just drop in the bread and let the Sunbeam take over. The bread lowers itself, turning on the current. When perfectly toasted, the toast comes up silently, and current turns off. It's that sensational. The new Sunbeam even regulates the toasting automatically, depending on the kind of bread. If the slices are moist it toasts them a little longer than if they are dry. If they are thin, it toasts them quicker than thicker slices. Moist or dry, thick or thin—you always get the same uniform golden color you want—automatically. Ask your dealer to demonstrate the new Sunbeam Toaster for you.
© SUNBEAM CORPORATION, Dept. 37, Chicago 50 • Canada: 321 Weston Rd., Toronto 9
Famous for Sunbeam MIXMASTER, IRONMASTER, COFFEEMASTER, SHAVEMASTER, etc.

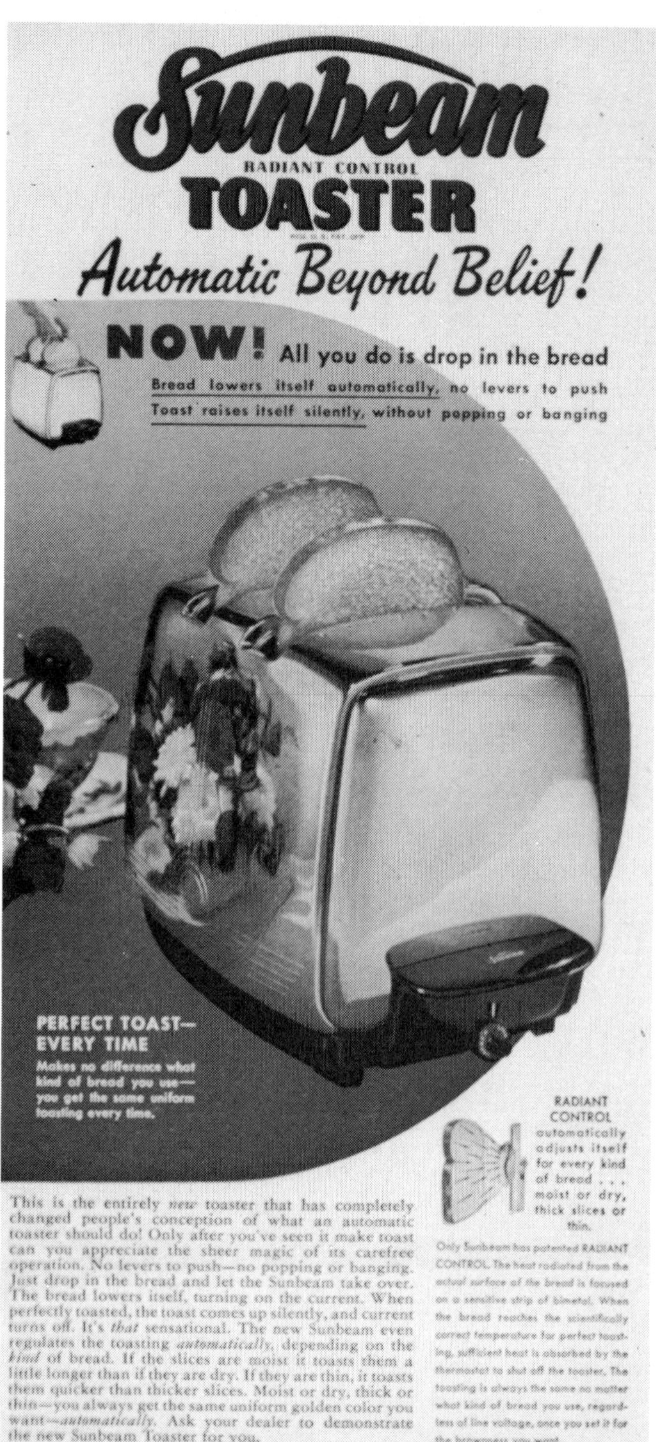

The 1950 model Sunbeam® Toaster with Radiant Control was "Automatic Beyond Belief!" When the bread was put in the toaster, it was lowered, and it rose automatically when toasted. (Courtesy Sunbeam® Appliance Company.) **$7.50-12**

Large Appliances

Dishwashers. By the late 1940s, magazine ads offered a number of different brands. The dishwasher was well on its way to public acceptance and mass production.

A combination automatic dishwasher and washing machine was introduced by Earle Ludgin and Company of Chicago in 1946. They said it could be converted from clothes washer to a dishwasher in less than a minute and a half; it was an easy matter to lift out the clothes washer parts and replace them with the dishwasher attachments, because all parts were lightweight.

In 1948, Hotpoint claimed that their dishwasher was the only one that dried electrically.

Does Your Husband Get "That Guilty Feeling"?

If your husband is like most other married men, even the *sound* of dishes being washed is annoying. For the clatter of each dish prods his conscience with that vexing question, "Should I go out and help?"

Let him read "The Wedding Ring on the Window Sill" because it provides a happy solution to his problem as well as yours. It tells the whole fascinating story of the magic of the General Electric Sink. How your most cherished china and crystal are washed, rinsed and dried electrically . . . hygienically clean and with perfect safety! How pots and pans too, come out gleaming bright.

But that's only part of the story. It also tells how the G-E Disposall, part of the Electric Sink, disposes of all your garbage electrically. Your hands never touch dishwater or garbage!

Send for your copy today. Fill out the space below, tear out and mail to the General Electric Co., Dept. SG-263, Bridgeport, Conn.

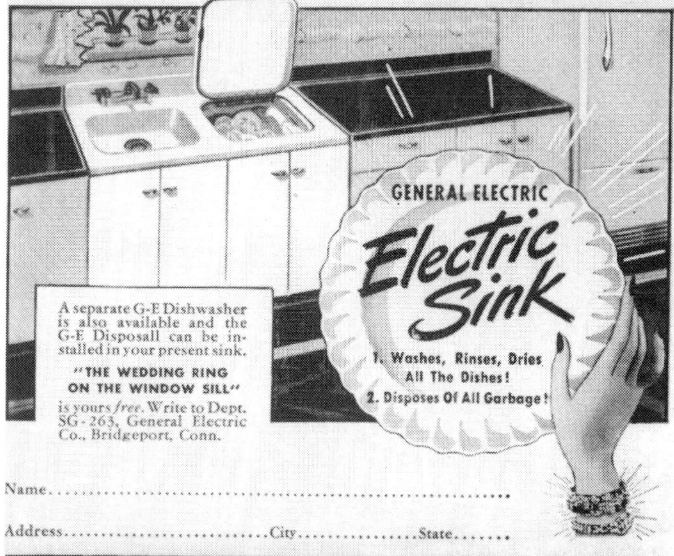

GENERAL ELECTRIC

General Electric's "Electric Sink" ad in 1940 asked, "Does Your Husband Get 'That Guilty Feeling'?" The noise of doing dishes is annoying, but should the husband offer to help? No, his problem could be solved with the purchase of G.E.'s electric dishwasher. (Courtesy General Electric Corporation.)

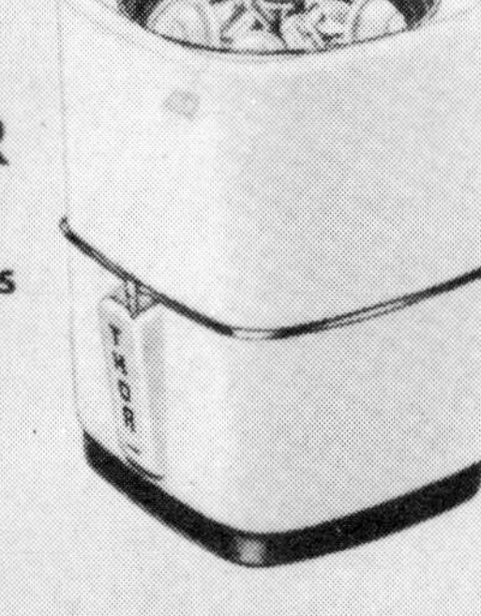

The THOR combination automatic clothes washer and dishwasher is shown in this 1947 advertisement. A Thor individual clothes washer cost $199.50, individual dishwasher $219.50, and the combination clothes washer and dishwasher sold for $269.95. Apparently this type of combination appliance did not prove acceptable to the majority of consumers, even though there was a financial savings.

it's new! it's automatic! it's Universal!

The gas range that washes dishes!

A complete, full-size Universal Gas Range and wonderful James Dishwasher . . . all in one!

Here's kitchen space-saving so new, so different, *so conveniently practical* you have to actually see it to believe it.

When not in use, the mobile James Dishwasher disappears into the range. At dishwashing time, you simply roll it to the sink and plug it in. No plumbing or installation costs. The James *automatically* washes, rinses and dries all dinner dishes for eight people in *less* than ten minutes.

The range is wonderful too. With one-piece easy-to-clean top, big automatic oven, and Universal's exclusive In-A-Drawer charcoal broiler, it has all the beauty, built-in quality, and perfect cooking performance that have been Universal's for over 80 years.

Be sure to see this amazing dishwasher-in-a-range now at better stores everywhere. It's one of a complete new line of 1953 Universal Gas Ranges designed to fit every need, every kitchen, and every purse.

De Luxe Mobile James Dishwasher *has 100-piece capacity. Heats, and softens water automatically. Washes, rinses, sterilizes and dries spotlessly.*

Universal "CP" Model Range *with automatic lighting top burners, oven, broiler. Fully insulated skyscraper construction. For city or bottled gas.*

See your Universal Gas Range dealer for a generous trade-in allowance.

A *Universal* gas range will glorify your kitchen

Made by Cribben and Sexton Company, Chicago 12, Illinois

The unusual Universal gas range and dishwasher combination was made by Cribben and Sexton Company, Chicago, Illinois, in 1953.

Disposers. After World War II, there were many advertisements for food waste disposers by a variety of manufacturers. Some said it was the most helpful appliance in the kitchen, because it got rid of garbage without odor, handling, or a garbage can.

Freezers. Frozen food was introduced in the 1930s, but it was not an immediate success because people had not cared for cold-storage, and they equated that with frozen food. It wasn't until the 1940s that housewives saw the convenience, quality, flavor, and economy of having like-fresh food year 'round.

Frigidaire made the first chest-type home freezer in the 1930s. Home freezers did not command a market until the 1940s, after World War II.

Many home freezer manufacturers made freezers that were small enough to hold one-hundred pounds of food, or as large as twenty-four cubic feet. Different models offered a variety of features, including removable shelves, food baskets, counterbalanced lids that opened easily and stayed up without being held, toe recess, and even a food protection insurance policy.

An American Kitchens Disposer ad in 1949 said that it was foolish to put up with messy garbage and risk disease when, for only a few cents a day, garbage could be disposed of with their automatic disposer.

The Tyler Fixture Corporation, Niles, Michigan, manufactured Harder Freez, an economical 12-cubic-feet chest type, and 9 and 18 cubic feet upright freezers in 1947.

In 1946, this Deepfreeze home freezer held 322 pounds of food. Its rounded lines were considered beautiful.

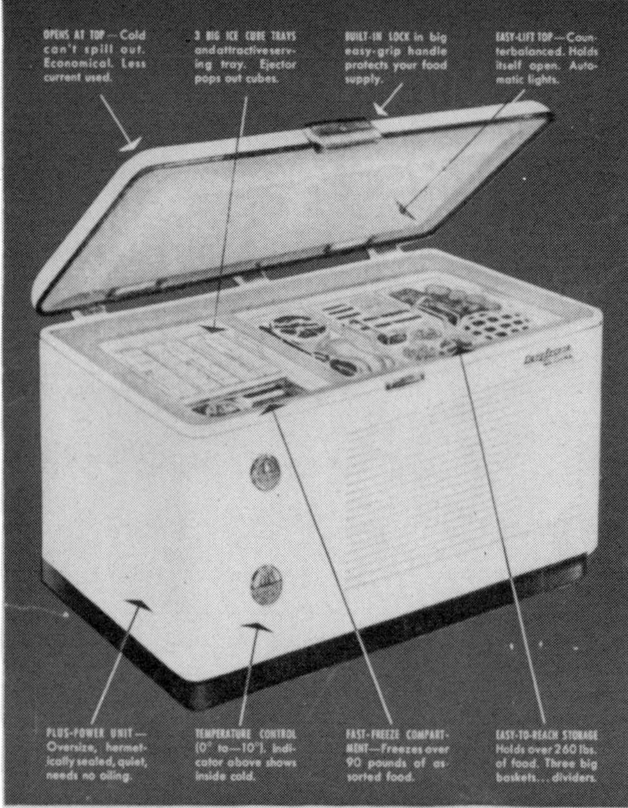

De Luxe Model C-10, 10 cu. ft., holds over 350 lbs. assorted food, $449.50. Others from $199.95, installed

Pays for itself with the money it saves

Before you decide to buy any home freezer, you owe it to yourself to get the facts. Learn how a genuine Deepfreeze home freezer saves time, work and money—how it brings you better living and pays for itself with the money it saves—how it can be bought for a small down payment on easy terms. See your Deepfreeze home freezer dealer for complete details.

The Deepfreeze home freezer 1948 model had changed dramatically from the 1946 model. The manufacturer was the Motor Products Corporation, Chicago, Illinois.

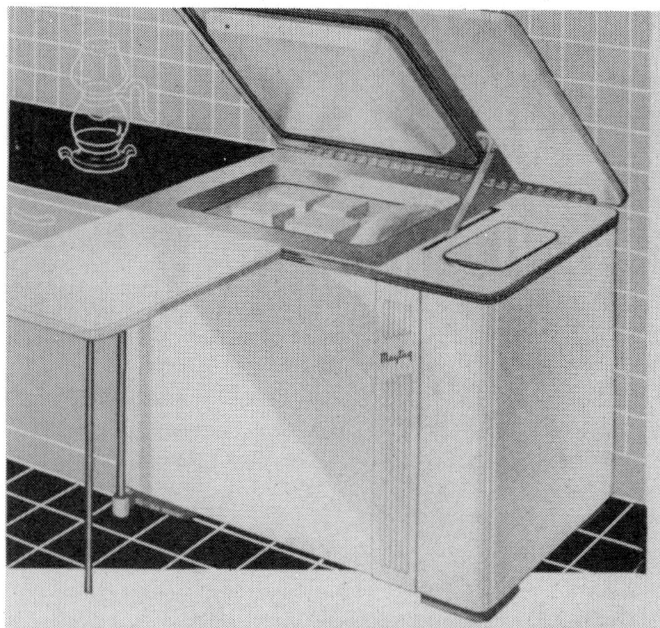

No other gives you all the advantages of the Maytag home freezer!

Fold-down leaf attachment as breakfast table—among many uses.

Counter-balanced lid opens easily—stays up without being held.

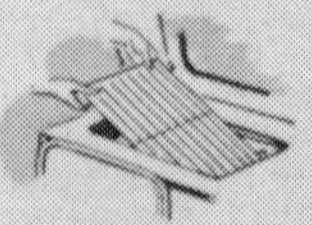

Handy wire racks are arranged for easy storing and removal of foods.

Quick defroster—for foods that require it—utilizes the motor's heat.
(Table leaf and dividers sold as accessory items.)

See this *truly different* freezer. Designed for use in your kitchen . . . stores foods right at your finger tips.

Not only does it keep the foods in the most convenient place possible; it also serves as an excellent kitchen table.

Perfectly flat top is of white, acid-resisting porcelain enamel—table size and height. Recessed bottom gives toe-room for working convenience. Extra work space is provided, if desired, by the optional, fold-down leaf attachment.

Frozen food capacity, six cubic feet. Holds 300 pounds of meat, or 240 pounds of mixed packages (average)—meat, fruit and vegetables.

You'll discover countless ways to use the Maytag freezer for better, more joyous living. And it will save you many steps and many hours of shopping, to say nothing of money saved by quantity buying.

Your nearby Maytag dealer will gladly show you all about it. Pay as you use it . . . small down-payment and convenient monthly terms. Don't wait. See it right away! The Maytag Company, Newton, Iowa.

The 1948 Maytag home freezer was "truly different." It not only kept food, but it also served as a table. The flat top was tablesize and gave toe room for working convenience. Extra workspace was provided by a fold-down leaf attachment that could be used as a breakfast table.

Ranges. Deep-well cookers were offered on electric ranges in the 1940s. The deep-well cooker was set down into the cooking surface, making it flush with other burners. The cooker was an economical feature, was efficient for small or large quantities, and would cook anything! It could bake, steam, and boil, and was especially good for slow-cooking meals.

After World War II, manufacturers came out with many models of the streamlined, modern ranges. There were many new features designed. Deep-well cookers were still prevalent in electric ranges, but some manufacturers offered a dual service thrift-cooker that could be elevated for top-of-range use. This increased surface capacity by 33 percent. Other manufacturers offered triple service, with a pressure cooker or non-pressure cooker, or as the fourth top-of-the-range cooking unit.

Other innovations on the electric ranges included improved surface units that had greater, more even, and faster heat; seven speed surface units; utensil drawers or compartments; and plate warmers.

Gas ranges also had new features offered by different manufacturers. They included automatic signals to show which burner was on, a broiler that used infrared rays just like hot charcoal, oven illumination, safety locks on burners to prevent children from causing accidents — even a moisture-free Crisp-Chest for keeping cereal, crackers, potato chips, and condiments fresh.

Estate gas and electric ranges had oven lights, fluorescent top light, Bar-B-Kewer, and two convenience outlets in 1947.

The new Norge gas range in 1949 was equipped with new burners that spiraled flame under the entire bottom of a pan with no waste heat, a click simmer valve, balanced heat oven, and two utensil compartments.

$200 ELECTRIC RANGES ELSEWHERE

Can't Equal This Rang

for Quality, Economy

and Downright Efficiency

Check the Features:

Super Speed Chromalox Units
Four 5-Heat Switches with Pilot
5-Quart Deep Well Cooker
Automatic Oven Timer
Dependable Electric Clock
Efficient Minute Minder
Chrome Trimmed Lamp
2-Piece Condiment Set
Convenient Outlet Plug
Automatic Oven Heat Control
Automatic Oven Light Flashes "On" When Door Is Opened
Oversize Insulated Oven
Big 1-Piece Storage Drawer
Economical Warming Drawer

Easy Payment Terms
Only $5 Down

Check the List of Features Shown Above . . . Approved by Underwriters

This DeLuxe Quality Electric Range offers everything in modern cooking! It's years ahead in ease of operation, perfect in mechanical details and beauty of design. It has a wealth of features that help make your kitchen work easier and more pleasant for many a year to come! No doubt you've already looked at electric ranges in your neighborhood . . . you've heard about the good points of each and every one . . . you know the prices and monthly payments. Now compare those ranges with this one . . . note its extra fine quality . . . its beautiful, modern lines and lustrous finish . . . study the features above . . . read the facts below . . . compare our prices and Easy Payment Terms.

Frankly We Say it . . . $200 electric ranges elsewhere have a hard time to equal it. No matter how you look at it, Sears give you "still more for your money." Electric cooking, with a Sears Electric Range, means a sparkling, clean kitchen; faster, more healthful cooking, greater economy and a new freedom from kitchen drudgery.

Gleaming White Porcelain Enamel from top to bottom features the entire range, which is of one-piece, heavy steel construction. Attractively designed black base is made with set-in toe space. Entire top has acid-resisting finish. Modern hardware is White Plaskon, chrome trimmed. Smoothly designed top and backguard is one-piece porcelain enameled steel. Just imagine how pleasant it will be to work with this electric range!

$134.95 Cash

Conveniently arranged at one side of smooth working top, are three Chromalox Super Speed units—one of 2000 watts, two of 1200 watts—plus the deepwell cooker. Oven is insulated with a thick layer of glass wool; has a sanitary porcelain finish interior, and when the heat-tight door is opened a light turns on automatically, fully lighting the inside. Fitted with a powerful, 2200-watt baking element and a 2200-watt broiler element; large, smokeless aluminum broiler pan and rack. Oven Timer and Oven Heat Control govern everything.

Modernistic Flood Lamp at back illuminates cooking top. Under it is a self-starting electric clock; Oven Time and Heat Control; 5-speed switches and pilot light which glows when any of the top switches or the warming drawer switch is on. Two one-piece metal storage drawers—one, a 1-piece plated warming drawer with rounded corners and a 500-watt Chromalox unit.

Size: Oven, 17 in. wide, 19½ in. deep, 15 in. high. Height to cooking top, 36 in. Height overall, 48 in. Fits space, 40x24 in. Shpg. wt., 313 lbs.

22 EM 1925F—Deluxe Electric Range. Cash Price **$134.95**
Easy Payment Price ($5 Down, $8 monthly) **$147.95**

Shipped from Chicago, Philadelphia, Boston, Kansas City, Minneapolis or Newark, Ohio. Order from our Mail Order House nearest you.

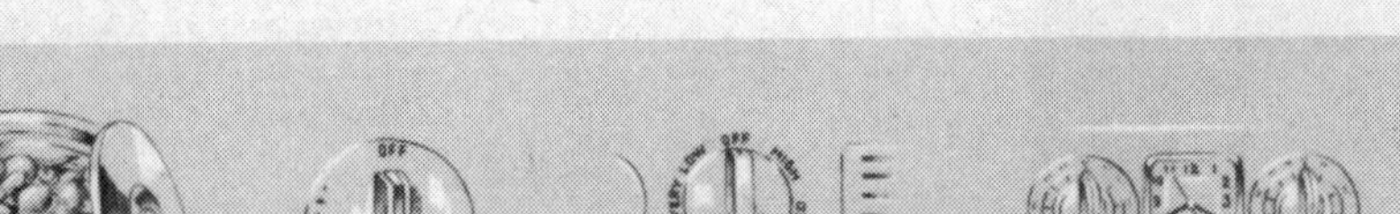

Five Cooking Speeds

THRIFT COOKER

ig economy feature! Cooks a de-
cious meal for as little as 1c. Effi-
ent for small or large quantities.
ooks anything . . . meat, vege-
bles, dessert . . . together or sep-
rately. Bakes, steams, boils. 3
apor-tight pans keep each food
om absorbing odors from other
ods. Is especially good for slow
ooking. Sets flush in deep well.

OVEN HEAT CONTROL

Simple and easy to operate . . . one turn of dial gives you desired temperature. Automatically keeps oven at exact heat you desire for accurate baking results. Because it maintains this constant, even temperature, it is unnecessary for you to open oven door until cooking is finished. Equipped with pilot light which glows when oven is on.

NEW 5-HEAT SWITCHES

Every cooking speed from "simmer" to "sizzle." Gives you ideal range of cooking heats . . . High, Medium, Low, Simmer and Very Low. 5-heat silver contact switches have rotary action operation in either direction. Easy to operate . . . a slight turn and they snap into position. Clearly marked so you can tell position of switch at a glance.

OVEN TIMER

Automatically turns oven ON and OFF at predetermined times. Makes it possible for housewife to set timer at 10:00 o'clock in morning so oven will turn on at 3:00 o'clock and turn off at 5:00 o'clock in afternoon. Gives housewife whole day for any occupation she desires. Conserves electric current. Tends to oven cooking with mechanical precision.

CHROMALOX UNITS

Smooth, easy-to-clean surface. Entire unit encased in metal. Spilled liquids or sharp blows from utensils will not damage them. 5 heats to meet every cooking need range from "High" for extra fast cooking to "Very Low" for warming.

SEARS PAGE 575

The 1940 Sears Roebuck catalog featured the top-of-the-line electric stove for $134.95. It had a 5-quart deep-well cooker (on back left), oven heat control, new five-heat switches, oven timer, and easy-to-clean, durable Chromalox units. Other electric ranges were from $84.95. Gas ranges could be purchased from $39.95 to $71.95. Kerosene, coal, and wood-burning stoves were usually less money. (Courtesy Sears, Roebuck and Company.)

NEW, IMPROVED "SPEED COOKING" IN THIS SPARKLING GENERAL ELECTRIC RANGE!

EXCLUSIVE!

- **Built-in Pressure Cooker saves ⅔ cooking time!**
- **Also Improved CALROD* Units!**
- **New cleanliness for your kitchen!**

WHAT A HONEY—this new General Electric "Speed Cooking" Range!

It brings you new speed that'll make meal-getting *so much easier*. New, sunshiny cleanliness that'll save lots of scrub-up time.

NEW Calrod units that are the last word in fast, even heat. And built for a long, dependable life.

This newly designed Calrod lets 40% more coil come in contact with the cooking utensil—makes sure the entire cooking surface is evenly heated. And there's *faster response*—thanks to a longer, more closely spaced coil.

Read all about the wonderful, work-saving features this new General Electric beauty gives you. *No other range has them all!* So hurry to your General Electric Retailer's, today! General Electric Company, Bridgeport 2, Conn.

AUTOMATIC ELECTRIC **RANGES**

General Electric Ranges, full-size models, as low as $189.75. "Stratoliner," shown here, $334.75. Prices include Federal excise tax, one-year warranty, delivery anywhere in Continental U.S. State or local taxes (if any) and installation not included.

TRIPL-UNIT has Pressure Cooker, fourth surface unit! No other range has it!

1. Yes ma'am! A 6-quart Pressure Cooker fits into the deep-well Calrod unit. Speeds up cooking by ⅔! Makes everything taste *extra* good!

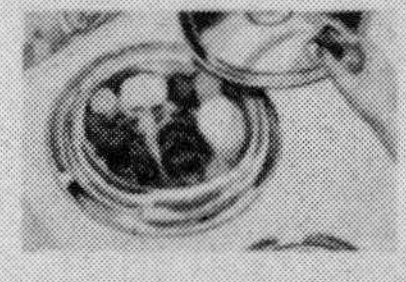

2. Utensil also equipped with nonpressure top, for thrifty deep-well cooking, or surface use.

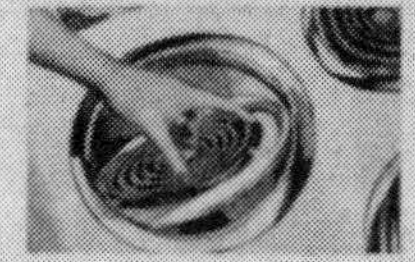

3. And look! If you need a fourth surface unit, you can have it! Simply lift the deep-well unit up—presto—it glides to the top!

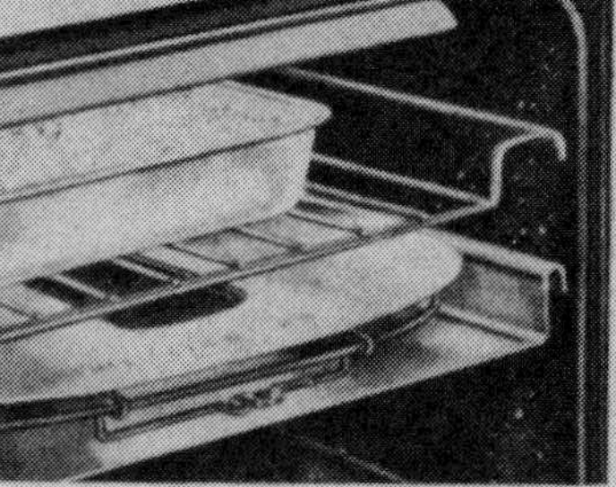

No other range has this big TRIPL-OVEN, with the new easy-clean tray!

Removable tray underneath oven Calrod unit does away with hands-and-knees scrubbing. Slips out for washing!

The new Tripl-Oven *preheats automatically*. And it's BIG! There's a huge Master Oven. Inside that, a larger-than-ever Super Broiler. Also a Speed Oven (made by shutting off part of oven you don't need) that *heats faster than any other range oven!*

No other range has these convenient color signals—TEL-A-COOK LIGHTS!

Saves peeking or guessing! Different colored lights on the control panel tell instantly what unit's on and at what heat. A quick warning, too, if a unit is accidentally left on.

New, washable No-Stain Oven Vent; new Automatic Oven Control!

No-Stain Oven Vent traps oven vapors—helps keep your kitchen gleaming. It's concealed under right rear unit—can be slipped out, washed!

Automatic Oven Timer is improved, almost human! Lets you take the whole afternoon off while your dinner *cooks itself!*

*Trade-mark Reg. U. S. Pat. O

GENERAL ELECTRIC

General Electric's 1947 range featured the TRIPL-UNIT deep-well cooker, pressure cooker, and fourth surface unit; a large oven that preheated automatically; removable tray under oven unit for easier cleaning; and Tel-A-Cook Lights on the control panel that told which unit was on and at what heat. The range shown was priced $334.75; others were from $189.75. (Courtesy General Electric Corporation.)

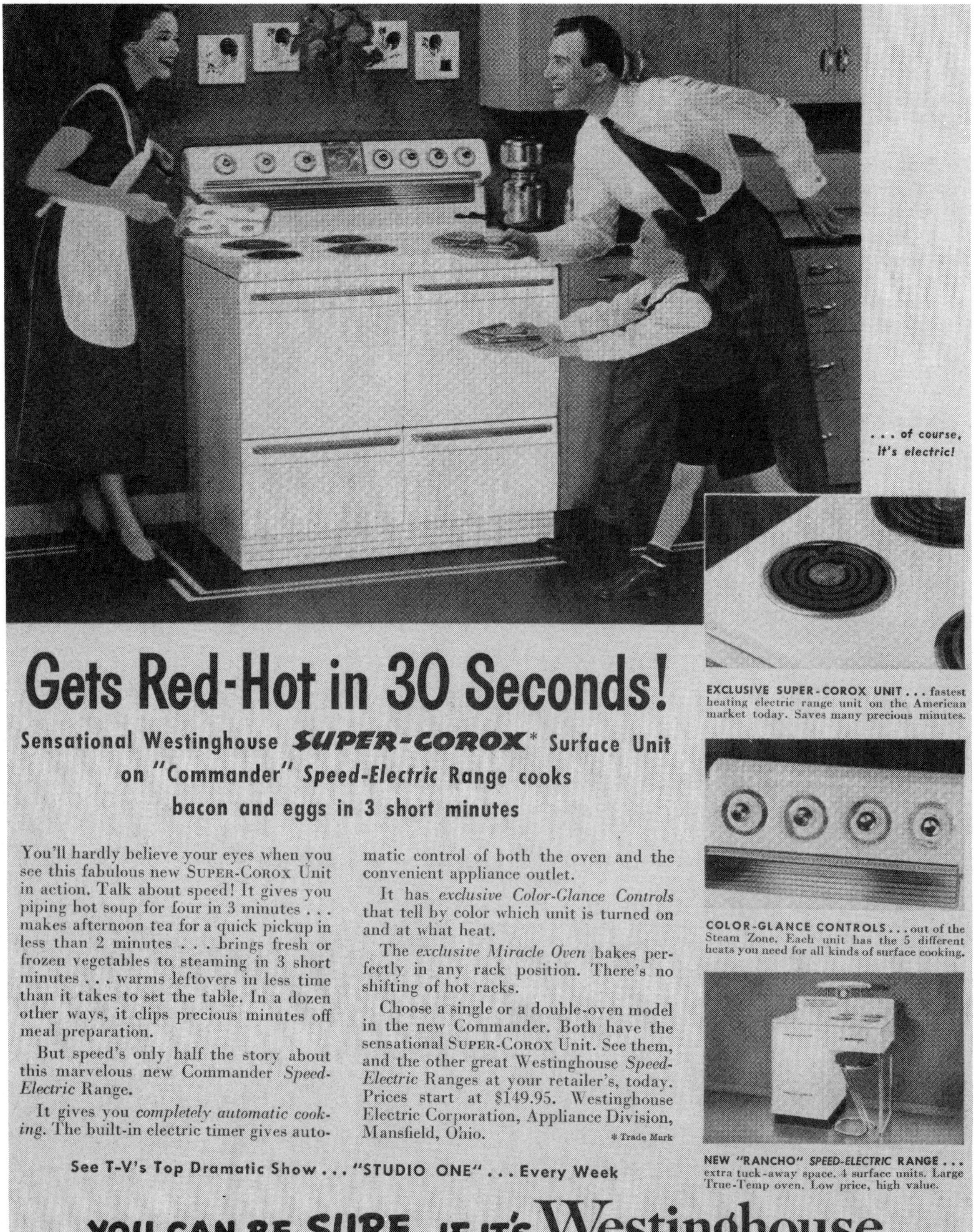

. . . of course, it's electric!

Gets Red-Hot in 30 Seconds!

EXCLUSIVE SUPER-COROX UNIT . . . fastest heating electric range unit on the American market today. Saves many precious minutes.

Sensational Westinghouse SUPER-COROX* Surface Unit on "Commander" *Speed-Electric* Range cooks bacon and eggs in 3 short minutes

COLOR-GLANCE CONTROLS . . . out of the Steam Zone. Each unit has the 5 different heats you need for all kinds of surface cooking.

You'll hardly believe your eyes when you see this fabulous new SUPER-COROX Unit in action. Talk about speed! It gives you piping hot soup for four in 3 minutes . . . makes afternoon tea for a quick pickup in less than 2 minutes . . . brings fresh or frozen vegetables to steaming in 3 short minutes . . . warms leftovers in less time than it takes to set the table. In a dozen other ways, it clips precious minutes off meal preparation.

But speed's only half the story about this marvelous new Commander *Speed-Electric* Range.

It gives you *completely automatic cooking*. The built-in electric timer gives automatic control of both the oven and the convenient appliance outlet.

It has *exclusive Color-Glance Controls* that tell by color which unit is turned on and at what heat.

The *exclusive Miracle Oven* bakes perfectly in any rack position. There's no shifting of hot racks.

Choose a single or a double-oven model in the new Commander. Both have the sensational SUPER-COROX Unit. See them, and the other great Westinghouse *Speed-Electric* Ranges at your retailer's, today. Prices start at $149.95. Westinghouse Electric Corporation, Appliance Division, Mansfield, Ohio.

* Trade Mark

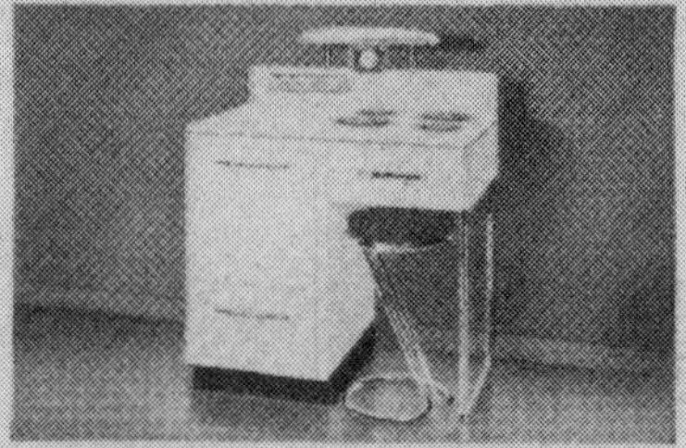

NEW "RANCHO" *SPEED-ELECTRIC* RANGE . . . extra tuck-away space. 4 surface units. Large True-Temp oven. Low price, high value.

See T-V's Top Dramatic Show . . . "STUDIO ONE" . . . Every Week

YOU CAN BE SURE..IF IT'S Westinghouse

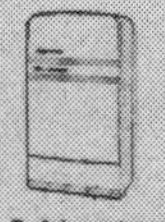

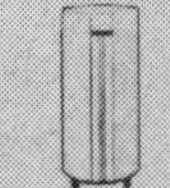

The Westinghouse range featured its Super-Corox surface unit on this 1950 Speed Electric range. The units heated red-hot in thirty seconds. (Courtesy White-Westinghouse Corporation.)

Refrigerators. Ice refrigerators were still available in the 1940s and, were economical, required no defrosting, were free from breakdowns, and were silent. Even so, they couldn't hold their share of the market.

By 1941, automatic refrigerators were considered indispensable in every household that could afford one. Gas refrigerators used an absorption system, while electric units used a compression-type method powered by an electric motor. The salesman used a model to inform product demonstrators at gas companies and dealerships of the convenient features of the Servel gas refrigerator.

By the late 1940s, many changes had been made to the automatic refrigerator. There were larger freezers, the beginning of two-door refrigerators, trigger-release ice cube trays, moist-cold compartments, egg holders, and adjustable shelves.

In 1948, the L&H automatic range made by A. J. Lindemann and Hoverson Company, Milwaukee, Wisconsin, had an extra-large oven, Duo-Cook Deep Well, and hinged heating units.

The 1941 Philco electric refrigerator had a frozen food compartment across the top and shelves on the door, which gave it 26 percent more usable space.

A salesman's sample case and the front of the sample Servel refrigerator. The refrigerator was 7½" × 4" × 2¼", with the Servel flame emblem on the door. Although this sample had the same basic design as those in the late 1930s, it had a different freezer unit in the center. It appears to have been made in 1945 and 1946. Twelve demonstration cards were in the sample.

The back of Servel had a diagram of the cooling mechanism, which had no moving parts. This made it quiet, as there was no starting and stopping of a motor. There is a box of wooden matches, half-full, that says: "STAYS SILENT...LASTS LONGER because it freezes with no moving parts." By lighting a match under the glass projecting tube, the moving orange liquid demonstrated how gas flowed through the freezing unit.

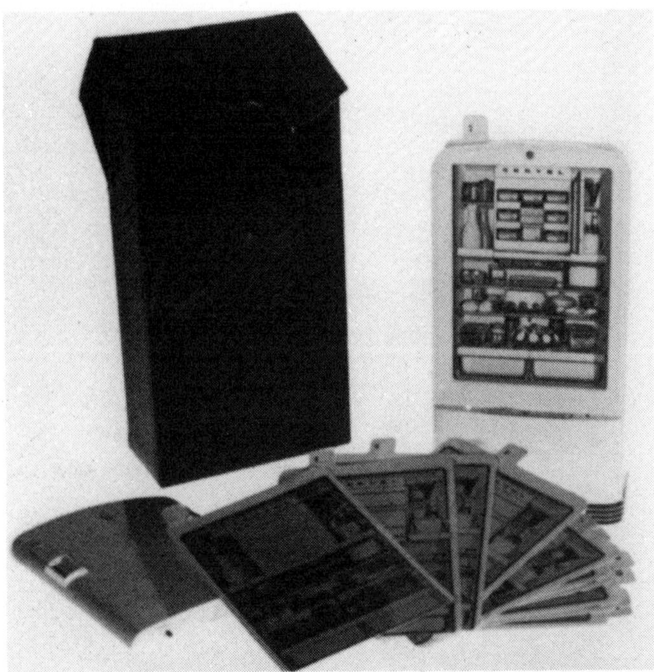

The door pulls off the front to show the interior with food arrangement and a larger freezer than earlier models in the illustration. Card #1 had a color interior. The rest of the cards demonstrate that this model provided a variety of flexible food and shelf arrangements. All shelves were adjustable, and ample provision was made for storage of meat, fruits, and vegetables, with drawers that were also movable and stackable.

The 1949 Admiral Dual-Temp refrigerator kept foods fresh without wrapping or covering. No defrosting was required for the Moist-Cold fresh food compartment, but was necessary in the freezer compartment.

Servel gas refrigerators were twenty years old in 1949.

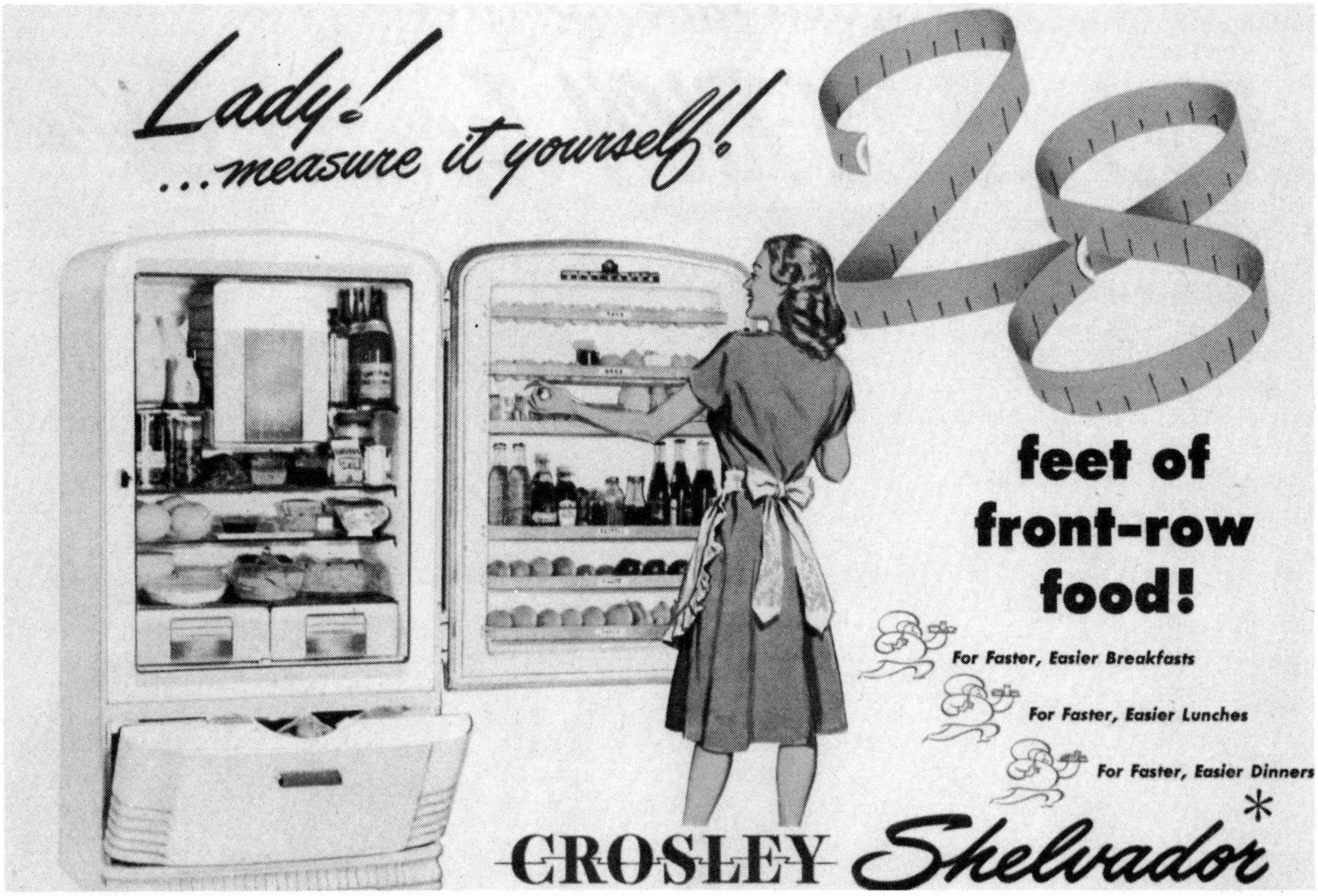

Lady!
...measure it yourself!
28
feet of
front-row
food!
For Faster, Easier Breakfasts
For Faster, Easier Lunches
For Faster, Easier Dinners
*
CROSLEY Shelvador

In 1947, the Crosley Shelvador refrigerator offered 28 feet of front-row food, which allowed a quick "food inventory" at a glance. The kitchen-size freezer could store 100 pounds of food. This refrigerator was manufactured by the Crosley Division of the Avco Manufacturing Corporation, Cincinnati, Ohio.

LOCKER-TOP
HOLDS 70 LBS.
OF FROZEN
FOODS

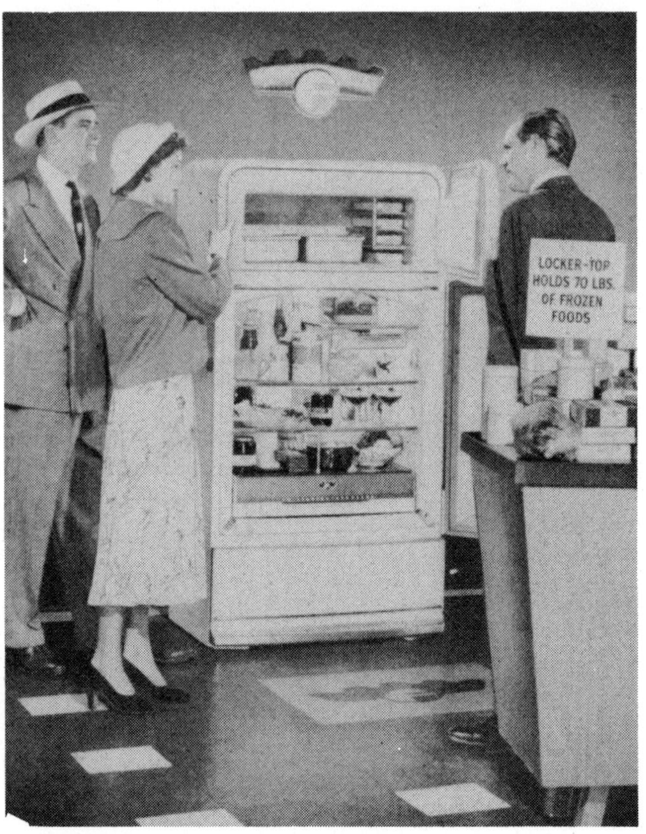

The 1949 Frigidaire was a two-door refrigerator with two cubic feet of freezing space that held up to seventy pounds of food. Frigidaire was one of the first manufacturers to make a two-door refrigerator with freezer on top.

Furniture. Free-standing kitchen cabinets, tables, and cupboards continued to be popular until, but not after, World War II. The emphasis on kitchen modernization in 1935 continued into the 1940s with built-in kitchen units.

After World War II, kitchen modernization resumed, with the emphasis on electric appliances. In 1946, Sears Roebuck was still offering wooden cabinets with chrome-plated door and drawer handles and work surfaces of either black or red linoleum.

In the late 1940s, numerous kitchen furniture manufacturers offered dinette sets with streamlined designs. They were popular because they were colorful. And their durable plastic upholstery, laminated plastic table surfaces, and shiny chrome made them easy to care for. Even the lightest pastel colors could be wiped clean with the whisk of a damp cloth.

The 1949 Cosco advertisement offered a variety of stools and utility tables.

ah!

how glamorous...!

Glamourize your kitchen, give it new charm and beauty with a CHROM*Craft* dinette...made of gleaming, tubular chrome steel, and upholstered in colorful, stain-proof, flame-proof, tear-proof, masland DURAN. And there are five smart table-top styles to choose from...porcelain, enamel, linoleum, oak and NEW PLASTIC. You won't believe your eyes they're so beautiful... priced for your budget, too. That's why CHROM*Craft* is Mrs. America's favorite dinette!

CHROMCraft

the finest name in chrome dinettes!

HAVE YOU SEEN THE

Mixcrafter?

It's the exciting, new portable server for your living room, den or rathskeller. Plenty of room for bottles, seltzer, soda, glasses and ice! Handy... when not in use, just roll it aside. Comes in a variety of smart colors. Ideal for the home... the life of every party.

AT YOUR FAVORITE FURNITURE AND DEPARTMENT STORES

CHROMCraft DINETTE FURNITURE
DIVISION OF
AMERICAN FIXTURE & MANUFACTURING COMPANY
2300 LOCUST ST. ST. LOUIS 3, MISSOURI

ChromCraft Dinette Furniture was made of gleaming, tubular chrome steel, and was upholstered in colorful, stain-proof, flame-proof, tear-proof, Masland Duran (a plastic leather). There were five tabletop surfaces to choose from: porcelain, enamel, linoleum, oak and NEW PLASTIC.

"Step Saver" Matched Steel Units for an Ultra-Modern Kitchen

$48.00 Value
5 Pieces As Listed

$28.95 Cash
$3 DOWN

A GRAND VALUE! CHECK THE FEATURES

Heavier steel construction; reinforced corners. Large working top.
Triple coated, stain-proof, Porcelain enamel base tops. Easy to keep clean.
Lustrous, baked-on Enamel finish.
A $48 value. You save over 35% on complete set. Easy Terms on Page 1038.

You can solve ANY space or storage problem with some "Step-Saver" combination. Study your kitchen, analyze your needs—then order the combination that best suits you. Choose it from the individual pieces shown at right. You'll save most, though, by ordering the ensemble shown below.

(E) $6.98 24-IN. BASE | (A) $12.95 40-IN. BASE | (C) $6.98 DOUBLE CABINET | (D) $4.98 SINGLE CABINET (G)

Above is the combination which is suited to most housewives' needs. It consists of double and single shelf cabinets, 40-inch base and wall cabinet, and steel back.

Portable Steel Units You'd Pay One Third More for Elsewhere!

Here's your chance to let "Step Saver" matched units make your kitchen as convenient and beautiful as the ones you see in magazines. Everything you want—at Sears customary easy-to-pay prices. Check these features: steel construction thru-out, spot welded. Ample toeroom and cleaning or sweeping space beneath units. Flush combination doorpulls and latches—flowing lines—no protruding handles to catch your cleaning cloth. All base tops triple-coated, stain-proof, porcelain-enamel. Lustrous, baked-on enamel finish, neat modern-type stencil decoration. Colors: White or Ivory with Black legs, choice of Black or Red trim. **State finish. Shipped from** factory near So. Bend, Ind. or Philadelphia, Pa. You pay freight from shipping point.
1 EM 2080F—(shown left) 1 Double, 1 Single Door Shelf Cabinet, 40-in. Base, Wall Cabinet and Back. Shpg. wt., 200 lbs. **$28.95**
1 EM 2079F—Similar, with 24-inch Base and Wall Cabinet. Shipping weight, 175 pounds **$20.95**

(A) 1 EM 2083F—40-in. Base. Top, 40x25-in., 32½-in. high, 4 shelf spaces. Shpg. wt., 72 lbs. About 11 cu. ft. capacity .. **$12.95**
(B) 1 EM 2084F—40-in. Wall Cabinet. 20-in. high, 11-in. deep. Has 2 shelf spaces. About 4 cu. ft. capacity. Shpg. wt., 30 lbs. **$4.98**
(C) 1 EM 2081F—Double Door Cabinet. 24-in. wide, 11-in. deep, 63-in. high, 5 shelf spaces. 8 cu. ft. capacity. Shpg. wt., 50 lbs. **$6.98**
(D) 1 EM 2082F—Single Door Cabinet. 18-in. wide, 11-in. deep, 63-in. high, 5 shelf spaces. 5½ cu. ft. capacity. Shpg. wt., 40 lbs. **$4.98**
(E) 1 EM 2086F—24-inch Base. Top 24x20-inches, 32½ inches high, 2 shelves, drawer, 7 cu. ft. capacity. Shpg. wt., 60 lbs. . **$6.98**
(F) 1 EM 2085F—24-in. Wall Cabinet. 20-in. high, 11-in. deep, 2 shelf spaces. 2 cu. ft. capacity. Shipping wt., 19 lbs **$3.48**
(G) 1 EM 2087F—Broom Closet. 18-in. wide, 11-inches deep, 63 inches high. Shelf, hooks, catches, etc. Shipping wt., 34 lbs. **$4.98**

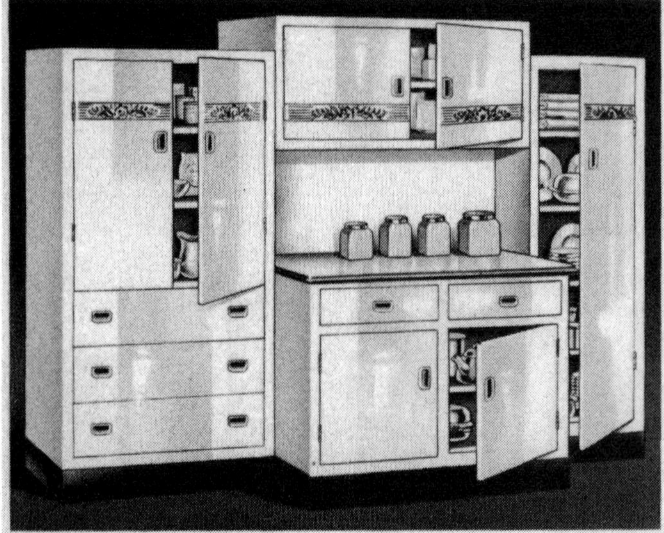

$11.98 Cash KITCHEN SAFE | $19.96 Cash 40-IN. CABINET & BASE | $4.98 Cash DISH CABINET | $34.98 Cash 5-PC. OUTFIT

$3.98 Cash DISH CABINET | $9.77 Cash WALL CABINET & BASE | $16.89 Cash 5-PC. OUTFIT

"Kitchen King"—Reduced $3

Just think: 2 roomy drawers in base for cutlery and silver; 3 grand double-width drawers in safe, with 3 shelf spaces for china above. 5 shelf spaces in dish cabinet for utensils and supplies. You needn't move from the work base to reach china, food or linen!

Strong, medium weight steel construction thru-out. Styled up to the minute with flush-to-the-floor Ebony Black base and flush doorpulls. Decorative stencil motif adorns ensemble. Base has White **porcelain** enamel stainproof work surface that cleans like a dish. Deep, roomy double cupboard below with 2 shelf spaces for bulky pots and pans and lid rack inside door. Five grand shelves in dish cabinet, 3 in safe. Snowy White enamel with Black base and black or red trim or rich Ivory with Black base and black or red trim. **State finish.** This is the ensemble to give you convenience as you've never known it before! Enjoy its many advantages while paying for it on Sears Easy Payment plan as shown on Page 1038. **Shipped only from factory near South Bend, Indiana.** You pay freight from shipping point. Connecting steel back included when both base and wall cabinet are ordered.

1 EM 2046F—5-Piece Ensemble: Dish and Wall cabinets, Kitchen Safe, Work Base, Back. Shipping weight, 265 pounds **$34.98**

Base Only: Height, 33 inches; Width, 40 inches; Depth, 25 inches. Double door cupboard, 2 shelf spaces, 2 drawers. Shipping weight, 95 lbs. **$14.98**

Kitchen Safe Only: Height, 63 inches; Width, 30 inches; Depth, 11 inches. Double door cupboard, 3 roomy shelf spaces above; 3 big drawers below. Shipping weight, 95 pounds **$11.98**

Dish Cabinet: Height, 63 inches; Width, 18 inches; Depth, 11 inches. 5 shelf spaces. Shipping weight, 38 pounds **$4.98**

Wall Cabinet: Height, 20 inches; Width, 40 inches; Depth, 11 inches. 2 shelf spaces. Shipping weight, 30 pounds **$4.98**

Quality Ensemble at Low Cost

Priced much lower than its value. Ideal for small kitchens. Medium gauge steel, spot-welded for lasting strength. Baked-on enamel finish, as easy to clean as a dish! Modern flush door pulls. Base has porcelain enamel, stainproof steel top, and handy cutlery drawer and cupboard. The complete 5-piece outfit is only $2 down and $2 a month on Sears Easy Terms. See page 1038 for details.

Colors: White or Ivory—with Black or Red trim. **State choice. Shipped from factory near South Bend, Ind. or Philadelphia, Pa.**; you pay freight from nearer point. Matching steel back included when both base and wall cabinet are ordered.

1 EM 2032F—COMPLETE 5-PIECE ENSEMBLE. As pictured. Consists of two dish or linen cabinets, base and wall cabinet, and steel back to fit between base and top. Shipping weight, 155 pounds **$16.89**
1 EM 2032F—Dish or Linen Cabinet. 5 handy shelf spaces. Size, 63x13½x10 inches. Door opens from left. Shipping weight, 27 pounds ... **$3.98**
1 EM 2032F—Dish or Linen Cabinet. Same as above but with door opening from right. Shipping weight, 27 pounds **$3.98**
1 EM 2032F—Base Cabinet. Stainproof porcelain enameled top, 24x20 inches. Height, 33 inches. Handy drawer. Shipping weight, 60 lbs **$6.48**
1 EM 2032F—Wall Cabinet. 2 wide shelf spaces. Size, 24x20x11 in. Hardware for mounting included. Shpg. wt., 19 lbs. **$3.29**

☐ SEARS PAGE 595D

Sears Roebuck tempted housewives with their Step Saver ultra-modern steel units in 1940. (Courtesy Sears, Roebuck and Company.)

Begin Your Dream Kitchen Now—for as Little as $2 a Month

LUSTER CRAFT Matched Wood Cabinets! Buy One at a Time or an Entire Ensemble!

Luster Craft—everything you've ever dreamed of for your kitchen! How often you've seen lovely pictures in magazines and said, "If I could only afford it, that's the kind of a kitchen I'd have!" Well, you CAN have it—and now! Here is the smoothly matched beauty, the quality and convenience of expensive units—at a price you'll gladly pay. Economy in its strictest sense, whether you buy for Cash or Easy Terms.

Cabinets built of select, hardwood, kiln-dried to withstand warping. Soundly blocked construction. Styled along simple modern lines. Finished inside and out in washable, **white enamel**, with colorful, wear-resisting, **linoleum-type countertops** and 12-inch splash backs bound in polished aluminum. Ebony-black, flush-to-the-floor bases recessed for additional toe room. There is plenty of cupboard and drawer space, labor-saving features like pan racks, covered and metal-lined bread drawers and flour bins. Units are portable—you can set them up to suit your needs. Easy to move. **Colors:** White with Black, Blue, Green or Red counters, splash-backs, drawer and door pulls. **Be sure to state choice when ordering.**

Sink Ensemble with Two 24-Inch Wall Cabinets

Sink Base. Pressed steel sink, 23x15 in. Depth, 7 in. Triple-coated with stain-proof white porcelain enamel. Brass, chromium-plated, double-mixing swivel faucet and basket strainer drain with removable crumb cup. Drain extends to trap connection. Sink housed in base 72x25 in.; 36-in. high. Approx. 34 cu. ft. of storage space. 4 big, roomy cupboards; 2 with pan racks. 2 shelf spaces in ea. 4 small and 4 large drawers.

Wall Cabinets above. Approx. 4 cu. ft. of storage space in each. See full descriptio under (E) below. Trimmed to match counter-tops. Just imagine—only $6.00 down f this ensemble, complete with sink and two 24-in. wall cabinets. Easy Terms—Page 103 **Shipped from** factory near Cincinnati, Ohio; **you pay freight from there.**

1 EM 2067F—Complete Sink Ensemble. Includes 72-in. Sink Base and two, 24-in. Wall Cabinets. Shipping weight, 245 pounds. Cash $69.0

1 EM 2029F—72-In. Sink Base Only. Shpg. wt., 195 lbs. $59.00

Ⓐ $5.00 Down Ⓑ $5.00 Down Ⓒ $4.00 Down Ⓓ $3.00 Down Ⓔ $2.50 Dow

Ⓕ Ⓖ

Do Your Own Planning—Choose the Combination That Suits Your Need

All Bases are 36 in. high. No wearisome bending—you work at them in perfect comfort. When placed together, bases provide continuous working surface. All are 25 in. deep, with roomy shelf spaces for bulky utensils. 12-inch Splash Backs included. Drawers are solidly built, smooth-sliding. For $1.00 extra, a covered, metal-lined bread drawer may be added (when not included). In 5 widths, as listed below.

All Wall Cabinets (except 30-in. unit) are 24 in. high, 12½ in. deep. For $1.25 additional, you may have a removable 20-lb. flour bin. Doors equipped with spring catche and decorative door pulls to match counter tops. For construction, trim, etc., see description of matching units above. **Specify color trim, pieces wanted.**

All units **shipped from** factory near Cincinnati, Ohio. You pay freight from there

Ⓐ 72-In. Ensemble

About 45 Cu. Ft. Storage

1 EM 2029F—72-inch Wall Cabinet only. 6 compartments, 2 shelf spaces. Approx. 12 cu. ft. of storage space. Shpg. wt., 75 lbs. Cash. $13.98

1 EM 2029F—72-inch Cabinet Base only. Like sink base at top, but without sink. 2 small extra drawers. Approx. 34 cu. ft. of storage space. Wt., 160 lbs. Cash. $35.98

1 EM 2029F—Complete 72-inch Cabinet Ensemble as in view A; also shown in large illus. at top. $5 Down, $5 a month on Terms. See Page 1038. Shpg. wt., 235 lbs. Cash $48.95

SEARS PAGE 595C

Ⓑ 60-In. Ensemble

About 38 Cu. Ft. Storage

1 EM 203 F—60-in. Wall Cabinet only. 5 cupboards, 2 shelf spaces in each. Approximately 10 cubic feet of storage space in all. Shipping weight, 60 pounds. Cash $11.98

1 EM 2031 —60-inch Base only. 5 small, 4 large drawers. 3 large, roomy cupboards. Pan racks on doors. Approximately 28 cubic feet of storage space. Shipping weight, 150 pounds. Cash $32.50

1 EM 2031F—Complete 60-in. Cabinet Ensemble as in view B. $5 down, $5 a month on Easy Terms. See Page 1038. Shipping weight, 210 pounds. Cash $42.50

Ⓒ 48-In. Ensemble

About 30 Cu. Ft. Storage

1 EM 2052F—48-inch Wall Cabinet only. 4 cupboards, 2 shelf spaces in each. Approximately 8 cu. ft. of storage space in all. Shpg. wt., 50 lbs $9.98

1 EM 2052F—48-in. Base only. 4 small and 4 large drawers; 2 cupboards. Pan racks on doors. Approximately 22 cubic feet of storage space. Shipping weight, 120 pounds $24.98

1 EM 2052F—Complete 48-in. Cabinet Ensemble as in view C. $4 Down, $5 a month—see Page 1038. Shipping wt., 170 lbs. Cash $33.95

Ⓓ 36-In. Ensemble

About 22 Cu. Ft. Storage

1 EM 2069F—36-in. Wall Cabinet only. 3 cupboards, 2 shelf spaces in each. Approximately 6 cu. ft. of storage space. Shipping weight, 40 pounds $8.98

1 EM 2069F—36-in. Base only. 5 small drawers; covered, metal-lined bread drawer. 2 cupboards, pan rack on one door. Approx. 16 cu. ft. storage space. Shipping wt., 105 lbs. $19.98

1 EM 2069F—Complete 36-in. Cabinet Ensemble as in view D. $3 down, $4 a month on Terms. See Page 1038. Shpg. wt., 145 lbs. Cash. $27.95

Ⓔ 24-In. Ensemble

About 15 Cu. Ft. of Storage

1 EM 2047F—30-in. Wall Cabinet. (Inset F.) Use over stove or refrigerator. 2 shelf spaces. Ht., 18 in. Depth, 12½ in. Approx. 4 cu. ft. of storage. Shpg. wt., 35 lbs. ... $6.98

1 EM 2058F—24-in. Wall Cabinet only. 2 shelf spaces. Approx. 4 cu. ft. of storage room. Shipping weight, 25 pounds $6.98

1 EM 2058F—24-in. Base only. small drawers; 2 cupboards, 2 shelf spaces each. Pan-rack. Approx. 1 cu. ft. of storage room. Shipping weight, 80 pounds $14.98

1 EM 2058F—24-in. Drawer Base (See Inset G.) 6 drawers. Shipp weight, 90 pounds.............. $1

1EM2058F—24-In. Cabine semble, view E. Shpg. wt. 105 lbs. $2

In 1940, Sears Roebuck offered wooden kitchen units for the "dream" kitchen. (Courtesy Sears, Roebuck and Company.)

for a PALACE-SIZE kitchen—

Lucky you, with a kitchen big enough for a little living . . . because this hospitable set was made for you! The table is tidily topped with Daystrom's own plastic, made for hard wear and easy care. It's wonderful how it shrugs off stains, scratches and scars! Two center leaves drop in to seat eight easily. The spring-seated chairs are richly upholstered in Duran. All Daystrom furniture is superbly designed in sleek, shining chrome, *electroplated* on sturdy steel. Table, 4 chairs, about $159.50*. Step-stool, about $9.95*.

or a PINT-SIZE dinette!

Here's a cheerful nook with a livable look, for folk who haven't space to spare. The trim little table has two extension leaves that zip open for extra room. Yes, every inch of Daystrom furniture is washable. A swish of a damp cloth cleans the plastic top, keeps chromed surfaces shining as sixpence and the Duran breezily bright. At furniture and department stores throughout U.S. and Canada, marked "Daystrom." Table, with 4 chairs, $104.50*. Other Daystrom sets from $49.95* to $169.50*.

*Slightly higher in West and South. Subject to change without notice.

• Don't worry! All Daystrom table tops are laminated plastic—resist heat, scratches, stains, even burning cigarettes!

-it's DAYSTROM furniture!

Furniture for casual living—featured by stores from coast to coast.

Daystrom Corporation, Olean, N.Y. Daystrom Pacific Corporation, Pasadena, Calif.

AN  ASSOCIATE

Daystrom was one of the leading names in chrome furniture. In 1949, kitchen and dinette tables were made for pint-size or palace-size rooms, with prices from $49.95 to $169.50.

Accessories. Accessories were important in the kitchen but had to be sturdy. Homemakers were reminded that, first and foremost, the kitchen was a place to work. But accessories could be appealing as well as practical.

Sears Roebuck offered many colorful designs for their pantryware from 1948 to 1950. Garden Fruit, Geranium, and Robin Rogue were popular. Bud Blossom, with tinted nosegays on white or yellow, were for sale in the 1950 catalog.

The development of polystyrene in 1938 and polyethylene in 1942 introduced plastics that had all the advantages of earlier plastic, plus many more. They could be molded faster and they cost less. Postwar plastic housewares became a fast-growing industry. They were colorful, durable, easty-to-care-for, lightweight, and would not chip, peel, or rust.

Two other products of Federal Tool (not shown) are a glass shaker and an ice chopper. The mixer sold for 25¢ in 1942. The quart-size glass ice chopper with hardened blades sold for 35¢ that same year.

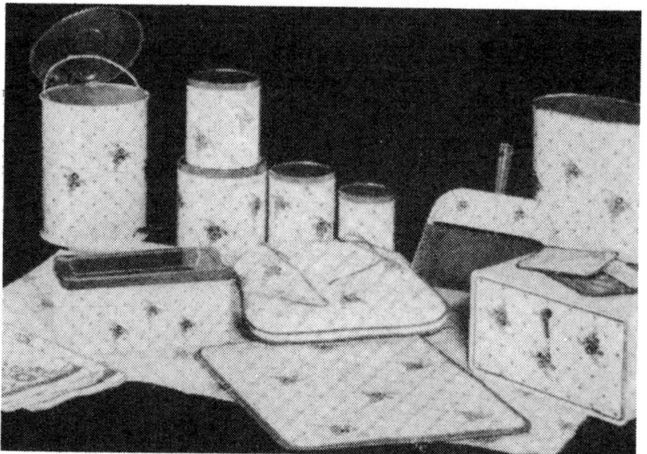

In 1940, Empeco's Floral Diamond tinware was priced from 15¢ to $1. Cannon tea towels were 10¢ each, and oilcloth by Columbus Coated Fabrics Corporation sold for 10¢ a yard or in made-up pieces. Snack-nook cushion 29¢, potholder set 10¢. All were of the Floral Diamond pattern.

A four-piece set in plastic-topped glass. Syrup jug, mustard and horseradish jars complete the set, made by Federal Tool Corporation. It sold for $1 in 1942 in a variety of colors.
$1.50-3.50 each

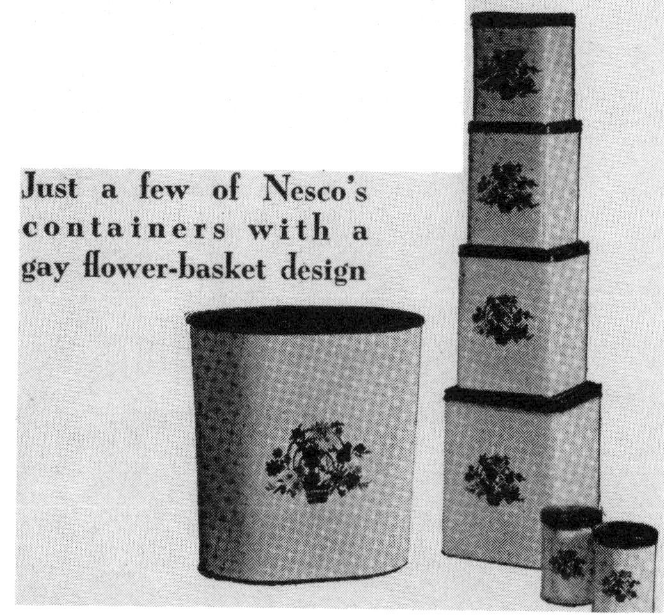

A sample of another Nesco pattern in 1940 was the Flower-Basket design.

Canister set $18-22

Waste can $5-9

Breadboxes $10-20

2½-quart bowl with four 12-ounce dishes. Red or yellow.
Oven-and-Table Set
$2.95

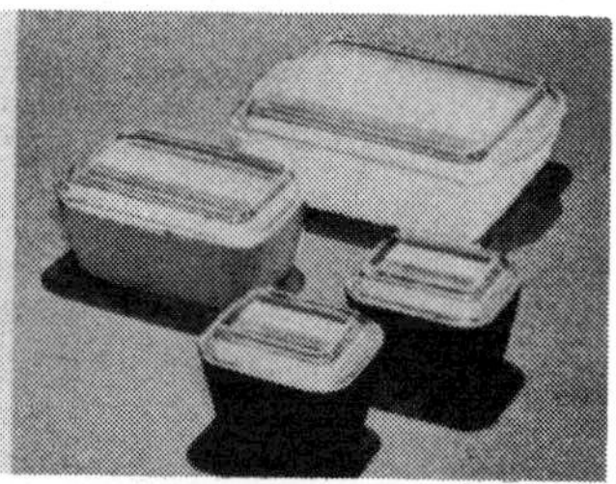

4 gay-colored dishes with clear glass covers. For baking, serving, storing.
Oven-and-Refrigerator Set
$2.95

Wonderful mixing bowls to use a dozen ways. A size for every use.
Color Bowl Set
$2.95

2½-quart size for buffet suppers. Bake in it, serve in it. Red or yellow.
Covered Casserole
$2.25

"Wonderful, wonderful Pyrex Ware goes smart in color!" The first three sets were $2.95 each; the covered casserole was $2.25. Pryex Ware was a product of Corning Glass Works in 1951.

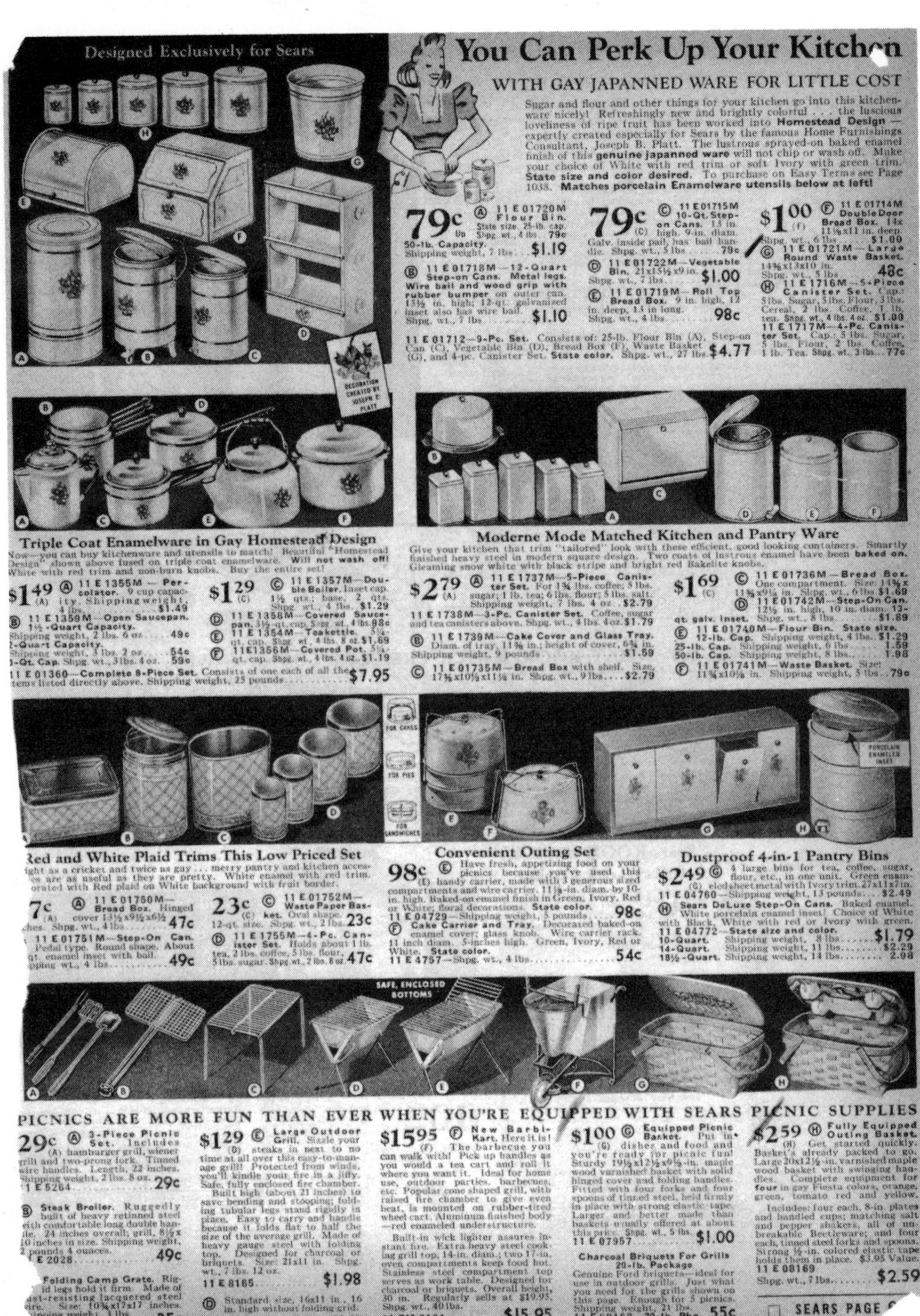

You Can Perk Up Your Kitchen

WITH GAY JAPANNED WARE FOR LITTLE COST

Sugar and flour and other things for your kitchen go into this kitchenware nicely! Refreshingly new and brightly colorful . . . the luscious loveliness of ripe fruit has been worked into **Homestead Design** — expertly created especially for Sears by the famous Home Furnishings Consultant, Joseph B. Platt. The lustrous sprayed-on baked enamel finish of this **genuine japanned ware** will not chip or wash off. Make your choice of White with red trim or soft Ivory with green trim. **State size and color desired.** To purchase on Easy Terms see Page 1038. **Matches porcelain Enamelware utensils below at left!**

79c (A) 11 E 01720M Flour Bin. State size. 25-lb. cap. Shpg. wt., 4 lbs. 79c
50-lb. Capacity. Shipping weight, 7 lbs. . . $1.19

(B) 11 E 01718M—12-Quart Step-on Cans. Metal legs. Wire bail and wood grip with rubber bumper on outer can. 15½ in. high; 12-qt. galvanized inset also has wire bail. Shpg. wt., 7 lbs. . . . $1.10

79c (C) 11 E 01715M 10-Qt. Step-on Cans. 13 in. high. 9-in. diam. Galv. inside pail, has bail handle. Shpg. wt., 5 lbs. . . . 79c

(D) 11 E 01722M—Vegetable Bin. 21x15½x9 in. Shpg. wt., 7 lbs. . . . $1.00

(E) 11 E 01719M—Roll Top Bread Box. 9 in. high, 12 in. deep, 13 in long. Shpg. wt., 4 lbs. . . . 98c

$1.00 (F) 11 E 01714M Double Door Bread Box. 14x11⅛x11 in. deep. Shpg. wt., 6 lbs. . . . $1.00

(G) 11 E 01721M—Large Round Waste Basket. 14⅜x13x10 in. Shpg. wt., 5 lbs. . . . 48c

(H) 11 E 1716M—5-Piece Canister Set. Cap.: 5 lbs. Sugar, 5 lbs. Flour, 3 lbs. Cereal, 2 lbs. Coffee, 1 lb. tea. Shpg. wt., 4 lbs. 4 oz. $1.00

11 E 1717M—4-Pc. Canister Set. Cap.: 5 lbs. Sugar, 5 lbs. Flour, 2 lbs. Coffee, 1 lb. Tea. Shpg. wt., 3 lbs. . . 77c

11 E 01712—9-Pc. Set. Consists of: 25-lb. Flour Bin (A), Step-on Can (C), Vegetable Bin (D), Bread Box (F), Waste Basket (G), and 4-pc. Canister Set. **State color.** Shpg. wt., 27 lbs. $4.77

DECORATION CREATED BY JOSEPH B. PLATT

Triple Coat Enamelware in Gay Homestead Design

Now—you can buy kitchenware and utensils to match! Beautiful "Homestead Design" shown above fused on triple coat enamelware. **Will not wash off!** White with red trim and non-burn knobs. Buy the entire set!

$1.49 (A) 11 E 1355M — Percolator. 9 cup capacity. Shipping weight, 4 lbs. . . . $1.49

(B) 11 E 1359M—Open Saucepan. 1½-Quart Capacity. Shipping weight, 2 lbs. 6 oz. . . . 49c
2-Quart Capacity. Shipping weight, 3 lbs. 2 oz. . . . 54c
3-Qt. Cap. Shpg. wt., 3 lbs. 4 oz. . . 59c

$1.29 (C) 11 E 1357M—Double Boiler. Inset cap. 1½ qts.; base, 2 qts. Shpg. wt., 4 lbs. $1.29

(D) 11 E 1358M—Covered Saucepan. 3½-qt. cap. Shpg. wt., 4 lbs. 98c

(E) 11 E 1354M—Teakettle. 5¼-qt. cap. Shpg. wt., 4 lbs. 8 oz. $1.69

(F) 11 E 1356M—Covered Pot. 5¼-qt. cap. Shpg. wt., 4 lbs. 4 oz. $1.19

11 E 01360—Complete 8-Piece Set. Consists of one each of all the items listed directly above. Shipping weight, 25 pounds. . . . $7.95

Moderne Mode Matched Kitchen and Pantry Ware

Give your kitchen that trim "tailored" look with these efficient, good looking containers. Smartly finished heavy steel in modern square design. Two coats of lustrous enamel have been **baked on.** Gleaming snow white with black stripe and bright red Bakelite knobs.

$2.79 (A) 11 E 1737M—5-Piece Canister Set. For 1¾ lbs. coffee; 5 lbs. sugar; 1 lb. tea; 6 lbs. flour; 5 lbs. salt. Shipping weight, 7 lbs. 4 oz. . $2.79

11 E 1738M—3-Pc. Canister Set. Coffee, sugar and tea canisters above. Shpg. wt., 4 lbs. 4 oz. $1.79

(B) 11 E 1739M—Cake Cover and Glass Tray. Diam. of tray, 11⅜ in.; height of cover, 6¾ in. Shipping weight, 9 pounds. . . . $1.59

(C) 11 E 01735M—Bread Box with shelf. Size, 17⅜x10½x11⅛ in. Shpg. wt., 9 lbs. . . . $2.79

$1.69 (C) 11 E 01736M—Bread Box. One compartment. Size: 14⅜x11⅝x9¼ in. Shpg. wt., 6 lbs. $1.69

(D) 11 E 01742M—Step-On Can. 12½ in. high, 10 in. diam. 13-qt. galv. inset. Shpg. wt., 8 lbs. . . . $1.89

(E) 11 E 01740M—Flour Bin. State size. 12-lb. Cap. Shipping weight, 4 lbs. $1.29
25-lb. Cap. Shipping weight, 6 lbs. . . . 1.59
50-lb. Cap. Shipping weight, 8 lbs. . . . 1.98

(F) 11 E 01741M—Waste Basket. Size: 11⅜x10½ in. Shipping weight, 5 lbs. . 79c

FOR CAKES

FOR PIES

FOR SANDWICHES

PORCELAIN ENAMELED INSET

Red and White Plaid Trims This Low Priced Set

ight as a cricket and twice as gay . . . merry pantry and kitchen acces es are as useful as they are pretty. White enamel with red trim. orated with Red plaid on White background with fruit border.

7c (A) 11 E 01750M—Bread Box. Hinged cover 13⅛x9⅛x6½ ches. Shpg. wt., 4 lbs. . . . 47c

11 E 01751M—Step-On Can. Pedal type. Round shape. About qt. enamel inset with bail. pping wt., 4 lbs. . . . 49c

23c (C) 11 E 01752M—Waste Paper Basket. Oval shape. 12-qt. size. Shpg. wt., 2 lbs. 23c

(D) 11 E 1755M—4-Pc. Canister Set. Holds about 1 lb. tea, 2 lbs. coffee, 5 lbs. flour, 5 lbs. sugar. Shpg. wt., 2 lbs. 8 oz. 47c

Convenient Outing Set

98c (E) Have fresh, appetizing food on your picnics because you've used this handy carrier, made with 3 generous sized compartments and wire carrier. 11⅛-in. diam. by 10-in. high. Baked-on enamel finish in Green, Ivory, Red or White; floral decorations. **State color.**
11 E 04729—Shipping weight, 5 pounds. . . . 98c

(F) Cake Carrier and Tray. Decorated baked-on enamel cover; glass knob. Wire carrier rack. 11 inch diam. 5-inches high. Green, Ivory, Red or White. **State color.**
11 E 4757—Shpg. wt., 4 lbs. . . . 54c

Dustproof 4-in-1 Pantry Bins

$2.49 (G) 4 large bins for tea, coffee, sugar, flour, etc., in one unit. Green enameled sheet metal with Ivory trim. 27x11x7 in.
11 E 04760—Shipping weight, 13 pounds. . . . $2.49

(H) Sears DeLuxe Step-On Cans. Baked enamel. White porcelain enamel inset! Choice of White with Black, White with red or Ivory with green.
11 E 04772—State size and color.
10-Quart. Shipping weight, 8 lbs. . . . $1.79
14-Quart. Shipping weight, 11 lbs. . . . $2.29
18½-Quart. Shipping weight, 14 lbs. . . . 2.98

SAFE, ENCLOSED BOTTOMS

PICNICS ARE MORE FUN THAN EVER WHEN YOU'RE EQUIPPED WITH SEARS PICNIC SUPPLIES

29c (A) 3-Piece Picnic Set. Includes hamburger grill, wiener grill and two-prong fork. Tinned wire handles. Length, 22 inches. Shipping weight, 2 lbs. 8 oz.
1 E 5264. . . . 29c

(B) Steak Broiler. Ruggedly built of heavy retinned steel with comfortable long double handle. 24 inches overall; grill, 8½x10 inches in size. Shipping weight, 2 pounds 4 ounces.
E 2028. . . . 49c

Folding Camp Grate. Rigid legs hold it firm. Made of ust-resisting lacquered steel ire. Size: 10⅜x17x17 inches. ipping weight, 3 lbs.
2092. . . . 35c

$1.29 (E) Large Outdoor Grill. Sizzle your steaks in next to no time at all over this easy-to-manage grill! Protected from winds, you'll kindle your fire in a jiffy. Safe, fully enclosed fire chamber. Built high (about 21 inches) to save bending and stooping; folding tubular legs stand rigidly in place. Easy to carry and handle because it folds flat to half the size of the average grill. Made of heavy gauge steel with folding top. Designed for charcoal or briquets. Size: 21x11 in. Shpg. wt., 7 lbs. 12 oz.
11 E 8165. . . . $1.98

(D) Standard size, 16x11 in., 16 in. high without folding grid.
11 E 8166—Shpg. wt., 6 lbs. $1.29

$15.95 (F) New Barbi-Kart. Here it is! The barbecue you can walk with! Pick up handles as you would a tea cart and roll it where you want it. Ideal for home use, outdoor parties, barbecues, etc. Popular cone shaped grill, with raised fire chamber to give even heat, is mounted on rubber-tired wheel cart. Aluminum finished body —red enameled understructure.

Built-in wick lighter assures instant fire. Extra heavy steel cooking grill top, 14-in. diam.; two 17-in. oven compartments keep food hot. Stainless steel compartment top serves as work table. Designed for charcoal or briquets. Overall height, 30 in. Regularly sells at $19.95. Shpg. wt., 40 lbs.
11 EM 8164. . . . $15.95

$1.00 (G) Equipped Picnic Basket. Put in dishes and food and you're ready for picnic fun! Sturdy 19½x12½x9½-in. maple wood varnished basket with solid hinged cover and folding handles. Fitted with four forks and four spoons of tinned steel, held firmly in place with strong elastic tape. Larger and better made than baskets usually offered at about this price. Shpg. wt., 5 lbs.
11 E 07957. . . . $1.00

Charcoal Briquets For Grills 20-lb. Package
Genuine Ford briquets—ideal for use in outdoor grills. Just what you need for the grills shown on this page. Enough for 5 picnics. Shipping weight, 21 lbs.
11 E 08168—20-lb. Pkg. 55c

$2.59 (H) Fully Equipped Outing Basket. Get started quickly. Basket's already packed to go. Large 20x12½-in. varnished maple wood basket with swinging handles. Complete equipment for **four** in gay Fiesta colors, orange, green, tomato red and yellow.

Includes: four each, 8-in. plates and handled cups; matching salt and pepper shakers, all of unbreakable Beetleware; and four each, tinned steel forks and spoons. Strong ½-in. colored elastic tape holds them in place. $3.95 Value.
11 E 08169
Shpg. wt., 7 lbs. . . . $2.59

SEARS PAGE

The 1940 Sears Roebuck catalog said you could perk up your kitchen with gay jappaned ware for little cost. The Homestead pattern was designed exclusively for Sears. It had matching porcelain enamelware utensils. Other choices were Modern Mode kitchen and pantry ware in white with a black stripe and red knob, or red-and-white plaid trimmed sets. (Courtesy Sears, Roebuck and Company.)

NESCO DECORATED KITCHEN WARE

Snow white finish. White base, red and green decorations blends beautifully with the gay red blossoms and green leaves. The construction of the Clover Blossom Ware is the finest throughout, with snug covers, well turned beads, and strong flat seams. All food containers are fabricated from sanitary, bright finished tinplate.

DROP DOOR BREAD BOX

Ideal box for shelves or work space under cupboards. Wire door supporting rods prevent door from striking table or shelf. Ventilated. Bright tinplate interior. Size 12⅞ inches x 11½ inches x 12⅝ inches.

No. 5455 .... Per dozen **$36.00**

Packed one to carton

KITCHENETTE BREAD BOX

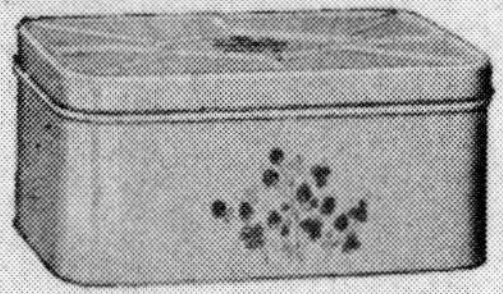

Fits into small kitchen shelf or cupboard space. Lift type cover with sturdy hinges and sanitary tinplate interior.

No. 5450 .... Per dozen **$14.40**

Packed ¼ Doz. to carton

CAKE COVER SET

Handy for carrying cakes or sandwiches to picnics. Set consists of cover, metal tray and wire handle.

No. 5420 .... Per dozen **$16.80**

Packed ½ dozen to carton

STEP-ON CAN

Smooth working cover raising mechanism. Close fitting cover. Hot dipped liner fits snugly.

No.	Size, In.	Cap. Qts.	Per Doz.
5410	9⅜x12⅝	10	**$16.20**
5414	11x14½	14	**27.60**

No. 5410 packed ½ dozen. No. 5414 ¼ dozen.

ROUND WASTE BASKET

Popular 24 qt. size with wide top. Heavy raised bottom and well rolled bottom add extra strength. Size 13½"x10⅜"x14⅜".

No. 5424 .... Per dozen **$13.20**

Packed ½ dozen to carton

ROUND CANISTER SET

Four piece set with ample capacities for food storage. Sanitary tinplate interiors. Snug fit covers. Set consists of 1 lb. Tea Canister; 2 lb. Coffee Canister; 6 lb. Sugar Canister; 6 lb. Flour Canister.

No. 5434 .... Per dozen **$13.20**

Packed ½ dozen to carton

SQUARE CANISTER SET

Four piece set with sanitary tinplate interiors. Snug fitting covers. Set consists of 1 lb. Tea Canister; 2 lb. Coffee Canisters; 6 lb. Sugar Canisters; 6 lb. Flour Canisters.

No. 5444 .... Per dozen **$14.40**

Packed ½ dozen to carton

MATCH SAFE

A safe container that can be hung near stove. Holds a full box and is self feeding.

No. 5481 .... Per dozen **$3.00**

Packed 1 dozen to carton

DUST PAN

Rubber edge and hooded top. Comfortable steel handle with convenient hole for hanging.

No. 5442 .... Per dozen **$4.80**

Packed 2 dozen to carton

SLANT DOOR BREAD BOX

Two ventilated compartments with clean bright tinplate interiors. Top door is self closing while bottom has an improved hasp. Size 12⅞x11¼x11¼ in.

No. 5456 .... Per dozen **$42.00**

Packed one in carton. Wt. 5 lbs.

ROUND WASTE BASKET

24 quart size with wide top. Heavy raised bottom and well rolled edge. Size top 12½ in., bottom 10⅜ in., Height 14⅜ in.

No. 5440 .... Per dozen **$27.00**

Packed one half dozen. Wt. 21 lbs.

SALT AND PEPPER SET

Large size screw top with just the right amount of free flowing openings. Bright tinplate interiors. Size 2⅝x4 in.

No. 5484 .... Per dozen **$5.40**

Packed one dozen. Wt. 5 lbs.

Sav-Ur-Bak Dust Pan

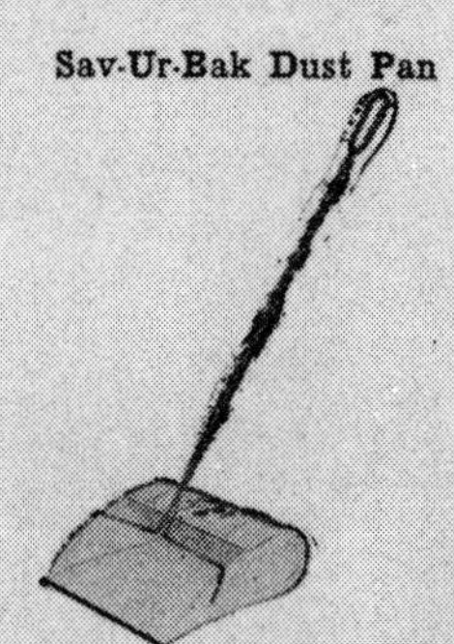

Convenient 26 in. wire handle eliminates stooping. Large hooded storage. Rubber edge. Size 10x9 in.

No. 5445 .... Per dozen **$13.20**

Packed one half dozen. Wt. 9½ lbs.

In 1948, Smith Brothers Hardware Company offered Nesco decorated kitchenware in Clover Blossom. It had red and green decorations on a white base.

Cookware. By 1940, the cookware that could be purchased was the same variety as in the previous decade, but with the addition of copper bottom stainless steel utensils. Revere Ware was introduced in 1938 and became an immediate success. Its production was stopped until after World War II, but then Revere Ware sales skyrocketed. Anchor Hocking started production of its Fire-King light blue glass ovenware.

Columbus Plastic Products, Inc., Lustro-ware plastic housewares had modern style in 1950. The color choice was mandarin red or sunshine yellow. This is just a small sampling of the array of plastic kitchenware that was flooding the market.

This 1950 Nesco ad showed stainless steel utensils and Garden Girl kitchen containers in red, yellow, and white. They were made by the National Enameling and Stamping Company, Milwaukee, Wisconsin.

The 1940 Sears Roebuck catalog featured the new copper bottom stainless steel kitchenware. It heated faster, saved fuel, and had greater cooking efficiency. The prices ranged from $2.29 for a covered one-quart saucepan, to $4.98 for a 1½-quart, five-way double boiler. A starter set consisted of the double boiler with two-quart inset and three-quart saucepan base; four-quart covered pot with bale handle; 10″ covered skillet; and two-quart saucepan. The set cost $18.75. (Courtesy Sears, Roebuck and Company.)

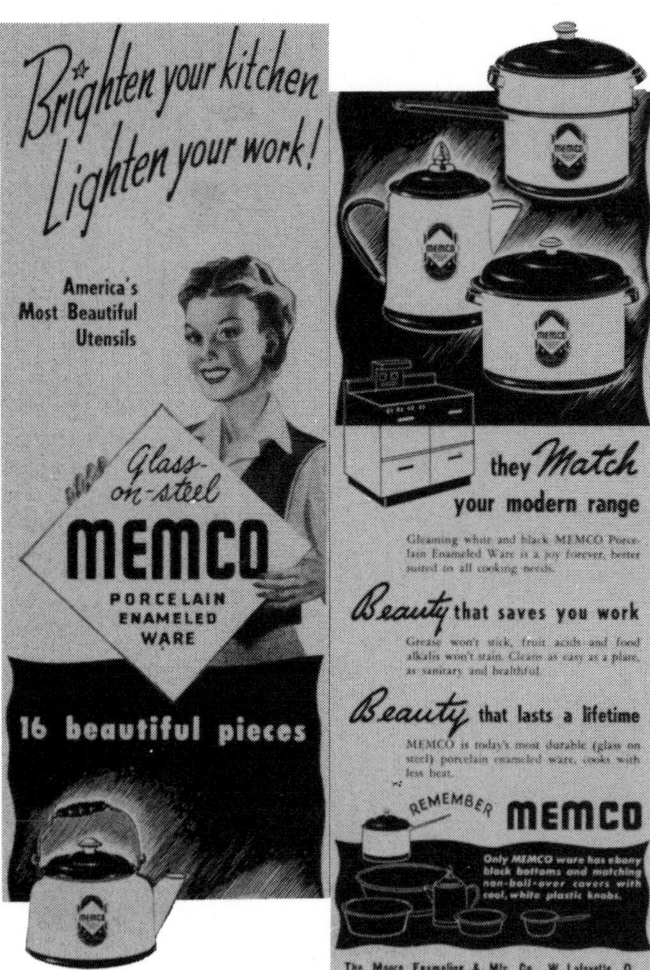

Memco Porcelain Enamelware, manufacturers of glass-on-steel cookware, matched modern range with the gleaming white and black cookware in 1947. Porcelain-enamelware was sparkling white, with either black or red trim in the 1940s.

Club Aluminum Hammercraft Waterless Cookware had twenty utensils available in 1949. The hammered finish took hard knocks and resisted scratches, the smooth stain-resistant interior finish made it easy to clean. This cookware was said to cook the easy, thrifty, full-flavor, top-of-the-stove way. Club cooked the "waterless" way on low heat, saving vitamins, minerals, and fuel, and providing a cooler kitchen, too.

Here's what You've been Waiting for!

The NEW REVERE WARE PRESSURE COOKER

This 4 qt. Pressure Cooker of lustrous stainless steel with a thick copper-clad bottom is truly lovely to look at! And it will last and last . . . remaining after years of hard usage as bright and beautiful as the day you first used it.

Even more important, you don't have to guess about the right pressure. Just dial the pressure you desire on the unique new metal weight gauge and an audible signal informs you when the correct pressure is reached. And you needn't worry about dropping or losing the gauge. It's *permanently* attached.

MORE FEATURES YOU'LL APPRECIATE

1. NEW Revere long-life, tight sealing gasket.
2. COOL, evenly-balanced Bakelite handles to fit your hands.
3. EASY and simple to use. Saves time and fuel, and retains vitamins and minerals in food.
4. FREE, a brand new recipe book! A product of several years in Revere's test kitchens, it contains appetizing recipes for vegetables, meat and luscious desserts. This handy book also includes complete instruction on how to take care of your Revere Pressure Cooker.

And remember—Revere has developed all these revolutionary improvements in design to make Pressure Cooking easier for you! So why not get your Revere Ware Pressure Cooker today?

REVERE COPPER AND BRASS INCORPORATED
Rome Manufacturing Company Division, Rome, New York

ASK YOUR DEALER TO SHOW YOU THESE NEW "KITCHEN JEWELS"

REVERE UTENSIL RACK—made of stainless steel, with movable brass hangers, 22 ins. long.

REVERE STARTER SET—includes a 6-in. Skillet, a 1-qt. Sauce Pan, a 1½-qt. Sauce Pan, each with Cover, and a Special Rack 22 ins. long. Pieces not sold individually. An extraordinary value, $12.50.

P.S. *Make sure you get Revere Ware. Look for the trade mark in the thick copper bottom.*

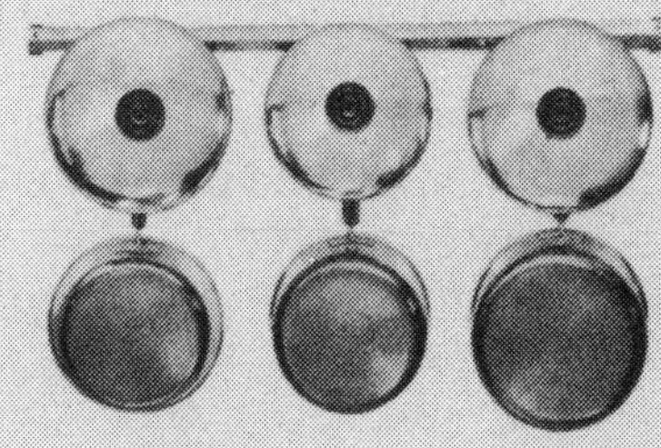

In 1949, a variety of kitchen utensils was offered in the Revere Ware line. This line of cookware was stainless steel with a thick copper-clad bottom and Bakelite handles. Farberware introduced their aluminum-clad stainless steel cookware in 1949.

Toy Kitchen Collectibles

Many a playtime started out with "let's play house," and valuable lessons of homemaking were learned. Toys were miniature versions of the tools mothers used, but designed for the very young homemaker. These honest-to-goodness work toys ranged from eggbeaters to stoves.

In the 1930s, there were electric kitchen toys available for children. Several toy electric ranges really cooked. These were approved by underwriters' laboratories and could be operated without danger of fire or shocks. Some models had both stove-top burners and heat units in the oven to bake pies, apples, and cookies. They were priced from $4.95. A miniature toaster could handle two small slices of bread and could be purchased for less than $1. There was a waffle iron that baked as well as Mother's and cost less than $2. An electric iron sold for 98¢.

To equip the play kitchen, there were all kinds of tools and utensils that were often exact duplicates of the adult products. A set of cooking utensils, made of aluminum, included a covered saucepan, frying pan, covered kettle, roaster, and colander, each only 35¢. An assortment of cooking tools and utensils could be purchased in sets or separately. The list included eggbeaters, spatulas, miniature funnels, half-cup measures, paring knives, potato mashers, ladles, mixing spoons, and many more.

For the young baker, there were pastry sets and small mixing bowls in yellow, red, blue, or green. Among a variety of baking tools were cookie cutters in amusing shapes, a measuring scoop, flour sifter, rolling pin, and baking sheet. Pie pans, cake pans, and muffin tins (for bite-size treats) were popular. Covered baking dishes, custard cups, pie plates, and pudding bowls of ovenproof glass were sold in novelty sets. Some were finished with borders in red and white.

Of course, once the cooking was finished, it had to be served. The table was set with dainty tea sets of china, enamelware, and aluminum cutlery (knife, fork and spoon sets).

What fun at the party!

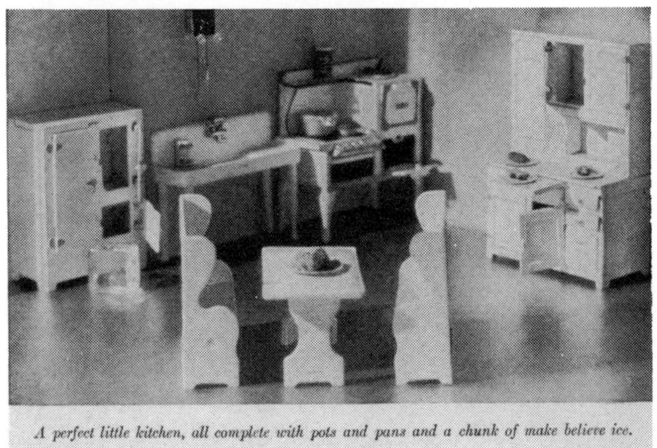

The 1926 Marshall Field Christmas booklet featured doll furniture made especially for that company. The perfect little kitchen included an icebox, sink, range, kitchen cabinet, table, and chairs, complete with pots and pans and even a chunk of make-believe ice.

The sale price of this twenty-three-piece lustre china with flower designs was $1.19 in 1930. **$30-45 set**

▶
Tootsietoy sold an unassembled, unfurnished dollhouse for $3 in 1926. The dollhouse had a living room, two bedrooms, dining room, kitchen and bath. Individual rooms of furniture sold for $1 a set. The seven-piece kitchen set was white and included icebox, sink, kitchen cabinet, range, table, and two chairs. **Kitchen set $15-30**

TOOTSIETOY DOLL HOUSE FURNITURE

TOOTSIETOY DOLL HOUSE
Unfurnished

Living Room, 2 Bedrooms, Dining Room, Kitchen and Bath. It comes knocked down. Made for TOOTSIETOY FURNITURE. $3.00

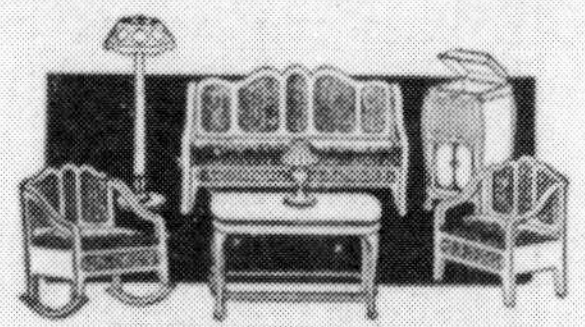

Living Room—Gold, Oak or Mahogany—7 pieces—$1.00

Bedroom—Gold, Mahogany, Oak, Pink or Blue—7 pieces—$1.00

Dining Room—Gold, Oak or Mahogany—8 pieces—$1.00

Kitchen—White—7 pieces—$1.00

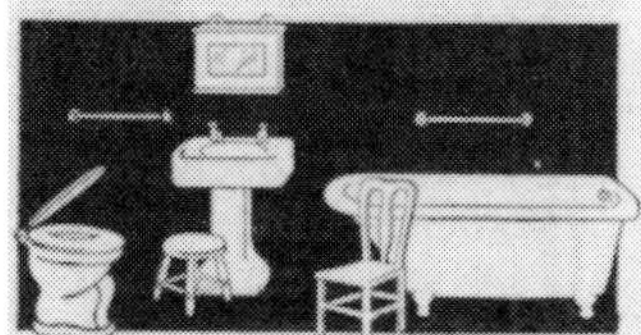

Bathroom—White—8 pieces—$1.00

There is Nothing Like TOOTSIETOY Doll House Furniture!

EVERY girl who sees TOOTSIETOY Doll House Furniture immediately falls in love with it—it's so pretty and cute and at the same time it looks just like real furniture—TOOTSIETOY is made to the scale of an inch to the foot—upholstered—and comes in a wide range of colors.

TOOTSIETOY is Made of Metal

There is TOOTSIETOY FURNITURE for every room in the house. Living Room, Bedroom, Kitchen, Dining Room and Bathroom. Each set sells for $1.00—or **5 rooms for $5.00.**

The Tootsietoy House is made especially for TOOTSIETOY Doll House Furniture. It has 6 rooms and sells for $3.00. Completely furnished. $9.00

Ask for TOOTSIETOY at the Toy Stores—if you have any difficulty in getting it we will ship what you want direct.

Send $9.00 for Tootsietoy Doll House and furniture for 6 rooms.
" $5.00 " Furniture for 5 rooms without doll house.
" $3.00 " Tootsietoy doll house without furniture.
" $1.00 " each single set if you wish to buy separately.

DOWST MANUFACTURING COMPANY
4541 Fulton Street, Chicago, Ill.

Sandy Andy toys were "Playthings That Made Playtime Happier." The "Sandy Andy" Laundry Set consisted of eight pieces: enameled metal washtub, glass surface washboard, clothes reel, bag of clothespins, galvanized wringer with rubber rollers, clothes basket, ironing board, and iron. Complete, $3.25.

The vacuum cleaner worked by friction and suction to pick up bits of paper or ashes when pushed along the floor. It was 28¼″ high, had an enameled finish in different colors, and sold for $2.50 at any toy store in 1927.

The games were priced from $1 to $2.

Goldilock's Home

We were given the plans of Goldilock's home and we have reproduced it so that *now* all the little girls have an opportunity to obtain one like it.

This is a real doll house sturdily constructed of wood, furniture made of wood and finished like real furniture. The drawers pull out and Dining and Living Room chairs have velvet seats. There is an extension table with two leaves. The dresser has a real mirror and so forth.

The house is made of three and five ply birch panel lumber, solid corner posts. The house comes in sections knocked down. It can be assembled in a few minutes. The construction is such that after it is assembled it is positively firm and rigid.

The rooms are 14" square and 9" high. The total height of house is 32". Base dimension is 18" x 32". A special feature is that the doll house is unpainted, making it possible for you to paint the house in any color combination you wish. This house will be handed down as an heirloom. Do not confuse this wooden house with the cardboard houses on the market.

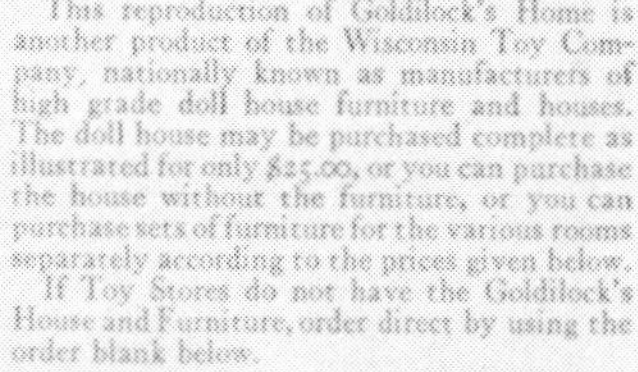

This reproduction of Goldilock's Home is another product of the Wisconsin Toy Company, nationally known as manufacturers of high grade doll house furniture and houses. The doll house may be purchased complete as illustrated for only $25.00, or you can purchase the house without the furniture, or you can purchase sets of furniture for the various rooms separately according to the prices given below.

If Toy Stores do not have the Goldilock's House and Furniture, order direct by using the order blank below.

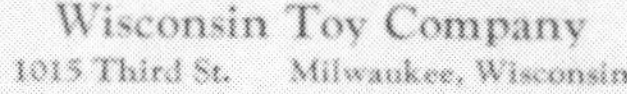

Wisconsin Toy Company
1015 Third St. Milwaukee, Wisconsin

Kitchen, White Enamel—$3.25

Bedroom, Pink, Blue or Ivory Enamel—$2.75

Living Room, Mahogany Varnished—$3.00

Dining Room, Walnut Varnished—$4.00

Bathroom with Bowl—$3.25
(Can be placed in attic)

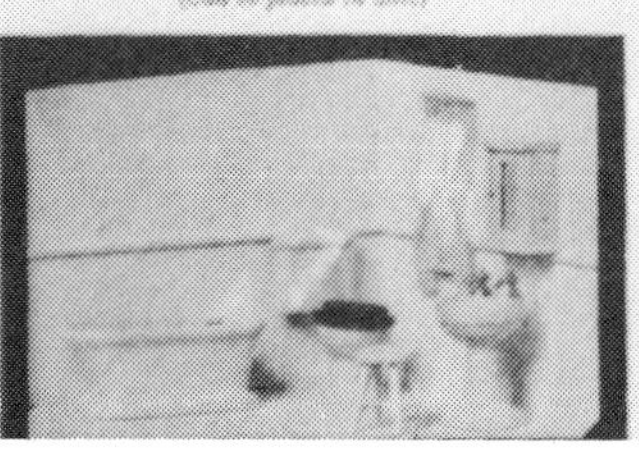

WISCONSIN TOY COMPANY
1015 Third St., Milwaukee, Wis.

Gentlemen:

Please find, enclosed, $...... for which please send me postpaid

Completely furnished Doll House As Illustrated	$25.00	( )
Doll House without furniture	12.50	( )
Kitchen Set	3.25	( )
Bedroom Set (State Color)	2.75	( )
Dining Room Set	4.00	( )
Living Room Set	3.00	( )
EXTRA		
Bathroom Set (Can be placed in Attic)	3.25	( )

Name ....

Goldilock's Home could be purchased for $25 furnished or $12.50 unfurnished. The house and furniture were made of wood. The doors opened and the drawers pulled out. The five-piece white enameled kitchen set was priced at $3.25. Other rooms ranged from $2.75 to $4. **Kitchen set $18-20**

Kitchen, 20 Pcs. Group Price $5.50

Set K. Cupboard, Sink, Table and Chair	$3.75
2 Forks	.15
3 Plates @ $.05	.15
3 Bowls @ $.05	.15
Rag Rug (hand made)	.85
Stove	.45
Frying Pan	.05
2 Flat Irons @ $.05	.10
Coffee Pot	.10
Milk Pitcher	.05
Candle Stick	.15
	$5.95

TYNIETOYS

This word means a choice of five Colonial Doll Houses of varying sizes from the two room "Farm House," $17.50, to the nine room "Colonial Mansion," $200.00. Also complete furniture for every room, from the flat iron, 5c, to the playing grand piano, $8.00.

The houses are solidly built of plywood with real brass door knobs and hinges. The windows are non-breakable, and not removable.

A delight to grown-ups and children. The furniture follows the lines of Chippendale, Hepplewhite and Sheraton; is well constructed, braded and glued.

The finish is Mahogany, Maple or painted lovely colors.

The scale is one inch to the foot, so that each piece is in perfect proportion.

The workmanship is endorsed by the leading Arts and Crafts Societies of the country.

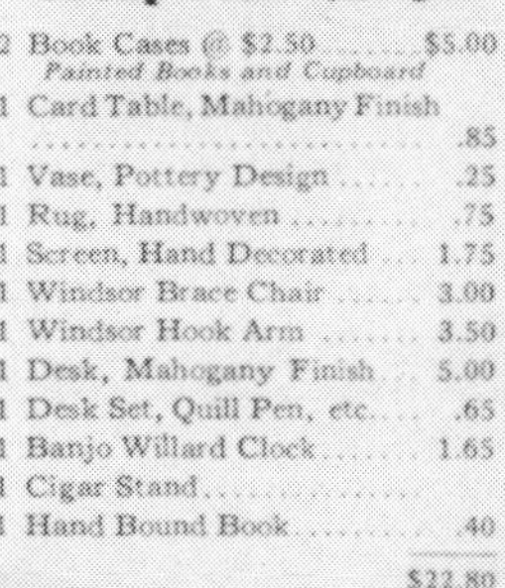

Library and 3 Pcs. Group Price $21.50

2 Book Cases @ $2.50 *Painted Books and Cupboard*	$5.00
1 Card Table, Mahogany Finish	.85
1 Vase, Pottery Design	.25
1 Rug, Handwoven	.75
1 Screen, Hand Decorated	1.75
1 Windsor Brace Chair	3.00
1 Windsor Hook Arm	3.50
1 Desk, Mahogany Finish	5.00
1 Desk Set, Quill Pen, etc.	.65
1 Banjo Willard Clock	1.65
1 Cigar Stand	
1 Hand Bound Book	.40
	$22.80

Write for a Free Illustrated Catalogue of the 130 Pieces

TOY FURNITURE SHOP
Market Square Providence, R. I.

Tynietoys were sold by the Toy Furniture Shop, Market Square, Providence, Rhode Island, in 1927. They sold dollhouses, from a two-room farmhouse for $17.50, to a nine-room colonial mansion for $200. The kitchen cupboard, sink, table, and chair were priced at $3.75 for the set. Other smaller items were from 5¢ to 85¢.

TOYS THE LITTLE GIRL LIKES BEST

$1.00

30-Piece Aluminum Coffee and Tea Set
All pieces Embossed. Coffee pot is 4x2⅝ in. Tea Pot is 4⅝x3¾ in., 6 plates, 6 saucers, 6 cups, 6 spoons and sugar and creamer in proportion. Shpg. wt., 1⁹⁄₁₆ lbs.
49H1872
30-Pc. Set........... $1.00

A Real Electric Toy Stove With 4 Dishes
Heavy sheet metal enameled in green; red enameled panels. Height, 8⅞ in.; width, 8½ in.; For 110-volt house lighting system. Shpg. wt., 4⁷⁄₁₆ lbs.
49H7304
Complete Set.... $1.00

98c

Big 5 Housecleaning Set
Just think of a Bissel toy sweeper with revolving brush, a real yarn mop, a colored yarn duster, a good quality 32-in. broom and a metal dust pan. Shpg. wt., 3⁵⁄₁₆ lbs.
Complete 5-pc. set. 79H9185..... 98c

12 Giant Balloons 21c
Three squawkers, one extra large, and alone a 10 cent value. Oblong shapes range from 19 to 28 in. long, round shapes from 25 to 30 in. in circumference when inflated. Shpg. wt., ⅛ lb.
49H9108 ...... 21c

Indoor or Outdoor Croquet Set 98c
Four mallet set made of hardwood and nicely varnished and striped. Mallets 22¼ in. long. Complete with wire arches, two wood stakes, stake and wire holders, set of rules. Hinge top wood box, size 27x5⅜x4⅝ in. $1.50 value.
79H180
Shpg. wt., 5⅝ lbs.... 98c

Junior 4-Club Golf Set
With Two Rubber Balls
Imitation leather golf bag with ball pocket and shoulder strap. Has metal base and rim. A 29-in. hardwood head driver, iron head niblick, mid-iron and putter, in proportion, and two golf type rubber balls.
49H9145
Shpg. wt., 2 lbs..... 98c

For Complete Line of Toys See Our Last Fall Large Catalog

Nationally Known Joy Ball
34-inch circumference. Made from durable, heavily coated rubberized waterproof cloth. For outdoor or indoor play. Extra heavy handmade stem type two-piece rubber bladder. (Not ordinary balloon bladder.)
49H7716
Shpg. wt., ¹³⁄₁₆ lb...... 48c

Bladder Only for Above
Stem type handmade, heavy, pure gum rubber bladder.
49H7725
Shpg. wt., ⁵⁄₁₆ lb....... 25c

Baby Chick White Rubber Rattle
Always popular with baby. Soft teething ring, handle and rattle. Whistle feature. 4¼ in. long.
49H4400
Shpg. wt., ⅛ lb..... 15c

Seven Bell Rattle
Nickel plated bells. Black enameled wood handle. 5 in. long.
49H2480
Shpg. wt., ⁵⁄₁₆ lb..... 13c

Ball Bearing Roller Skates
98c
Rubber Cushion Shock Absorbers

$1.25 New Ball Bearing Skates 98c
Wheels have inside ball race and hardened steel cones. Most others do not. Strong, heavy steel frame adjustable from 7½ to 8½ in. Front and rear axles mounted in rubber cushions. Toe clamps and leather back strap, not just webbing. Key included. Shpg. wt., 4 lbs.
49H7808—Per pair.......................... 98c

Among the toys "the little girl likes best" in 1932 were a coffee and tea set, an electric stove, and a housekeeping set. The thirty-piece Embossed Aluminum Coffee and Tea Set included plates, cups and saucers, and flatware for $1. The Real Electric Stove was green enameled metal with red panels, 8⅞" × 8½". The stove plus four dishes sold for $1. The Big 5 Housekeeping Set was complete with a Bissel toy sweeper, a yarn mop, colored yarn duster, broom, and dustpan for 98¢. (Courtesy Sears, Roebuck and Company.) **Electric stove $15-28**

75

Now—
for your little girl
A Real Kitchen Cabinet!
"Just Like Mother's"

Imagine how your little girl will delight in owning a kitchen cabinet "just like mother's!" A real cabinet —built just her size.

For years to come it will bring her pride and joy as well as hours and hours of helpful instructive training.

The Playroom Kitchen Cabinet is shown above. See that roll front. It really runs up and down—just as smoothly as on big cabinets. See those cunning doors that open and close—with genuine spring catches. There's a real porcelain work top, too,—and regular base cupboards. Playroom Kitchen Cabinets are built by experienced cabinet-craftsmen.

Surprise and Delight Her— This Christmas

You can find no finer Christmas gift for your little girl than this wonderful Playroom Kitchen Cabinet. Compare it with playthings of equal size and equal quality—you will instantly recognize that the price is remarkably low.

Every cabinet is 39 inches high and finished in beautiful white, green or ivory. In construction, hardware and finish, it is built to last for years.

Send no Money—Order Now!

Simply send the order coupon below or write a letter. The cabinet will be sent by express—you pay on delivery, plus a slight shipping charge.

PLAYROOM EQUIPMENT COMPANY
1814 Tribune Tower, Chicago, Ill.
☐ Enclosed find $12 which please ship Playroom Kitchen Cabinet.
☐ Please ship Playroom Kitchen Cabinet, C.O.D. $12
Color Choice—White ☐ Green ☐ Ivory ☐
(If color is not specified, white will be shipped)
Name.................................
Address..............................
City.................. State..........

The Playroom Equipment Company made a "real" kitchen cabinet built just for a child. It had a roll front, doors that opened, and a porcelain work top. Every cabinet was 39" high and was finished in white, green or ivory. It could have been purchased for $12 in 1927.

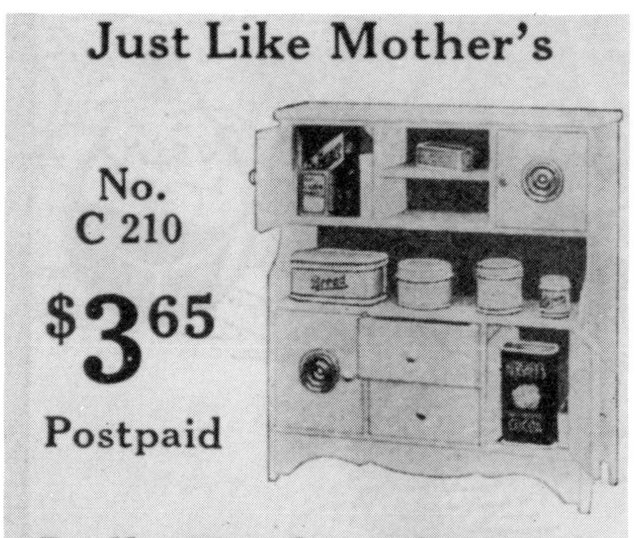

Dolly Kitchen Cabinet

A dandy big cabinet for dolly, well made and finished in washable ivory enamel with blue trim. It's a darling little model just like the big one in Mamma's kitchen. Entire height, 16½ inches, width, 15¼ inches; work table, 8 inches from floor. Four compartments with hinged doors. Two handy drawers. All items displayed are furnished with the cabinet. A plaything like this harbors and nourishes that motherly instinct which is in the heart of every little girl. Most stores would ask at least five dollars for it.

The Dolly Kitchen Cabinet was 16½″ high by 15¼″ wide. The cabinet included items just like Mother's. It was finished in washable ivory enamel with blue trim. In December, 1927, it sold for $3.95 postpaid.

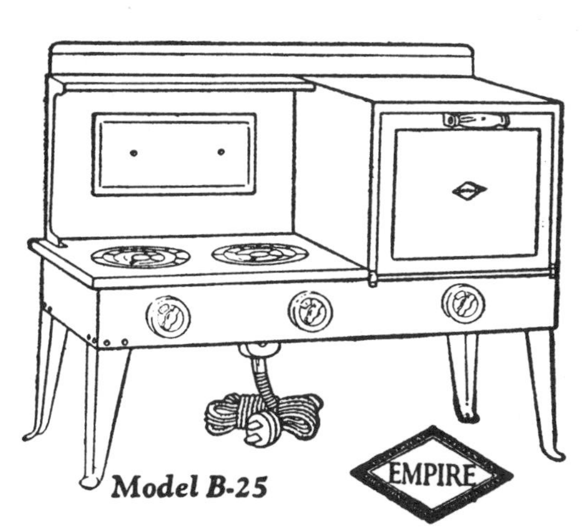

Just Like a Big Range

Cooks a real meal, bakes cake, boils, broils or fries, electrically operated. Comes with utensils to fit. Teach your little girl to cook now. See them at your dealer's.

METAL WARE CORPORATION
Sales Office: **111 W. Washington St., Chicago**
Factory: **Two Rivers, Wisconsin**

The Empire electric toy range could be used to bake, boil, broil, or fry a real meal just like Mother's in 1927.

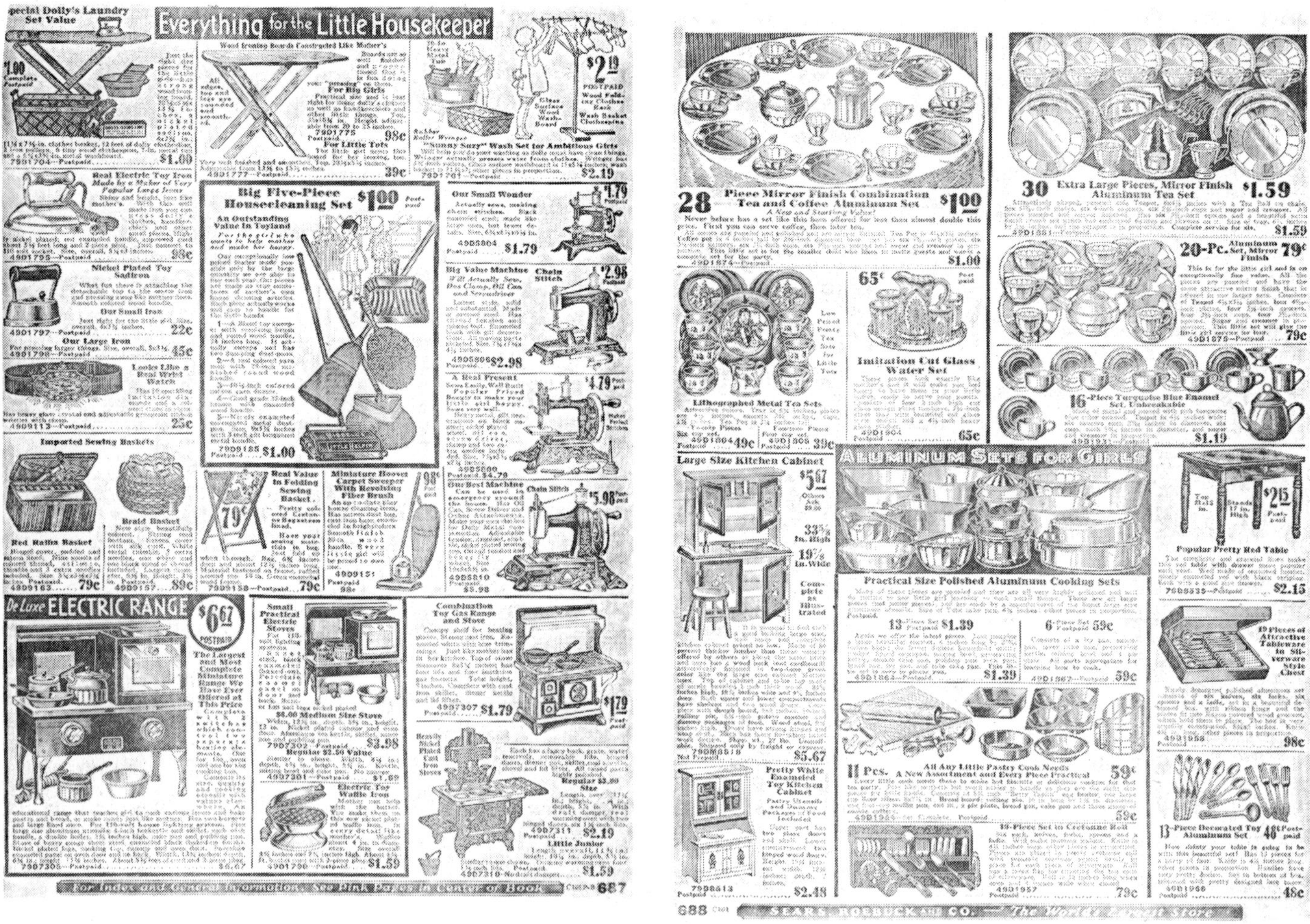

"Everything for the Little Housekeeper" was available from Sears Roebuck in their 1930-1931 catalog. (Courtesy Sears, Roebuck and Company.)

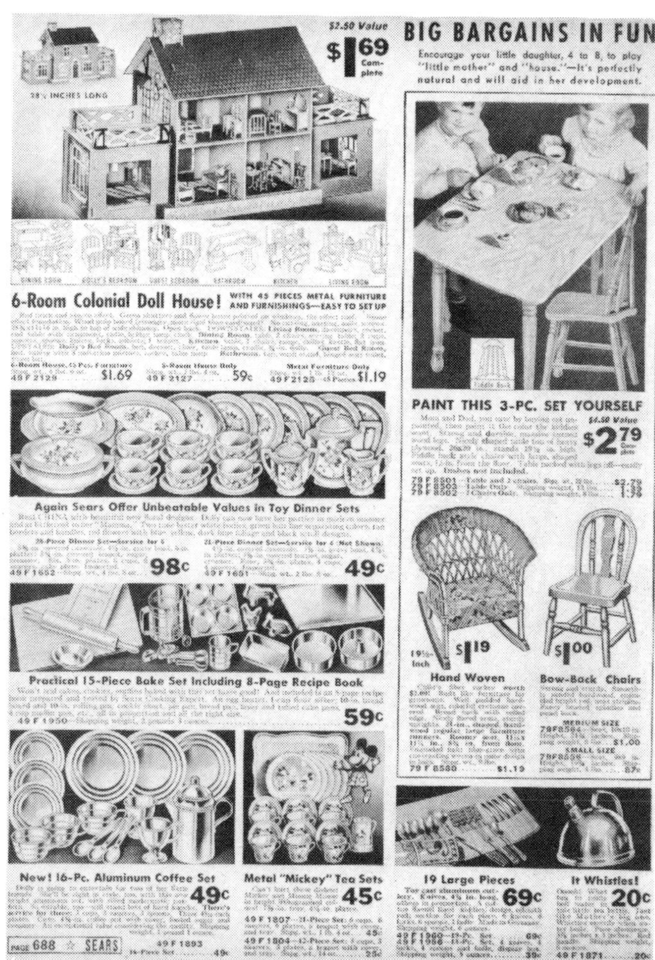

There were "Big Bargains In Fun For The Little Housekeepers" in the 1937-1938 Sears Roebuck catalog. A twenty-eight-piece china toy dinner set was priced 98¢ and a twenty-one-piece set was 49¢.

"Won't real cakes and cookies, muffins baked with this set taste good!" Sears Roebuck said of their fifteen-piece bake set, which included a recipe book, all for 59¢.

A 21" high green enameled wooden highchair was 69¢, while the 24" crib was only 67¢. In 1937, the Orphan Annie stove sold for 49¢. (Courtesy Sears, Roebuck and Company.)

Highchair $10-15

Orphan Annie Stove $15-35

Alice gives children the Golden Key to Table Manners

in these gay tea-party sets of Richelain . . . .

"At this moment the door of the house opened, and a large plate came skimming out, straight at the Footman's head: it just grazed his nose, and *broke to pieces* against one of the trees behind him." (From *Alice's Adventures in Wonderland.*)*

"What a shame," said Alice, ignoring the Footman's alarm and stooping to pick up the fragments. "Such a pretty plate, too. Now, wouldn't it be wonderful if only someone would invent tea things which would not break easily. They would save such a lot of worry for mothers and spankings for children!"

* * *

Now, just fancy. Here's Alice's wish come true at last in gay little tea-party sets of Play-Proof Richelain cups, saucers, sugar bowls, cream pitchers, and all made of this marvelous new material which is lighter but much stronger than glass or china. Dishes to delight the eye and thrill the heart of any child!

These little dream sets of Richelain are made in a rainbow of lovely colors—blue, green, yellow, cream, orchid and red. They are styled in the most modern manner by one of the country's foremost designers, who originally designed them for his own children! Each set is a complete tea service for four and is arranged in a beautiful "Alice in Wonderland" tea-caddy box!

This box is simply scrumptious! On the cover there's a picture of Alice herself surrounded by her quaint Wonderland companions that children love so well. The King, and The Duchess; the Mad Hatter and March Hare; Tweedledee and Tweedledum; the Cheshire Cat, Humpty Dumpty and the Lobster. And inside the cover (Ah! here's something that will please Mother), a set of rules for good table manners, all written in jolly jingle form, by the noted children's author, Dixie Willson—rules that children will love to read and memorize! The kind of teaching that makes a lark of learning!

Can you imagine a more beautiful or practical gift for a child? And what an adorable Christmas present! Little Housekeeper set, $3.00. Little Sister set, $1.50. See them at leading department or toy stores—or write to THE RICHARDSON COMPANY (Lockland) Cincinnati, Ohio. New York Office: Tom McGinty, 200 Fifth Ave.

NRA

CHILDREN'S *Toy Tea Sets*

These children's Toy Tea Sets were made of "play-proof" Richelain. It was a material that was lighter but stronger than glass or china and came in a rainbow of colors. The Little Housekeeper set was $3 and the Little Sister set, $1.50.

Manufacturers

A. & J. Manufacturing Company. Refer to *Kitchens and Gadgets.*

Acme Specialty Company, Orr-Flesh Building, Piqua, Ohio. The Sterling eggbeater and can opener, automatic toaster, and noodle cutter were all illustrated in their catalog.

Aluminum Cooking Utensil Company, 1071 5th Avenue, New Kensington, Pennsylvania. The Wear-Ever trade name was adopted in 1903. The company later became part of Alcoa.

American Central Manufacturing Corporation, Connersville, Indiana, later became the American Central division of Avco Manufacturing Corporation. They made American Kitchens.

American Fixture and Manufacturing Company, 2300 Locust Street, St. Louis, Missouri, were makers of ChromCraft Dinette Furniture.

American Stove Company. The New Process Stove Company was a division of American Stove Company and was located in Cleveland, Ohio, in the early 1900s. Magic Chef ranges were made by American Stove, which was located at 65 Chouteau Avenue, St. Louis, Missouri, in the 1930s.

Armstrong World Industries, Inc. The Armstrong Company was founded in 1860; in 1895 the name became the Armstrong Cork Company and remained so until 1980, when it was changed to Armstrong World Industries, Inc. They manufacture floor coverings.

Aurora Precision Devices, P.O. Box 365, Aurora, Illinois, was distributor of Seal King.

Automatic Wire Goods Manufacturing Company, Inc., New York, New York. Two of their products were a rotary beater and lifter.

Borg-Warner Corporation of Detroit, Michigan, in the 1930s acquired Norge, makers of electric ranges and refrigerators. The Norge division was sold in the 1960s.

The William Campbell Company, 1701 Union Avenue, Alliance, Ohio. Their electric fireless cooker range was advertised in the 1920s.

Capitol Kitchens, Roselle, New Jersey.

Capitol Products Company, Winstead, Connecticut, manufactured toasters.

Cincinnati Galvanics Company manufactured a food press.

Citra Products, Winter Haven, Florida, manufactured grapefruit corers.

Cleveland Metal Products Company. In the 1920s, the address was 7342 Platt Avenue, Cleveland, Ohio. The firm manufactured the Perfection Oil Cook Stoves and Ovens.

Club Aluminum Company. The address was 1238-50 Fullerton Avenue, Chicago, Illinois, in the 1920s. The name became the Club Aluminum Products Company at a later date. They merged with Monarch Aluminum Manufacturing Company to become Club Products Company. The company was acquired by Standard (a conglomerate) in 1968.

Coleman Lamp and Stove Company had offices in Wichita, Chicago, Philadelphia, Los Angeles, and Toronto in the 1930s. They manufactured irons, lanterns and stoves.

Columbus Plastic Products, Inc., of Columbus, Ohio, started business in the late 1930s. By 1946, the Zippo-line was phased out, replaced by the "Lustro-Ware" line. In 1966, the company was acquired by the Borden Company. In 1982, it ceased operating the Lustro-Ware division, which had made clothesline reels.

Columbus Spring And Specialty Company, Columbus, Ohio, made a clothesline reel.

Congoleum Corporation was founded in 1916. With a merger in 1924, it became the Congoleum-Nairn Corporation until 1975, when the name was changed to Congoleum Corporation. Since the beginning they have manufactured floor coverings.

Corning Glass Works. The company was founded in Massachusetts in 1864, moved to New York and became the Corning Glass Works in 1875. Pyrex glass ovenware was first marketed in 1915.

Corona. This name appeared on a mincer.

Crane was founded in 1855. Today their headquarters are in New York. In the 1930s and 1940s, they manufactured plumbing for kitchens and baths.

Daystrom Corporation, Olean, New York, manufactured furniture.

Delta Manufacturing Corporation, Philadelphia, Pennsylvania, made toasters.

A. F. Dormeyer, 2640 Greenview Avenue, Chicago, Illinois. A. F. Dormeyer developed a beater in 1927 manufactured by the MacLeod Manufacturing Company. Company name was changed to Dormeyer Manufacturing Company in early 1930s.

Dover Manufacturing Company, of Dover, Ohio, manufactured irons.

Dowst Manufacturing Company, 4541 Fulton Street, Chicago, Illinois, made Tootsietoy dollhouse furniture.

Dulane, Inc., 8550 West Grand Avenue, River Grove, Illinois, was the manufacturer of Fryryte deep fryers.

Ekco Housewares Company was founded in 1888. They are a housewares manufacturer.

Electric Household Utilities Corporation, Chicago, Illinois. The Hurley Machine Division manufactured Thor appliances.

C. E. Erickson Company, Inc., of Des Moines, Iowa, was the name on a broom holder.

Everedy Company, Inc., Frederick, Maryland. The company manufactures Cap-Master, the Everedy Jelly bag and stand, and the Everedy Climax Bottle Capper.

W. J. Fabrick, of Elgin, Illinois, was the manufacturer of Seal King.

Federal Tool Corporation, 412 North Leavitt Street, Chicago, made syrup jars.

Fletcher-Terry Company, Forrestville, Connecticut, made Aero-Whip.

Florence Stove Company, Gardner, Massachusetts, made oil, gas, and electric ranges.

General Electric was founded in 1878. Originally it was called the Edison Electric Company. Hotpoint is an appliance division.

G. M. T. Company. G. M. Thurnauer founded the company in 1881. It was an importing company for hundreds of housewares items.

Hamilton Beach Manufacturing Company was founded in 1910. In 1920, it became part of Scovill Manufacturing Company in Waterbury, Connecticut. Scovill continues to manufacture Hamilton Beach appliances.

Hamilton Manufacturing Corporation of Columbus, Indiana, were makers of Cosco kitchen furniture. The company was formed in 1945 and later became known as Hamilton-Cosco, Inc.

The Hoosier Manufacturing Company, 1227 Broad Street, New Castle, Indiana, manufactured kitchen furniture from the late 1800s until 1942, when they closed.

The Huenefeld Company, 511 Spring Street, Cincinnati, Ohio, in 1917 manufactured Boss Oil-Air Stoves and Boss Ovens.

Huot Manufacturing Company, 550 North Wheel Street, St. Paul, Minnesota, made meat tenderizers.

International Nickel Company, Inc., 73 Wall Street, New York, New York, manufactured Monel Metal used for kitchen equipment by various manufacturers. The company was founded in 1877 and is now known as Inco, with headquarters in Toronto, Ontario.

Jiffy-Way, Inc., Owatonna, Minnesota, made the Jiffy-Way egg grading scale.

The Kitchen Craft Company, Health Hill, West Bend, Wisconsin, in the 1920s made waterless cookers.

Kitchen Maid Corporation, 412 Snowden Street, Andrews, Indiana, manufactured kitchen furniture in the 1920s, 1930s, and 1940s.

Kompass and Stoll Company, Niles, Michigan, manufactured kitchen furniture.

Kraft-Phenix Company was the result of a merger in 1928. The company was founded in 1903. In 1978 the name became Kraft, Inc. Cookie cutters were one of their premiums in the 1930s.

Lake Center Corporation, 2744 Nicollet, Minneapolis, Minnesota, manufactured It's A Honey toy electric irons.

Langer Manufacturing Company, New York, New York, made the Hostess cake breaker and kitchen saw.

Lamont, New York, New York, manufactured Kut-Ezy can openers.

Lindemann and Hoverson Company, Milwaukee, Wisconsin, manufactured L & H ranges.

Lorraine Novelty Manufacturing Company, Inc., 461 Fourth Avenue, New York, New York, made a cheese slicer.

Malleable Iron Range Company, Monarch, Beaver Dam, Wisconsin, manufactured ranges.

Master Metal Products, Inc., Buffalo, New York, made Sanette step-on cans.

McGraw Electric Company was established by Max McGraw in 1900. In 1926, all of McGraw Electric was sold to Westinghouse Electric and Manufacturing Company. Toasters were one of their products.

Metal Ware Corporation, Sales Office: 111 West Washington Street, Chicago, Illinois. Factory: Two Rivers, Wisconsin. Metal Ware made the Empire toy range.

Miller and Sons, Valley City, North Dakota, made the all-width bread knife in the 1940s.

Moore Enameling and Manufacturing Company, West Lafayette, Ohio. The trade name Memco was used on their nut chopper and cookware.

N. K. Morris Manunfacturing Company, Avon, New Jersey, made the Baltomore Slicer.

Motor Products Corporation, North Chicago, Illinois, made Deepfreeze home freezers.

Mouli Manufacturing Corporation, 91 Broadway, Jersey City, New Jersey (in 1948), manufactured graters, mincers, and juliennes.

Mullins Manufacturing Corporation, Warren, Ohio, Youngstown Kitchens.

W. Munro Manufacturing, Camden, New Jersey, made razor holders.

NaMac Products Corporation, a subsidiary of Wm. R. Wagner and Company, Inc., 1027 North Seward Street, Los Angeles, California, in 1948 made the Worlbeater.

National Manufacturing Company, Worcester, Massachusetts, made the Victor sifter.

National Rubber Machinery Company, Akron, Ohio, made National Disposers.

New System Bakery, Woodsfield, Ohio, was the name on a bread knife.

Noma Electric Corporation, Hamilton, Ohio, manufactured Estate gas and electric ranges.

Northern Refrigerator Company, 782 Crofton Avenue Southwest, Grand Rapids, Michigan, was the manufacturer of the Glacier refrigerator.

Pet Manufacturing, Inc., Dayton, Ohio, made a toy refrigerator.

Playroom Equipment Company, 1814 Tribune Tower, Chicago, Illinois, made playroom kitchen cabinets.

Porter's was the name on a toy sweeper.

C. H. Reed and Associates, Jackson, Michigan, made Diamond cutters.

Revere Copper and Brass, Inc., Rome, New York, has been in the cooking utensil business since the 1890s. The Revere ware line was introduced in 1938.

The Richardson Company, Cincinnati, Ohio, carried children's toy tea sets.

Robinson Knife Company made knives and forks with catalin handles.

Schneider, of Toledo, made cheese and cake slicers.

G. I. Sellers and Sons Company, 1004 Thirteen Street, Elwood, Indiana, (in 1918) made kitchen furniture.

Servel, Inc., was founded in 1929 and located in Evansville, Indiana. It merged its residential division with the Clevite Corporation in 1967. By the 1970s, the only gas residential models manufactured were for recreational vehicles.

The Silex Company dates from the early 1900s. It was acquired by the Proctor Electric Comapny in 1960 to become the Proctor-Silex Corporation. Then, in 1966, it became a subsidiary of the SCM Corporation. The Silex coffeepot and Proctor irons and toasters are their products.

Specialty Manufacturing Company, St. Paul, Minnesota. One of their products was the Acme egg grading scale.

Standard Sanitary was formed in 1899 and has continued to be in the plumbing business. Enameled cast iron plumbing fixtures were their most important product. The one-piece lavatory, built-in bathtubs, and the single tap for hot and cold water were their innovations. Today the corporation is known as American Standard, Inc.

Sterno S. Sternau Company, Brooklyn, New York, was the original name. Later the company name was changed to the trade name Sterno.

Sunbeam Corporation, Chicago-Toronto. The company started as Chicago Flexible Shaft in 1897. Sunbeam was the trade name used on their products starting in 1921, but it did not become the company name until 1946. They manufacture small appliances, including egg cookers.

Tappan Stove Company, Mansfield, Ohio, manufactured Tappan ranges.

Toy Furniture Shop, Market Square, Providence; Rhode Island, sold Tynietoys.

Tyler Fixture Corporation, Niles, Michigan, manufactured Harder Freez freezers.

M. H. Tyler, Muncie, Indiana, made meat tenderizers.

United Drug Company, 43 Lyon Street, Boston, Massachusetts, (in 1941) was founded in 1902. They sold their electric curling irons through the Rexall, Liggett, Owl, and Sontag drugstores.

Valley Forge. This name appeared on a spreader.

Vaughan Novelty and Manufacturing Company. Refer to *Kitchens and Gadgets.*

Wagner Manufacturing Company, was started in 1891 in Sidney, Ohio. Wagner Cast Aluminum Ware was their product. In 1952, it was purchased by the Randall Company of Cincinnati, which sold the company to Textron in 1959.

The Washburn Company was a houseware manufacturer whose trademark was Androck. Refer to *Kitchens and Gadgets.*

Weir Stove Company, Taunton, Massachusetts, made the Glenwood Range.

Westinghouse Electric and Manufacturing Company, East Pittsburgh, Pennsylvania. The company was founded in 1886 by George Westinghouse, an inventor. They manufactured kitchen appliances. Today it is known as White-Westinghouse.

White Consolidated Industries, Inc., has acquired the following appliance names: Kelvinator, Gibson, Westinghouse, Bendix, Philco, Hamilton, Cold-Guard, Perfection, Vesta, Crosley and Frigidaire.

White Enamel Refrigerator Company, 1500 University Avenue, St. Paul, Minnesota, made the Bohn Sanitor Kitchen Table.

White Frost Refrigerator Company, 573 North Mechanic Street, Jackson, Michigan.

Whitehead Metal Products Company, 304 Hudson Street, New York, New York. In the 1930s, they made Whitehead Kitchens.

Wisconsin Toy Company, 1015 Third Street, Milwaukee, Wisconsin, made dollhouse furniture.

Wolverine Supply and Manufacturing Company, Pittsburgh, Pennsylvania, made Wolverine toy refrigerators before they became known as Wolverine Toy Company.

Wolverine Toy Company, Pittsburgh, Pennsylvania, made toy irons before they moved to Boonville, Arkansas, where they are located today.

Wonder Sales, 620 North Michigan Avenue, Chicago, Illinois, sold knife sharpeners.

Wyndale Manufacturing Corporation, Indianapolis, Indiana, made the Popper-Plus electric corn popper.

Trademarks

Specialty Manufacturing Company

egg grading scale

ACME EGG-GRADING SCALE

Ekco Housewares Company

1907 egg beater

C. 1915 to 1920 strainer spoon

C. 1915 to 1920 measuring spoon

MADE IN U.S.A.
PAT'D

Unknown Company

handle on card

ADJUSTA-FIT

Fletcher-Terry Company

cream whipper

Aero-Whip
PATENT APPLIED FOR
IT'S SPATTER PROOF
CREAM WHIPPER
THE FLETCHER, TERRY COMPANY
FORESTVILLE, CONNECTICUT, U.S.A.

Unknown Company

can opener

ALLAROUND LINE
MADE IN U.S.A.

Miller & Sons

bread knife

All-width BREAD SLICER
MILLER & SONS. VALLEY CITY, N.D.

Unknown Company

toy kettle

Amsco
TOYS

Washburn Company

flour sifter

Turner & Seymour Manufacturing Company

can opener

Turner & Seymour Manufacturing Company

egg beater

Unknown Company

french fry cutter

The BURNS

Everedy Company, Inc.

jar opener and wrench

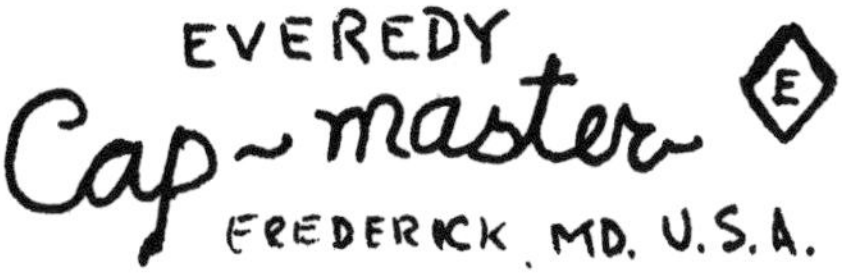

Unknown Company

utility knife

Cincinnati Galv. Company

food press

CIN'TI
GALV
CO.

Citra Products

grapefruit corer

CITRA

Corona

chopper

Norton Company

knife sharpener

Unknown Company

slicer, corer

THE
DANDY

Delta Manufacturing Corporation

toaster

Unknown Company

curling iron

Ekco Housewares Company

french fry cutter blade box

United Drug

curling iron

ELECTREX
UNITED DRUG CO
BOSTON MASS

Unknown Company

can opener

Eversharp
CAN OPENER

Unknown Company

whip

— TRADE —
FLUFFY BEATER
MARK

G. M. Thurnauer

can opener

G.M.T. Co.
U.S.A.
STAINLESS

Unknown Company

can opener

GRUNERT

Unknown Company

on cookie cutter card

Washburn Company

flour sifter

Hand-i-Sift Jr.

Unknown Company

tomato knife

HENRY'S
STAINLESS

Unknown Company

screen cleaner

HI-GENE

Huot Manufacturing Company

chopper-serrater

HUOT

Lake Center Corporation

play iron

IT'S A Honey

Unknown Company

mixer

JIFFY-MIXER

Jiffy-Way, Inc.

egg scale

"JIFFY-WAY"

Unknown Company

bowl-plate scraper

KITCHEN KING

Knapp-Monarch

orange juicer

Knapp-Monarch

orange juicer

Unknown Company

can opener

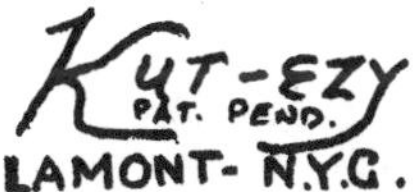

Lorraine Novelty Manufacturing Company

cheese slicer

LORRAINE
NOVELTY MFG. Co. INC.
461 Fourth Avenue, New York, N.Y.

Unknown Company

fruit knife

MARVEL
STAINLESS STEEL
MADE IN U.S.A.

Acme Specialty Company

meat tenderizer

MEAT TENDERER PAT. 4-9-07. SUPERIOR WARRANTED

Turner & Seymour Manufacturing Company

knife sharpener

MONARCH

Mouli Manufacturing Company

shredder-grater

"MOULI"

Unknown Company

knife

Unknown Company

pan scraper

Unknown Company

curling iron

PENCO
371A SERIES

Pet Manufacturing Company

toy washing machine

Unknown Company

carpet sweeper

Robinson Knife Company

knife

Robinson Knife Co.

Vaughan's Novelty Company

wall can opener

SAFETY ROLL JR. NO. 25
TRADE MARK REG. U.S. PAT. OFF.

Samson Cutlery Company

batter spoon

SAMSON

W. J. Fabrick

jar sealer

SEAL KING

Unknown Company

chopper

STAINLESS STEEL

Ekco Houseware Company

flatware

STA-BRITE STAINLESS

STAINLESS STEEL

S. Sternau Company

Before 1920

Sterno
Canned Heat

After 1920

STERNO CANNED HEAT

Sunbeam Corporation

egg boiler

Unknown Company

knife sharpener

SUPER-TRIC
PAT. PEND.
U.S.A.

Unknown Company

toy sweeper

Landers, Frary and Clark

toaster

THERMAX

McGraw Electric

toaster

TOASTMASTER

Unknown Company

yarn baller

UNIVERSAL BALLER

Valley Forge

cheese spreader

VALLEY FORGE
STAINLESS STEEL

Unknown Company

jar lifter

Unknown Company

flour sifter

VICTOR
MADE IN U.S.A.

Westinghouse Electric & Manufacturing Company

toaster

Wolverine Toy

play iron

NaMac Products Corporation

eggbeater

Columbus Spring & Specialty Company

utility clothesline

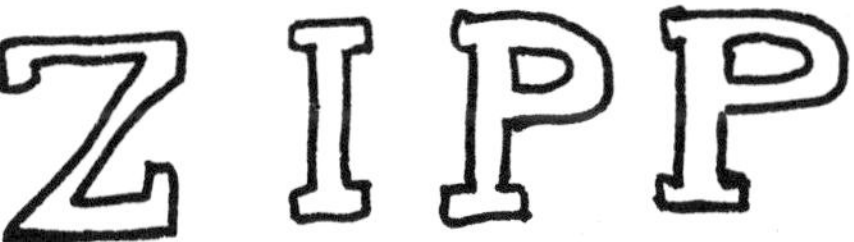

Columbus Plastic Products, Inc.,

utility clothesline

ZIPPO

Bibliography

Agan, Tessie. *The House, Its Plan and Use.* Chicago, Philadelphia, New York: J. B. Lippincott, 1948.

American Home. New York, New York: American Home Corporation, 1920-1950, monthly.

Antique Week - Tri-State Trader. Knightstown, Indiana: R. T. Mayhill Publications, 1979-1984, weekly.

Baird, James, ed. *Cooks Catalogue.* New York, New York; Evanston, Illinois; San Francisco, California; London, England: Harper and Row, 1975.

Berney, Ester S. *A Collector's Guide to Pressing Irons & Trivets.* New York: Crown Publishers, 1977.

Better Homes and Gardens. Des Moines, Iowa: Meredith Publishing Company, 1922-1952, monthly.

Celehar, Jane H. *Kitchens and Gadgets 1920-1950.* Des Moines: Wallace-Homestead Book Company, 1982.

Claire, Mabel. *Lazarus Cook Book and Kitchen Guide For The Busy Woman.* New York: Greenburg Publisher, 1932.

Cussins & Fearn Company. Columbus, Ohio, 1921 and 1938 catalogs.

de Haan, David. *Antique Household Gadgets and Appliances c. 1860-1930.* Woodbury, New York: Barron's, 1977.

Delineator Magazine. New York: Butterick Publishing Company, 1929-1939, monthly.

Dodds, John Wendell. *Everyday Life In Twentieth Century America.* New York: G. P. Putnam's Sons, 1965.

Ehrenkranz, Florence; Inman, Lydia. *Equipment In the Home.* New York: Harper Brothers Publishers, 1958.

Encylopedia of Collectibles. Inkwell to Lace. Alexandria, Virginia: Time-Life Books, 1979.

Fisher, Katherine A., Director. *Good Meals and How To Prepare Them.* Good Housekeeping Institute, 1927.

———. *Good Meals and How to Plan Them.* Good Housekeeping Institute, 1927.

Franklin, Linda Campbell. *From Hearth to Cookstove — Collectibles of the American Kitchen 1700-1900.* Florence, Alabama: House of Collectibles, 1975.

Frederick, Christine. *Efficient Housekeeping.* Chicago: J. B. Lippincott Company, 1925.

Giedion, Sigfried. *Mechanization Takes Command. A Contribution to Anonymous History.* New York, New York: Oxford University Press, 1948.

The Home. Magazine Circulation Company, Inc., 1924.
Ladies' Home Journal. Philadelphia, Pennsylvania: Curtis Publishing Company, 1898-1936.
Lifshey, Earl. *The Housewares Story — A History of the American Housewares Industry.* National Housewares Manufacturers Association, 1973.
Lynes, Russell. *The Domesticated Americans.* New York, New York: Harper and Row Publishers, 1957, 1963.
Montgomery Ward Catalog. Chicago, Illinois: Montgomery Ward Company, 1922, 1930.
Moskowitz, Milton, ed. *Everybody's Business — An Almanac — The Irreverent Guide to Corporate America.* San Francisco: Harper and Row, 1980.
Nickell, Paulene and Dorsey, Jean Muir. *Management in Family Living.* New York: John Wiley and Sons, Inc. London: Chapman and Hall, Limited, 1942.
Peet, Louise Jenison, and Sater, Leonore E. *Household Equipment.* New York: John Wiley and Sons, Inc. London: Chapman and Hall, Limited, 1934.
Sears, Roebuck and Company Catalogs. Chicago, Illinois: Sears, Roebuck and Company, 1902-1950.
Smallzried, Kathleen Ann. *The Everlasting Pleasure: Influences On American Kitchens, Cooks and Cooking From 1565 to 2000.* New York: Appleton Century Crofts, Inc., 1956.
Spinning Wheel. Hanover, Pennsylvania: Everybody's Press, monthly.
Smith Brothers Hardware Company, Columbus, Ohio. Cut Easy Catalog No. 51. Columbus, Ohio: Smith Brothers.
Steinmetz, Rollin C. *History of The American Kitchen 1776-1976.* Kreamer, Snyder County, Pennsylvania: Wood-Made Cabinetry, 1975.
Strasser, Susin. *Never Done, A History of American Housework.* New York: Pantheon Books, 1982.
Time-Life Books, ed. *Time-Life Books, This Fabulous Century, 1900-1950.* New York: Time, Inc., 1969.
Woodson, Wesley E. *Human Factors Design Handbook.* New York: McGraw-Hill Book Co., 1981.
Woman's Home Companion. New York and Springfield, Ohio: Crowell and Collier Company, monthly.
The George Worthington Company Catalog: 1936. Cleveland, Ohio: George Worthington Company.

Index

Illustrations and photographs are indicated in boldface type.

About the Author

When Jane Celehar and her husband John moved to Ohio in 1977, their collection of antiques, and in particular, kitchenware, arrived with them. It was an ideal time for Jane to embark on a whole new way of life.

Jane is a native of New Jersey and spent many years in Massachusetts raising a family and serving her community. All the while, her interest in people and inquisitive nature added to a storehouse of resources for her future.

Fascinated by the many kitchen gadgets of the more recent past, the Celehars continued their search in Ohio. Attempts to find information about these "treasures" led Jane to extensive research that eventually become the foundation of her first book, *Kitchens and Gadgets 1920-1950.*

The painstaking process was rewarded with positive acceptance and a host of new opportunities. Always a good listener and eager student of people, she began lecturing and found a varied audience interested in her topic. The response encouraged her to write a second book, *Kitchens and Kitchenware 1900-1950.* It complements the first with a broader view of the kitchen and its equipment. Many pages from old catalogs and magazines show how the housewife's life was transformed from one of backbreaking toil to a less physically taxing one by modern conveniences.

While completing this book Jane found her avenues of opportunity and challenge widen. From author-speaker to entrepeneur, she now directs a full service organization that offers unique and customized seminars and programs for meetings and conventions.

Any collector seems to be on the lookout for new "finds." This author carries that same zest looking for ways to invest her time and energy.